A-Z

Economics & Business Studies

Nancy Wall
Ian Marcousé
David Lines
Barry Martin

DIGITAL EDITION

PHILIP ALLAN
UPDATES

Philip Allan Updates, an imprint of Hodder Education, an Hachette UK company, Market Place, Deddington, Oxfordshire OX15 0SE

Orders

Bookpoint Ltd, 130 Milton Park, Abingdon, Oxfordshire OX14 4SB
tel: 01235 827720
fax: 01235 400454
e-mail: uk.orders@bookpoint.co.uk

Lines are open 9.00 a.m.–5.00 p.m., Monday to Saturday, with a 24-hour message answering service. You can also order through the Philip Allan Updates website: www.philipallan.co.uk

ISBN 978-0-340-99110-7

First published 1996
Second edition 2000
Third edition 2003
Fourth edition 2010

Impression number   5   4   3   2   1
Year   2014   2013   2012   2011   2010

Typeset by Macmillan, India

Printed by Antony Rowe Ltd, Chippenham, Wiltshire.

Environmental information
Hachette UK's policy is to use papers that are natural, renewable and recyclable products and made from wood grown in sustainable forests. The logging and manufacturing processes are expected to conform to the environmental regulations of the country of origin.

Contents

How to use this book

The *A–Z Economics and Business Studies Handbook* is an alphabetical textbook designed for ease of use. Each entry begins with a one-sentence definition. This helps the user to add precision to the completion of reports or case studies.

Entries are developed in line with the relative importance of the concept covered. *Synergy* is covered in a few lines, whereas central ideas such as the *product life cycle* or *price elasticity* receive a whole page. These entries would provide sufficient material to enrich an essay. Numerate topics are developed through the use of worked examples. All formulae are set out explicitly.

The study of economics and business studies can be developed further by making use of the cross-referenced entries. For example, the entry for *unemployment* refers the reader to *cyclical unemployment* and *structural unemployment*. Cross-referenced entries are identified through the use of bold italics. Therefore essay or project writing should benefit from following the logical pathway indicated by italicised entries.

Economics and business students have always had difficulties with the language of the subject. This stems from several factors:

- both subjects have their own jargon
- different firms have their own terminologies, and their own ways of using words
- the media and politicians use or invent new terms (such as 'private finance initiative'); some of these prove temporary, while others need assimilating into course content
- textbooks recommended by the awarding bodies use technical terms in different ways.

The *A–Z Economics and Business Studies Handbook* is a glossary providing a single solution to these problems. Where terms have more than one meaning, both are explained. In addition, the entries have enough detail to make the book a valuable reference/revision companion. This fourth edition provides full coverage of the GCE A-level specifications.

More words are included than you are actually required to know for the specifications. This ensures that, as often as possible, you can find the words you have come across during your studies. It does not mean that you need to be familiar with all of the terminology in the book.

To aid the revision process, carefully selected lists are provided at the back of the book. Those facing examinations can use the lists to make the best use of the handbook during their revision time. The revision recommendations are split into units, for ease of use.

You should find these lists valuable when you come to do your revision. The section on examiners' terms provides an explanation of the trigger words used on exam papers, such as 'analyse', 'discuss' and 'evaluate'.

A-Z Online

This new digital edition of the *A–Z Economics and Business Studies Handbook* includes free access to a supporting website and a free desktop widget to make searching for terms even quicker. Log on to **www.philipallan.co.uk/a-zonline** and create an account using the unique code provided on the inside front cover of this book.

Once you are logged on, you will be able to:
- search the entire database of terms in this handbook
- print revision lists specific to your exam board
- get expert advice from examiners on how to get an A* grade
- create a personal library of your favourite terms
- expand your vocabulary with our word of the week.

You can also add the other *A–Z Handbooks (digital editions)* that you own to your personal library on A–Z Online.

The *A–Z Economics and Business Studies Handbook* will help anyone who wants to understand current events in the economy. Many terms that are used in the financial media are fully explained so that their significance will become clearer. We hope that, as well as providing an invaluable resource for A-level economics and business studies, this handbook will be used more widely by people with an interest in the general field.

Acknowledgements

The book took a year to research and write. The authors were fortunate to have the assistance of a number of people and organisations. Among the organisations were the Banking Insurance and Finance Union (BIFU), the City Business Library, the Advisory Conciliation and Arbitration Service (ACAS) and the Advertising Association.

The individuals fell into two groups. First, the family aides. Maureen Marcousé did much of the research into employment practices and laws. Fiona Martin proved a hawk-eyed proof reader. Jill Lines provided ideas and support throughout. The other people to be thanked are the team at Hodder and Stoughton, especially the late Tim Gregson-Williams, plus the new Philip Allan Updates team headed by Katie Blainey.

Researching, writing and editing a book of this size requires teamwork and hard work. It also requires the occasional willingness to sacrifice technical accuracy in favour of clarity. A considerable amount of time went into checking the entries, but if any mistakes have slipped through, the authors apologise and accept full responsibility.

Nancy Wall, Ian Marcousé, David Lines and Barry Martin

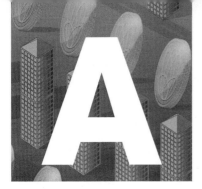

abnormal profit: see *supernormal profit*

absenteeism measures the rate of deliberate workforce absence as a proportion of the employee total. Ideally this statistic would exclude absence due to ill-health, though it may be impossible to distinguish between genuine absences and truancy.

$$FORMULA: \quad \frac{\text{staff total} - \text{number of staff present}}{\text{staff total}} \times 100$$

Main causes of absenteeism include: *alienation*, poor staff welfare systems, stress, poor working conditions.

Remedies include: pay systems linked to attendance, *job enrichment*, better *human relations*, better working conditions.

absolute advantage: a country has an absolute advantage in trade in a particular good with another country if it can produce that good using fewer real resources. This means that its costs will usually be lower in money terms. For example, Jamaica has an absolute advantage over the UK in the production of bananas because its climate is suited to banana production.

absolute poverty: a standard of living which fails to provide basic necessities of life. Poverty may also be relative, in the sense that some people have very much less income than others, and may therefore be unable to buy the things which are regarded as necessary in that society. Poverty can therefore be defined in different ways in different societies: a poor person in the UK will usually have a higher standard of living than a poor person in India.

Some international organisations have defined poverty as having to live on less than $1.25 per day. Low-income countries were defined by the *World Bank* in 2007 as those with annual income of less than US$936 per head. The table overleaf shows data for selected low-income countries.

The percentage living on less than $1.25 a day is calculated using *purchasing power parity (PPP)* figures; income per head uses current exchange rates.

absorption costing calculates the unit cost of an item after allocating a proportion of the estimated fixed *overheads*, i.e. each unit must absorb its fair share of the overheads.

PROS: • ensures that prices are set after all costs have been considered
• requires thought about the most accurate method for allocating overheads

CONS: • ignores the problem that fixed costs per unit can only be estimated accurately if demand/output can be predicted
• often undermined by imprecise methods of *overhead* allocation

Selected low-income countries, including India for comparison

	Income per head, 2007, US$	% of population with less than $1.25 a day
Bangladesh	470	50
Congo D.R.	140	35
Ethiopia	220	39
India	950	42
Kenya	680	20
Nigeria	930	64
Rwanda	320	77

Source: World Bank, World Economic Indicators, 2008

ACAS: see *Advisory, Conciliation and Arbitration Service (ACAS)*

accountability is the extent to which a named individual is held responsible for the success or failure of a policy or a piece of administration. When a company's management structure is clear, staff will know what authority has been given to them, and by whom. If that authority is exercised poorly, the employee should be held to account for his or her mistakes.

PROS: • clear accountability is the basis for providing two of Professor **Herzberg**'s 'motivators': achievement and recognition for achievement
• in order to correct mistakes it is essential to know how they came about – usually a function of people's decision-making or communication failures

CONS: • if a firm operates in an atmosphere of mistrust, accountability can be seen as a threat; managers may fear that overambitious sales targets have been set with a view to proving their incompetence

accounting period: the period of time, typically a year, over which an organisation records revenues and expenses, cash flows and changes in assets and liabilities. At the period end the final accounts are drawn up and can be compared with the previous period. The business should keep the same accounting period to ensure consistency.

accounting principles: a chosen set of accounting conventions that must be applied consistently if company accounts are to be useful to observers. These include: matching costs to related revenues (matching principle); valuing assets with prudence; making the assumption that the firm is a going concern; and establishing accounting rules to ensure objectivity, i.e. minimising personal judgement in the drawing up of accounts.

accounting ratios: see *ratio analysis*

Accounting Standards Board: the body which lays down the accounting standards that firms should follow and checks on whether the standards are being met. If concerned about an issue, the Accounting Standards Board may review the Statement of Standard Accounting Practice (SSAP) that governs the problem, or may issue a new *Financial Reporting Standard (FRS)* to cover it.

accounts: a systematic way of recording the financial history of an organisation over a certain time period. The principal accounts kept are the *balance sheet*, *profit and loss account* and *cash flow statement*.

accumulated profit is the total retained profit a firm achieves over its lifetime. Also known as *reserves*, accumulated profit forms part of the *shareholders' funds*. A common mistake is to assume that accumulated profit represents an asset that can be used or liquidated. It is a source of long-term finance that has already been invested in *fixed assets* or *working capital*. If a firm needs cash today, it must look at its assets not its past profits.

acid rain occurs when emissions of pollution from industrial activities are blown away but then absorbed into rain. This may fall in areas far removed from the original source of the pollution, so that acid rain becomes an international problem. Lakes have been badly affected in parts of Scandinavia because they are downwind from industrial areas in the UK and other parts of Europe.

ACP states are the African, Caribbean and Pacific states which had colonial links with member countries of the European Union. To some extent they have been able to negotiate favourable trading arrangements with the EU. India is not included despite its ex-colonial status.

acquisitions: a term used to refer to businesses which have been or are being taken over. (See also *mergers*, *takeovers* and *Competition Commission*.)

activity rates: see *participation rates*

adding value: the process by which firms add to the price consumers are prepared to pay for a product. This may take a very simple form: for example, cleaning your car or motorbike before you sell it makes it seem worth more in the eyes of the purchaser. Therefore you have added value. Note that this has no effect on the actual performance of the car or motorbike, so the notion of 'value' is very subjective. (See also *value added*.)

administration: when a company in severe financial difficulties brings in an administrator whose task is to protect the best interests of the shareholders by keeping the business going. The administrator may need to sell off an *asset* or assets, but is most unlikely to close down the whole firm. If the financial problems cannot be resolved, a *receiver* might be called in. He/she would act in the best interests of *creditors*, possibly by liquidating all the firm's assets.

ad valorem tax: a tax which is charged as a proportion of the price. The tax will be set as a percentage of the price charged by the retailer, and then included in the final price to the customer. A good example is *value added tax (VAT)*.

advertising is paid-for communication through the media. Most can be categorised as either *informative advertising* or *persuasive advertising*, or a combination of the two. Many different media may be used including radio and TV, newspapers and magazines, billboards, catalogues and websites. The objective is to shift the *demand curve* to the right, so that at any given price more will be sold than before the advertising campaign. The effect is to engineer a change in consumer tastes or fashions.

Though many different types of firms advertise, advertising spending is most likely to be high when there is intense *non-price competition*, as often happens under *oligopoly*.

3

advertising agency: a firm specialising in creating, planning and executing a client's advertising strategy. Agencies are usually divided into three main departments, all of which draw upon the work of market research:

PLANNING:
- decides which type of consumer to target the advertising at, and the strategy for doing so

CREATIVE:
- designs and writes the advertisements and commercials, including the slogans and catch-phrases

MEDIA:
- plans and buys the media time or space to reach the target market as cost-effectively as possible

advertising campaign: the complete realisation of a client firm's strategy, i.e. all the advertisements appearing for a certain product within a specified time period.

advertising elasticity measures the extent to which changes in advertising spending affect **demand**. If a relatively small change in spending caused a major shift in demand, the product would be termed 'advertising elastic'.

FORMULA:
$$\frac{\text{percentage change in demand}}{\text{percentage change in advertising spend}}$$

> **Worked example: if a firm doubled its advertising spending and demand rose from 20 000 to 28 000 units as a result, its advertising elasticity is:**
>
> percentage change in demand = 8 000 ÷ 20 000 × 100   = + 40%
> percentage change in advertising spending   = +100%
> advertising elasticity $= \dfrac{+40\%}{+100\%} = 0.4$

advertising ethics are the moral issues raised by the persuasive power of **advertising**. Laws prevent advertisements from containing untruths, but do not force firms to state the whole truth. This allows companies to use advertising images that exaggerate or mislead. An ethical company should reject such an approach. In recent years a further ethical issue is the way in which firms incite children to use pester power.

Advertising Standards Authority (ASA) is a self-regulatory organisation set up to ensure that advertisements are kept socially acceptable. It administers the **Code of Advertising Practice (CAP)**. Critics suggest that because it is financed by advertisers, the ASA is not harsh enough on advertisements that appear to break the code.

advertising strategy is the plan for meeting advertising objectives. Frequently, these objectives consist of targets that are not directly linked with sales volume, such as improving consumers' awareness of a brand name. The strategy will set out the **target market**, the preferred media for reaching these potential customers, and the overall style of the advertising. The **advertising agency** puts the strategy into practice.

Advisory, Conciliation and Arbitration Service (ACAS) was set up in 1975 as an independent source of expertise in preventing or settling industrial disputes. It is the organisation that companies, unions or individuals turn to when seeking an expert, unbiased conciliator or mediator. Upwards of 150 000 individual conciliation cases are handled each year.

ACAS has a reputation for unbiased advice that has been helped by its policy of not commenting publicly on the strength of the case of either side to a dispute. (See **conciliation** and **arbitration**.)

AER: see *annual equivalent rate (AER)*

after-sales service is the appreciation that customer needs do not end when a sale has been made. Spare parts and maintenance may have to be provided, and friendly, supportive advice should always be available. Efficient after-sales service may be a vital factor in encouraging a high level of repeat purchase.

ageing population occurs where people are living longer and therefore the average age of the population is rising. Japan and a number of European countries have rapidly ageing populations. The UK population is ageing more slowly. The economic implications include the necessity of providing more health care and pensions. Also, there may be problems arising as the ratio of the working population to the dependent population becomes lower. A larger transfer from the **working population** to the retired population may become necessary. The pressures created by this trend can lead to rethinking of pension policies.

ageism is discrimination based on a person's age. European legislation forced the British government to outlaw this in 2006. It is no longer legal to reject job applicants because they are 'too young' or 'too old'.

agenda: the notification to those attending a meeting of the topics to be discussed and the order in which each will be tackled.

agent: an independent person or company appointed to handle sales and distribution within a specified area. An agent's income comes from the commission or mark-up they make on each sale.

PROS:
- for a small firm the appointment of agents removes the need for the high set-up and overhead costs of a distribution network
- as agents work solely for a percentage of the **sales revenue** they may work harder than a salaried **salesforce**

CONS:
- if the agent sells many different products, he or she may not give yours enough attention

aggregate demand refers to the total demand for goods and services from all sources in the economy. It includes:
- consumer spending
- *investment* by firms in plant, machinery and stocks
- government spending
- the net effect of *international trade*, i.e. exports minus imports.

An increase in aggregate demand may lead to an increase in output provided there is underutilised productive capacity in the economy. If there is no spare capacity, and the economy is producing using all available, suitable resources, rising demand is likely to lead to inflation. (See also **circular flow of national income**.)

The level of aggregate demand will influence the level of activity in the economy. A low level of aggregate demand is likely to be associated with high levels of unemployment. This situation is usually described as **cyclical unemployment**. It is usually accompanied by a high level of business failures and sometimes also by declining real incomes.

Rising levels of aggregate demand will increase profitability, encouraging firms to increase output and take on more *labour*. This will tend to have a *multiplier* effect on the economy.

Aggregate demand is affected by changes in all its constituent components:

- A fall in savings can lead to an increase in consumption and vice versa.
- Changes in interest rates affect levels of investment.
- Tax changes affect disposable incomes and therefore both consumption and investment. Government expenditure changes feed directly into the level of aggregate demand.
- Rising imports reduce demand for domestically produced goods and services. Export levels have a direct effect.

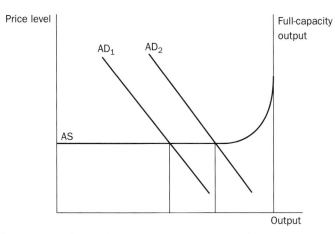

An increase in aggregate demand leads to increased output if there is underutilised productive capacity in the economy

aggregate demand curve: *aggregate demand* can be graphed by plotting output on the horizontal axis and the price level on the vertical axis. It will be downward sloping because lower prices will allow higher levels of output demanded for any given income level. In combination with the *aggregate supply curve*, it can be used to analyse macroeconomic events.

aggregate demand shock: any sudden change in a component of aggregate demand which has a noticeable effect on the economy. For example, a change in interest rates may rapidly affect both consumer and investment demand, so that there is a shift in the aggregate demand curve.

aggregate supply: the total of all goods and services produced in the economy. In the short run, aggregate supply may increase in response to rising *aggregate demand*. In the long run, it can increase only if more resources (e.g. oil) become available or if there are improvements in technology or if efficiency is increased in some other way. (See also *full-capacity output*.)

In the long run, aggregate supply has increased in the UK by a little over 2 per cent per year. This is the *long-run trend rate of growth*, made possible by investment and improved technologies. Better, more efficient management can also help. These are sometimes associated with increases in *human capital* – the expertise available in the economy.

Long-run aggregate supply is shown diagrammatically as a vertical line which shifts to the right as the capacity of the economy to supply goods and services increases. At any one time the total amount which can be supplied is fixed, being determined by the quantity of resources available to produce. As the stock of capital increases and people acquire more knowledge and skills, the line shifts outwards, increasing full-capacity output. The result will be a process of economic growth, provided demand is increasing to absorb all the goods and services which can now be produced. The increased quantity of resources will make it easier to achieve rising standards of living and to avoid inflationary pressures.

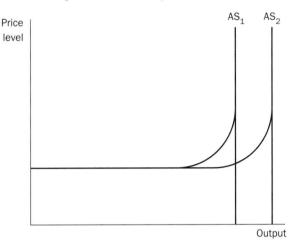

Rising aggregate supply

aggregate supply curves show aggregate supply diagrammatically. Short and long-run *aggregate supply* can be distinguished. In the short run, the aggregate supply curve slopes upwards because an increase in *aggregate demand* will raise profits and encourage producers to expand. However, unless there are ample supplies of underutilised *labour* and capital, prices will tend to rise in the process. (See diagram above.) In the long run, aggregate supply is determined by the stock of resources, land, labour and capital. So the long-run aggregate supply curve is a vertical line. This can only be shifted outwards by an increase in the stock of resources, e.g. through investment in plant, machinery, development of new technologies or education and training. These kinds of changes take time.

aggregate supply shock: a sharp change in the capacity of the economy to supply goods and services. This may occur if there is a natural disaster, a war, or a sudden change in the price of an important commodity such as oil. These kinds of events will cause the *aggregate supply curve* to shift.

AGM: see *annual general meeting*

aid is provided by wealthier developed countries to countries with low per capita incomes. It includes payments made by charities. However, the political aspects of foreign aid can be extremely complex. It may be given as a grant or a loan, and loans may be at market or at concessional rates of interest. Some kinds of aid are more effective in meeting poor countries' needs than others. Much depends on how the money is spent. Spending on some major construction projects such as dams has attracted criticism because it has been unsuited to the long-term needs of the country concerned. There are serious controversies surrounding much aid spending. Some of the money which is classed as aid is spent on defence. Many developing countries have tried to negotiate larger aid donations, without much success.

aims are the long-term intentions that provide a focus for setting *objectives*. They are usually expressed qualitatively, sometimes in the form of a *mission statement*. A typical corporate aim might be 'to produce the finest chocolate in Europe'. From this starting point a firm can build a series of quantifiable targets, such as to increase its consumer quality rating from fifth in Europe to third within three years.

alienation is the state of mind that results from a boring, unpleasant and meaningless job. It is most likely to occur in a situation of high *division of labour*, or when the workforce rejects the approach or objectives of senior management. Once established, alienation is very hard to dispel. Improved *human relations* or *job enrichment* could only work after the apathy and mistrust have been overcome.

allocation of resources: economic decisions about the uses which should be made of land, *labour* and capital leading to an overall allocation of resources, which generally matches the pattern of consumer demand. Consumer demand creates profitable opportunities for *entrepreneurs* to organise inputs of *factors of production* so as to meet that demand. In this way the allocation of resources responds to the pattern of demand exhibited by consumers. However, the idea of the allocation of resources can be applied much more widely to a range of decisions which may be taken by individuals or by governments.

- People decide how to allocate their own resources when they choose between work and leisure or whether to save more or consume more.
- Governments make resource allocation decisions when they consider making changes to different categories of spending: they may consider whether to allocate more towards defence or education or towards health care or unemployment benefit.

It is not always the case that the allocation of resources conforms to the pattern of consumer demand. Firms and governments can sometimes control certain aspects of the allocation of resources through monopoly power or through administrative decisions. Where this happens, there is said to be a *distortion* of the allocation of resources so that it does not accurately reflect consumer preferences. (See also *market economy* and *market failure*.)

allocative efficiency describes the extent to which the *allocation of resources* matches consumer preferences. The most efficient allocation of resources will be the one which fits the genuine needs and wants of consumers most closely. An economy can move closer to allocative efficiency when ways are found to help firms to respond effectively to consumer demand. For example, in a *centrally planned economy* such as North Korea, some producers may be bound by administrative decisions and will not necessarily be able to produce the type of goods which consumers want most. The transitional economies, such as Hungary and Poland which have moved a long way towards being market economies, have become more allocatively efficient because enterprises producing items which consumers do not want have gone out of business. Government controls of any kind are liable to reduce the responsiveness of markets to consumer demand. However, they may be able to protect consumers from the market power of large businesses.

Alternative Investment Market (AIM): a market for buying and selling shares in firms which are too small or too young to be quoted on the full London Stock Exchange. AIM became the successor to the Unlisted Securities Market (USM) in 1995 and has become a successful way to float small (but often risky) companies.

amalgamation: the merging of two or more divisions of a business, perhaps as part of a *rationalisation* process.

amortisation: the *depreciation* of *intangible assets* such as *goodwill*.

annual equivalent rate (AER): the effective annual interest rate paid on credit purchases or received on bank accounts. It shows the compound interest rate and is considered more accurate than its legal predecessor, the *annualised percentage rate (APR)*.

annual general meeting (AGM): a meeting held by a *public limited company (PLC)* to which all shareholders are invited in order to:
- approve the year's accounts
- vote on resolutions and the election or re-election of board directors
- have the opportunity to put questions to the company chairman.

annualised hours agreement: the acceptance by an employee of working hours that are measured per year instead of per week. As a result, the company is able to obtain higher working hours at seasonally busy periods of the year without needing to offer overtime payments. This is an example of *flexible working*.

annualised percentage rate (APR) measures the interest charges on a loan or credit as a percentage of the loan amount outstanding. This is an attempt to ensure that borrowers can compare the true cost of credit from different lenders. APR contrasts with the highly misleading flat-rate method of interest calculation, which makes the interest charge appear much lower than it really is. Lenders are legally required to quote the APR on loans so that the necessary consistency is achieved.

annual report and accounts: at the end of each accounting year a company must produce a set of accounts to be sent to every shareholder and to *Companies' House* (for public scrutiny). For public limited companies (PLCs) the annual report must include: a *balance sheet*, an *income statement*, a *cash flow statement*, a *directors' report* and an *auditor's report*.

Ansoff, Igor (b.1918) developed the notion of corporate strategic planning, arguing that a business needs to look at its resources and, in a formal way, match them against its competitive environment. He attempted to formalise this process into a series of 'rules' that managers could apply. This has been criticised for ignoring the dynamics of the business environment, which require strategies to be evaluated and altered as necessary. The most widely used feature of his work on business strategy is *Ansoff's matrix*.

Ansoff's matrix measures the degree of risk associated with certain strategies. The closer a business stays to its existing products and markets, the lower the risk. Hence the recommendation to *stick to the knitting*. Introducing new products into diversified markets carries the most risk. Ansoff showed this in a matrix form (see diagram overleaf).

9

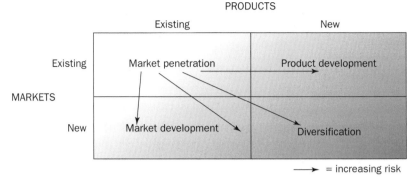

Ansoff's matrix

anti-competitive activities: where a firm in a dominant market position uses its powers to restrict or eliminate competition. Such actions undermine free competition within a marketplace and may therefore lead to poorer customer service or higher prices. For example, in 2008 British Airways was fined £121.5 million by the **Office of Fair Trading (OFT)** for price fixing in the passenger and cargo markets for air travel.

Anti-competitive activities can take many forms:
- *price fixing* agreements that avoid competing on price
- *market-sharing agreements*, where competing firms keep to separate geographical areas
- *cartels*, when competing businesses agree on their marketing strategy
- exclusive dealing, i.e. forcing suppliers to deal exclusively with the dominant firm
- refusing to supply distributors who handle competitors' products
- *full line forcing,* i.e. where the dominant firm requires distributors to stock all of its product line, thus preventing a rival from getting a toehold even in a niche
- tie-in sales, where the dominant firm requires the purchaser to buy a package which not only includes the good of primary interest but others as well. For example, a consumer may be offered a guarantee only on the understanding that the product is serviced by the supplying firm
- aggregated discounts, i.e. where a distributor is given a discount for the total sales over a year or any other lengthy period. This encourages the distributor to stay with the dominant firm and discourages competitors.

Such activities come under the Competition Act 1998, and are therefore subject to review by the Office of Fair Trading (OFT) and the **Competition Commission**.

antitrust laws are the laws in the USA which control the growth of large businesses in order to prevent monopoly power from developing.

appraisal is the process of assessing the effectiveness of a process or an employee. It is usually conducted by comparing goals with outcomes. An employee appraisal might be conducted through a questionnaire but is more commonly a one-to-one discussion between employee and manager. The conversation will focus upon the employee's performance, perhaps in relation to pre-set indicators such as timekeeping, customer sales levels and contribution to teamwork. The appraisal interview may take place annually or more frequently; it will usually end with discussion of career prospects and training needs.

appreciation occurs when the value of something rises. Capital appreciation means a rise in the value of an asset such as a factory building or land. *Currency appreciation* means a rise in the exchange rate such that the same amount of one currency will buy more than before of another. This means that import prices will be lower and exports will lose some competitiveness.

apprenticeship: a form of training for young people, focused upon learning the skills and methods required to carry out a single job. It usually consisted of three or more years of on-the-job training plus some practical and written tests. Apprenticeships faded out in the 1970s and 1980s as new technology reduced the need for craft skills and modern employment practices emphasised multi-skilling and job flexibility. There has recently been an attempt to revive this approach to training through *modern apprenticeships*.

appropriation account: the section of the *profit and loss account* that shows how the firm has used its after-tax profits (its *earnings*). Part may be paid to *ordinary shareholders* as dividends, part to *preference shareholders*, and the remainder will be retained within the company as investment capital. The part of the appropriation account that is retained adds to the balance sheet *reserves*.

APR: see *annualised percentage rate (APR)*

arbitrage is trading between two or more markets when profitable opportunities arise. For example, if the pound equals 1.25 Swiss francs in Zurich and 1.28 in London, a profitable arbitrage deal can be made by buying pounds in Switzerland and selling them in London. In this way currency dealers' actions ensure that different market rates keep in line with each other.

arbitration is resolving a dispute by appointing an independent person or panel to judge the appropriate outcome. The arbitrator will listen to both sides to the dispute and then make his or her decision. If both sides have agreed it in advance, this decision can be legally binding. Otherwise, either side could reject the arbitrator's decision. (See also *conciliation* and *Advisory, Conciliation and Arbitration Service (ACAS)*.)

arithmetic average (mean): the arithmetic mean or average of a distribution is a *measure of central tendency* which is calculated by dividing the total value by the number of occurrences.

$$FORMULA: \quad \frac{\text{sum of (variable} \times \text{frequency)}}{\text{sum of frequencies}}$$

The mean is a useful measure and can be subject to further calculations but it is distorted by extreme values and may not be a whole number or the same as one of the items in the distribution.

ARR: see *average rate of return (ARR)*

articles of association: one of two documents required by law to establish a limited company. It sets out the internal rules under which the company will operate and its relationship with its shareholders. Examples include: the way meetings are conducted, the types of shares and the rights attached to each type, and the powers of the directors.

Together with the memorandum of association, the articles are submitted to the **Registrar of Companies**. They can be viewed by anyone on payment of a fee.

ASA: see *Advertising Standards Authority (ASA)*

assembly line is the final stage in the manufacturing process, where components and each sub-assembly are fitted together to make the finished product. The assembly line usually works on the basis of high *division of labour*, with the use of conveyor belts to move the parts from one stage to the next.

asset: anything providing a flow of benefits to an organisation over a certain time period. Those reported as assets on a *balance sheet* are the ones which can be given a monetary value, usually because they have been bought and a value thus obtained. Assets show how an organisation has deployed the funding available. Assets represent what is owned by an organisation or what is owed to it.

asset-led marketing bases the firm's marketing strategy on its strengths (instead of purely on what the customer wants). An example of this was the use of the Mars Bar as the starting point for Mars to move into the ice-cream market.

assets employed: the book value of all the firm's assets minus *current liability*. It is calculated by adding fixed (long-term) assets to (short-term) working capital.

asset stripping occurs when a *predator* takes over a target company because it feels that the market price of the target's assets is higher than its *stock market* value suggests. Thus the stock market is undervaluing the target company whose assets can be stripped out individually and sold in total for more than the price the predator pays. The sum of the parts is greater than the whole (the opposite of *synergy*).

assisted areas: carefully defined parts of the UK in which government grants may be given to persuade firms to locate there. These grants are available for production and service businesses. They represent an element of the government's *regional policy*. For details of the assisted areas 2007–2013 go to www.berr.gov.uk (the Department for Business, Innovation and Skills).

asymmetric information: refers to a situation in which one party to a deal knows something that the other one does not. For example, when selling a house the vendor may know that the roof occasionally leaks, while the buyer does not. In such a situation, the normal checks and balances of competition are impaired.

auction is a method of selling based on gathering buyers together to bid for the item being sold. Buyers compete openly, with the highest bid being the winner.

audit: an independent check on the financial accounts of an organisation. It is conducted by auditors, who are professional accountants. In the wake of a series of banking and finance failures in 2008 and 2009, auditors came under repeated criticism for their failure to clarify accounting irregularities to the shareholders. It was pointed out that although the process should be independent, the fact that the client firm was selecting and paying the auditor might undermine that independence. (See also *internal audit* and *social audit*.)

auditor's report is part of an organisation's annual accounts and will be read carefully by shareholders, *creditors*, employee organisations and others to check for indications of concern. If satisfied, auditors will report that the accounts reveal a true and fair view of the organisation's affairs for the period. If the auditors qualify their remarks, there may be cause for concern.

authorised share capital: the value of *share capital* which a company may issue, i.e. sell, to raise funds. This is found in the memorandum of association. A company may choose not to issue all its authorised share capital, ensuring the ability to raise new funds from existing and new shareholders at any time in the future.

authoritarian leadership style assumes that information and decision-making are best kept at the top of the organisation. This may be because the senior managers lack trust in the competence or good faith of their staff, or it may reflect acute pressures on the firm that force the directors to make rapid, difficult decisions. (See also *leadership style*.)

authority is the power given to an employee by his or her boss, e.g. decision-making power. Authority is delegated from boss to subordinate, but responsibility for anything that goes wrong should remain with the boss.

autocratic leadership style: see *authoritarian leadership style*

automatic stabiliser: part of the economic system which helps to iron out fluctuations in the *economic cycle*. The most common example is social security expenditure and, in particular, unemployment benefit. As the economy goes into *recession*, more people become unemployed, and so government expenditure rises to pay benefits to those out of work. This maintains demand at a higher level than would otherwise be the case were the unemployed simply left with no money at all. The other important automatic stabiliser is income tax. As income rises in the *boom* phase of the economic cycle, income tax receipts rise more than proportionately because income tax is *progressive*. Similarly, if incomes are falling during a recession, tax receipts will fall more than proportionately. In this way, the tax system takes more spending power out of the economy in a boom than it does in a recession, so helping to counteract the fluctuations in aggregate demand and diminish their impact.

automation uses machinery to replace human labour. This may reduce total costs, but could result in a more inflexible production process. This makes a firm more vulnerable to changes in consumer taste or increases in competition. Modern, *lean production* techniques emphasise the need for flexible automation, using computer-controlled machines that can quickly be reprogrammed to perform different tasks.

autonomous group working is a term used to describe the delegation of set tasks to a team of workers. The workers are given the power to: decide how best to complete the task; decide if there should be a team leader and, if so, who; and decide who should do what. It is a process of decentralised teamworking.

average cost is the total cost divided by the number of units produced. It is also known as unit cost.

FORMULA: $\dfrac{\text{total cost}}{\text{units of output}}$

Worked example: a firm buys materials at 50p per unit and spends £1000 on weekly overheads: the production level is 4000 per week.

So average costs are: $\dfrac{(£0.5 \times 4000)\ £1000}{4000} = \textbf{75p}$

Average costs vary according to the level of output. In general they fall at first as output is increased, because the **fixed costs** are being spread across a larger quantity of output. This can be seen in the diagram.

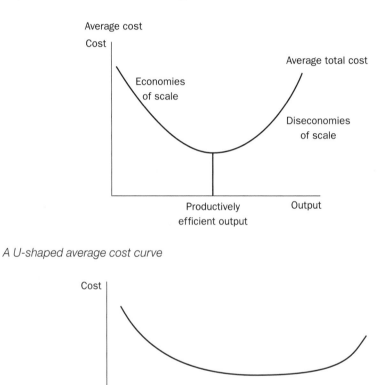

A U-shaped average cost curve

Long-run average cost curve with a range of efficient outputs

Average costs may also fall because there are **economies of scale** to be reaped. At higher levels of output it may be more efficient to use larger machines and invest in different technologies. This can cause costs to fall considerably at higher levels of output.

If levels of output continue to increase, then it is possible that there will be **diseconomies of scale**. These will cause average costs to rise with output. These may possibly be caused by the difficulties of communication and co-ordination in a large organisation.

These two contrasting trends give the textbook average total cost curve its characteristic U-shape. However, in practice there may be a large range of possible outputs at which average costs are more or less constant. This gives the curve a long flat bottom.

The minimum average cost, lowest point on the ATC curve, is associated with *productive efficiency*. When all resources are being used as efficiently as possible, it follows that average costs will be at a minimum.

average fixed costs are the costs of the fixed factors of production, land and capital, per unit of output. They fall in the short run as output increases because the fixed costs are spread more thinly over the larger number of units produced.

$$FORMULA: \quad average\ fixed\ costs = \frac{total\ fixed\ costs}{units\ of\ output}$$

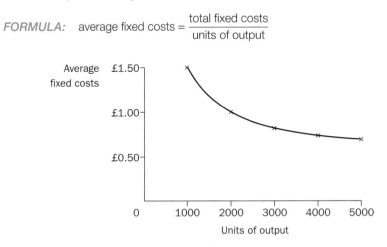

Average fixed costs falling as output rises

average rate of return (ARR): a measure of profitability which can be used to assess the relative merits of alternative investment projects. It relates the average annual profit to the amount spent on the investment. This can then be compared with current interest rates.

$$FORMULA: \quad \frac{total\ profit\ over\ project\ life \div number\ of\ years}{capital\ outlay\ on\ project} \times 100$$

It is not enough to be able to cover the interest rate alone. The investment decision should depend on whether the intended project is the most profitable available given the risks involved.

average revenue: total revenue derived from sales divided by the number of units sold.

average variable costs are the costs of variable factors of production such as *labour*, raw materials and components. In the short run they may rise as output rises, because efforts to produce more without increasing the amount of capital (a fixed factor) may make production less efficient.

$$FORMULA: \quad average\ variable\ costs = \frac{total\ variable\ costs}{units\ of\ output}$$

B2B is a short-hand way of saying Business To Business; an internet company that sells to other businesses, not to consumers. Some B2B firms offer services to other businesses, such as employee recruitment; others sell internet hardware, software or telecommunications.

B2C is a short-hand way of saying Business To Consumers; an internet company that sells directly to the public rather than to firms. Typical examples include Lastminute.com and Amazon.com.

backdata is past research information that can be used to interpret new findings. For example, if a survey finds that 47 per cent of beer drinkers say they would buy a new American malt liquor, how could one translate that into a sales forecast? Only by comparing the result with backdata on the research and actual performance of past product launches. If a new German lager had, a year ago, received a 45 per cent result and, since then, had actual sales worth £40m, a sales forecast of more than £40m could be made for the malt liquor.

backward (or upstream) vertical integration means buying out a supplier, e.g. a chocolate manufacturer buying a sugar producer.

PROS TO THE COMPANY:	• close links with supplier aids new product development
	• control over supply quality, quantity and delivery times
PROS TO THE CONSUMER:	• more innovative products available
	• more reliable supply of goods
CONS TO THE COMPANY:	• assumed guarantee of demand may make supply division complacent
	• increases firm's dependence on one industry (opposite of *diversification*)
CONS TO THE CONSUMER:	• complacency may lead to cost increases and then to price rises
	• firm's control over its supplier may reduce variety of goods available

bad debt: an unpaid customer's bill for goods or services sold on *credit* which is now thought unlikely to be settled, perhaps because the customer is in *liquidation*. As a credit sale has already been included as revenue in the organisation's books, the bad debt needs to be charged to the profit and loss account. Small firms can be hard-hit by bad debts, especially if they depend on a few large customers.

balance of invisibles is the term used to describe that part of the **balance of payments** account which registers exports and imports of invisible payments and receipts. Exports and imports are categorised as either visible or invisible. Visible trade is that which involves goods, such as cars and machinery, i.e. those which you can clearly see and touch. Invisibles include services such as banking, insurance and tourism, which you cannot see and touch. Traditionally, the UK has run a surplus on invisibles thanks mainly to its finance sector, which has paid for its deficit on the **balance of trade**.

balance of payments: a record of all transactions associated with imports and exports, together with all international capital movements. It consists of the **current account**, the capital account and the financial account. The current account shows trade in goods and services, income from employment and investments abroad, and transfers which may be made by governments or individuals.

UK balance of payments, 2007, £ billion

	Credits	Debits	Balance
Current account			
Total goods	220.7	310.0	−89.3
Total services	147.6	106.0	41.6
Income			
employment abroad	2.0	1.8	−0.6
investment income	284.6	275.3	9.3
Current transfers	15.7	29.4	−13.7
Current account balance	**670.6**	**728.7**	**−52.6**
Capital account			
Totals	−	−	2.6
Financial account			
UK investment overseas less)	−	−	39.8
overseas investment in UK)			
Net errors and omissions	−	−	10.1

Source: ONS, Pink Book 2008

Visible exports and imports consist of goods, while services are often referred to as invisibles. The balance on current account is the total of visible and invisible exports and imports. It is not always possible to identify all payments: unrecorded transactions are shown as 'errors and omissions'.

The capital account is of little significance, accounting for changes associated with immigration and emigration together with transfers of EU funds and foreign aid payments.

The financial account shows the capital outflow from the UK caused by investments overseas and the capital inflow resulting from foreign investment in the UK. These investments may consist of factories or offices built by foreign companies in the UK. Or they may be payments for shares, property or other assets, or money flowing into or out of UK bank accounts (known as portfolio investment). Net UK investment overseas shows the balance between the two.

balance of payments deficit/surplus on current account: this occurs when total imports exceed total exports. If this remains fairly small and is balanced by capital inflows on the financial account, it may be of no great consequence. However, by 2007 (see table on page 17) the deficit was significant. As the financial crisis developed in 2008, capital inflows fell as overseas investors saw London as a less safe location for their funds. The consequence was a sharply depreciating pound.

A surplus occurs when the exports exceed imports. The surplus can be used to increase *foreign exchange reserves*. Large *current account imbalances* can threaten economic stability.

balance of trade is the term used to describe that part of the *balance of payments* account that registers exports and imports of visible goods. The UK has been importing more visible goods than exports since the last quarter of the nineteenth century, and this has been paid for by the surplus on invisibles.

balance sheet: a statement of an organisation's *assets* and *liabilities* at a point in time, usually the last day of the financial year. The balance sheet gives an indication of a firm's financial health and strength. Liabilities must equal assets, thanks to the accounting convention of double-entry bookkeeping. From 2005 public limited companies were required to follow a new format for balance sheets. This format fits in with international accounting standards. A shortened version is shown below:

Balance sheet for A–Z plc, 31 December 2009

Balance sheet item	Explanation	£000s	£000s
Non-current assets	Fixed, i.e. long-term assets		450
Inventories	Stocks, e.g. goods awaiting sale	125	
Receivables	Customers who owe you money	160	
Cash		45	330
Payables	Short-term (current) liabilities		(260)
Non-current liabilities	Long-term liabilities, e.g. loans		(135)
NET ASSETS			385
Share capital		25	
Reserves	Accumulated, retained profit	360	
TOTAL EQUITY	Shareholders' funds		385

balanced budget: if the government exactly balances tax revenue and expenditure it is said to have a balanced budget. In fact, on an annual basis this happens rather rarely. Most often there is a budget deficit, sometimes a budget surplus, and very occasionally the budget nearly balances. Over a period of time the annual budget deficits and surpluses may balance each other out. Gordon Brown had a 'golden rule' as Chancellor of the Exchequer, that expenditure should not exceed tax revenues by more than the level of public investment. Borrowing to invest can be justified because of the expected future income which the investment will create. However, this rule has been blown away by the need for the government to borrow to recapitalise the banks and provide a stimulus to the economy in 2008.

ballots: the process of voting for or against a course of action. Ballots authorising *industrial action* must meet the requirements of the *Employment Act 2008*. These demand that ballots must be secret, must offer voters an alternative which stops short of strike action and must include a warning that strike action may lead to dismissal. Only if the industrial action receives more than 51 per cent support will the union be immune from being sued.

bank: a bank is a financial intermediary which takes deposits from people or businesses that wish to save, and lends money to people or businesses that wish to borrow. By doing this on a large scale, and by exploiting the fact that not all of its deposits will be withdrawn at any one time, a bank can expand its lending over and above the total of deposits which it receives from savers. Normally, banks are supposed to be carefully regulated to ensure that they do not over-lend. (This safeguard broke down in the period of increased lending, 2005–07; it eventually became clear that many banks had taken big risks with sub-prime mortgages based on an expectation that house prices would rise indefinitely.)

Traditionally, banks make their money by 'borrowing long and lending short'. Borrowing long means taking deposits which are unlikely to be withdrawn and which are available at relatively low *interest rates*. Lending short, i.e. making loans for short periods, will be profitable because a higher interest rate can be charged. The margin between the two rates gives the bank its income.

Banks supply a wide range of financial services. Some also specialise. Retail banks take deposits from all kinds of small and large customers. *Investment banks* exist to meet the needs of large businesses and specialise in funding large projects and advising on finance for individuals with significant wealth. In recent years a number of *building societies* have become banks.

Normally governments do not get involved in banking business, but the threatened bank failures in 2007–08 led the UK government to nationalise Northern Rock and take a very large share of Lloyds TSB/HBOS and Royal Bank of Scotland (RBS). It remains to be seen how this story will end.

bank bills: very short-term loans, usually for three months only. They can be bought and sold on the *money market*. There is no interest to pay on them but the maturity value will be larger than the loan, giving a rate of return to the lender. Bills can be issued by the Bank of England to fund government borrowing: these are called Treasury bills.

Bank of England: the central bank of the UK. It is responsible for the note issue and for the determination of *monetary policy* including interest rate and exchange rate policy. It is also responsible for ensuring that *public sector net borrowing* is funded through the sale of bills and bonds. Until 1997 the Bank of England acted as a watchdog for all banking activities in the economy. This *bank supervision* is now carried out by the *Financial Services Authority*, an independent body whose other main objectives are to ensure that financial services such as insurance, accounting, stockbroking and investment advice operate honestly and competently. This may change.

Traditionally there was always close collaboration between the *Chancellor of the Exchequer* and the Governor of the Bank of England. This changed when the *Monetary Policy Committee* was set up in 1997. This gave the Bank operational independence in setting interest rates. However, during the 2007–09 financial crisis the government had to become much more involved because the rescue of failing banks required *recapitalisation*, achieved with large amounts of government money. The stability of the system could only be underpinned by the government's ability to raise tax revenue.

There was no other way to restore confidence in the banking system. It is likely that once all the banks are self-supporting again, the government will withdraw and leave the Bank of England operating independently again. It is open to question whether the then government will choose to make the Bank fully and legally independent, similar to the US Federal Reserve or the *European Central Bank (ECB)*.

The MPC has been a crucially important body while the banks have been in crisis. It is responsible for decisions relating to *quantitative easing* as well as *bank rate*, as policies to reduce the impact of recession.

The role of the Bank of England will change dramatically if the UK adopts the *euro* as its currency. The determination of monetary policy will shift to the ECB.

bank rate: this is the interest rate set by the *Monetary Policy Committee* of the *Bank of England*. This is the rate which the Bank charges when the banks need to borrow on a short-term basis to cover day-to-day customer withdrawals. It is thus a basis for determining interest rates throughout the banking world, and influences rates on loans taken out by individuals and firms. Typically, a bank rate of 5 per cent might mean that firms can borrow at interest rates of from 8 per cent upwards, while savers will receive interest rates of 3 per cent or less. The difference between the savers' and borrowers' rates represents the profit margin made by the 'high street' banks such as Barclays.

The bank rate is the main weapon in *monetary policy*, which attempts to influence the level of economic activity. In an attempt to stop inflation from accelerating, the MPC raised interest rates during 2006–07. As signs of impending recession developed it began to reduce bank rate during 2008, slowly at first and then dramatically to an all-time low. Some people argue that it should have been reduced earlier and faster.

UK bank rate (%), August 2006 to February 2009

August 2006	4.75
November 2006	5.00
January 2007	5.25
May 2007	5.50
July 2007	5.75
December 2007	5.50
February 2008	5.25
April 2008	5.00
October 2008	4.50
November 2008	3.00
January 2009	1.50
February 2009	1.00
March 2009	0.50

Source: Bank of England

bank supervision: the process by which the *Financial Services Authority* (FSA) aims to ensure that banks do not lend more than they ought to, also known as bank regulation. If they do they may eventually be unable to meet the demands of their customers to withdraw their cash. This is known as bank failure: it happened to Northern Rock in late 2007, when the fall in its share price panicked depositors, who then created a 'run on the bank' for the first time in the UK since 1866. The bank had increased mortgage lending by taking on customers without adequate checks on their ability to keep up with payments. When house prices began to turn down and unemployment rose, it became clear that the bank's reserves were insufficient to cover the risky loans they had made.

Supervision means making sure that the banks are holding a sufficient quantity of liquid assets, enough to balance the growth of their lending, so that they do not run out of cash even if there is a downturn in economic activity. There was widespread criticism of the FSA for allowing this to happen. Watch out for changes to this system.

bankruptcy: an individual or an *unincorporated* body may request (petition for) bankruptcy or be declared bankrupt when unable to settle its *liabilities* or if acting in such a way as to lead *creditors* to think that it is unable to settle, e.g. by refusing to communicate with them. Note that the term bankruptcy should not be applied to *limited liability* companies. (See also *insolvency* and *liquidation*.)

bar chart: a diagram used to give a quick comparison between variables, e.g. monthly *sales revenue* of a company's three products. The values are plotted vertically and time horizontally. The heights of the bars represent the values. While good for impact, the bars lack precision and it may be difficult to ascertain actual values from the vertical axis. Also, distortion can be created by selecting the width of bar inappropriately and by starting the vertical scale at above zero.

bar coding is the recording of data in a form that can be read instantly by a laser beam. When used on packaging it enables each sale to be recorded, thereby providing accurate stock records.

barriers to communication are physical or attitudinal reasons why messages fail to be received. If an alienated worker is unwilling to listen, or intermediaries fail to pass on messages, there may be a serious problem.

barriers to entry occur when it is difficult for new firms to enter an industry. This most commonly arises because there are substantial *technical economies* of scale being reaped by existing firms, and a new entrant to the industry, starting up in a small way, would have higher costs. Many manufacturing industries have barriers to entry because the production process is very *capital intensive*. Other economies of scale, financial and marketing (especially where there is extensive advertising), may be important too.

Barriers to entry may be legal arising from *patents*. When an invention is patented, only the holder of the patent is allowed to produce it for a specified number of years. This means that no other company can copy the product until the patent expires. Other barriers include exclusive dealership arrangements, any kind of collusive agreement between existing firms in the industry, *sunk costs* and *limit pricing*.

barriers to trade: see *import controls*

barter is the swapping of goods or services to conduct a non-monetary transaction. It is likely to be needed when the deal is between different countries, one of which has a currency which cannot be converted freely.

base year: where *time-series analysis* data are put into *index number* form, the year chosen to have a value of 100 in the index series is called the base year.

basic pay: an agreed regular wage excluding any bonus, shiftwork or profit-sharing supplements.

basket of currencies: when exchange rate changes are measured, an *index number* is created which shows the extent of the change for one currency against those of its main trading partners. The currencies selected for this are known collectively as a basket of currencies. (See also *exchange rate index*.)

batch production is the manufacture of a limited number of identical products, usually to meet a specific order. Within each stage of the production process, work will be completed for the whole batch before the next stage is begun. This provides some *economies of scale* compared with *job production*, but not as many as through *flow production*.

bear market: a period of pessimism and falling share prices on the *stock market*. Individuals who anticipate this happening sell shares in the expectation that they will be able to buy them back in the future at a lower price. To a certain extent it results in a self-fulfilling prophecy, in that if everyone sells, more shares will come onto the market, and their price will indeed fall. A bear market is the opposite of a *bull market*. The 2007–09 bear market saw share prices halve, following a long bull market.

beggar my neighbour policies: measures which restrict trade with the intention of protecting domestic industries, but have the effect of reducing trade overall. The term is used to describe the events of the 1930s when many governments brought in *import controls* to protect their domestic producers from competition from cheap imports. This had the effect of reducing the exports of many countries, so reducing aggregate demand and worsening the plight of the many countries caught up in the depression. The onset of recession in 2008 brought fears that governments would again try to protect their economies in this way.

behavioural theories of the firm: theories based on business objectives other than profit maximisation. For example, small businesses may have objectives relating to an easy life, possibly *satisficing*. Managers of large businesses may seek power or perks rather than profit as such. Or they may seek to maximise output and turnover.

benchmarking means setting competitive performance standards against which progress can be measured. These standards are based on the achievements of the most efficient producers within a marketplace (if you can find out their figures). They ensure that production managers focus upon the competitive environment, instead of looking purely at this year's achievements compared with previous years. Benchmarking is seen as a vital element in achieving *world-class manufacturing*.

benefits in kind: people receive many benefits from the welfare state which are not given in the form of money. Health care, education and other services provide benefits in kind which add to people's well-being but do not increase their money income in the short run.

BERR: the Department for Business, Enterprise and Regulatory Reform, which has been renamed the *Department for Business, Innovation and Skills (BIS)*.

bias is a factor that causes data or an argument to be weighted towards one side. Statistical bias occurs when a *sample* has – by chance or by mistake – an overweighting towards one subgroup (e.g. too many pensioners within a research sample). Personal bias occurs when a decision maker consciously or subconsciously favours one side over another.

bilateral talks or arrangements are those that occur between two parties. Therefore discussions on trade between the American and British governments could be termed bilateral trade negotiations.

bilateral monopoly occurs where there is a single seller and a single buyer. A *trade union* which represents all the workers in an industry and a dominant employer can create a bilateral monopoly, as in the case of the British Medical Association which negotiates doctors' pay, and the National Health Service which employs most of them.

bilateral trade occurs when two countries swap equal quantities of exports and imports. More often trade is multilateral, characterised by surpluses and deficits between pairs of countries, so that the UK might export engineers' services to Saudi Arabia, which might in turn export oil to Japan, which in turn exports cars to the UK.

biotechnology is the attempt to harness nature for commercial purposes such as the manufacture of medicines. Whereas pharmaceutical drugs, food colourings and flavourings have traditionally been based scientifically on chemistry, the intention is that advanced biology will become more important in future. Biotechnology is best known for genetic engineering, but it is the vast worldwide market for medicines that most attracts investors into this high-risk, high-tech area.

birth rate: the average number of live births occurring in a year per 1000 population.

BIS: see *Department for Business Innovation and Skills (BIS)*

black economy is the term used to describe all those transactions which do not appear in the national income statistics. Some of these are legal, others are not. The black economy includes the wages of people who are on means-tested benefits while actually working more than the few hours allowed. It also includes payments, e.g. to babysitters, which do not need to be recorded for tax purposes. It is estimated that 3–5 per cent of tax revenue is lost through illegal activities taking place in the black economy.

blacklist: a list of names of people or companies that a firm or country will not deal with.

black market: when a market is controlled, e.g. by rationing, a black market develops, where people who have things to sell and people who want to buy them evade the controls. A black market developed in the UK during the Second World War and more recently countries with strict foreign exchange controls have experienced black markets in *currencies*.

blind product test is a consumer test of the qualities of two or more rival products. What makes it a 'blind' test is that the brand name and therefore image of the product is hidden from the consumer.

blue chip: a company that is so large, well established and soundly financed that it can be regarded as a secure investment or employer. The term was called into question when huge blue chips such as HBOS and the Royal Bank of Scotland (RBS) suffered share price collapses during 2008.

blue collar union: a *trade union* that represents manual workers.

body language is the conscious or unconscious use of the body to convey unspoken messages. A shrug of the shoulders may convey indifference, while an aggressive stance may undermine a manager's attempt to apologise to a subordinate.

bonds: a borrower may issue a bond, which is a promise to repay a certain sum of money at a date some time in the future (from one to 20 years or so). In return for the loan which is the price of the bond, interest will be paid, usually at a fixed rate. Bonds may be traded on the **Stock Exchange**, and the price will reflect the attractiveness of the interest rate relative to current market rates. Bonds issued by the **Bank of England** to finance government spending are known as Treasury Bonds, also as gilts, because the government will always be able to repay on maturity, since it has the right to tax. (Hence, they are said to be 'as good as gold'.) Bonds issued by companies are known as corporate bonds. Because the rate of interest and the maturity value are fixed, bonds are much less risky than shares, but are likely also to have a lower rate of return.

bonus: an amount over and above normal salary paid to employees who are considered to have done their job particularly well. They can be used to try to ensure loyalty or to act as an incentive. Sometimes they are used to pay very large amounts, the wisdom of which has been questioned by some shareholders and members of the public, especially in relation to bankers whose banks became very weak during the 2007–09 financial crisis.

book value: the **balance sheet** value of an asset. For **fixed assets** this is the historic cost minus accumulated depreciation. For stocks it is the lower of cost and net realisable value. In either case, the stated book value depends on assumptions made by the business, and is therefore only as reliable as the individuals concerned and the information they have available to them.

boom: the phase of the **economic cycle** in which economic growth is at its most rapid. As recovery gathers pace, economic growth becomes faster until in a boom it is growing at a rate which cannot be sustained in the long run. The economy will be characterised by relatively low levels of **unemployment** and little underutilised capacity.

In the later stages of a boom, bottlenecks or supply constraints develop. Employers find it hard to recruit some scarce types of skilled **labour**. Firms producing **investment** goods develop long order books, so that buyers have to wait. Wages will tend to be bid up in an attempt to recruit more people. This increases costs and may lead to increasing prices so that **inflation** accelerates. In any case, the ease with which firms can sell their output in a growing market encourages them to raise prices. In these ways inflation may accelerate. This was the situation in the UK at the end of 2007; growth for the year was just under 3 per cent, which was probably unsustainable, being somewhat above the **long-run trend rate of growth**.

If governments implement counter-inflation policies, the heat will be taken out of the economy and the downswing of the cycle will begin. Even without such policies the economy is likely to slow down because expectations that growth is likely to slow will reduce the rate of investment, which in turn reduces **aggregate demand**.

Boston matrix: a method of analysing the current position of the products within a firm's portfolio, in terms of their **market share** and growth within their marketplace. Devised in America by the Boston Consulting Group, this system of product portfolio analysis is far more sophisticated than the **product life cycle**. The Boston matrix points out not only the importance of market share, but also that firms want products that can support each other's development. Product life cycle theory implies that declining brands have no future other than to die, whereas the Boston matrix shows that an ageing brand can be a **cash cow** to be milked for the benefit of a 'rising star' or to finance the changes needed to a 'problem child' (see diagram).

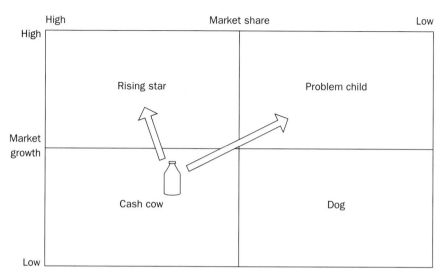

The Boston matrix

bottlenecks may refer to hold-ups in production for a business or supply constraints in the economy generally. They are caused by an inability to increase supply to match an unexpected surge in demand.

● Within an individual firm, bottlenecks might be caused by poor management planning: trying to rush more output through the factory than is possible using the available labour, material or capital resources.

● In the economy, bottlenecks occur when there is a *boom*. There may be shortages of skilled *labour* which make it difficult for firms to hire the kind of people they need in order to expand. This can lead to prices of scarce resources being bid up as buyers compete for them. This can be the start of an acceleration in *inflation*. Or there may be shortages of other inputs, e.g. microchips, forcing producers of a huge range of products to slow down their rate of output.

bottom line: jargon for the bottom line of a *profit and loss account*, or the estimated *net profit* on a specific activity or project. Care must be exercised to see which version of profit is meant.

brainstorming: a group activity in which members are encouraged to say the first answer that strikes them about how to solve a problem, no matter how weird. Having obtained as many ideas as possible, the group will consider each one in more detail. It is a way of encouraging more creative solutions than the normal carefully considered, safety-first ideas that managers may put forward.

branding: establishing an identity for your product that distinguishes it from the competition. Marketing managers often talk about the personality of their brands as if referring to people. Successful branding adds value to an item and can ensure *brand loyalty*.

brand leader: the brand with the highest percentage share of a specific market or segment. This has become an increasingly valuable position as retailers have become more powerful over recent decades. Supermarkets such as Tesco have such strong *own-label* products that they do not have to stock every national brand within a sector. Usually, they stock the brand leader, their own label and just one other brand. Therefore the second biggest selling brand often has to compete fiercely with the numbers three and four for shelf space, and that means cutting prices to the bone. Only the brand leader is able to negotiate on equal terms with the retail giants.

brand loyalty exists when consumers repeat-purchase your product on a regular basis. Such customers are unlikely to be price sensitive, therefore your product's *price elasticity* will be low. This enables you to increase the price level without much effect upon demand. Brand loyalty can be active or passive:

- active loyalty stems from a conscious decision on the part of your customers that they prefer the taste, look, quality or image to that of the competition
- passive loyalty stems from consumer inertia, from people's tendency to become used to a purchasing pattern from which they do not bother to change; for new products, this is the hardest marketing problem to overcome.

brand mapping: see *mapping*

brand proliferation occurs when a large business sells a number of different brands in an attempt to target a number of different market segments or achieve a competitive edge. The high cost of marketing them all may act as a *barrier to entry*.

brand standing: a measure (in effect an audit) of where one firm's brand stands in consumer affections compared with rivals. This is monitored regularly by the use of *market research* into the images, attitudes and usage of those within the *target market*.

Brazil, Russia, India and China (BRIC) economies were identified by investment bank Goldman Sachs in 2001 as emerging economies with outstanding growth potential. All four are large countries with large populations, but it is arguable that the growth prospects of India and China seem much more soundly based than those of Russia and Brazil.

breach of contract: breaking a term laid down in a legal contract and therefore being liable to be taken to court or to be sued.

break-even chart: a line graph showing total revenue and costs at all possible levels of *output* or *demand*, i.e. at every point from an output of zero through to maximum capacity. This enables the reader to see at a glance the profit at any output level that interests them (by looking at the vertical difference between revenue and costs).

The chart comprises three lines: *fixed costs*, total costs and total revenue. They are plotted with pounds on the vertical axis and output on the horizontal axis.

- fixed costs form a horizontal straight line
- total costs line starts at fixed costs and rises as a diagonal straight line
- total revenue line starts at 0 and rises as a diagonal straight line

To construct the chart, first set out a grid with the following headings:

Quantity	Revenue	Variable costs	Fixed costs	Total costs

In the quantity column should be no more than three figures:
- 0 units
- maximum output (which might have to be assumed)
- a convenient point between them (probably halfway).

Worked example: compile a table of data for a firm with fixed costs of £40 000, variable costs of £1, a selling price of £2, and a factory capable of producing 50 000 units.

Quantity	Revenue	Variable costs	Fixed costs	Total costs
0	£0	£0	£40 000	£40 000
25 000	£50 000	£25 000	£40 000	£65 000
50 000	£100 000	£50 000	£40 000	£90 000

From this information the graph can be drawn as shown below, with pounds on the vertical axis and output on the horizontal.

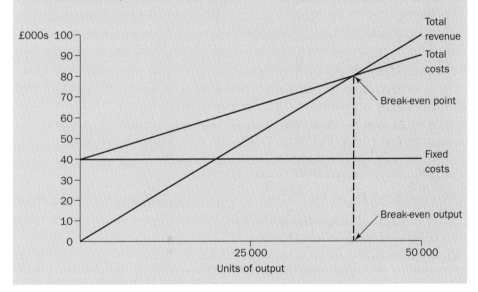

break-even point: the intersection of total revenue and total costs on a *break-even chart*. It can be calculated without drawing the chart as shown below:

$$\text{FORMULA:} \quad \text{break-even output} = \frac{\text{fixed costs}}{\text{contribution per unit}^*}$$

*selling price – variable cost

Worked example:

$$\frac{£40\,000}{£2 - £1} = 40\,000 \text{ units}$$

break-even revenue: the value of sales required to cover all the firm's costs. This can be found in one of two ways:

- First calculate the **break-even point**, then multiply that number by the selling price.

- Use the formula: $\dfrac{\text{fixed costs}}{\text{contribution per £ of sales}}$

Worked example: a clothes shop makes, on average, 40p contribution per £ of sales. Its fixed operating costs are £1000 per week. What weekly revenue does it need to break even?

$$FORMULA: \dfrac{\text{fixed costs}}{\text{contribution per £ of sales}} = \dfrac{£1000}{£0.4} = £2500$$

BRIC: see *Brazil, Russia, India and China (BRIC) economies*

British Rate and Data (BRAD): a monthly publication that lists all the advertising media available in the UK, from *The Times* to *The Grocer*. Each entry gives the address of each medium, together with the cost of buying advertising space. It is available at many local libraries and is ideal for discovering real advertising costs for projects or business plans.

British Standard 7750 is a certification of environmental management standards. It is a tool by which an organisation can recognise whether it is achieving acceptable environmental standards. It has largely been overtaken by the international standard ISO 14000.

British Standards Institute (BSI): the body responsible for setting quality and performance standards over a wide range of product fields. Seeing the BSI *kitemark* logo on a product should give consumers confidence that it has been manufactured to a high quality and safety standard.

brown goods: a collective term for electrical household goods that were traditionally made with wood casings, such as televisions and hi-fis.

BS 7750: see *British Standard 7750*

BSI: see *British Standards Institute (BSI)*

Budget: the Budget is the occasion on which the *Chancellor of the Exchequer* sets out taxation and expenditure plans for the year. Detailed changes will be made to both *direct* and *indirect tax* rates as they affect firms and individuals. There may also be changes in certain areas of expenditure such as health and *social security*. Because it has a direct effect on almost everyone, which can be measured in money terms, the Budget attracts a great deal of attention.

Budget day is usually in March each year. Each November the Chancellor of the Exchequer sets out the government's spending plans. Both occasions provide all-embracing statements of economic policy, including detailed forecasts of expected levels of economic activity.

The Budget performs a macroeconomic management function, as well as involving detailed adjustments to policies which affect the allocation of resources. An example of the latter occurs when there are changes in expenditure taxes on fuel, which have environmental objectives.

A significant part of the Budget speech will review *macroeconomic policy*. Tax and expenditure changes will lead to changes in the overall budget deficit or surplus. This will have an effect in turn on the level of *aggregate demand* and the prosperity of the economy.

budget: a forward financial plan usually involving a *cash flow forecast*, forecast sales and forecast costs. A budget is a kind of route map that should have been set in the light of the company's objectives for the period. Budgets can be used as a discipline, a coordinator, a motivator, a monitoring and control device and a trigger for remedial action, as well as a test of forecasting ability.

budget deficit: the amount by which government expenditure exceeds tax revenue. The deficit can be financed by borrowing. The *Bank of England* will sell Treasury *bonds* and bills in sufficient quantities to raise the funds. Useful amounts may also come from *National Savings*. In general the government can borrow at low rates of interest because it can guarantee to be able to pay back the money, because of its right to tax. However, if it needs to borrow a great deal more to finance the deficit, it may be necessary to raise *interest rates*. This may have the effect of discouraging investment and therefore future economic activity.

A budget deficit may be caused by structural or cyclical factors:

- structural: a long-term tendency for spending to exceed revenue, perhaps because government spending is more popular politically than government taxation
- cyclical: in a *recession*, tax receipts inevitably fall because people are out of work, and firms are making less profit. In addition more people out of work means more spending on social security benefits such as unemployment benefit.

Cyclical causes should be self-correcting when the economy recovers. Structural causes will not disappear unless tackled directly. Borrowing for *investment* makes sense when the income generated by the investment is likely to be sufficient to pay the interest on the debt. The annual budget deficit is known as the *public sector net borrowing* requirement. The combined deficits from the past are called the *National Debt*. (See also *fiscal rules*.)

budget surplus: the amount by which tax revenue exceeds government expenditure. (See also *Budget* and *budget deficit*.) The surplus in any one year is called the *public sector debt repayment (PSDR)*.

buffer stock may mean a stock of inputs held by a business, or stocks of commodities, held in case of shortages across the economy.

- A minimum stock level of items needed for production will be held by a firm, just in case something goes wrong. Possible causes include a supplier's failure to deliver, the discovery of substandard supplies or an unexpected increase in demand. The more efficient the firm and its suppliers, the lower the buffer needed. Those aspiring to a *just in time (JIT)* production system set their sights on removing the buffer stock completely. This would release capital to be put to more profitable use elsewhere in the business.
- Stocks of some commodities, such as wheat, are held in many countries and can be used in the event of shortages at some time in the future. Some are held by government bodies and some in the private sector. For many commodities, both demand and supply can vary. The demand for oil is affected by the level of economic activity, worldwide; the supply can be affected by wars. So prices do fluctuate from

time to time. Releasing buffer stocks onto the market – or buying up a glut – helps to keep prices stable. The supply of agricultural products varies because of weather and other problems. So keeping a buffer stock can help to prevent very low prices during a glut or very high prices at times of shortage.

building society: an organisation that provides interest-paying savings accounts, using the funds to provide households and small businesses with mortgages (long-term loans to buy property). These societies started as small, local organisations and kept a 'mutual' structure, meaning that any profits were reinvested into the business. The Building Society Act 1986 encouraged the societies to offer full banking facilities such as overdrafts. This led many to turn themselves into plcs, making them the same as other banks. In the pursuit of rising profits, former building societies such as Halifax and Bradford & Bingley were centrally involved in the reckless lending that led to the *credit crunch*.

bulk buying means purchasing in large enough quantities to secure a lower price per unit. This is an important economy of scale (see *economies of scale*) and is a reason why firms are attracted to *horizontal integration* (mergers). Traditionally, even small firms thought it sensible to buy in large quantities, gaining discounts but needing to hold stocks for a long time. This desire to buy in bulk has become unfashionable due to the focus on *just in time (JIT)* production and *stock control*.

bulk decreasing good is one which loses size and/or weight during its manufacturing process, e.g. steel and glass making. Because the reduction in bulk decreases transport costs, industries which do this tend to be located close to their supply of raw materials. (See *industrial location*.)

bulk increasing good is one which increases in size and/or weight during its manufacturing process, e.g. car body shells and soft drinks. Because adding weight and/or size increases transport costs, industries which do this tend to be located close to their market and the consumers. (See *industrial location*.)

bull market: a period when prices on the *stock market* are on a rising trend. Individuals who anticipate this happening buy shares in the expectation that they will be able to sell them in the future at a higher price. Sometimes this can get out of hand, so that the speculation on a high rising market begins to develop a momentum of its own, which has no relationship to the real value of the companies themselves. Such a market can only be sustained by its own momentum, and once a hint of doubt sets in it collapses very rapidly. Exactly this happened in the 1929 *Wall Street Crash* and again in 2003–07. Both were followed by a long, deep *recession*. A bull market is the opposite of a *bear market*.

bundling: selling products together in a package, rather than individually. This can be anti-competitive if it makes it hard for suppliers of reasonably priced alternatives to compete. If no one wants their products because they were forced to buy the bundle from a competing supplier, that business will have an unfair advantage. Computers and software provide the obvious example.

bureaucratic: a process or management that is rooted in paper-based checks and counterchecks on decisions or actions. As a consequence, creativity is likely to be stifled and decision-making both slow and cautious.

business confidence is widely assumed to be a major factor in decisions regarding firms' staffing plans, investment plans and stock levels. It is measured regularly by many research groups, of which the best regarded is the *Confederation of British Industry (CBI)*'s Quarterly Survey. Many believe that confidence can produce a self-fulfilling prophecy, with an optimistic outlook causing the investment spending and stockbuilding that makes the economy grow. This can lead governments to 'talk up' the economy in recessionary times.

business cycle: see *economic cycle*.

business environment is the combination of factors which lie outside an individual firm's control, but which have an effect on its performance. Such factors include economic circumstances, changing technology, government legislation and policy, the social environment, *pressure group* activity and the ethical climate.

business ethics: see *ethics* and *ethical code*

Business Link: the government's one-stop advice centre for new small firms. Operating regionally, Business Link offices can put *entrepreneurs* in touch with experienced advisers who can prevent firms making common mistakes such as failing to register for *value added tax (VAT)*. It is part of the *Department for Business, Innovation and Skills (BIS)*.

business objectives: targets set by the board of directors that affect decision-making throughout the organisation. Examples might include:
- to break even
- to make a 20 per cent return on the capital invested in the business
- to become known as the technological leader within a marketplace (for example, Sony in the audio and video markets).

A *business plan* will be devised to attempt to achieve the objectives set.

business plan: a report detailing the marketing strategy, production costings and financial implications of a business start-up. The plan is useful for helping the *entrepreneur* to think his or her idea through, though it is mainly drawn up to persuade investors or lenders to inject capital into the business. The main sections of a business plan are:
- a *marketing plan* showing the market gap, product positioning and competition within the chosen marketplace
- an account of the entrepreneur's business experience and financial commitments
- a *cash flow forecast*
- a projected *profit and loss account* and *balance sheet* for the end of the first year
- details of the finance needed from the investor, and the forecast rate of return on the investor's capital
- a brief account of the long-term forecasts and plans of the business.

business responsibility: the idea that businesses should take their decisions in a way which considers the needs and interests of all their *stakeholders*. As well as shareholders and employees, these include customers, suppliers, creditors and the community. Some managers see business responsibility as being part of effective management and believe that it can be achieved without reducing profits because it is in the long-term interests of all. Most firms say that they abide by the laws of the countries in which they are operating but some go beyond that and actively try to improve employment conditions or look for production methods which minimise environmental impact.

business taxation includes *corporation tax* and business rates.

buyers' market: if there are large numbers of sellers trying to sell to a relatively small number of buyers, then the buyers will be able to force a drop in price. This is sometimes used to describe the housing market when the number of houses for sale exceeds the number of potential buyers at current prices.

buying power is the strength of pressure a customer can place on a supplier. If a business has huge buying power, it can force the supplier to charge low prices and give generous credit terms.

A–Z Online

Log on to A–Z Online to search the database of terms, print revision lists and much more. Go to **www.philipallan.co.uk/a-zonline** to get started.

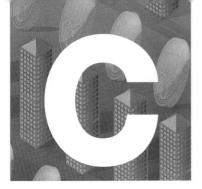

CAD: see *computer-aided design (CAD)*

calculated risks: some risks can be assessed by using probability data to decide how likely it is that each possible outcome may actually happen. This gives the business some idea of the size of the risks it is facing and may help in the decision-making process.

call centres: the highly regimented offices where high volumes of telephone calls can be made or received in factory-like conditions. There may be 500 staff working under very close scrutiny, including tape recording of every call and even closed circuit television surveillance. Many commentators have suggested that call centres are the modern-day equivalent of the factories that *F W Taylor* once visited or shaped.

CAM: see *computer-aided manufacture (CAM)*

cannibalisation is the effect of a new product launch on sales of a firm's existing brands. If Mars launched a mint Mars Bar they would worry that its sales would eat away at sales of the standard Mars Bar. This would need to be taken into account when estimating the profitability of the new product.

CAP: see *Code of Advertising Practice (CAP)* or *Common Agricultural Policy (CAP)*

capacity is the maximum amount an organisation can produce in a given period in the short run, i.e. without extra *fixed assets* and/or *fixed overheads*. Capacity is often difficult to estimate as more output can often be produced by a more intensive use of *plant*, e.g. motivated workforce, better materials, better maintenance or *shift work*.

capacity utilisation can be measured for an individual business or for the economy as a whole.
* For a business, it shows the extent to which the maximum capacity of a firm is being used, i.e. actual output as a percentage of maximum potential output.

$$\textit{FORMULA:} \quad \frac{\text{actual output per period}}{\text{full-capacity output per period}} \times 100$$

A firm's capacity utilisation is of considerable financial importance, because of the impact of fixed *overheads* per unit on profit margins. If a 40 000 unit factory has fixed overheads of £400 000 a year, full-capacity working carries *fixed costs per unit* of £10. Should demand halve to 20 000 units, fixed costs per unit double to £20. So high capacity utilisation keeps fixed costs per unit down, by spreading the overheads over many units of output. Low utilisation can push a firm into severe loss-making, forcing it to consider a strategy of *rationalisation*.

- Capacity utilisation for the economy as a whole is an important indicator. It shows how close the economy is to *full-capacity output* and will help to show when the pressure of *aggregate demand* is likely to lead to accelerating *inflation*, because the amount of unused resources in the economy is diminishing. Capacity utilisation fell sharply in 2008 as the financial crisis led to aggregate demand growing first more slowly and then actually declining.

capital: to an economist, capital is one of the *factors of production*, the others being land, labour and entrepreneurship. To the business person, it means funds invested in the company, either from the shareholders (*share capital*) or from lenders (*loan capital*). Both, however, recognise that capital is stored-up wealth, which, when combined with the other factors of production, can be used to make goods and services more efficiently. The return to capital may be *interest*, *profits* or *rent*. These provide compensation to the owner of the capital for not having the use of it at the present time for consumption purposes.

capital adequacy ratio defines the amount of capital needed by banks to ensure that they do not run out of funds when customers ask to withdraw their deposits. The amount is fixed in relation to the amount and types of loans which the bank is providing to customers.

capital consumption measures the amount of capital needed to replace equipment which has worn out during the course of one year. The term is used in the national accounts to show how much of total (gross) investment can be attributed to normal wear and tear or depreciation and how much reflects a net addition to the nation's stock of capital or productive capacity.

capital deepening occurs when more capital equipment is provided for each person employed. It will normally lead to an increase in *productivity* or output per person employed.

capital employed is the total of all the long-term finance of a business, consisting of loans, *share capital* and *reserves*. It provides the funds for obtaining the company's assets; therefore capital employed must equal assets employed.

capital expenditure: spending on new *fixed assets* such as machinery or new buildings. This affects the *balance sheet*, as a cash purchase would cause cash to fall while the fixed asset total rises. Capital spending does not, however, have any direct effect on the *profit and loss account*. This is because the cost of capital expenditure is only charged to the profit and loss account through *depreciation*, i.e. the cost is spread over the useful lifetime of the asset.

capital gain: a gain arising from the increase in value of an *asset*, which becomes apparent when the asset is sold for more than its historic cost or is subject to professional revaluation, e.g. property. A capital gain is accounted for in the balance sheet through an increase in *shareholders' funds*.

capital goods: another term for *fixed assets* such as *plant* or machinery.

capital intensive means that the way a good or service is produced depends more heavily on capital than the other *factors of production*. Examples of production systems which are very capital intensive include steel production and oil refining. A capital-intensive production process will require very high spending on plant and machinery, causing fixed costs to represent a high proportion of total costs.

capitalism: the system in which the price mechanism is used to determine how resources are allocated. Land and capital are owned by individuals who will decide how they are used on the basis of the profit that can be obtained. Similarly, they will pay employees according to the amount needed to attract them to undertake the required work. Most economies are actually mixed economies, with market forces determining many decisions and some governments taking other economic decisions. The advantage of capitalism is that the allocation of resources is determined primarily by consumer demand for final products.

capital: labour ratio measures the proportion of those two factor inputs in the production of a good. A good with a high capital : labour ratio is said to be *capital intensive*, and *labour intensive* when the reverse is true. Some economists have argued that a purely quantitative measure such as this is unhelpful. The quality of the capital and the labour (e.g. how well the workforce is trained) is more important.

capital market: the banks and other lenders that provide funds for long-term business investment. The capital market can be compared with the money market, which provides shorter-term loans, although in practice the line between the two is increasingly blurred.

capital movements are flows of capital from one currency to another. The location of the money may or may not change: it could be moved from a dollar account in New York to a sterling account in London, but it might equally be moved from a dollar account in London to a sterling account in London. Money which is 'footloose' in this way and moves from one currency to another in search of the best rate of interest is sometimes called *hot money*.

capital: output ratio measures the amount of capital employed in producing a given amount of output. A high capital : output ratio will indicate *capital intensive* production because wage rates are relatively high and some labour-saving investment has taken place.

capital stock: the amount of capital currently available for use in the economy. Changes in the capital stock provide a guide as to the productive potential of the economy.

capital widening occurs if employment is increasing and there is investment in new plant and machinery to give them the capacity to produce. This contrasts with *capital deepening*, which enlarges the amount of capital available to a given number of people.

captive market is a group of potential customers who are virtually unable to obtain alternative supplies because one company has a *monopoly* position. Isolated villagers would represent a captive market for a small village shop and are likely to be charged high prices as a consequence.

carbon emissions trading: see *emissions trading schemes*

carbon offsetting: firms and governments can buy carbon offsets to reduce the impact of activities that result in greenhouse gas emissions. These can be used to comply with regulatory caps on their total emissions. Individuals can also buy carbon offsets to counter the effects of emissions resulting from personal air travel.

cartel: a group of firms which agree to limit output in order to keep prices higher than they would be if there were free competition. The best-known cartel is OPEC (the *Organization of Petroleum Exporting Countries (OPEC)*) which at times in the past has restricted output so that world oil prices would rise. This is different from the standard cartel in that governments are involved.

Firms which collaborate in this way may have *market-sharing agreements* in which they each have a geographical area where they can operate without fear of competition. Or they may agree a minimum price or limit their range of products or non-price competition.

Cartels are now relatively infrequent for two reasons:

- In most developed countries, **competition policy** makes cartels illegal. By restricting competition, cartels lead to lower levels of output and higher prices for consumers.
- Cartels are quite hard to create and maintain, because the high prices act as an incentive for other firms to enter the market. Also, participating firms may try to cheat by offering secret discounts or not sticking to their output quotas. The parties to the agreement have to have a large share of the market in order to achieve the desired effect.

The process by which cartels achieve their objectives is called **collusion**. Evidence of this will encourage the Office of Fair Trading and the **Competition Commission** to investigate. In 2008 the Competition Commission investigated the way that supermarkets show price comparisons with other chains, usually showing all the same prices. They concluded that this was a sign of a 'de facto cartel'.

cash means literally notes and coin. However, it is usually used now to mean very liquid assets, as in 'cash in the bank', i.e. money held in instant access accounts.

cash balance: a firm's net cash position at a point in time, as shown by the bank statement.

> *FORMULA:* cash at start + cash inflows – cash outflows = cash balance

cash cow: a brand that has a high share of a declining market. Firms use their cash cows to generate the cash to invest in newer products with greater growth prospects. The cash generation (or 'milking') is achieved by pushing prices up as high as possible while minimising expenditure on **research and development (R&D)**, **market research** or **advertising**. (See **Boston matrix**.)

cash flow is the sum of cash inflows to an organisation minus the sum of cash outflows, over a specific period. Inflows can arise from cash sales, **debtors** paying up, interest received or disposal of assets. Outflows can be caused by cash purchases, settling **creditors**, or asset purchases. As not all these items pass through the **profit and loss account**, cash flow and **profit** are different concepts. Profit may be affected by non-cash items such as credit given and taken, **depreciation** and stock valuation.

cash flow forecast: a detailed estimate of a firm's future cash inflows and outflows per month. From this can be derived the monthly **cash flow** and, by adding together each month's figures, the cumulative cash position. As the worked example below demonstrates, a firm may face a period of negative cash flow that is purely temporary. As long as it has been forecast, **overdraft** arrangements can be made with the bank to ensure that temporary finance is available.

Worked example: cash flow forecast

(All figures in £000s)

	Jan	Feb	Mar	Apr
Cash at start	45	30	(20)	(5)
Cash inflows	115	130	150	170
Cash outflows	130	180	135	145
Net cash flow	(15)	(50)	15	25
Cumulative cash	30	(20)	(5)	20

cash flow statement: an account that shows the sources and uses of cash within a firm over its financial year. Whereas a *cash flow forecast* is based upon estimates of the future, a cash flow statement records what has happened in the past, i.e. it shows historic cash flow. It is one of the three financial documents that must be published each year by every public limited company.

caveat emptor means 'let the buyer beware'. In other words, however much consumer protection legislation there is, buyers always have a responsibility to take reasonable care over their purchases.

CBI: see *Confederation of British Industry (CBI)*

CDO: see *collateralised debt obligations (CDO)*

cell production splits a continuous-flow production line into self-contained units. Each cell will produce a significant part of the finished article, enabling the cell workforce to feel committed to their *complete unit of work*. It is part of what the management consultant Schonberger calls 'building a chain of customers', which he believes to be a vital part of *just in time* (*JIT*) production.

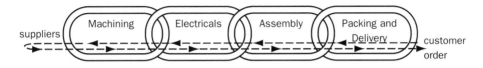

central bank: all countries have a central bank whose traditional function was to issue notes and coins, and to regulate the banking system. Britain's central bank is the *Bank of England*; in *euro* currency areas it is the *European Central Bank (ECB)* and in the USA it is the *Federal Reserve Bank*.

centralisation is drawing decision-making powers from the local or lower-level parts of an organisation, and concentrating them within the head office or centre. Its opposite is *decentralisation*.

PROS: • centralisation allows consistent policies to be applied throughout the firm
　　　　• it ensures that quick decisions can be made without consultation

CONS: • centralisation reduces the input of the day-to-day experts (the shop-floor staff) into the firm's decision-making
　　　　• it risks demoralising branch managers, who may feel powerless or mistrusted

centralised organisation: one in which decision-making powers are kept at the top of the hierarchy rather than delegated. The same term applies to geographic centralisation, in which local branches (or shops) work within a pattern tightly laid down by head office.

centrally planned economies: see *command economy*

Central Office of Information (COI): the government department that deals with all the *advertising* and *public relations (PR)* campaigns for the government. Examples of the COI's work would include drink-drive campaigns and recruitment advertising for the armed forces.

centring: a technique used in the *moving average* method of forecasting to ensure that the moving average trend data coincides directly with a time period. In a four-quarter moving average, for example, two successive four-quarter averages are added together, and the result divided by two. This establishes a centred average which shows the trend figure for the third quarter. Centring is needed whenever the moving average is based on an even number of pieces of data.

Worked example: centred averages

YEAR 1	Sales average	Four-quarter average	Centred average
Quarter 1	900		
Quarter 2	1200	1150	
Quarter 3	1300		1175
Quarter 4	1200	1200	
YEAR 2			
Quarter 1	1100		

CEO: see *chief executive officer (CEO)*

Certification of Incorporation: issued by the *Registrar of Companies*, this gives a company its legal personality and enables it to trade.

ceteris paribus is a Latin phrase meaning 'other things being equal'. This is a vital assumption in a lot of economic analysis, for it enables one to assume that no variables are influencing a situation other than those under consideration. An example would be that when measuring a product's sales following a price increase, one can only draw conclusions about the product's *price elasticity* if one assumes other things are equal, i.e. *ceteris paribus*.

chain of command is a vertical line of authority within an organisation enabling orders to be passed down through the *layers of hierarchy*. (See also *organisational chart*.)

chairman (or chairperson): the elected chair of the meetings of an organisation. A company chairman will not only run the meetings of the board of directors, but may also take responsibility for the long-term aims and objectives of the business, leaving the managing director to determine and execute the strategy and to run the business day to day.

Chambers of Commerce are groups of business people in a town or city who gather together as a *pressure group* to look after the interests of local firms. They provide information and help for small companies as well as promoting trade fairs and exhibitions.

Chancellor of the Exchequer: the person responsible for running the nation's economy. He sets out the government's tax and spending plans once a year. He also sets the inflation target, which the Bank of England must set interest rates to meet.

change is a constant feature of business activity. The key issues are whether it has been foreseen by the company – and therefore planned for – and whether it is within the company's control. Extensive change may come from sales growth: requiring new management structures, new *layers of hierarchy*, new divisions or *profit centres*. Such organisational change may be difficult, but one could say, fairly, that failure would be due to bad management. Yet there may be failure. Growth may lead the company to become stiflingly *bureaucratic*, causing bright young people to leave. Or extensive delegation to profit centres may backfire, as managers struggle to live up to their new responsibilities.

More problematic is unforeseen change. A small business that has a product which suddenly becomes very popular has many serious threats. An overstretched management may let costs get out of control: overtime payments, company cars, expenses and so on. *Quality control* may slacken in the rush to meet orders, leading to high returns (and therefore refunds) and a poorer reputation. Capital spending on new, bigger capacity will drain cash from the company. Worse, it may prove wasted if demand falls away as rapidly as it came. This example combines two problems: unforeseen change and change that is outside the company's control. Yet the firm could have brought the change within its control by ensuring steady, moderately geared, liquid growth, rather than frenetic, risky expansion.

External change is usually the hardest to control or even influence. Changing tastes or fashions, new laws or taxes, increased competition, or changes in the economy: all are major external constraints. The firm will try to affect these areas (by advertising or through *pressure group* activity), but may not succeed; in which case it must ensure that it is prepared to respond quickly and appropriately to whatever change occurs. *Contingency planning* is needed to succeed in this aim. This will cover the marketing tactics and production planning needed in the short term. Long-term health will often depend on the product range and degree of *diversification* in the business. A sharp tax increase on whisky will not damage a company with extensive beer, wine and soft drinks interests.

change management: the process of planning, preparing, implementing and evaluating changes in business strategies or working methods. The key underlying factor in change management is trust. For only if staff have faith in the motives and competence of the managers concerned will they help to implement the desired change. Successful management of change requires:
* people whose motivation and trust makes them willing to accept and even harness it
* brand names with the consumer loyalty to ensure continuing, high sales revenues
* knowledge and confidence in several different markets
* the financial resources to be able to invest in new products or methods.

Chapter 7: the section of the US Federal Bankruptcy Act 1978 that provides for the *liquidation* of a company which cannot reasonably be expected to return to a viable operating condition. Typically, a company in financial trouble will first turn to *Chapter 11* of this Act. If the company cannot be turned round it may end up in Chapter 7: liquidation.

Chapter 11: a section of US Federal Bankruptcy Act 1978 that allows a firm in financial difficulties to protect itself from its creditors for a period of time. Filing for Chapter 11 fends off the threat of *liquidation* while managers attempt to return the firm to financial health.

characteristics of entrepreneurs: the personality and character traits that make *entrepreneurs* different from most people. These include:
* initiative, i.e. making something happen before others join in
* hard-working
* resilient, i.e. able to keep going when times get tough (doesn't give up)
* creative, i.e. able to think of clever, perhaps original, solutions to problems
* self-confident
* taking calculated risks, i.e. able to cope with risk and to manage risk by thinking through the downside versus the upside.

charismatic leader: one who motivates employees to strive to meet an objective through the force of his or her personality. Such leaders were treated as the heroes of the stock market booms of 2003–07. After the collapse of HBOS and other banks in 2008 there was much more reflection on whether charismatic leaders can become too powerful within 'their' companies.

charity: a *non-profit-making organisation* established with the aim of collecting money from individuals and spending it on a cause, which is usually specified in its title. There are tax benefits to the givers, who are also not liable for the debts of the organisation. Although charities are not established to make profits, they can earn surpluses. Some are large-scale organisations employing many people across the world, such as Oxfam, Friends of the Earth, Médecins sans Frontières and Save the Children.

chief executive officer (CEO): the director in charge of all operations within a business. In Britain, the term 'managing director' has usually described this function, but the American version CEO seems to be gaining popularity. The CEO is answerable to the chairman of the board of directors, although some companies combine these functions. This results in an individual having a degree of power that concerns those with an interest in *corporate governance*.

Chindia: a collective term bracketing the world's high-population growth stars, China and India. The implication is that both have similar futures. In fact China and India are very different economies with different strengths and weaknesses.

chinese walls: the wall of silence that is supposed to exist in *investment banks* between those advising firms on *takeover bids* and the bank employees who are stock market dealers. If the dealers hear of a bid in advance, they could make huge profits by buying shares that are about to rise in value, but will lay themselves open to accusations of *insider dealing*.

chinese whispers: the way in which distortion occurs in a message passed orally along a chain of people.

CIM: see *computer-integrated manufacture (CIM)*

circular flow of national income: the way in which income flows around the economy, from firms to households and back to firms in a continuous process. Payments to employees are income, as are profits and rent. Income from all these sources is spent on goods and services. This spending becomes the revenue received by firms. Hence, the flow of money is circular. The model can be extended to take in savings and investment, taxes and government expenditure and imports and exports. These *withdrawals* and *injections* respectively reduce or increase the circular flow.

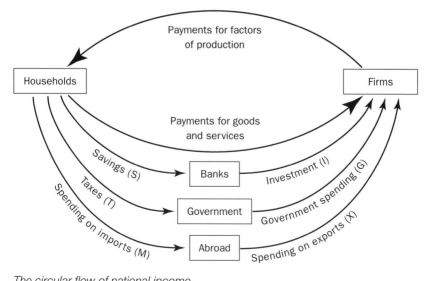

The circular flow of national income

circulating capital: the funds flowing through a business enabling it to carry out its usual operations. Also known as *working capital* and defined as *current assets* minus *current liabilities*.

citizenship: the extent to which a business acts as a good citizen, such as in clearing up its own mess and pollution, behaving well towards others and acting in the best interests of the whole community.

The City refers to the City of London and its financial services sector. The latter includes the banking system, the *Stock Exchange*, the money markets, the insurance industry and commodity exchanges.

civil law: legislation which covers offences that are not automatically prosecuted by the police. The civil law gives the individual the right to pursue a grievance by taking another person or corporation to court.

classical economics was developed by, among others, Adam Smith, David Ricardo and J S Mill, between 1776 when Adam Smith's *The Wealth of Nations* was published, and 1848 when J S Mill's *Principles of Political Economy* was published. These economists laid down the general principles of the market economy, perfect competition and the theory of comparative advantage. They were concerned mainly with the principles of microeconomics and the assumption of *perfect competition* was crucial to their analysis. They held that government intervention was mainly unhelpful and that the operation of self-interest would bring about efficient production in the long run. The classical economists continue to influence thinking right up to the present day, being the forerunners of what is now known as neoclassical economics.

classical management theory was formulated by observing how large organisations worked, and concluded that the main management functions were: forecasting, planning, organising, commanding, coordinating and controlling. The main theorist, *Henri Fayol*, believed that a clear hierarchy and the specialisation of tasks were the keys to effective management.

class intervals are the dividing lines chosen in order to group data into categories for purposes of analysis, e.g. there might be 12 days when sales volume was greater than 25 and no greater than 30. The class interval is five units. (See *frequency distribution*.)

climate change: the warming trend that has been observed along with the change in composition of the earth's atmosphere. Although there have been many observations relating to a warming trend overall, scientists expect climate change to lead to less predictable weather and different effects in different places. This will have striking economic effects in the years to come, leading to increased migration, changes in output for many products and changes in prices. Some of these may be affected by policy decisions. The *Stern Review* (2006) set out proposals for UK policy.

climate change levy: a tax on the use of fossil fuels by businesses and public sector organisations. The objective is to reduce emissions of greenhouse gases that are thought to be causing global warming. Organisations are being given an incentive to economise in their use of electricity, gas, petrol and coal. This is in line with international commitments. There is a discount scheme which can save organisations up to 80 per cent of the levy if they have met energy or carbon saving targets.

closed question: a question to which a limited number of pre-set answers are offered, e.g. Do you buy a newspaper nowadays? Yes ☐ No ☐

PROS: • ticking boxes is much quicker and easier for the respondent, so closed questions ensure a higher response rate
• a limited number of answers makes them easy to process and analyse

CONS: • provides no scope for comment or qualitative input
• impossible to anticipate all the possible answers

closed shop: a workplace where employees must belong to a *trade union*. It can only occur by agreement between the employer and the union. The enforcement of 100 per cent union membership was made illegal in the Employment Act 1988.

cluster sample: respondents drawn from a relatively small area selected to represent a particular aspect of a product's *target market*. For example, the cluster may be a seaside town chosen by a producer of sun lotion.

Code of Advertising Practice (CAP): the document that sets out the boundaries of what is acceptable within an advertisement, as laid down by the *Advertising Standards Authority (ASA)*. For example, the Code states that advertisements for alcoholic drinks should not feature people who are or who look under 25. If a member of the public complains about an advertisement to the Advertising Standards Authority, the test will be whether the advertisement breaks the Code.

code of practice: a form of *self-regulation* devised and run by an employers' organisation that lays down appropriate standards for firms operating within an industry. It is a way of improving the industry's public image and of avoiding government legislation and regulation. Although codes of practice are most obvious within industries with poor reputations such as time-share holidays, many conventional sectors also have them. Critics believe that rogue companies will always surface within a system of self-regulation. Advocates of codes of practice believe that industry experts can supervise their own industry more effectively and more economically than the state.

coincident indicator: a monthly economic statistic that can be taken as an indication of the health of the economy currently. A good example would be the demand for motor cars.

collateral is the security offered to back up a request for a loan. Usually the only acceptable form of collateral to a bank is property, since that tends to appreciate in value, whereas other business assets depreciate. For small business start-ups, the owners' personal property is often the only asset substantial enough to provide the security demanded by the banks.

collateralised debt obligations (CDOs) are parcelled-up batches of mortgage debts that are sold on as investments. The purchaser of a CDO is looking for a higher annual interest rate payout than is available on more conventional investments such as National Savings or 'gilt-edged' (government) securities. CDOs were a fundamental part of the property and banking boom that led to a bust in 2007–09. They were a way of making *sub-prime mortgages* appear less risky than proved to be the case. The term 'toxic debt' was often used in the *credit crunch* that led to many banking collapses. CDOs were that toxic debt.

collective bargaining is when one or more *trade union*(s) negotiate with management on behalf of a whole category of employees within an organisation or plant. Such negotiations usually cover pay, fringe benefits, working conditions and working practices. A benefit to the firm of collective bargaining is that a single negotiation can settle pay issues and potential disputes for a year. Less appealing to the employer is that the single negotiation gives the trade unions more power through solidarity.

collusion occurs when firms act in concert with each other, perhaps over *market-sharing agreements* or price fixing. The word has strong implications of working together for reasons that are not in the public interest, and it is illegal under competition law. There is no reason why firms should not share marketing data or *research and development (R&D)* effort.

command economy: an economic system controlled by the decisions of those at the centre of government. This contrasts with the Western model of free or social markets in which economic decisions are made by producers in response to demand from customers. The command economy rejects the notion of the *invisible hand* in favour of a system that hopes to distribute resources more fairly, but seems to be more *bureaucratic* and less able to supply goods of the right quality and quantity to meet consumer demand. The collapse of the command economies of the USSR and the Eastern bloc countries and the low living standards which prevailed before their collapse indicates the inefficiency that results from such a system.

commercial banks are those banks whose activities are directed at making a profit by borrowing from customers at an interest rate lower than that at which they lend. This makes them different from a *central bank*. Because customers who deposit their money with banks only ever need a small portion of that money in cash, commercial banks can lend the rest to other customers, who in turn only need a small proportion as cash, and so the remainder can again be lent to yet further customers… and so on.

Commission for Racial Equality: since October 2007 this has been part of the *Equality and Human Rights Commission*.

commodity: any good – as opposed to a service – which can be bought and sold. The term is usually applied to markets in which there is almost no product differentiation. These include commodities traded in commodity markets, such as unprocessed tea, sugar, rubber, wool, metal ores and so on. Businesses may also talk about a consumer market as 'having become a commodity market'. This would mean that customers have come to choose products or brands solely on the basis of price.

commodity prices can be very volatile. Most commodities can be stored and demand and supply are not always in equilibrium. Markets may be slow to respond to changes. Time lags can delay producers' responses to changes in demand and make prices even more volatile.

Many commodities have rather inelastic supply. Relatively small changes in demand and supply can lead to large changes in price. For example, when the demand for metal ores rises during a *boom*, little can be done in the short run to increase supply and the price may rise sharply, rationing existing supplies amongst the buyers prepared to pay the highest prices. Developing countries that are heavily reliant on one or a few commodity exports are vulnerable to the very unstable prices that they experience. Copper prices fell 60 per cent in late 2008 as recession took hold, creating a very difficult situation for Zambia and the Democratic Republic of Congo.

Common Agricultural Policy (CAP) is the scheme by which agricultural production within the *European Union (EU)* is organised. It was set up by the Treaty of Rome as a way of helping small-scale and relatively inefficient European farmers to survive.

In 2006, EU support for farmers (under the CAP) accounted for 45 per cent of its £75 billion budget.

PROS: • it stabilises farm incomes
  • it enables marginal producers to stay in business, e.g. sheep farmers on Welsh hills
  • it has helped to make Europe self-sufficient in food production

CONS: • it is expensive to operate
  • it is open to corruption
  • it raises food prices above world levels; this hurts consumers, and it hurts poor consumers more than rich ones

common external tariff: the import duties which are set by the European Union to cover certain imported goods for all member countries. The common external tariff favours producers within the EU and discriminates against producers outside the EU.

communication is the interaction between people, focusing primarily on the transfer of information. A communicator chooses an appropriate transmission mechanism in order to communicate with the intended receiver of the message. Communication can only be said to have succeeded once a response (**feedback**) has been achieved.

People can feel swamped by too much communication – especially if it is passive, such as memos to all members of staff. **Herzberg** and others have emphasised the importance of direct communication in the psychology of motivation.

communication channels are routes through which communication occurs. Examples include team briefings, **works councils**, plus the **chain of command** within an organisation. Communication channels can be 'open' or 'closed'. The latter means that access to the information is restricted to a named few. The former ('open') means that any staff member is welcome to see, read or hear the discussions and conclusions.

communication net (or network) is a diagram representing the actual communication structure within an organisation. The most common types are the circle and the wheel. As the diagram below indicates, the circle gives strong, team-based communication whereas the wheel gives control to the person at the hub.

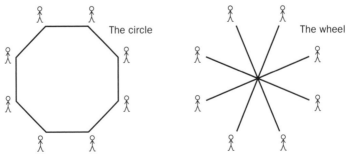

Communication networks

communication overload occurs when employees can no longer identify important pieces of information because they are too bogged down by trivial messages. A busy manager may return to her desk and find an inbox containing 120 e-mails.

44

Companies' House is where the *Registrar of Companies* holds the financial and ownership details on all the limited companies in the country. As laid down in the Companies Act 2006, all these records have to be available to the public. Students working on a project requiring the latest accounts for a company will find that the Cardiff and London bases for Companies' House can provide the information required (for a fee of around £15). It is also possible to obtain the information online at www.companieshouse.gov.uk.

company: see *private limited company* and *public limited company (PLC)*

company culture: see *culture*

company objectives: see *corporate objectives*

company secretary: appointed directly by the board of directors, the company secretary is the chief administrative officer of a business, usually responsible for the company's legal affairs.

company union: a Japanese approach whereby all workers within a firm are automatically represented by a trade union structure that is employed by the firm itself. Critics regard the lack of independence as a fundamental flaw.

comparative advantage: the idea that countries can benefit from specialising in the production of goods at which they are relatively more efficient. In this way consumers within each country gain the maximum benefit from international trade. At first, this may seem strange, because a country like the United States would seem to have an advantage at producing all goods when compared with a less developed country such as Somalia. However, it is easy to see that while the US may be one hundred times more efficient than Somalia in the production of maize, it is probably one thousand times more efficient at the production of cars. It therefore benefits everyone if the US produces cars, and Somalia maize, and then they trade.

compensation principle shows that society gains from a certain change if the gainers gain more than the losers lose. In other words, the gainers could compensate the losers and still be better off. It is actually rather difficult to use the compensation principle in practical situations, because it is often hard to quantify gains and losses in money terms.

competence-based qualifications are those based on identified achievements such as writing a letter or operating a word-processing package.

competition: the process by which businesses strive against one another to capture a larger market. In price competition they may try undercutting each other's prices. This is known as *competitive pricing*. The impact of competition on prices is plain to see. For example, since BT's monopoly of telephone calls came to an end, the cost of phone calls has fallen sharply. This is partly because of new technologies but also because of competition.

The impact of competition depends on the number and strength of other firms selling products within the relevant market sector. The more similar the products, the fiercer the competition. Firms need to cope either by becoming super-efficient, or by developing highly differentiated products (*non-price competition*). The ideal is to have a product with an appealing *unique selling point (USP)*, such as Apple's iPod.

Perfect competition refers to a situation in which there are many sellers of an identical product. Imperfect competition may still be very strong competition but involves fewer sellers.

Competition Commission: the organisation responsible for investigating markets in the UK to ensure that they are kept in line with **competition policy** and that firms cannot engage in anti-competitive business practices. To be effective, the Commission must work in full cooperation with the Office of Fair Trading and the European Commission. It has two main functions:

- to investigate planned mergers and to determine whether they will lead to excessive monopoly power
- to act as a court of appeal for firms which have been found to be engaging in **anti-competitive activities** such as a **cartel**.

The **Office of Fair Trading (OFT)** can refer a particular market situation or possible merger to the Competition Commission. Any merger which is likely to lead to a 25 per cent or greater share of the market will be investigated by the Commission.

The Commission can now take legal action to enforce its recommendations. As the OFT has got stricter with the companies it investigates, it seems likely that the Competition Commission will deal with more appeals from aggrieved businesses which are finding that the legislation has a serious effect on their activities. In general, any abuse of a dominant position in the market will come under scrutiny.

competition policy: the government's approach to ensuring that competition is active enough to provide consumers with goods and services that are high quality and fairly priced. The government seeks to avoid consumers being 'ripped-off' by ensuring that:

- **monopolies** do not form takeovers or mergers (regulated by the **Competition Commission**)
- privatised monopolies such as gas supply and water distribution are regulated toughly by organisations such as OfGas and OfWat
- anti-competitive behaviour by firms is monitored by the **Office of Fair Trading (OFT)**.

In many ways, the power of **European Union (EU)** law has driven UK governments to adopt stronger competition policies than have traditionally existed in Britain. The introduction of prison sentences for infringements of competition law has greatly increased the impact of the Competition Commission and the OFT.

Monopoly theory shows that a firm with market power may restrict output and raise prices. This can be shown to reduce consumers' real incomes. Firms which use their market power may require an unnecessarily large quantity of real resources to produce their output, which is quite simply wasteful and inefficient. Hence the perceived need to control market power in the interests of the consumer.

competitive advantage: an aspect of a business that enables it to withstand competition. The theorist Michael Porter suggested that there are two main types of competitive advantage:

- the ability to produce at lower costs than competitors (the secret of Ryanair's success); this allows the firm to undercut the prices of any competitor
- clear product differentiation that offers some added value to customers, e.g. the distinctiveness of BMW car design and image is something that people will pay extra for.

competitiveness: the degree to which a firm succeeds in selling its product when there is competition in the marketplace. Competitiveness relates to consumers' perceived value for money and may rest on:

- a price advantage, which may reflect **productive efficiency** and lower costs than those of competitors

- a willingness to accept lower profits
- an advantage in design, quality, reliability or customer service or some other important product feature, maybe a *unique selling point (USP)*, all aspects of *non-price competition*.

International competitiveness is important to economies and to governments because it enables both domestic producers and exporters to expand, leading ultimately to economic growth. It is usually associated with strong *productivity* growth or a commitment to innovation. It can be measured by examining *unit costs* in comparison with those of other economies. Without competitiveness, both domestic producers and exporters face strong competition from foreign producers. Imports will rise and exports fall, leading generally to falling aggregate demand and depressed trading conditions.

competitive pricing means setting a price for a product or service based on the prices charged by competitors. This can be subdivided into two types:
- In a market with low *product differentiation*, where all producers are price takers, no one has the market power to set a price higher than the competition.
- In a market dominated by a *price leader*, a less important brand would have to price at a discount in order to sell a significant sales volume.

competitive tendering is the practice of encouraging *private sector* firms to compete to undertake tasks that were formerly done by council employees. This encourages those applying to find new, more efficient methods of carrying out the task, but often results in lower wages and/or poorer conditions of service for the employees.

complaints procedure: the process whereby a customer complaint is resolved to his or her satisfaction and the problem communicated to management to prevent its repetition. Some organisations have a special department for dealing with complaints. This is likely to be efficient, but may insulate other staff from hearing the causes of customer dissatisfaction.

complementary goods are products that complement each other, such as bread and butter, cars and tyres, fish and chips. Because usage and demand are connected in this way, if the price of one product rises, demand for its complement is likely to fall. The amount by which these movements take place is determined by their *cross-price elasticity*.

complete unit of work means organising the production process so that the task of each worker or team represents a significant part of the whole. This move away from high *division of labour* is regarded by Professor *Herzberg* as a key factor in providing *job enrichment*.

components are manufactured parts used within production or assembly. They might be bought in from suppliers or produced within the factory.

compound interest: the way that the value of a lump sum can build up if the interest is constantly reinvested, adding to the capital sum.

computer-aided design (CAD) enables designers and draughtsmen to store, retrieve and modify their work using multi-dimensional images.

computer-aided manufacture (CAM) involves the computer in a variety of manufacturing tasks beyond the use of robots on the *production line*. These include *stock control* and ordering goods.

computer-integrated manufacture (CIM) is the use of computers to coordinate every aspect of production, from product design through *stock control* to production scheduling and control.

concentration ratio is the extent to which a market is dominated by a small number of large firms (at one extreme) or a large number of small firms (at the other). It can be measured in a number of ways, e.g. by *capital employed*, turnover or number of employees.

conciliation is the attempt to get both sides in a dispute to reconcile their differences. An independent conciliator might be found from ACAS, the *Advisory, Conciliation and Arbitration Service (ACAS)*. He or she would listen to the views of both sides, look for possible common ground, then encourage both sides to meet to discuss a compromise.

conditions of employment are the details of pay, working hours and holiday time that are set out in an *employment contract*.

Confederation of British Industry (CBI): the premier employers' association, listing most of the country's leading firms in its membership. The CBI's main functions are:
- to be a lobbying service for industry within the government and elsewhere, promoting the legislation and economic policies favoured by the *private sector*
- to promote the image of industry as a worthwhile career, especially among students
- to provide its membership with well-researched, nationally applicable research such as the CBI's *Quarterly Survey of Economic Trends*.

confidence level: a measurement of the degree of certainty to be attached to a conclusion drawn from a *sample* finding. For example, if a pre-election opinion poll puts the Conservatives 3 per cent ahead of Labour, how confident can one be of a Tory victory? Clearly, not 100 per cent certain since the research finding is not based on the whole population. Market researchers only feel happy to draw conclusions from findings that have a 95 per cent chance of being right (i.e. 19 times out of 20). The term given to that is a '95 per cent confidence level'.

conflicting objectives: governments often face a situation in which they can only achieve one of their policy objectives at the expense of another. The most obvious example is the short-term *trade-off* between inflation and unemployment. There were many occasions during the 1970s, 1980s and early 1990s when it would have been possible to reduce unemployment by increasing *aggregate demand* in the economy, but the consequence would have been increasing inflation due to *excess demand* in the economy. This looked like becoming a problem again in 2007, until the *credit crunch* happened.

congestion charges involve the payment of a fee on bringing a vehicle into the area where they apply. It acts as an incentive to avoid unnecessary journeys, so reducing traffic congestion. The London congestion charge, introduced in 2003, is generally regarded as having successfully reduced congestion and an example of what *road pricing* can achieve.

conglomerate: a firm which is comprised of a series of disconnected businesses. This provides the strength derived from *diversification* but has the potential weakness of a lack of focus. The modern approach to the management of a conglomerate is to delegate power very extensively to the different businesses within the group. This is to enable each business to act as its own core with its own strategy and focus.

conglomerate mergers occur between firms which have no clear connection with each other's business, either horizontally or vertically (see *horizontal integration* or *vertical integration*). The advantage to the firm of such a move is that it spreads risk, and may increase overall profit potential.

conscience spending occurs when consumers spend because they feel, for a variety of reasons, that they 'ought' to buy the good or service. Charities often exploit this situation in their advertising and, especially at Christmas, by offering cards or small gift items for sale.

consensus is the area of agreement between people. It may be tacit rather than explicit. In other words it may not have been discussed and agreed formally. It is a key principle of Japanese management that a strategy should not be implemented until a consensus has been arrived at.

conservation concerns the way in which depletable resources are used. When production involves the use of real resources which cannot be replaced, there will be a case for conserving those resources in such a way that they do not become excessively scarce too quickly. In this way conservation measures may apply to petrol, on which taxes have been raised so as to discourage consumption.

constant prices are used when it is important to measure a variable in a way that avoids including the effect of inflation. For example, real income is measured in constant prices. This will involve the selection of a *base year*, so that the variable is expressed in, for example, 2008 prices.

constraints: limitations on a firm's ability to meet its objectives. Internal constraints are within the firm's control; *external constraints* are beyond it. Often, however, internal and external constraints interact, muddying the dividing line between them. For instance, a rise in interest rates (external) is primarily a problem for firms with high borrowings (internal).

constructive dismissal occurs when an employee resigns from a job because the employer has acted unlawfully, or broken the contract of employment. A black worker who has suffered racist abuse from a manager could take the company to an industrial tribunal on grounds of constructive dismissal.

consultation: asking for the views of those who will be affected by a decision. These views should then be taken into account by the executive responsible for taking the decision. It is important to distinguish between consultation and *delegation*. The latter means passing decision-making powers down the hierarchy, whereas consultation keeps power at the top.

consumable: any product that is not a *consumer durable*, i.e. can only be used or consumed once. Typical examples include food, detergent and petrol. In addition, all services would be classified as consumables.

From the business point of view, their significance is that:

- consumables do not share the *market saturation* problems of durables, therefore demand is more constant
- due to the possibility of regular purchasing it is easier to build strong *brand loyalty* towards consumables
- consumables are less subject to falling demand during a *recession* (whereas durables suffer as customers postpone replacement purchases).

consumer: a person who purchases or consumes a product. Manufacturers of children's products are aware that their consumers are often not the purchasers. This is why advertisements for products such as breakfast cereals are often a strange combination of health information (for parents) wrapped up in jazzy, fun cartoon images (for children).

The consumer is an important player in the market because a decision to buy creates a potentially profitable situation for the supplier. There is then an incentive to ensure that the products desired are made available at a price which generates some profit. Equally, decisions not to buy may end in a producer going out of business or cutting back production. This is the basis of *consumer sovereignty*.

consumer credit is the means by which people buying goods can delay payment and so spread the cost. Purchasing in this way often requires a deposit and carries a rate of interest. One of the most common types of consumer credit is *hire purchase*.

Consumer Credit Act 2006: the regulations covering the purchase of goods on *credit*. Its intention is to prevent consumers signing unfair contracts and also to ensure that purchasers know exactly what interest rate they are to be charged for the credit they receive.

consumer durables are goods which are owned by households but which are not immediately consumed by them. Examples include washing machines, dishwashers, cars and televisions. In effect, they are the *capital goods* of households.

consumer expenditure is the sum total of all spending by consumers in the whole economy over a period of time. It is a component of *aggregate demand*. The level of consumer expenditure and its likely future growth are sometimes important variables for a business which is considering whether to expand.

consumer prices index (CPI): the UK's new way of measuring annual *inflation*, which excludes the cost of housing, in order to provide more consistent data trends. See *retail prices index (RPI)* for an explanation of how this data is gathered. It is used by the Treasury as the basis for setting the *inflation target*.

consumer profile: a quantified picture of a company's customers, showing the proportions of young to old, men to women, middle class to working class and so on. (See *demographic profile*.)

consumer protection refers to that group of laws passed to control the worst excesses of past business practices towards their customers. It includes health and safety regulations and the prevention of *anti-competitive activities*.

consumer resistance is the term given for the factors that prevent potential customers from buying a particular product. The reasons for resistance may be active or passive. If people dislike the idea of whisky mixed with cream, they will actively resist trying or buying an Irish cream liqueur. *Brand loyalty* may lead to passive resistance.

consumer sovereignty is sometimes referred to by the saying 'the consumer is king'. This means the consumer, by his or her purchasing habits, determines what is produced in the marketplace and the way resources are allocated. An increase in demand will tend to make it more profitable to produce the item in question. This encourages firms to produce more. Similarly, if demand falls, losses may be made and these create an incentive for producers to move resources into some other line of production. In this way the *profit-signalling mechanism* transmits the information given by consumer demand to producers, so that the allocation of resources is kept in line with the pattern of demand.

In practice, **market imperfections** can greatly reduce consumer sovereignty. Market power and advertising can push consumers into choices that for them are less than optimal. (See also **supernormal profit**.)

consumer surplus: a consumer good will be valued more highly by some consumers than by others, yet they will all pay the same price for it. Some consumers would be willing to pay a price higher than the actual market price. The term consumer surplus refers to the value of the extra satisfaction which these consumers get from the item, over and above what they have had to pay for it. The consumer surplus is shown on a supply and demand diagram by the triangle enclosed by the demand curve and the price line. The demand curve shows how consumers value the product and all those who are prepared to pay a higher price get some extra satisfaction.

Put another way, consumers demand a quantity of the product such that the **marginal social benefit** they get from it is at least equal to the price. If it is worth less than the price, then clearly they won't buy it. But for the many consumers who would still buy the product at a higher price, the marginal social benefit of the product is actually greater than the price, by the amount of the consumer surplus. Many consumers are getting the product for less than they would be prepared to pay.

Consumer surplus is maximised at the equilibrium price. If either the supply or the demand curve shift in either direction, consumer surplus will change too.

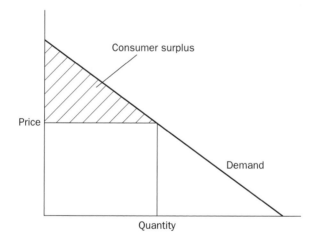

consumption means the level of all spending on consumer goods and services in the economy as a whole. It is an important component of **aggregate demand**. (See also **consumer expenditure**.)

contestable markets: it may be comparatively easy for newcomers to the industry to break into a contestable market. This means that existing businesses, already in the field, face a constant threat of increasing competition. We might expect that prices will be generally lower in contestable markets, merely because of the possibility of competition. If they announce very large profits, firms already in the industry may be advertising the possibility of large profits for others and this may encourage **new entrants**.

So even if there are a very few firms in the market, the threat of competition from new entrants may keep prices low. No-frills airlines provide an example of a contestable market. In the reverse case, where there are **barriers to entry**, existing businesses are protected from competition. Where economies of scale are a substantial barrier to entry, only very large firms may be able to produce efficiently. Entry costs will be high, the risks for a new competitor may be great and the market will hardly be contestable at all.

Very few markets are perfectly contestable because there are almost always some **sunk costs** which give an existing producer at least a small advantage. These sometimes relate to advertising and brand familiarity. Or they may be fixed costs associated with plant and machinery that has little or no alternative use. This means that the cost of **exit** will be high. An incumbent firm faced with competition from a new entrant, which has to cover all the costs of new investments in plant and machinery, could cut prices in order to delay the loss of its market share.

contingency planning means preparing for unwanted or unlikely possibilities. Since Perrier Water's setback when it was found to contain traces of benzene, firms include disaster planning as one contingency. Plans might also be prepared in case of:

- a severe **recession**
- **bankruptcy** of a major customer
- a sudden surge in demand.

Contingency plans can be prepared on computer models that provide the opportunity to ask and answer **what if...? questions**. Of course, complete surprises such as the 2004 tsunami may never be planned for successfully.

continuous improvement: see **kaizen**

continuous research consists of **surveys** that are carried out on a regular basis, such as every month. Firms might do this to monitor brand awareness and **brand standing**.

PROS: • warns of any slippage in **brand loyalty** or image
       • helps measure the success of advertising campaigns

CONS: • regular research will be expensive over the year, therefore may not be economic for a small firm
       • accuracy relies on asking the same questions each month, which is less flexible than ad hoc research

contract: a legal agreement between two parties which defines the relationship in terms of what is expected on both sides. It will detail the actions to be taken and the payments to be made. It provides a degree of certainty that contains the risks involved in any agreement.

contract of employment: see **employment contract**

contracting out means placing with independent suppliers a task that used to be done in-house, i.e. within the organisation. **Private sector** firms, councils or nationalised industries might contract out services such as cleaning, refuse disposal, or even the production of components. Contracting out is a reversal of **vertical integration**. Sometimes it is called **outsourcing**.

PROS: • might lead to lower costs as the contractor's wage rates do not have to be as high as those within the organisation
       • putting the service out to **tender** invites new management thought on how to improve efficiency

CONS: • the subcontractor's employees may be less motivated towards providing the quality the organisation wants
       • from the employees' viewpoint, working for a subcontractor may mean more intensive work for less pay

contractionary policies are used when the economy appears to be growing unsustainably fast or when **inflation** is becoming a problem. The policies are of two kinds:

- *monetary policy*, which would require high interest rates, is decided by the **Bank of England**
- *fiscal policy*, in the form of either tax increases or government expenditure cuts, or both, is decided by the Treasury.

In both cases, the objective is to reduce the rate of growth of aggregate demand so that inflationary pressures are reduced. Reducing demand will slow down firms' attempts to recruit more **labour**, thus reducing the demand for scarce skills and making it harder for people to negotiate higher pay.

contribution is total revenue minus total **variable costs**. Therefore contribution minus **fixed costs** equals profit. It is a measure of the amount each product or department contributes towards covering the fixed overheads of the business. Once the latter have been covered, all further contribution is straight profit. The contribution of a product line or of even a department is its revenue minus the costs which would disappear or could be avoided if it were discontinued. Contribution gives a clearer picture by removing general **overheads** or fixed costs which are difficult to allocate.

Revenue £150 000

minus £60 000 Variable costs equals		
		Contribution £90 000
Contribution of £90 000		minus Fixed costs of £56 000 equals
		Profit of £34 000

Worked example: calculating profit by use of contribution

If a firm sells 20 000 units at £7.50, has £3 of variable costs and £56 000 of fixed costs, what is its profit?

Answer:	Total contribution	−	fixed costs	=	profit
	(£4.50 × 20 000)	−	£56 000	=	
	£90 000	−	£56 000	=	£34 000

contribution costing: the valuation of a product's cost solely on the basis of **variable cost**, i.e. excluding **fixed costs** or **overheads** which are difficult to allocate (especially in multi-product companies).

contribution pricing: the setting of prices based on the principle that as long as an item is sold for more than the *variable cost*, it is making a contribution towards the *overheads* of the business. This notion may lead a firm towards one of two approaches to pricing: *price discrimination* and *loss leaders*. For exam purposes, the main consequence of contribution pricing is its effect on the acceptance of additional customer orders at cut prices. A standard exam question runs as follows:

> Worked example: contribution pricing
>
> **The BG Co has sales of 2000 units at £5. Its fixed costs are £3000, variable costs are £3 and average costs are £4.50. BG's sales director has just phoned through with an extra order for 500 units at £4 each. Should it be accepted?**
>
> Answer: the immediate thought is that if average costs are £4.50, it must be unprofitable to accept an order at £4. That is wrong, however, because if fixed costs have already been covered and variable costs are £3, any price above £3 is profitable. The order will in fact generate an extra 500 × £1 = £500 profit (assuming BG Co has the capacity to produce the extra units).

control: one of the two key factors involved in successful *delegation*; the other being trust.

convergence: refers to the process of bringing the *European Union (EU)*'s economies and currencies into line with each other. This was an essential prerequisite for *Economic and Monetary Union (EMU)* and the single currency. Unless all the member countries have similar levels of economic activity, rates of inflation and interest rates, the euro could cause major economic upheavals. The main focus for convergence is upon public sector borrowing and inflation rates.

convertible currency: one which can be exchanged for another currency without limit. At its simplest level, this means if you go abroad you can take as much *sterling* out of the UK as you like, or exchange it before you go. At another level it means that companies can move large sums out of and into currencies as they wish.

cooperative: an organisation run by a group of people, each of whom has a financial interest in its success and a say in how it is managed. That group might be the producers (as with agricultural cooperatives handling the packing and storage of several farmers' crops), the workers or the customers (as with retail cooperatives).

coordination means ensuring that the work of many different people interlinks within a single plan. It is a major management function which can become hard to achieve when a great deal of decision-making power is delegated. The difficulty of coordinating the workings of a large organisation is one of the key *diseconomies of scale*.

copyright is the legal protection against copying for authors, composers and artists. Unlike *patents*, there is no requirement to register an author's copyright. The law on copyright is governed by the Copyright, Designs and Patents Act 1988.

core activities are the operating divisions that a firm sees as central to its *corporate objectives*. Other, more diversified functions may be seen as peripheral to the firm's purpose, and therefore sold off or closed down.

core inflation: a measure of inflation that excludes items that are likely to distort the data for the underlying rate of inflation. *Consumer prices index (CPI)* is the preferred measure in the UK.

core staff are those people – managers, technicians and skilled workers – who are essential to a company. They give the organisation its distinctiveness. Because they are essential, the organisation seeks to bind them to itself with secure, full-time employment at high salary levels and with good conditions and *fringe benefits*.

corporate advertising: an *advertising campaign* to boost the image of a company rather than to sell a particular brand.

PROS: • can increase sales of a whole range of products if, like Heinz, the company name is also the brand name
   • can make the company more attractive to potential shareholders, suppliers and employees

CONS: • can be regarded as a luxury, especially in times of recession
   • has often been used to correct image problems caused by the company's own unethical behaviour (e.g. banks overcharging or oil companies polluting)

corporate bonds are loans to companies which carry a fixed rate of interest and have a fixed maturity value. They may be held by individuals, by banks or other financial intermediaries. They may be traded on the *Stock Exchange*, should the holder require *liquidity*. The price at which they are traded will vary according to interest rates and the comparative profitability of other investments.

corporate culture: the attitudes and behaviours of staff that are the norm within an organisation. (See *culture*.)

corporate governance is an American term raising questions about who controls the boardrooms of public companies and whose interests do they and should they serve? In theory, the shareholders have voting powers over company directors, but in practice these are rarely exercised. Practical power resides with institutional investors such as pension funds, but they rarely step in unless they see the company dividends or share price threatened. In Britain, issues of corporate governance became prominent after a series of City and company scandals revealed a moral vacuum at the top of many businesses. Unfortunately, the problems had not been resolved before the banking boom and bust that led to the 2008/09 recession.

corporate identity: the design package that aims to create the company image desired by a firm. This may consist of a *logo*, a company uniform, the colour and style of the firm's stationery or even company cars and vans.

corporate image: the view of a company held by its customers, employees, and the public at large. For a bank, the ideal image might be: large, reputable, long-established yet innovative, approachable. *Market research* would aim to find the image characteristics desired by the customers, which would in turn influence decisions on *corporate advertising* and *corporate identity*.

corporate objectives are the *goals* of a whole enterprise. These should be based upon the firm's mission/aims. The corporate objectives govern the targets for each division or department of the business. They provide a mechanism for ensuring that authority can be delegated without loss of coordination. Among the most common corporate objectives are:
• to ensure long-term, stable growth in real terms
• to spread risk and achieve growth through *diversification*

- to concentrate upon the firm's core skills
- to maximise *market standing*
- to add value through continuous technological *innovation*
- to achieve *profit maximisation* in the short to medium term.

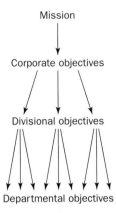

corporate responsibility is the idea that organisations have to consider environmental and ethical factors in their decision-making as much as those concerned with profit. The Cadbury Report (1992) spurred many companies into action, so that, for instance, ICI now issues a separate environmental report; and many companies undertake *environmental audits* of their activities to examine the impact they are having.

corporate saving occurs when firms retain some of their profits, keeping them in reserve for the future. Often they will use their savings to replace capital equipment, or expand the business, in the future.

corporate social responsibility (CSR): the ways in which companies address issues beyond their *bottom line*, i.e. their profit. In many firms CSR may be an important, positive aspect of the business *culture*; in others it may be a cynical way to respond to – or prevent – unfavourable publicity. (See also *social responsibilities*.)

corporate structure: the way a company is organised. It may be tall, flat, matrix, hierarchical, centralised or decentralised depending on its size, aims and *leadership style* (see *tall hierarchy*, *flat organisation (or hierarchy)*, *matrix management*, *hierarchical structure*, *centralised organisation* and *decentralised organisation*).

corporate venturing occurs when a large firm decides to invest in a smaller, probably fast-growing business. It is then behaving like a venture capital firm such as 3i. Optimists see corporate venturing as a valuable way of giving small firms access to equity capital and advice from an experienced 'sister' firm. Sceptics believe this is a way for large firms such as Microsoft to keep an eye on the potential competitors of tomorrow.

corporation tax is the tax which companies have to pay as a percentage of their profits. (Although tax rates can be changed each year in the *Budget*, the level has usually ranged between 30 and 35 per cent.) Smaller firms pay a lower rate, of between 10 and 25 per cent.

correlation is a measurement of how close a causal link there is between two or more sets of numerical data. Highly correlated data would form a predictable pattern, such as that for

Worked example: Company A pays 34 per cent tax on profits while the smaller Company B pays 25 per cent.

	Company A	Company B
	(£000)	(£000)
Revenue	9500	1200
Total costs	7300	840
Pre-tax profit	2200	360
Corporation tax	748	90
Profit after tax	1452	270

every £100 extra spent on advertising, sales rise £500. If the correlation is total, the data will form a straight line, as shown below.

A danger with statistical correlations is making assumptions about cause and effect. Perfume advertising is at its heaviest in the weeks prior to Christmas. Sales follow the same pattern. Yet it would be foolish to suppose that this proves the effectiveness of the advertising. Perfume companies advertise at Christmas because that is when the public is most receptive to their advertising. The sales and advertising data are correlated, but that does not in itself prove which factor is the cause and which is the effect.

Correlation between advertising and sales

corruption: using bribes to influence politicians or officials to secure a favourable decision. Corruption has a very bad effect on the **allocation of resources** because decisions are made on the basis of the bribe rather than the well-being of the community concerned or the market forces which reflect consumer preferences. It undermines the effectiveness of democratic systems which are designed to reflect the wishes of the electorate. It greatly reduces the efficiency with which market economies work.

cost-based pricing: setting a price on the basis of production costs rather than market conditions. This can only be sensible for a firm with little or no direct competition. The two main cost-based pricing methods are mark-up and **cost-plus pricing**.

cost–benefit analysis examines all the costs of a particular project or decision, be they *external costs* or *internal costs*. The internal costs are private costs which are experienced by the producer, sometimes called the financial costs. For example, the chemical plant will count the financial cost to itself of all the inputs to the production process. In addition to these costs, there will be external costs which are paid by a third party who is not a producer or a consumer. These usually reflect the pollution created in the neighbourhood of the plant, which affects the people who live there. These are social costs and may be hard to quantify.

Including both private and social costs can give a better idea of the true cost to society of some projects. The Victoria Line in the London Underground, the Channel Tunnel and numerous motorway projects were subjected to cost–benefit analysis. The difficulty is that although some social costs and benefits can be quantified, others cannot. The benefits of faster moving traffic can be estimated for the people who will spend less time in traffic jams during working hours. The benefits of improved health through reduced pollution are more difficult to define, although treatment costs are quantifiable. This means that cost–benefit analysis has to be based partly on value judgements about the relative importance of different factors in the decision. However, looking at all costs and benefits does mean that decisions are not made solely on financial evidence.

Wherever private and social costs and benefits diverge, and social costs and benefits are hard to quantify, there must be careful consideration of the social priorities that might influence decisions relating to costly investment projects. Given the cost overruns that plagued the building of the Channel Tunnel, it is hard to imagine that decision takers would have decided in favour if they had known the true cost of the project in advance. But in South East England it is quite hard now to imagine life without it. Maybe the external benefits of increased economic development made it economically viable, despite the high cost.

cost curves relate the cost of the product to the quantity produced. (See also *average cost* and *marginal cost*.)

cost differential: a difference in cost between competing producers. This could be due to *economies of scale*, or the use of different technologies or *differentiated products*.

costing is the process of determining the cost of producing or supplying a product or service to the customer. It may be based upon historic information, or standard costing may be used to monitor the present and forecast the future.

cost minimisation: the attempt to cut operating costs as low as possible. This is sometimes put forward as a business objective, but few managers would see it as valuable. Most firms want to optimise costs, in other words get the right level of costs. Cadbury does not want to make chocolate as cheaply as possible. It wants costs to be as low as possible while meeting its taste/quality standards.

cost of living: the cost of a selection of goods and services considered necessary to a normal life. This is measured by the *retail prices index (RPI)*, which is based on price data for a wide range of products and retail outlets. The term 'cost of living' tends to be used rather vaguely because it is itself a very imprecise idea. The problem is that it varies from one household to another and specific price changes have a different impact in different types of household.

cost of sales is the accountant's calculation of the direct costs that can be attributed to the *sales revenue* generated over a trading period. The cost of sales can then be deducted from revenue to show the **gross profit**. This is the first stage in constructing the trading account of a firm's **profit and loss account**.

The calculation of cost of sales is quite tricky because of the accounting principle known as the matching principle. This makes it necessary to exclude from the purchases total any costs of building up stocks for sale in the next financial year. In order to achieve this, cost of sales is calculated below.

FORMULA: opening stock + purchases − closing stock = cost of sales

Worked example: a firm's trading account

	£	£
Sales revenue		100
Opening stock	20	
Add purchases	50	
	70	
less closing stock	(15)	
Cost of sales	55	55
Trading or gross profit		45

cost-plus pricing means adding a set profit percentage to the estimated total costs per unit.

PROS:
- cost-plus ensures that any cost increases will be passed on to the customer in the form of higher prices, thereby protecting the firm's profit margins
- it may be the only way of pricing a job for which the amount of work cannot be predicted, such as **research and development (R&D)** into a supersonic military aircraft

CONS:
- cost-plus can only be applied in a situation where no effective competition exists; this is because it means setting prices with no reference to the market situation. So although it is the ideal pricing method, few companies are in a position to use it
- by ignoring market conditions, the firm may be missing out on the further profit opportunities offered by **price discrimination**

Worked example: a firm with fixed costs of £40 000 per month and variable costs of £1 per unit wants to price its product on the basis of 25 per cent cost plus. Monthly sales are estimated at 100 000.

Total costs per unit	= fixed costs per unit	+	variable costs per unit
	= £40 000 ÷ 100 000	+	£1
	= £0.40	+	£1

Total costs p.u. + 25% = £1.40 × (125/100) = £1.75

So the price is **£1.75**

cost-push inflation occurs when rising production costs force firms to increase their prices to protect their profit margins. In particular, **trade unions** are accused of making wage demands greater than productivity increases, causing employers to raise the prices of their goods, hence causing **inflation**. The usual response to this is that trade unions are only protecting their members' living standards, and if prices rise in the rest of the economy, it is unfair to expect workers to suffer a reduction in their standard of living. The causes of inflation are complex, and would be said to result from the interaction of cost-push with **demand-pull inflation**.

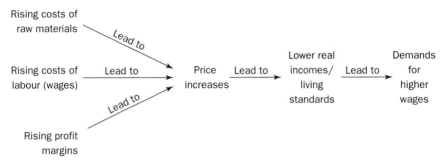

The causes of cost-push inflation

costs: see **fixed costs**, **variable costs**, **average cost**, **average fixed cost** and **marginal cost**

costs of growth: the negative aspects of the growth process, such as pollution and congestion and the depletion of resources generally. As negative **externalities** increase in number the benefits of **economic growth** are reduced.

Council of Ministers: the **European Union (EU)**'s main decision-making body. Its membership comprises one government minister from each of the 25 member states. The minister chosen will depend upon the issue under discussion. If the meeting is focusing upon the European economy, the **Chancellor of the Exchequer** is likely to be the UK's representative.

council tax is a tax raised on the value of houses by local authorities. If it is assumed that larger houses are owned by people who are better off, it is broadly related to ability to pay. People on benefits are generally exempt. Council tax funds a part of local expenditure, the rest coming from central government.

counter-cyclical policy is used to iron out fluctuations in economic activity (see **economic cycle**). When the economy is booming, the government will try to stop it 'overheating' by reducing its own spending on goods and services. In times of **recession** it will follow the opposite course. To a certain extent this is automatic; in a recession there is more unemployment, so government spending has to rise to pay for more unemployment benefit. The automatic element is known as the **automatic stabiliser**.

The tricky part is deciding when to apply policy measures which are not automatic. Getting the timing wrong will make the situation worse. If the Chancellor believed the economy was coming out of recession he might reduce government spending on, say, roads. If, however, the recovery did not happen as expected, the reduction of incomes in the road-building industry would make the recession worse.

counter-inflation policy: if inflation is accelerating, the Bank of England may adopt contractionary monetary policies, by raising interest rates. This will have the effect of reducing *aggregate demand* and pressure on resources. (See also *monetary policy*.)

CPI: see *consumer prices index (CPI)*

creative accounting is the name given to legal but questionable accounting practices that massage the figures (and therefore ratios) in published company accounts. The two focal points for creative accounting are the stated profit for the trading period and the balance-sheet ratios relating to financial health. During the 1990s, the *Accounting Standards Board* brought in new measures to minimise the scope for presenting legal but misleading accounts.

Among the main creative accounting techniques are:

- brand accounting, meaning to obtain a valuation for brand names a company owns, and then place them on its *balance sheet*; this boosts *shareholders' funds* and therefore cuts the firm's apparent *gearing* level
- capitalisation of interest, by which the interest costs of financing a property development are recorded as an addition to the value of the property asset, instead of as a business cost
- *off-balance-sheet financing*
- *window-dressing*.

creative destruction: the idea that barriers to entry and big profits create an incentive for big businesses to research and develop innovative products and processes. These ultimately lead to greater efficiency, price cuts, larger markets and higher standards of living. This idea is associated with the work of Joseph Schumpeter, and contrasts with the view that highly competitive markets promote greater efficiency.

creative tension: the stimulation to thought and motivation that can come from exchanging views with others on a problem that has no clear-cut solution.

creativity is the spark that can provide an innovative solution or decision. It may be a quality that certain individuals possess naturally, but it will only become evident within an organisation that nurtures it. Some *top-down management* lays down company policies for dealing with virtually every eventuality. This removes the flexibility of operation that is the essential background for creative solutions to problems. A firm wishing to foster creativity might:

- encourage *group discussions* among the workforce based on *brainstorming*
- accept that all ideas are worth considering
- encourage open, *direct communication*
- accept that mistakes are to be learnt from, not condemned.

credit exists as soon as someone has acquired goods or services without paying for them at once or by paying for them with someone else's money. A credit sale means that an organisation acquires the *current asset* of *debtors* rather than cash. A sale is recorded in either case.

credit creation: the process by which banks expand their lending by a multiple of any new deposits they receive. Not all their customers will want to withdraw their deposits at any one time. This allows the banks to keep just a percentage of their assets in the form of liquid reserve assets and to use the rest to make loans. As borrowers spend the money, it is deposited once more in the bank, allowing a further expansion of credit. This is the process that went too far, too fast in the period 2005–07 as banks made excessively generous loans for house purchase. This led to the **credit crunch** and the process of credit creation stalled as banks sought to avoid making any more risky loans.

credit crunch: the sudden switch from plentiful credit to credit shortage that began in August 2007. It started with the freezing of wholesale money markets when banks stopped trusting each other. With banks struggling to obtain the cash they needed, central banks and governments stepped in. This stopped banks from collapsing, but did not give banks the confidence to lend. Therefore householders and businesses found themselves crunched by lack of credit.

Causes of the crunch:

- reckless lending by banks to consumers and businesses that borrowed recklessly
- the collapse of house prices in America following years of housing boom and the bundling of **sub-prime mortgages** into **collateralised debt obligations (CDO)**
- banks that grew too fast, partly because executives were offered excessive bonuses for achieving growth; the banking tradition of prudence (caution) was ignored
- lack of effective regulation because governments in America and Britain had become convinced that the **invisible hand** of the free market would serve everyone's best interest.

Effects of the crunch:

- major banks in Britain and America collapsed, including Northern Rock, Lehman Brothers; others, such as the Royal Bank of Scotland (RBS), were part-nationalised
- from Autumn 2008 there were dramatic falls in economic output worldwide due to cutbacks in consumer confidence and spending; as a result, unemployment rose rapidly
- in every country, governments were forced to take a far more hands-on approach to running the economy, often using **Keynesian** methods such as higher government spending
- many commentators speculated that the crunch would see a once-and-for-all shift in economic power from America–Europe to China–India.

credit insurance involves paying a fee (premium) in return for the guarantee that if a customer fails to pay for a credit purchase, the insurer will pay. It is therefore a guarantee against **bad debts**. Export credit sales can be insured through the **Export Credit Guarantee Department (ECGD)**.

creditors are those to whom an organisation owes money, perhaps through having purchased goods or services on credit so that payment is still outstanding. Creditors appear under **current liabilities** in the **balance sheet**.

creditors meeting: a meeting arranged to confirm the appointment of a **receiver** to a company that has just gone into **liquidation**. The creditors would also have the opportunity to ask the proposed receiver questions about the likelihood of any payments of the cash they are owed.

credit rating: a judgement made by bankers about the financial health of a business and therefore how safe it would be to provide it with goods on **credit**. The credit rating will be based upon the strength of the firm's **balance sheet** and on its recent financial history. The best known credit rating service is the American company Moody's. Any firm with Moody's top rating (triple AAA) is in a position to borrow at the best possible terms. Moody's and the other ratings agencies were heavily criticised in 2008 and 2009. They had given triple AAA ratings to investments based on **sub-prime mortgages**.

credit terms: the time allowed by a supplier before the customer must pay for the good or service received. This is usually 30, 60 or 90 days from the time the invoice has been presented, though customers may try to take longer to pay than this. Business credit is usually interest free.

criminal law applies to those committing a criminal offence such as fraud. Such offenders should be pursued by the police and prosecuted. This contrasts with **civil law**, which only results in lawbreakers being sued if an individual or organisation takes them to court.

crisis management: the response of an organisation to a severe, probably unexpected threat to its well-being or even survival. Many firms use **contingency planning** to cope with predictable crises (such as a fire at a key supplier's factory), but the actual crisis will rarely go according to plan. Therefore a named top executive is likely to be put in charge. It is quite possible that this person will manage the crisis in a far more authoritarian manner than usual, due to the need for quick decision-making.

cross-price elasticity measures the responsiveness of demand for one good to a change in the price of another. So, if the price of apples falls, the demand for pears is likely to fall as consumers switch to purchasing apples. It is measured by applying the following formula:

FORMULA: $$\frac{\text{percentage change in quantity demanded of good X}}{\text{percentage change in price of good Y}}$$

The closer the competition between goods X and Y, the higher will be their cross-price elasticity.

CSR: see *corporate social responsibility (CSR)*

cultural differences: the variations in perceptions and attitudes between one country and another. These need to be considered when plans are being made to market a new or adapted product in more than one country. (See also **global localisation**.)

culture: the culture of an organisation is the (perhaps unwritten) code that affects the attitudes, decision-making and management style of its staff. Examples of different business cultures include:

- goal-orientated, bonus-seeking, youthful culture based upon success at any price
- hierarchical culture based on respect for seniority, tight official communication channels and the avoidance of mistakes
- lively, growth-orientated culture based upon commitment to the product and the company.

The culture will affect **resistance to change** within the business and therefore the ability of a new boss to impose his or her style or decisions upon subordinates. (See **Handy, Charles**.)

cumulative data is generated by adding up consecutive numbers within a series. For instance, a firm with sales of 100 units per month in the period January–March has cumulative sales of:

January	100
February	200
March	300

It follows that if April's cumulative figure is 380, monthly sales have fallen to 80 units. Alternative terms for cumulative data include accumulated data and year to date.

currency: the notes and coins which are used as a medium of exchange in the country concerned.

currency appreciation occurs when the exchange rate rises and the purchasing power of the currency increases. This might reflect an increase in demand for the country's export products or a capital inflow. Either of these would increase demand for the currency and drive up the exchange rate. (See also *appreciation* and *capital movements*.)

currency crisis: if dealers on the foreign exchange market expect the value of a currency to fall, they may start selling large quantities of it. This may make it impossible for the central bank to buy enough of the currency to keep up its value, because its foreign exchange reserves are limited. This would be termed a currency crisis. (See also *fixed exchange rate*.)

currency swaps are ways in which firms avoid the problems of international currencies which fluctuate in value. A swap takes place when a currency is simultaneously bought and sold. This may be done by purchasing a currency on the spot market and at the same time selling it on the forward market. This is a way of *hedging*.

current account: see *balance of payments*. The term also refers to bank accounts kept mainly for the purpose of making transactions.

current account imbalances are deficits and surpluses resulting from significant differences between level of exports and level of imports. If they become very large they can destabilise the economy. The USA had very large deficits during the Bush presidency. These were covered in large part by loans from China, which has a very high savings rate and a policy of investing abroad by buying US government bonds (which helped to finance the US budget deficit). This eventually led to loss of confidence in the dollar and depreciation of the currency. These imbalances remained significant in the run-up to the financial crisis in 2007 and after. (See also *global imbalances*.)

current asset: anything owned by an organisation which is likely to be turned into *cash* before the next *balance sheet* date, usually within one year. Typical current assets are *stock*, *debtors* and *cash*. The balance of current assets over *current liabilities* is called *working capital* and, in essence, finances the organisation's day-to-day running.

current liability: anything owed by an organisation which is likely to be paid in cash before the next *balance sheet* date, usually within one year. Typical current liabilities are *creditors*, *overdrafts*, *dividends* and unpaid tax.

customer behaviour: *consumer* decisions and actions taken during the year, which can be measured by recording delivery times and sales patterns (such as Christmas peaks). Such information will be held on a ***database***.

customer loyalty implies such positive purchaser attitudes as to ensure a high rate of repeat purchase. This could be achieved through the quality of a product or service, the level of sales and/or after-sales care, or from the power and attraction of the product image.

customer service: this covers all the activities that affect the customer's experience of dealing with an organisation. This will include the impressions created by the manner, appearance and training of staff, plus the reality of how well the customer's needs or wants can be satisfied. Businesses offering a high level of customer service will add value to their products, enabling them to charge a higher price, while ensuring customer loyalty. (See also ***after-sales service***.)

customs duties: the taxes levied on imports as they are brought into the country, also known as ***tariffs***.

customs union: a group of countries which agrees to trade freely within their borders and imposes a ***common external tariff*** on imports from outside the area. The European Union is a customs union. This may lead to ***trade creation*** and ***trade diversion***. Overall it will usually promote the growth of trade and specialisation, thus allowing member countries to become better off.

cyclical unemployment occurs when ***aggregate demand*** in the economy is slowing and is not enough to buy the output which can be produced when all resources are fully employed (***full-capacity output***). In these circumstances, cyclical unemployment could be reduced if ***aggregate demand*** increased.

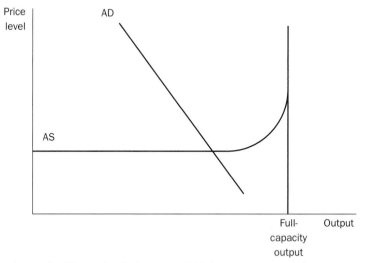

Aggregate demand will buy a level of output which leaves many people unemployed

Cyclical unemployment is sometimes lagged to the ***economic cycle***, perhaps by as much as a year. As demand falls, employers may postpone making people redundant as long as possible. Similarly, during the upturn, employers will wait to be sure that the increased demand is permanent before recruiting more staff.

Government policies to reduce cyclical unemployment could:
- reduce taxation and increase government expenditure
- try to reduce *labour* costs, for example by reducing the employer's National Insurance charges.

Governments have often in the past been unwilling to use counter-cyclical measures because of the perceived risk of higher aggregate demand causing excess demand and accelerating inflation. So cyclical unemployment persisted for a number of years, e.g. during much of the 1980s and during and after the recession of 1990–1992.

The recession of 2008–2009 appears at the time of writing to have caused less cyclical unemployment than the two earlier recessions. This may mean that the labour market really is more flexible than it used to be. (See also *flexible labour markets*.)

cyclical variation: in *time-series analysis*, this is the variation which can be attributed to the economic or trade cycle. For example, the increase in demand for *consumer durables* after a period of recession may be cyclical rather than indicate a change in the underlying trend.

Do you need revision help and advice?

Go to pages 324–35 for a range of revision appendices that include plenty of exam advice and tips.

damages: money awarded by a court to a plaintiff in compensation for something suffered or lost. The money will have to be paid by the defendant. This may occur if a firm has been sloppy about product safety and a customer injury results.

data: facts of any kind, whether in number or verbal form. Although this is the correct explanation, business people are inclined to use the term to mean numerate information only.

database: a collection of information, usually stored on a computer. Examples of databases used in business include lists of customers and suppliers. Such information can be quickly and easily accessed, added to and interrogated, so that, for instance, it might be possible to ask the database for the names of all customers living in the North-East of England.

Data Protection Act came into force in 1984 to protect individuals who have information about them held on computers. Organisations which hold such information have to register with the Data Protection Registrar, and have to agree to levels of accuracy and security. The Act gives people the right to see their personal file; for example, one held by a bank on a customer's creditworthiness. The 1998 Data Protection Act updated the legislation and gave employees the right to see their personnel files.

dawn raid: an unannounced, rapid raid intended to succeed through surprise. The term is used for *stock market* share raids, when a firm making a *takeover* buys up as many shares as possible before the bid announcement is made. This enables it to buy some shares cheaply, and to establish a base shareholding upon which to build. A dawn raid can also be used to describe the unexpected arrival of tax or *Office of Fair Trading (OFT)* officials to inspect a company's books.

day release is off-the-job training for employees who are given paid time off work each week to complete a college-based course that will lead to extra qualifications.

deadweight loss: the welfare loss to the consumer which occurs when an industry becomes a *monopoly*. The market power of the firms in the industry is such that they can push up prices and reduce the quantity supplied. This effectively reduces consumers' real incomes by diminishing the *consumer surplus* which they might have had. An example of deadweight loss would be where a drug company limits the supply of a new and effective drug for which it holds the patent. High prices could be charged but that would mean that some sufferers who could benefit from the drug will not be able to afford it (as with AIDS drugs in developing countries). Against this, there is always the possibility that a monopoly can rationalise production and achieve cost savings which will be at least partially passed on to consumers.

death duties: see *inheritance tax*

death rate: the number of people dying per thousand of population. This is an important component of the rate of population increase, particularly in developing countries where life expectancy has increased dramatically.

debenture: a fixed-interest, long-term security with underlying *collateral*, usually land. So a £100 000 10 per cent debenture dated 31 December 2015 would pay £10 000 a year before tax to the registered holders until 2015. If the company defaults, the collateral can be sold to repay the lender, much like a building society *mortgage*. Debentures are an alternative to shares as a means of raising long-term *capital*. They do not dilute control but create the risks associated with raising the *gearing* level.

debrief: a meeting to hear what a researcher or interviewer has discovered and to discuss what conclusions can be drawn.

debt: money owed by one individual or organisation to another. Debts are usually created with an agreement as to the interest payable and date of repayment. There may be a contract which can be enforced through the courts.

debt finance means using loans to pay for investments, rather than share capital. Most firms rely on a combination of debt and *equity* (share) finance. If there is heavy reliance on loan or debt finance and the business takes time to become profitable, interest payments may become a problem. This happened with the Channel Tunnel. Initially, finance came from share issues but as time went by there were cost overruns which were financed by borrowing from the banks. Eventually the company was unable to cover its interest payments out of current income and had to restructure its debts, giving the banks shares in exchange for their loans. This reduced the interest payable. (See also *gearing*.)

Debt Problem: since the 1970s, many *developing economy* governments have borrowed large sums from banks in the developed countries. The amounts of foreign currency they could generate by exporting were insufficient to cover their interest commitments, even after they had cut back their imports substantially. In time some were also unable to repay the capital. This became known as the Debt Problem.

Some countries negotiated *debt rescheduling*. Some banks wrote off part of the debt. Many of the countries that are still seriously affected are in Africa south of the Sahara.

The movement Jubilee 2000, which became Jubilee Plus, a coalition of charities and aid agencies, pressed hard for the debt to be written off for the poorest countries. Some progress was made but debt remains a problem. The United Nations, the *World Bank* and the *International Monetary Fund (IMF)* are still working on this.

debt ratio: the amount of a country's debt in relation to the level of its exports.

debt rescheduling may occur when a borrower (an individual, a firm or a government) with large loans cannot meet the repayments. The lenders can extend the term of the loans and postpone the repayment dates. They can also give an interest holiday, so that interest payments can be temporarily suspended to give time for the borrower to recover. On the international level, debt rescheduling means lengthening the periods over which governments can repay their debts, in order to reduce the problem. Rescheduling is often preferable to default.

debtors are the people who owe you money. On a *balance sheet*, they represent the total value of sales to customers for which money has not yet been received. The way an organisation manages its debtors is often a key to its *liquidity*. Successful credit control ensures that credit is not extended to potentially bad debtors and that late payers are chased (see *bad debt*).

decentralisation means devolving power from the head office to the local branches or divisions. This includes passing authority for decision-making 'down the line', thereby accepting less uniformity in how things are done. Traditionally, firms such as Sainsbury's and Marks and Spencer have been highly centralised.

PROS:
- decentralisation can *empower* local managers, encouraging them to be more innovative and motivated
- it reduces the volume of day-to-day communication between head office and the branches, therefore giving senior managers the time to consider long-term strategy

CONS:
- reduction in uniformity may unsettle customers, who expect every Sainsbury's to look the same or every McDonald's hamburger to contain just one slice of gherkin
- head office is in a position to measure the success of every aspect of the product and sales mix, therefore its instructions may prove more profitable than local managers' intuition

decentralised organisation: one in which decision-making powers and financial resources are passed down the hierarchy to empower junior and local managers. Whereas in a *centralised organisation* a local store manager has to apply the rules set out by head office, decentralisation enables junior staff to make decisions in line with local circumstances and opportunities. (See *empowerment*.)

decentralised wage bargaining occurs when negotiations are between individual employers and their employees, rather than between an *employers' association* and a *trade union*, operating at a national level. Decentralised bargaining allows local variations in *labour* market conditions to be reflected in local wage rates. It may help to generate jobs in areas of high unemployment if locally agreed wage rates are lower than national rates.

decile: the total accounted for by one tenth of a population. For example, if all the households in Britain were ranked in order of wealth, the lowest decile would be the 10 per cent of the population with the least wealth. To measure the distribution of wealth within society, the proportion of national wealth owned by the lowest decile could be compared with the highest decile.

declining industries: industries with products for which demand is falling. There are several causes:
- a shift in *comparative advantage*, such that competing imports are becoming available at prices below those which the domestic industry can achieve (as happens with textile products in developed countries)
- *technological change* leading to the development of new products which are superior to the old one (as when air travel reduced demand for ocean liners).

The major declining industries in the UK have been coal, iron and steel, shipbuilding, textiles and footwear and, to some extent, vehicles. Unfortunately all of these have been localised industries so the effects of decline have been particularly hard on some communities.

decreasing cost industry: an industry in which expansion leads to a fall in average costs of production. This would occur if there were *economies of scale* to be reaped as output rose. The situation is sometimes described as increasing returns to scale.

deficit: when income falls short of expenditure. The opposite is a *surplus*. The terms are used generally instead of profit and loss for *non-profit-making organisations* such as charities, or in economics when describing balances such as the government's finances or the country's *balance of payments*.

deflation is a term which is used in two different ways. It can be:
- A fall in the general price level. This is different from a fall in prices in a particular sector of industry (e.g. telecommunications) or a fall in the rate of *inflation* (which means that prices are rising more slowly than before). Up to and including the 1930s, prices generally fell from time to time and were as likely to fall as to rise.
- A period of reduced economic activity, when *aggregate demand* is falling, output and employment are cut and incomes fall. These, the conditions of a *slump*, can be accompanied by falling prices.

Deflation threatened a number of economies in 2009 as output and employment fell.

deflationary gap: see *output gap*

deflationary policies or *contractionary policies* are those which are designed to reduce demand by the use of either *fiscal policies* or *monetary policies*. This might occur when inflation is a problem.

deindustrialisation means the long-term decline in Britain's relative position as a world manufacturer. Writers using the term are usually looking for thoroughgoing changes in society and government policy in order to halt the trend. The main causes of deindustrialisation are said to be:

- *short-termism*
- the social class divide (*them and us*)
- poor education and vocational training.

All mature economies (i.e. those which have had a substantial manufacturing sector for a long time) experience a tendency for resources to shift out of manufacturing and into the service sector. This is most marked in the USA and the UK.

delayering is the removal of one or more *layers of hierarchy* from the management structure of an organisation.

PROS:
- leads to a wider *span of control*
- gives greater responsibilities and workload for each staff member
- reduces the number of intermediaries between the bottom and the top
- reduces overhead costs

CONS:
- staff may become overstretched (causing stress)
- may just be a euphemism for making people redundant

delegation means passing authority down the hierarchy (see *decentralisation* and *empowerment*). It can only work successfully on the basis of mutual trust. The boss must trust the subordinate to complete the tasks efficiently, while the subordinate must be sure that the boss is not just passing on dull or impossible tasks. The other key element in delegation is control. Can the boss bear to relinquish control over a task? If not, the delegation is phoney.

deliberate creativity: using a planned approach to generate innovative ideas from people who are not usually 'creative'. This is achieved by encouraging people to describe in detail an existing product or process, then visualise how things might be different if one variable was changed.

demand means the quantity of a good or a service that people want to buy at a range of different prices. Market demand refers to the level of demand which comes from everyone in a particular market. *Effective demand* means demand backed by the ability to pay for the product. *Aggregate demand* means demand for all goods and services available in the economy as a whole.

The level of demand for individual products may be influenced by:
* incomes
* tastes or fashions
* changes in the prices of other goods, be they **substitutes** or **complementary goods**.

Individual demand will be particularly influenced by incomes and family circumstances. (See also *demand curve*.)

demand curve: a line graph which relates the quantity demanded to a range of possible prices. The curve almost always slopes downwards to the right because, as prices fall, people tend to buy a larger quantity. This is known as a movement along the demand curve and leads to a change in the quantity demanded.

A shift in the demand curve will occur if tastes or incomes change or if there is a change in the price of a related good, either a **substitute** or a **complementary good**. This is often loosely referred to as a change in demand (as opposed to a movement along the demand curve). It is better to be clear and use the word 'shift'.

As telephone calls have become cheaper, people are using the telephone more often. Similarly, the falling price of mobile phones has increased the quantity demanded. These are movements along the demand curve.

Equally, rising incomes could mean that more people want to own mobile phones at all price levels. This means that the demand curve for mobile phones will shift to the right. It is often important to use the *ceteris paribus* assumption when analysing market changes. It allows us to deal with one change at a time and analyse its effect in isolation.

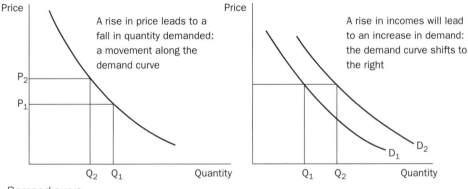

Demand curve

demand deficiency unemployment occurs when *aggregate demand* is too low to buy all the output that can be produced in the economy. It is unemployment which could be reduced if spending increased. It is also known as *cyclical unemployment* because it increases during the recession phase of the *economic cycle*. Sharp increases in unemployment of this kind occurred in 1990–92 and 2008–09. (See also *depression*.)

demand management refers to government policies which influence *aggregate demand* so that there is neither excessive inflation nor high unemployment. *Fiscal policies* and *monetary policies* can be used to control demand and prevent it either from growing faster than the capacity of the economy to produce or from slowing to well below that level. Demand management policies have been associated with the work of *J M Keynes*, and are sometimes called Keynesian policies. It can be difficult to predict exactly how much of a change in demand is needed to secure the government's objectives. The term itself has gone out of fashion but the policies are still in use.

demand-pull inflation occurs when *aggregate demand* is greater than the capacity of the economy to produce goods and services. This excess demand occurs when aggregate demand is growing fast and almost all the real resources in the economy are fully employed. Shortages, i.e. supply constraints, will appear, typically of skilled *labour*, and this will make it easy for people to negotiate pay rises. This in turn raises firms' costs and they will be quick to raise their prices to cover the increase. As the economy approaches its *full-capacity output*, it is impossible to increase output to meet the growing demand and any further increase in aggregate demand will quickly push up prices. Inflation will then tend to accelerate. In the diagram, aggregate demand grows from AD_1 to AD_2 to AD_3, but with the economy close to full capacity, the resources to increase output are scarce and their prices are bid up to P_3 by the rising demand.

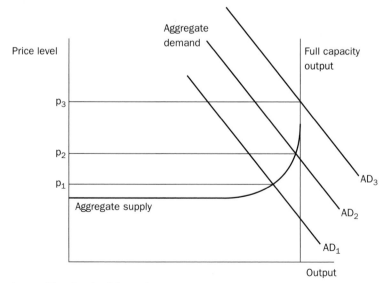

Excess demand leading to rising prices

Demand inflation appeared to be threatening the UK in 2007–08 as food and oil prices rose but rapidly subsided as the financial crisis caused aggregate demand to fall. (See *cost-push inflation*.)

demand schedule gives the quantities sold of a product at a set of different prices. It gives the data from which a *demand curve* may be drawn.

demarcation is the dividing line between one job function and another. For example, it used to be common for maintenance workers in factories to be split into mechanics and electricians. Nowadays, firms favour *multi-skilling*, which does away with demarcation lines and therefore prevents demarcation disputes.

demerger occurs when a firm is split into two or more parts, either by selling off parts or by floating them separately on the *Stock Exchange*. Demergers occur because:
- firms involved in *takeovers* often find that their new purchases offer fewer *economies of scale* than expected, so they prefer to focus on their original business
- takeovers are often financed by heavy borrowings, so in times of economic downturn firms may try to sell off non-core business to cut their debts or interest payments.

demerit good: a good which has been found through the political process to be socially undesirable. Illegal drugs provide the simplest example. They may be subject to *overconsumption*.

Deming, W E (1900–1995): an American engineer whose post-1945 work on product quality at the Hawthorne lighting plant led him to be invited to help the Japanese rebuild their industries after the Second World War. His emphasis on achieving quality through statistical process control was well learned and appreciated by the Japanese. They regard him as one of the founders of *total quality management (TQM)* and have named their premier quality award after him.

democratic leadership means running a business or a department on the basis of decisions agreed among the majority. This might be done formally through a voting system, but it is much more likely to be an informal arrangement in which the leader delegates a great deal, discusses issues, acts upon advice, and explains the reasons for decisions. The main difference between democratic and *paternalistic leadership style* lies in the degree of *delegation* and in the willingness to go along with the decisions of the majority.

demographic profile: a statistical breakdown of the people who buy a particular product or brand, e.g. what percentage of consumers are aged 16–25? What percentage are male? The main categories analysed within a demographic profile are the customers' age, gender, social class, income level and region. Main uses of profile information are:
- for setting quotas for research surveys
- for segmenting a market
- for deciding in which media to advertise (*Vogue* or the *Sun*?).

denationalisation means returning to the *private sector* a business that was previously operated by the *public sector*. (See *privatisation*.)

Department for Business, Innovation and Skills (BIS) is the government department responsible for helping British firms start up and compete effectively. It has particular responsibilities for competition policy, regional policy and overseas trade. In the recession of 2008/09 it also had to offer assistance to the car industry to prevent a huge loss of jobs.

dependency ratio: the percentage of people who are either in education or are too young or too old to take paid employment or who are unable to work because of disabilities. This group will be dependent on the working population to provide them with adequate real incomes.

dependent variable: a variable which is determined by changes elsewhere in the system and therefore depends on another variable. For example, we usually view the level of tax revenue as depending on the level of income, for a given set of tax rates. Income is thus the independent variable and tax revenue is the dependent variable.

depletable resources are things which are fixed in quantity and, once consumed, cannot be replaced. The term is used particularly in relation to energy: gas and oil are fossil fuels and once used, cannot be replaced, although it is possible to search for new sources. Similarly, tropical hardwoods are depletable in that they cannot be replaced at the rate at which they are currently being used.

depreciation has two different meanings:

- The fall in value of *fixed assets* as wear and tear take their toll and new technologies make the equipment less useful. Depreciation allowances are identified in the *profit and loss account* and may be used to replace the capital at the end of its useful life.
- An exchange rate, the value of which is falling on the foreign exchange markets, is said to be depreciating. It is losing value and purchasing power. It is also making exports cheaper and therefore easier to sell. (See also *exchange rate depreciation*.)

depression: a prolonged period of negative growth, or growth that is well below the long-term average. Whereas a *recession* occurs regularly as the bottom phase of a country's *economic cycle*, a full-scale depression is much rarer. It will be characterised by:

- falling *aggregate demand* and output
- redundancies and high unemployment
- falling incomes and consumer spending
- very low levels of *investment*; as output falls productive capacity is reduced
- falling rates of inflation.

Depression may be countered by *expansionary policies*. *Automatic stabilisers* such as the rise in unemployment benefits will help to protect incomes and contribute to more spending in the economy.

There will be *cyclical unemployment*, caused by insufficient levels of aggregate demand. In the diagram opposite, the level of aggregate demand is well below that needed to buy all the output which could be produced if the economy was working at *full-capacity output*.

Few would not argue that the depression of the 1930s was one such period. Japan suffered an economic depression between 1990 and 2000. During the severe downturn of 2008/09 some commentators feared the start of a new depression in the West.

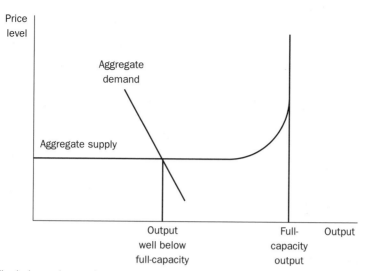

Output falls during a depression

deregulation is the removal of government rules, regulations and laws from the workings of business. This might include scrapping wages councils, or ending *monopoly* rights to supply services such as letter delivery or bus services.

PROS: • less regulation means fewer regulators need be employed by the government or local councils (cutting public spending and therefore cutting tax levels)
• less regulation should encourage more competition

CONS: • many rules affecting business were to stop exploitation; is this acceptable nowadays?
• competition does not necessarily provide what society wants, it may only provide what is profitable (such as buses in the daytime but not at night)

derivatives trading: paying for the right to buy or sell a commodity in the future, at a price fixed today. Derivatives trading can take place in foreign currencies, agricultural produce, metals or in any other tradable item. Two of the most common forms of derivatives trading are *hedging* and *options*. Firms can use hedging to reduce the risk of profits being hit by a sharp change in the price of a commodity. Options, however, are a highly geared, risky form of speculation. In 2008 the French bank Caisse d'Epargne lost $800 million due to reckless trading by one of its derivatives trading teams.

derived demand: employers' demand for *labour* is said to be derived demand, because they do not want labour for its own sake but for what it may be able to produce.

deskilling occurs when a new machine or process changes a job that was once a source of craft pride into a repetitive or mundane task such as feeding or minding a machine.

desk research means finding out information from already-published sources, perhaps from trade magazines, from government statistics or from an on-line computer *database*. It is also known as secondary research.

destocking is the deliberate attempt to reduce a firm's stockholding by cutting orders of materials or by cutting production levels. This is usually undertaken by organisations at the beginning of a **recession**, when orders begin to fall. Businesses can cut stocks of raw materials quickly by reordering less from suppliers. This represents a cut in the suppliers' levels of **demand**, which reinforces the recession. Stocks are usually financed by **overdraft** borrowing from banks on which interest is paid, so there is a strong incentive to destock when interest rates rise.

destroyer pricing: another term for *predatory pricing*.

destruction pricing: another term for *predatory pricing*.

devaluation is the deliberate decision by a government to reduce the value of its currency in relation to foreign currencies. This boosts the international competitiveness of the country's products, making it more expensive for British consumers to buy foreign goods, therefore making home-produced goods more attractive. Devaluation also boosts the competitiveness of exports, thereby improving the **balance of payments**. Nowadays the exchange rate may be allowed to depreciate, achieving the same effect in the context of floating exchange rates.

This happened with the pound in 2008, giving UK exporters some opportunities despite the recession, and attracting some tourists from abroad.

PROS: • makes a country's exports more competitive
• makes imports more expensive and less price competitive
• should therefore boost the country's **balance of payments**

CONS: • may represent an 'easy option' for firms, so that they don't have to control their costs
• imposes cost-push inflationary pressures on an economy due to rising import prices (see **cost-push inflation**)

developed economies: the countries with high per capita incomes and high levels of investment which have become prosperous during the 20th century. This group used to consist of Western Europe, USA, Canada, Japan, Australia and New Zealand. Recently, Hong Kong, Singapore and South Korea have raised their incomes to the point where they are generally regarded as developed countries. A number of others are not far behind them.

developing economies: a country with a developing manufacturing base, but which has a national income that is not yet big enough to provide sufficient saving to sustain the investment required for more growth. Many developing countries have been dependent on *primary sector* products for their growth in the past, but as prices for such products are notoriously unreliable, growth has often been intermittent.

development area: a geographical region designated by government to receive special help due to its depressed economic circumstances. The British government may offer selective regional assistance to encourage a business to locate within a development area. Increasingly the *European Union (EU)* has played a major role in offering grants to such areas to encourage regeneration.

development indicators include GDP per capita, car ownership, access to health and education and the *Human Development Index (HDI)*.

devolving power means delegating it to a person or organisation at a lower level within a hierarchy. (See *delegation*.)

dictatorial leadership: the use of power by giving out orders, rather than consulting or delegating. It implies what McGregor termed a *Theory X* attitude on the part of the leader, i.e. the assumption that employees have little ability or desire to contribute fruitfully to the decision-making process (see **McGregor, D**). The dictatorial leader is also likely to threaten or penalise those who fail to succeed in the tasks they have been set. (See **authoritarian leadership style**, **paternalistic leadership style** and **democratic leadership**.)

differentials are the proportionate differences in pay between one grade of worker and another. They are likely to reflect different levels of skill or responsibility. When differentials are narrowed, workers on the higher rate of pay may feel that their skills and status are being downgraded.

differentiated products: a highly differentiated product is one which people think of as so distinctive that it has no acceptable substitutes. With low differentiation, a product would be one among many, with many direct, acceptable competitors. As a result, products with weak differentiation need to charge relatively low prices in order to hold their **market share**.

There are two main sources of product differentiation:
- actual product advantages, such as better design, better manufacture and higher quality standards
- psychological factors such as **branding** and **advertising**.

In contrast, with **homogeneous products** it is impossible for the buyer to distinguish one supplier's product from another's. Differentiated products are a feature of **imperfect competition**. Firms can exert some degree of control over the market if their products are distinctive.

diminishing returns occur when, as a producer adds more of one factor of production to a fixed quantity of other factors of production, the output increases but less than proportionately. For example, if 10 people have 10 spades and are digging a trench, the addition of one extra person digging and allowing each person to take a break will allow the team to dig a longer trench in a given time. But if more people are added to the team, each extra one will add less and less to the distance dug, because the rest of the team will gain little benefit from further breaks.

direct communication means communication that is not through intermediaries. It is an alternative to the conventional system of communicating through official, formal channels.

direct controls: a general term to describe the government's power to influence business and the economy through direct intervention, such as legislation or administrative action. For example, direct controls may be imposed by the **Bank of England** on the **commercial banks** in order to limit their lending. The Bank also specifies the type and amount of lending rather than using more indirect methods such as **monetary policy**. Such controls are more likely to be imposed by an **interventionist** government, or at a time of grave economic crisis.

direct investment: see **foreign direct investment (FDI)**

direct relationship: where two variables move together, they are said to have a direct relationship. For example, output and employment tend to rise and fall together, though with a time lag.

direct sales: selling directly to the end-user, without going through an outlet such as a shop. This might be achieved through door-to-door selling, internet or telephone selling, direct response TV or press advertising.

directive leadership involves letting subordinates know exactly what is expected of them and giving specific directions on how they must go about their tasks. Subordinates are expected to follow the organisation's rules and regulations to the letter. A leader might adopt this approach because of a lack of confidence in the abilities and self-discipline of the subordinates.

director: a senior manager proposed by the *chief executive officer (CEO)* and elected by shareholders to represent them on the main decision-making committee, the board of directors. Directors may be either executive or non-executive. Executive directors are employees of the company, usually with the responsibility for running a large division or department. *Non-executive directors* are not company employees; they are experienced senior managers from other firms, appointed to give independent advice. It has always been hoped that non-executive directors would be sharp critics of the internal management, taking special care to look after the interests of the company's shareholders. Experience has not always borne this out, however, as too many have been friends or business associates of the chief executive.

directors' report: a statutory element in the annual report of a *public limited company (PLC)* which informs shareholders of: future developments, the firm's health and safety policy, any political or charitable donations, directors' shareholdings and *share options*, plus any changes in board personnel.

direct taxes are levied on the incomes of individuals and firms. They include income tax, corporation tax and council tax. They also include taxes on wealth, principally *inheritance tax*. Direct taxes are usually *proportional* or *progressive*. They also include *National Insurance charges (NICs)*. In contrast, *indirect taxes* are levied on expenditure and collected from the sellers of goods and services (e.g. VAT).

dirty float is the term used to describe a *floating exchange rate* which operates only within certain bands (see diagram). In other words, the *central bank* will intervene to prevent the exchange rate exceeding those limits. In 2009 China operated a dirty float system for its currency, to prevent its value rising too rapidly against the US dollar.

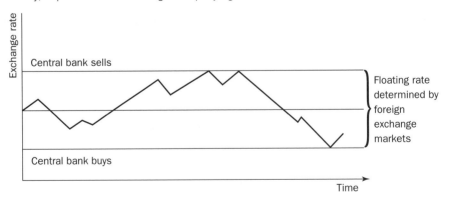

Disability Discrimination Act 2005: this forbids employees with disabilities being treated less favourably than others, and requires employers to make reasonable adjustments to provide working conditions and an environment to help overcome the practical difficulties of disability. From 2006 firms were also required to provide full access to customers with disabilities, e.g. for those using wheelchairs.

disaster planning is a common form of *contingency planning*, made more urgent by events such as the Kobe earthquake and the 2004 tsunami. It involves visualising possible types of disaster that might hit the firm, then deciding:
- which team of senior managers would be best suited to tackling the crisis
- where they would meet
- what resources they would require (telecommunications etc.).

disclosure of information is the process of releasing factual data to enable outsiders to make a judgement or decision. For many years British *trade unions* have complained that they cannot trust the stance of managers in industrial negotiations because of their failure to disclose key facts. Company secrecy over industrial accident rates, pollution emissions and recycling levels also makes it hard for environmental campaigners to pressurise firms into accepting their *social responsibilities*. This is why a *pressure group* may feel that the law should force firms to disclose more information in their *annual report and accounts*.

discounted cash flow (DCF): an *investment appraisal* technique based on *cash flow forecasts* and the *opportunity cost* of money. It uses a discount rate to assess the present value of a future income stream.

discouraged workers: people who have been unemployed for some time, despite making an effort to find work, sometimes give up the search for a job. Effectively, they drop out of the *labour* market in the sense that they are no longer making themselves available for work.

discretionary income: the income left to a household after deduction of income tax, national insurance and contracted outgoings such as mortgage payments.

discretionary policy refers to deliberate changes in tax rates or government expenditure which will affect the level of *aggregate demand*. In contrast, some changes in the level of taxation and spending are referred to as *automatic stabilisers*, because they will increase or reduce aggregate demand automatically as incomes and unemployment change over the course of the business cycle. (See also *fiscal policy*.)

discrimination: the practice of preferring an applicant for a job because of the person's race, gender or religion. Although discrimination is illegal there is a good deal of evidence of its continuation. Preferred groups generally are able to earn higher rates of pay and may have lower unemployment rates.

discriminatory pricing: see *price discrimination*

diseconomies of scale: factors causing higher costs per unit when the scale of output is greater, i.e. causes of inefficiency in large organisations. The main factors are:
- Communication costs: in small firms, internal communication is mainly oral, which is cheap and highly effective since *feedback* is inbuilt. Large firms have many *layers of hierarchy* so messages may be distorted as they pass through intermediaries. Consequently, much communication is done through memos, reports or written requests. These require the time and therefore pay of typists, filing clerks and messengers.
- Coordination costs: in small firms, decisions are usually made by the proprietor, perhaps after consulting staff. One person taking the decisions ensures *coordination* of the firm's strategy and actions. Large firms require *delegation*, as one person cannot make hundreds

of major decisions competently. Yet empowering managers to make their own decisions can result in different departments heading in different directions (see **empowerment**). So regular meetings are required to ensure coordination. This is why research shows that managers spend over half their time communicating. That time represents a considerable extra **overhead** cost for the firm to bear.

Senior managers often underestimate the problems caused by diseconomies of scale. A good example came in Morrisons' difficult takeover of Safeway.

disequilibrium occurs when there is **excess supply** or **excess demand**, either in a particular market or in the economy as a whole. For example, if there are large stocks of unsold butter, we can say that the market is in disequilibrium. The likely explanation will be that the price is too high for **market clearing** to take place. The diagram shows how a high price may cause excess supply. Reducing the price will bring the market back into equilibrium.

Equally excess supply can result from a fall in demand that leaves producers with stocks of unsold goods. If prices are flexible the disequilibrium will not last long but if not, adjustment may take time. In the service sector excess supply might consist of underutilised capacity, e.g. empty hotel rooms.

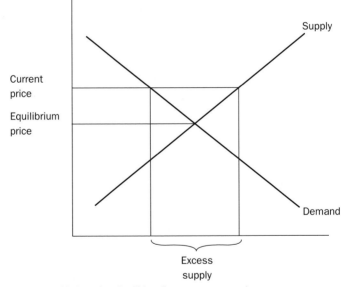

A price above the equilibrium level will lead to excess supply

On the macroeconomic level, high levels of **aggregate demand**, in excess of the economy's capacity to supply goods and services, would indicate disequilibrium. The likely outcome would be accelerating inflation and the government might want to use **fiscal policies** and **monetary policies** to reduce the level of demand.

disguised unemployment occurs when people who would like to work do not register, usually because they are not entitled to unemployment benefit, and therefore have no incentive to do so. The claimant count measure of unemployment fails to count these people. The **Labour Force Survey** usually produces a higher figure for unemployment because it can take account of people who do not register. (See also **unemployment**.)

dismissal: being dismissed ('sacked') from a job due to incompetence or breaches of discipline. Note that this is different from *redundancy*.

disposable income is the income left over after tax and *National Insurance charges (NICs)* have been deducted. Benefits such as income support and child benefits will increase disposable income, enabling people to spend more than they can earn. Because of taxes and benefits, disposable income is more equitably distributed than gross income.

disputes procedure: the formal process by which a dispute between management and *trade union* will be progressed. For example, it may be laid down by written agreement that a pay dispute will be put to an arbitrator appointed by the *Advisory, Conciliation and Arbitration Service (ACAS)* before any *industrial action* is taken (see *arbitration*).

distinctive competence is a competitive advantage that distinguishes one firm from another. It is the skill or asset upon which future strength can be built. For example, the French company Bic has developed exceptional know-how in the manufacture of disposable plastic products; that is their distinctive competence.

distortions: when prices are distorted, they fail to reflect the true costs of production. This means that either more or less will be consumed than would be if prices covered all the costs. For example, the apparent cost of motoring is less than the true cost because the road system is free to users. If road users paid the full cost of the roads they travelled (i.e. if roads were priced) they would probably choose to make fewer journeys. People who do not own cars would probably have to pay less tax for road building as the costs would be covered by road users. To the extent that road users were deterred by the pricing system from making journeys, there would be less congestion.

distribution: the entire process of getting products to where customers can buy them. This sounds easy, but actually requires considerable persuasion. Shop shelf space is limited, so if a retailer is to stock your product they must destock another. Furthermore, having obtained shop distribution, manufacturers have to battle constantly to keep it. (See *distribution targets*.)

distribution channels: the stages of ownership that take place as a product moves from the manufacturer to the consumer.

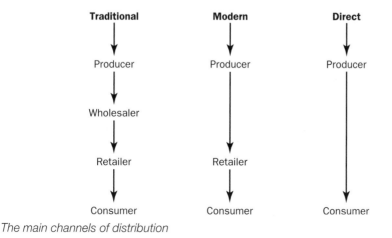

The main channels of distribution

distribution of income refers to the way in which total income is shared among the different groups in society. A very equitable distribution of income might involve the richest tenth of the population having no more than three times the income of the poorest tenth. In the UK, the distribution of income became considerably less equitable after 1977. There have been some attempts to reverse this process but the UK distribution of income remains one of the least equitable in Europe.

Income distribution by quintile group

Year	bottom	2nd	3rd	4th	top	Ave real income per household, £ p.a., 2006–07 prices
1977	8.3	13.4	19.5	24.1	34.7	14 631
1986	8.1	11.3	17.9	24.2	38.6	17 814
1996–97	7.3	11.3	17.1	23.9	40.4	21 125
2006–07	7.4	11.7	16.6	23.3	41.0	27 370

Source: ONS, Economic and Labour Market Review

The intention of taxation and social security benefits is usually to redistribute income from the richer towards the poorer members of society. The more *progressive* the tax system, the more effective this process will be.

A relatively unequal distribution of income may increase incentives to work but may also increase tensions between employers and employees. Some *developing economies* have a much more unequal distribution of income than developed economies.

distribution of wealth refers to the ownership of assets and how it is spread amongst different groups of people. Wealth can consist of bank balances, shares, property, businesses and anything else which provides a continuing income or can be sold. Wealth is a *stock*, in contrast to income, which is a *flow*. Income is paid continuously whereas wealth is held over a long period. A relatively equal distribution of wealth would imply that most people had some and few had either none or a great deal. The distribution of wealth may be affected by *inheritance taxes* and by changes in property prices or ownership.

distribution targets are set to motivate the *salesforce* to obtain distribution in as high a percentage of target outlets as seems feasible. This might be achieved by:
- offering a high *profit margin* to retailers
- heavy advertising in trade magazines
- giving sales staff big incentives to work and sell hard.

diversification is the spreading of business risks by reducing dependence on one product or market. It is an important business objective, be it for a small ice-cream producer wanting security from cool summers, or for *multinational* firms wanting to move into new growth markets. The opposite of diversification is *focus*.

PROS: • improves prospects for long-term company survival
- can enable a firm in a saturated market to regain a growth path
- provides new outlets for a firm's skills and resources

CONS: • many diversifications have disappointed due to *diseconomies of scale* or failure to understand fully the new marketplace (the customer, competition, etc.)

- the firm's core business may be weakened as resources are redirected towards new opportunities; the American writer Peter Lynch has called this phenomenon 'diworsification'

divestment means selling off parts of a business that no longer fit the long-term strategy. This might be because they are no longer profitable, or because the firm wants to focus its management on the *core activities*.

dividend policy: the proportion of profits after tax that a company's directors decide to pay out to shareholders in the form of annual dividends. The higher the payout, the less there is to reinvest to make the business bigger or more efficient. Higher retained profits should enable the firm to pay higher dividends in future. So the more profit that is retained today, the greater prospects of benefits tomorrow. Shareholders would have to agree to such a policy. They can vote on it at the *annual general meeting (AGM)*; if they disagreed with the policy they could sell their shares.

dividends are the share in the profits of a company distributed to its shareholders according to the rights which the shares give them. Dividends must be paid (after interest charges) on *preference shares* before *ordinary shares*. Preference share dividends are fixed but ordinary share dividends are declared annually by the directors and voted on at the *annual general meeting (AGM)*.

dividend yield is the annual dividend per share (DPS) expressed as a percentage of the market price of the share. The dividend is a matter of record but the market price may fluctuate constantly. If the share is being upgraded by the *stock market*, its price will rise and therefore the yield will fall. Dividend yield is an important consideration for share buyers who need an annual income from their savings to boost their regular earnings (for example, pensioners). Investors can compare a share's dividend yield directly with building society rates, to help decide where to place their savings.

$$FORMULA: \quad \frac{\text{dividend per share}}{\text{market share price}} \times 100 = \text{dividend yield}$$

division of labour means the way in which people specialise in particular types of job. There are two elements in the division of *labour*:

- A manufacturing process is usually split into a sequence of individual tasks. This is easily seen in an assembly line. Each person has a small task which is repeated for each product which comes past. This *specialisation* is usually faster and cheaper than having one person or a team assembling the entire product on their own. Costs are cut and prices can come down, bringing the product within the reach of a mass market. This was the type of process observed in the pin factory by *Adam Smith* and described in his book, *The Wealth of Nations*, published in 1776.
- All jobs are specialised in a modern economy and people move into the type of occupation in which they have a *comparative advantage*. This allows them to exploit their natural advantages and also to acquire specialist skills which will increase their productivity. Experience adds further to their advantages as they learn to avoid mistakes.

The breaking down of manufacturing processes into individual component tasks has made it possible over the past 200 years to mechanise most areas of production.

This has led to huge increases in productivity, and similarly large price cuts, but it has also *deskilled* many people. This means that many manufacturing processes have become very dull and it can be hard to motivate employees to maintain quality. In recent years ways have been found to reduce this problem through teamwork and *multi-skilling*, so that the division of labour has actually diminished in some workplaces.

divorce of ownership and control is a phrase conveying concern that although the shareholders own public companies, managements run them. This might lead to conflicting loyalties, with managements pursuing objectives that help their own careers or job satisfaction rather than looking after shareholders' best interests. Many past *diversification* moves and *takeover bids* seems to have offered little real benefit to shareholders.

dog: a term given by the Boston Consulting Group to describe a product with low *market share* within a market with low growth. The Group recommend that dogs be considered for discontinuation, in order to concentrate time and resources on more profitable brands. Dogs form one part of the *Boston matrix*.

Doha Round: the *World Trade Organization (WTO)* trade negotiations that began in 2001 and stalled in 2008. Earlier rounds of trade negotiations had been very successful in reducing barriers to trade in manufactures; with Doha it was hoped to reduce trade barriers for agriculture and services. Some progress was made, e.g. in patent protection of pharmaceuticals. But on the big issues relating to agricultural tariffs and subsidies, the developed countries and the third world countries were deadlocked. The principal protagonists were Brazil, India, China and South Africa. The USA and the EU were generally unhappy about making concessions. It seems quite likely that negotiations will restart but probably only after there has been some recovery in the world economy. In the meantime the threat of growing *protectionism* is very real.

dollar ($): the currency of the United States of America. Because of the importance of the US economy in terms of world trade, many goods are traded internationally in dollars. For example, oil produced in the North Sea by the UK will be sold to another country at a price given in dollars.

domestic competition: all those businesses that are rivals in the market and producing in the same economy. Strong competition can have a positive effect on the rate of innovation and the efficiency of the business.

dominant price leader: a firm which is first to raise prices and is then followed by the rest of the industry. Ford has sometimes been considered to be a dominant price leader in the UK car market. This type of situation may be accompanied by *tacit collusion*. No actual agreement is made – this would be illegal – but the industry simply follows the lead of the dominant firm and avoids competing on price.

dot com (.com): the magic addition to a company name that, in 1999 and 2000, could add billions of pounds to a company's stock market value. The magic was, of course, conjured up by the internet.

Dow Jones Index is the name of the New York Stock Exchange daily market index. Dating back to 1928, the index takes the average price of thirty major stocks, which together account for 25 per cent of its *market capitalisation*.

down-market: a product or advertisement aimed at working-class or low-income households; the opposite of *up-market*.

downside is the possible or actual consequence of a decision turning out badly. If the downside is relatively small compared with the potential benefits of a decision, the risk : reward ratio is said to be favourable.

downsizing: reducing the size of a business to meet a new, lower demand level; the term downsizing is often used as a euphemism for *redundancy*. Due to the negative connotations of the term downsizing, some firms now use a further euphemism – rightsizing.

downtime is when machinery is needed but not being used. This may be because of a breakdown, lack of spare parts, or when resetting the machine for a different product specification to be manufactured. Downtime might be measured in minutes or as a proportion of the day's working hours. It represents a waste of resources and adds to *fixed costs per unit* by restricting the volume of *output* from a given *production line*.

downward multiplier: when *injections* fall or *withdrawals* rise, the level of spending in the *circular flow of national income* falls. Some firms find that demand for their products has fallen. They cut back output and eventually employment. Incomes fall and *aggregate demand* falls again. Because of the cumulative nature of the decline in demand, the eventual fall in income will be larger than the fall in spending which brought it about.

Dragon: a term for a *venture capital* investor, derived from the BBC television series *Dragons' Den*.

drawings represent the salary taken out of an *unlimited liability* firm by its proprietors. What is left on the *profit and loss account* after drawings is the firm's retained earnings.

dumping means selling exports at less than their cost of production. Usually the exporter has spare capacity. Dumping is illegal under *World Trade Organization (WTO)* rules but it is often hard to decide what the production costs really are. There are two main reasons for dumping:
- production has increased rapidly and prices are falling – as with Chinese textile products
- the industry is in decline. This has been a particular problem in the steel industry where there is world over-capacity.

duopoly is where there are only two producers in a market. This may result in what appears to be a highly competitive market, usually based on *non-price competition*, such as *advertising*. However, there may also be a certain amount of *collusion*, either explicit or implicit, in order to guarantee high profits for both firms and to keep out other potential competitors. Because there are only two producers, the actions of one are clear to the other, and so each business decision will be based on how it is expected that the competitor will react to the decision, as well as how consumers will respond.

durables: see *consumer durables*

dynamic markets: while some markets are stable, others are constantly changing. Where incomes are growing, or consumer preferences are changing or there is technological change, conditions of demand and supply will be constantly shifting for some products. This leads to *reallocation of resources* and *structural change*. Businesses that are flexible and adapt quickly can find the resulting opportunities very profitable.

earnings: when applied to a company, means *profit* after tax. For individuals, it comes from wages, salaries and freelance or self-employed earnings. It contrasts with unearned income, which comes from interest, dividends, rent or profit from a business.

earnings per share (EPS): a ratio showing the after-tax *profit* available for distribution to shareholders. The company directors recommend and the shareholders vote on how much of that profit will be paid as dividends and how much will be *ploughed-back profit* that goes back into the company.

$$FORMULA: \frac{\text{profit after tax}}{\text{number of shares}}$$

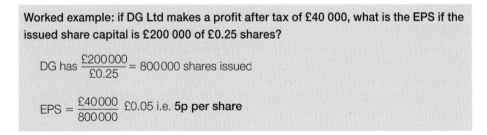

Worked example: if DG Ltd makes a profit after tax of £40 000, what is the EPS if the issued share capital is £200 000 of £0.25 shares?

DG has $\frac{£200\,000}{£0.25}$ = 800 000 shares issued

EPS = $\frac{£40\,000}{800\,000}$ £0.05 i.e. **5p per share**

ECB: see *European Central Bank (ECB)*

ECGD: see *Export Credit Guarantee Department (ECGD)*

easy entry: the situation where new businesses can start up and compete successfully with existing producers. The market is contestable; no producer has sufficient market power to effectively exclude new entrants. Normally this means that there are few if any barriers to entry. So potential economies of scale and initial advertising costs pose no problems and the necessary inputs are readily available.

e-commerce: a widespread abbreviation for electronic commerce, meaning purchasing goods through an on-line source, such as the internet. In 1999, 1 per cent of UK purchases were made in this way. Forecasters were suggesting rapid growth, to at least 10 per cent of purchases, which might have severe knock-on effects upon high-street retailing. By 2009 such boasts looked much less likely, though there have been some huge on-line successes, such as easyJet building its business by making more than 97 per cent of its ticket sales on the internet.

Economic and Monetary Union (EMU): the group of EU members that adopted the single currency, the *euro*. The process began in January 1999 and completed in mid-2002. By then all the members' own currencies were out of use and the euro was used for all transactions.

PROS: • more efficient, i.e. there are no exchange costs, no need for forward or spot markets and foreign exchanges
  • easier for producers and consumers to compare products and prices, which should stimulate competition and efficiency gains
  • it should ease transfers of people into a wider job market, as well as easing travel generally

CONS: • a feeling of a loss of national identity, through the loss of a national currency
  • in order to work, the nations involved will have to bring their economies into closer alignment, particularly rates of inflation. This is difficult, especially where countries have to deflate in order to bring this about

(See also *euro* and *European Central Bank (ECB)*.)

economic convergence: see *convergence*

economic cost: an *opportunity cost* resulting from the production process. Economic costs are not the same as commercial costs. The latter include only those which the producer actually has to pay. Economic costs can include those *external costs* which can be quantified in economic terms. These increase the cost to society of the activity concerned.

economic cycle: the fluctuations in output and employment which take the economy through a sequence of *boom*, *recession*, *slump* and *recovery*. (This is often also referred to as the business cycle or the trade cycle.)

The cycle varies in length and severity and must be looked at alongside the process of *economic growth*. This provides the background: a *long-run trend rate of growth*, around 2.2 per cent in the UK, about which output growth fluctuates. The phases of the economic cycle do not form a neat, predictable pattern, but interact with other events to form a complex sequence.

• The *boom* phase occurs when there is unsustainably fast growth, which causes *supply constraints* and accelerating inflation. Between 1993 and 2006 the UK economy grew steadily but without causing accelerating inflation, enabling Gordon Brown to say that the cycle of boom and bust was over. However, by 2006 inflation had begun to accelerate and there were signs of tightness in the labour market as well as very rapidly rising house prices. Above-average growth rates were unlikely to last.
• Booms may give way to *recession*. Businesses may realise that boom-time rates of growth are not going to be sustainable and cut back their investment plans. Confidence in the economy may evaporate. Or governments may implement *counter-cyclical policies* that take some of the heat out of the economy and reduce the level of activity. Often this means raising the *bank rate*, as happened in late 2006 and early 2007. The economy reaches a turning point and the downturn begins. The definition of recession is two consecutive quarters in which output falls, as in the second half of 2008. The effect of falling aggregate demand may be cumulative because of a *downward multiplier*.
• If income and output fall for more than two quarters, the recession is turning into a *depression* or slump. Unemployment increases rapidly, though with a time lag.

It may peak 12 months or more after output reaches its lowest level. This type of unemployment is termed **cyclical unemployment**. Levels of investment will be very low.

- **Recovery** may be a response to government policies to stimulate the economy. Or it may start when firms realise that they need to replace worn-out plant and machinery just to keep going. This will actually lead to an increase in investment, which will be cumulative as the multiplier takes effect. If growth rates rise too fast, the recovery may turn into a boom.

The data for **economic growth** (see page 90) shows the phases of the economic cycle described here quite clearly. In the past, the economic cycle was usually thought of as lasting roughly 10 years but there is no clear pattern for the past two decades and any trend can be affected by **shocks** in the world economy. Globalisation has changed the way the cycle works in ways that are not yet thoroughly understood. (See also **recession**.)

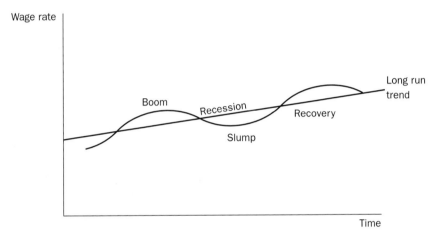

The phases of the economic cycle

economic development is the process by which a country may experience economic growth and a **reallocation of resources** away from agriculture and towards manufacturing. The term is usually used to describe what is happening in relatively poor countries which are referred to as **developing economies**. Rapid economic development is usually associated with high levels of investment and improvements in education and training opportunities and sometimes with a policy of allowing relatively **free trade** and an increasingly **open economy**.

economic efficiency implies that output is being produced at the lowest possible cost in terms of resources and in the types and quantities which most closely reflect patterns of consumer demand. Minimising costs in turn implies that there is **productive efficiency** (sometimes known as technical efficiency). This means that the production process uses the best available technology and is organised so as to eliminate wasted resources. When the structure of production reflects consumers' wants there is **allocative efficiency**, arising from **consumer sovereignty**.

economic expectations refer to people's anticipation of the way the economy is likely to develop in the future. Such expectations can have a profound effect. For instance, firms will not invest in new **plant** and machinery if they believe they will not get an adequate return, even if the rate of interest is low. Consumers will not spend money in the shops, whatever the level of prices, if they believe that the economy is in **recession** and that their jobs are at risk.

economic forecasting: the process by which economists use *economic models* to predict future trends in the main economic variables. The accuracy of forecasts depends on the extent to which the assumptions on which they are based actually correspond to reality. Forecasting is made difficult by the fact that *shocks* may occur which are quite unexpected and have far-reaching effects that are by their nature unpredictable.

economic growth means an increase in output and real incomes. It is usually measured using *gross domestic product (GDP)*. In seeking to increase GDP, much depends on the quantity and quality of the factors of production in use. Some growth takes place just by increasing the quantity of factors of production, e.g. through immigration.

The important elements in the growth process are:
- *Investment*, which increases the amount of capital per person employed and increases productivity. This may be generated domestically or may come from abroad.
- Education and training which enhance *human capital*, again making people more productive.
- *Technological change* which leads to the availability of bigger and better machines, and also helps to create better ways of managing people. It can increase the *quality* of the investment that takes place.
- Exports to new markets which increase demand for the country's products.

Pollution, deforestation and climate change can all reduce the positive effects of growth and this will not show in the GDP figures. There is a trade-off between rapid growth and environmental protection and sustainable growth will require more investment in clean technologies. In some countries the opportunity cost of rapid growth is a deteriorating environment.

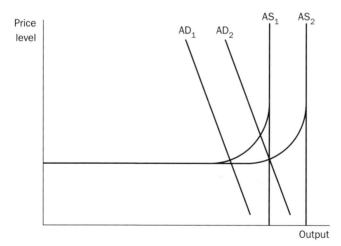

Rising capacity in the economy, as aggregate supply increases, means that output can grow without inflation accelerating

In practice, economic growth fluctuates with changes in aggregate demand and the *economic cycle* (see graph overleaf). It is often possible to follow policies that allow rapid growth in the short run. But if that rate of growth cannot be sustained in the long run then recession or worse may follow. (See also *long-run trend rate of growth*.)

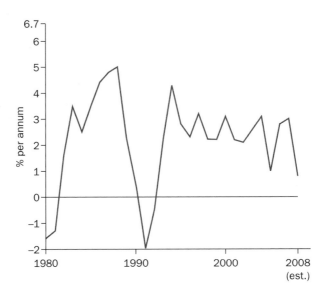

Economic growth rates fluctuate over the course of the economic cycle.
(Source: OECD Economic Outlook.)

economic indicators are the monthly statistics that provide information on a country's economic performance. *Leading indicators* give a prediction of future events, *coincident indicators* show the state of the economy today, and *lagging indicators* show the health of the economy in the recent past. All are subject to considerable error, so it is unwise to draw any conclusions from one month's data.

economic man is an assumption that human behaviour is based upon rational economic motives such as the desire for financial gain and fear of financial pain. It underpinned the writings of *Adam Smith* in the eighteenth century and *F W Taylor* in the early twentieth century. It is also at the heart of what *McGregor* called a *Theory X* attitude on the part of managers.

economic models are constructed from the relationships between different variables which enable economists to examine the connections between changes. A model may use only those variables which are most important within the situation being studied and thus can reduce the level of complication which must be considered. In this way, models enable us to gain important insights into the way the economy works.

economic performance can be examined using a number of different criteria:
- The rate of *economic growth* is measured using GDP data, suitably deflated to remove the effects of inflation and provide a measure of the real increase in income.
- *Inflation* and *unemployment* rates provide information on the scale of economic problems.
- *Productivity* data indicates whether progress is being made in terms of increasing output per person employed. This can be achieved by investing more in both physical and human capital and by increasing technical progress through research and development.
- *Competitiveness* can be measured using data on unit costs of production in different countries.
- The level of spending on investment and research and development indicates whether efforts are being made to produce in more efficient ways.

economic policy encompasses a large range of different types of policy which have some impact on the economy. These are the broad categories of policy:

- Macroeconomic policy involves taxation, government expenditure and interest rates, all of which can be used to influence the level of **aggregate demand** and output in the economy.
- Microeconomic policies are used to foster competition, encourage particular types of industrial development and influence the **allocation of resources**.
- Trade policies can be used to adjust **import controls** and sometimes to influence the level of exports.
- Exchange rate policies determine the extent to which the exchange rate floats or is managed.

EU rules generally forbid most direct aid to businesses.

economic profit is the difference between total revenue from the sale of the product and the opportunity costs of all the resources used in production. It is a reward for the taking of unquantifiable risks by the entrepreneur. Profit in excess of the full opportunity cost of the resources encourages entrepreneurs to divert more resources to production because it shows that there is a high level of demand for the product. (This is the **profit-signalling mechanism**.)

economic stability requires **sustainable growth** rates, low **inflation**, low unemployment and avoidance of significant trade **imbalances**, in the long term. This requires policy objectives that relate to the long term rather than the short term. Policies that help political parties to win elections can be very inimical to stability (if they keep their promises). Giving responsibility for **monetary policy** to the Monetary Policy Committee and making the Bank of England operationally independent is more likely to lead to stability than leaving it in the hands of the government of the day.

economic union involves the creation of an area composed of several different economies which all agree to use the same economic policies and regulations. Successful economies almost all have large markets, in which there are major opportunities for competent producers. This may be because the economy itself is large (as in the case of the US) or it may be because they are very **open economies** (as with Singapore) and trade extensively with the outside world. One way to create a large market is to form an economic union. As of 2009, the **European Union (EU)** has roughly 497 million people. All 27 member countries operate according to harmonised economic rules laid down by the European Commission, so producers can design their products according to the same requirements wherever they sell within the EU.

economic welfare refers to the extent to which people have the resources needed in order to lead a satisfying life. The welfare state aims to ensure that everyone has the minimum requirements for living in reasonable comfort, without providing any real luxuries. In practice it does not always provide all the basic necessities. The study of economic welfare involves deciding how particular changes affect people's sense of physical well-being. Some of the judgements required depend on how well-being is defined.

economics is a social science that studies how society allocates its scarce resources in order to satisfy its unlimited human needs and wants, in the most efficient way possible. Thomas Carlyle, the 19th century writer, described it as 'the dismal science' because at that time some economic theories appeared very pessimistic. Because of technological change, economic theories have become rather more optimistic.

The interesting feature of economic theory is that it is constantly catching up with events; the conventional wisdom seldom stays the same for long. This makes it much more exciting to study than a subject full of established truths. In fact, economics is not so much a set of theories as a way of thinking about economic relationships.

economies of scale are the factors that cause average costs to be lower in large-scale operations than in small-scale ones. In other words, doubling the *output* results in a less than double increase in costs; the cost of producing each unit falls because factor inputs can be used more efficiently. Economies of scale fall into a number of categories, divided into internal and external economies. The following are internal:

- managerial economies, i.e. with a large workforce it is possible to divide up the work process and then recruit people whose skills exactly match the job requirements; staff can then be trained and become highly effective at carrying out their limited tasks
- technical economies, such as the use of automated equipment; this is only feasible when the *fixed costs* of the machine can be spread thinly over many units of output
- purchasing economies are the benefits of bulk buying, i.e. obtaining supplies of materials and components at lower unit costs, thereby cutting variable costs
- financial economies stem from the lower cost of *capital* charged to large firms by the providers of finance. Banks charge lower rates of interest and equity investors are more willing to accept a low *dividend yield* from bigger firms. This is because large firms are usually more diversified and less vulnerable to *liquidation* than small firms
- risk-bearing economies can be achieved when the business is large enough or diversified enough to carry them without being forced to close when unexpected events make trading difficult.

External economies are the advantages of scale that benefit the whole industry, and not just individual firms. So if an industry is concentrated in one geographical area it is likely that a pool of labour will be attracted and trained, perhaps by a local college, which will have specialised skills useful to the whole industry and from which each firm will benefit. Similarly, a large grouping of firms will attract a network of suppliers, whose own scale of operation should yield economies such as lower component costs. There may be research institutes in the area that can provide access to technological developments.

Economist Intelligence Unit (EIU): a sister company to the *Economist* magazine that provides carefully researched *secondary data* on particular countries or markets.

EDI: see *electronic data interchange (EDI)*

effective demand is the desire to buy backed by the ability to pay. Textbooks often suggest that the price of a *commodity* is determined by *supply* and *demand*. In such cases the author really means effective demand.

effective exchange rate: the exchange rate as measured by the *exchange rate index*, which values the currency as a weighted average of the currencies of the nation's major trading partners. The weights are proportional to the amount of trade involved.

efficiency generally means using resources in the most economical way possible. This means that *average costs* will be at a minimum. Output from a given quantity of resources will be maximised. The jargon term for this is **productive efficiency**. It can be measured by examining **productivity** in one of its forms:

- labour productivity means output per person employed
- capital productivity means output per unit of capital invested.

The higher the level of productivity, the more efficiently the resources are being used. Waste is kept to a minimum.

The term efficiency can also mean **allocative efficiency**, which refers to the extent to which the allocation of resources tallies with the real preferences of consumers. An economy is said to be allocatively efficient when the goods and services produced are on sale at prices which reflect true costs of production and in quantities that accurately reflect levels of consumer demand.

Allocative efficiency is sometimes also known as **economic efficiency**.

EFTA: see *European Free Trade Association (EFTA)*

EGM: see *extraordinary general meeting (EGM)*

elasticities measure responsiveness to change. For fuller details see **price elasticity** of demand, **income elasticity** of demand, **supply elasticity** and **advertising elasticity**.

electronic communications technology: all the forms of information technology that involve communication. At the time of writing these include: e-mail, fax, text-messaging, enhanced telephones (such as voice-mail), **electronic data interchange (EDI)**, computer **networks**, tele- and video-conferencing and interactive television (often through touch screens). The speed of technological change means that many of these may be obsolete within a few years, making it risky for firms to invest heavily in them.

electronic data interchange (EDI) is on-line communication between computers, usually personal computers communicating with mainframes. It is used by retail branches to transmit details of their day's trading to a central computer, which orders replacement supplies from the distribution depot. In turn, the depot's EDI link with suppliers brings fresh supplies from the manufacturers.

embargo: an order forbidding trade with a particular country, perhaps imposed by the United Nations against a country that has broken international laws or conventions.

emerging markets: a term used by banks and businesses to mark out countries with low income levels but high growth rates, i.e. with good prospects for the future.

emissions are substances which pollute air or water, coming from the activities of individuals or firms. Liquids and solids may be discharged into rivers or the sea. Solid particles and gases may be discharged into the atmosphere.

emissions trading schemes give companies the right to allow a certain quantity of polluting gases to escape into the atmosphere. They can sell all or a portion of their rights if they do not need them. This ensures that those companies which create air pollution above a certain level actually pay for the right to do so. The price of the right to pollute creates an incentive to pollute less. The industries involved are energy, iron and steel, glass and cement. An alternative name for emissions trading schemes is carbon trading schemes.

The EU scheme has been in place since 2005 but the permitted emissions levels are currently quite high. They will only have a significant effect on the level of pollution if they are reduced. A similar scheme is proposed for the US.

employee appraisal: see *performance appraisal*

employee share ownership (ESOP): a programme for providing a public limited company's employees with a share stake in the business. If each individual's shareholding is large enough, this might encourage greater sympathy with the firm's profit motive and therefore eliminate a feeling of *them and us*. Unfortunately, both staff and directors are inclined to turn their shares into cash at the earliest opportunity, undermining the exercise.

employers' association: an organisation representing the views and interests of the companies within a sector or industry. It is financed by members' subscriptions and is expected to provide value for money by:

- its success as a *pressure group*; for example, in influencing the taxes the government imposes or cuts on products
- its research success, either by compiling sales figures from all the firms within an industry, or by initiating studies that can help the members cope with foreign competition. Part of the motivation towards this research may be *public relations (PR)*
- providing a negotiating team that can agree minimum pay and conditions throughout the industry with employees' trade union representatives.

Employment Act 2008: the main piece of legislation that sets out the rights and duties of employees and employers. The government stated the purpose of the new law as 'increasing protection for vulnerable workers and lightening the load for law-abiding businesses'. Employment law covers:

- the *national minimum wage* and the penalties for employers who ignore it
- the difference between *redundancy* and *dismissal*
- the 90-day consultation process required before a large company declares redundancies
- the rights of workers to join and be represented by a *trade union*.

employment contract: a legal document that sets out the terms and conditions governing an individual's job. It details the employee's responsibilities, working hours, rate of pay and holiday entitlement. By signing it, an employee agrees to abide by its terms. If, therefore, the employee joins in with strike action, he or she can be dismissed for having broken the contract.

employment protection: the laws which protect the position of the employee at work. Employees are protected from unfair dismissal and are entitled to statutory redundancy payments, according to the length of time they have been with the employer. There is some concern that there is a *trade-off* between protecting the employee and encouraging employers to create more jobs. Employment protection is stronger in some EU countries than in the UK and this may help to explain why these countries have higher unemployment rates.

empowerment is providing the means by which subordinates can exercise power over their working lives. Whereas *delegation* might provide the power for a subordinate to carry out a specific task, empowerment is more all-embracing. It implies a degree of self-regulation; the freedom to decide what to do and how to do it.

EMU: see *Economic and Monetary Union (EMU)*

end-game strategies are plans for dealing with the decline phase of the *product life cycle*. Theory suggests that the only response to decline is to cut marketing spending and cut prices. However, the huge profitability of the UK cigarette market suggests that more positive end-game strategies are possible.

end product: the good the consumer buys, as opposed to any *intermediate goods* used to produce the end product. End products can include consumables such as Mars Bars or Sunny Delight, or consumer durables such as an iPod or a digital radio.

Enron: the US energy business that grew to be the largest in the world by 2000, only to collapse amidst financial scandal in 2001. It has become a byword for the risks of investing in shares, and the problem of *corporate governance* in times of booming stock markets.

enterprise is the organisation of *factors of production* in such a way as to generate profits. The term also means showing initiative and *entrepreneurship*.

Enterprise Act 2002: legislation intended to reform competition law, strengthen consumer protection and alter Britain's approach to insolvency. Key measures include:
- removing political involvement from competition decisions
- toughening the law to allow for up to five years in prison for those operating a *cartel* that fixes prices, limits production or uses *collusion* to rig bids for contracts
- reducing the restrictions placed upon an *entrepreneur* who has suffered *bankruptcy*.

enterprise culture: a social climate which applauds the profit motive in general and starting a small business in particular.

Enterprise Investment Scheme: a government initiative offering tax incentives to encourage direct equity investment in companies which are not quoted on the Stock Exchange. Individuals can obtain 20 per cent tax relief on share purchases made this way and firms can raise up to £1 million per year through the scheme. It is a form of government subsidy of venture capital.

entrepreneur: an individual who is willing to take risks and who makes the decision to go into production. The entrepreneur develops a product and decides how it will be produced using *factors of production*. He or she carries the risks associated with bringing the product to the marketplace. Sometimes the entrepreneur is described as the fourth factor of production.

entrepreneurship: the skills and attitudes that enable people to take bold, risky decisions and carry them out.

entry refers to the process by which a firm may set up in business and become part of the industry. *Easy entry* implies that the industry will be at least fairly competitive because profits will attract additional producers who will then compete with each other. An individual or an existing business can start off a new line of production and find ways to sell the product at a profit. Exit is the reverse process. Entry and *exit* are an important part of the process of *structural change*. *Barriers to entry* make it difficult for new businesses to get started.

environmental audit: an independent check on the pollution emission levels, wastage levels and recycling practices of a firm. If measured annually and published, such an audit could encourage companies to invest in improved environmental practices. Since the 1990s Body Shop, BP and IBM have all conducted and published environmental audits annually. Unless forced to do so by legislation, however, it is hard to see why poorly performing companies should carry out this exercise.

environmental degradation: the process by which economic activity leads to the destruction of real resources, e.g. spills from a chemical plant which lead to long-term contamination of the soil around it, and from many other causes. Environmental degradation may involve externalities but this can be avoided if ways can be found to make the producers cover the *social costs*.

environmental economics is the study of environmental problems and lays particular emphasis on evaluating the costs and benefits of different kinds of solutions to the problems posed by pollution, congestion and the general destruction of resources. Most environmental problems are associated with *market failure* and *externalities* which enable producers to avoid paying the full resource costs of production.

Traditionally, economics regards national income figures as a fair measure of the standard of living. However, these are constructed on the basis of recorded accounts. To the extent that there are *external costs* and *external benefits* arising from economic activity, these accounts may not reflect the true improvement in welfare. Environmental economics tries to measure the standard of living in ways which allow for the costs of economic growth.

environmental market failure occurs when buyers of the end product are not paying for the external costs of production. This means that the product price is less than the true costs to society as a whole of the production process. *Overconsumption* may result. If the external costs can be internalised by making the producers pay whatever it costs to avoid doing environmental damage, prices will rise and the market will give the correct signals to consumers.

environmental policy: a written statement of a firm's approach to dealing with the environmental disturbance or hazards it may face or create. A paper-towel manufacturer, for example, might adopt a policy that covers:
- planting a new tree for every one its suppliers cut down
- including an average of at least 30 per cent recycled paper in its products
- getting at least 20 per cent below the minimum pollution emission standards ruling within the *European Union (EU)*.

equality means that people do not experience large differentials in income within a society. Total equality has seldom been achieved in any society, but some countries have for long periods had a much greater degree of equality than others. Sweden has been most notable in this respect while the USA has tended to have very little equality in its income distribution, though rather more equality of opportunity through its education system. (See also *equity/ efficiency trade-off*.)

Equality Act 2006: this legislation widened the law against discrimination to include schools (previously there had been a focus on employment). It also set up the *Equality and Human Rights Commission*.

Equality and Human Rights Commission: an independent but government-financed body set up in 2007 with the aim of reducing inequality, eliminating discrimination and promoting human rights. It was set up by the *Equality Act 2006* to replace:
- the Commission for Racial Equality
- the Equal Opportunities Commission
- the Disability Rights Commission.

The new Commission intends to address the causes of inequality in society, including unequal provision of education.

equal opportunities: a situation where employees and potential recruits have equal chances of being employed or promoted, whatever their sex, race, colour, religion or disability. The pursuit of this goal has been frustrated by personal and organisational discrimination.

A political consensus in the 1970s enabled the Equal Opportunities Commission and the Commission for Racial Equality to be set up. The former sought to promote sex equality, the latter to overcome discrimination on grounds of race. They have both now been absorbed into the *Equality and Human Rights Commission*.

Many large firms employ an equal opportunities officer whose job is to monitor procedures, attitudes and outcomes regarding discrimination within the business. The officer will check that:
- each job description, advertisement and application form has no inherent bias
- the shortlisting of candidates is carried out on objective criteria (such as educational achievement)
- interviews are conducted fairly
- the statistics of those appointed (or promoted) suggest that minority groups have been given equal opportunities
- the proportion of disabled employees meets the government target of 3 per cent (this only applies to firms with over 20 employees).

Although these systems could work effectively to provide equal opportunities, the evidence shows that many firms give this issue a low priority. Success will require either tougher laws or a change in social attitudes.

equation of exchange: connects the quantity of money (M), the velocity of circulation (V), the price level (P) and the number of transactions (T).

> *FORMULA:* $MV = PT$

This is sometimes known as the Fisher equation. PT is the total value of all output, which is equivalent to national income. MV is the amount of money needed to pay for it, since the velocity of circulation is simply the number of times each unit of currency circulates within a given time period. If the velocity of circulation is constant and the number of transactions only grows slowly, then it follows that inflation will be directly related to the quantity of money in circulation. This sounds simple but in reality, the velocity of circulation varies so the outcome can be uncertain.

The *credit crunch* revived interest in the work of Irving Fisher. It is hard to tell at the time of writing how the money supply and the velocity of circulation are behaving but these ideas may turn out still to have useful applications.

equilibrium in the marketplace means that the quantity supplied is exactly the same as the quantity demanded. This means that there is an equilibrium price at which the market clears. No one is left with unwanted stocks of unsold goods and consumers get all they want at the going price. There will be neither *excess supply*, nor *excess demand*. This process of *market clearing* comes about because the price is free to change. However, markets are constantly changing so equilibrium may not last long.

equilibrium prices apply in *labour* and capital markets as well as the market for goods and services. A wage rate which is above the equilibrium level can lead to unemployment and an excess supply of labour, and vice versa. A very high interest rate may lead to an excess supply of funds in the capital markets, with banks willing to lend but a shortage of viable investment opportunities.

The idea of equilibrium allows us to identify the problems in markets which plainly do not clear, e.g. the housing market when many potential sellers are unable to find buyers at the price they would like to get. Price theory predicts that houses will sell if prices fall to the equilibrium level. Sellers who *must* sell frequently discover this, even if the exact level of the equilibrium price is not at first obvious.

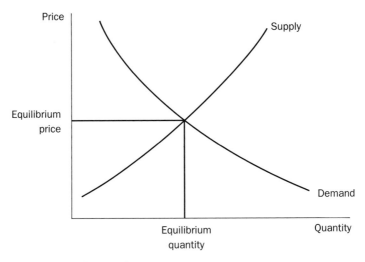

Equilibrium in the market for goods

equilibrium unemployment includes all those types of *unemployment* that can occur even when the wage rates are such that labour markets should clear, i.e. structural, frictional, technological, regional and seasonal unemployment.

equity: a term associated with the notion of fairness. Equity requires that incomes be reasonably close, without large variations between the highest and the lowest incomes. It requires also that the benefits of economic growth be reasonably equally distributed. (See also *equity/efficiency trade-off*.)

equity capital is the name given to shares; equity being the word for 'equal'. Therefore equity capital means *share capital*. In the UK, equity shareholders have one vote per share and each share has an equal right to distributed profits. Some books, however, treat equity as if it means all *shareholders' funds*, i.e. share capital plus *reserves*.

equity/efficiency trade-off: decisions which are taken in the interests of promoting efficiency may have the effect of increasing inequality. For example, incentives which encourage people to increase *productivity* may lead to an increasingly unequal distribution of income.

For governments, there may be a choice between *equity*, i.e. creating a relatively equal distribution of income, and *efficiency*, which may require some incentives. Incentives to work and take risks imply that some people receive rewards in the form of earnings or profits which make them much better off than most other people. Yet without incentives, economic growth may be slow and therefore fail to deliver the improvement in standards of living which people expect.

This area is very controversial. It is not clear that measures to reduce inequality, such as *progressive taxes* and spending on social services, actually reduce economic growth and the quest for efficiency. Scandinavian countries have on the whole a fair degree of equality and average or better growth rates.

ethical code: a document setting out the way a company believes its employees should respond to situations that challenge their integrity or social responsibility. The focus of the code will depend on the business concerned. Banks may concentrate on honesty, and chemical firms on pollution control. It has proved difficult to produce meaningful, comprehensive codes; Natwest Bank, for example, took two years to produce its ten-page document.

A typical code might include sections on:
- personal integrity – in dealings with suppliers and in handling the firm's resources
- corporate integrity, such as forbidding *collusion* with competitors and forbidding *predatory pricing*
- environmental responsibility – highlighting a duty to minimise pollution emissions and maximise recycling
- social responsibility – to provide products of genuine value that are promoted with honesty and dignity.

Critics of ethical codes believe them to be *public relations (PR)* exercises rather than genuine attempts to change behaviour. What is not in doubt is that the proof of their effectiveness can only be measured by how firms actually behave, not by what they write or say.

ethical investment: *stock market* investment based on a restricted list of firms that are seen as ethically sound, for example:
- they do not make products such as cigarettes or arms
- they act responsibly towards the environment
- they are good employers.

If many share buyers applied ethical principles, responsible firms would receive a reward in the form of a rising share price.

ethical marketing: promoting a product or service in a way that creates goodwill from consumers concerned about social and environmental issues. This sometimes seems to be done in a wholly cynical way, such as a supermarket trumpeting a 'Computers in Schools' programme worth less than 0.1 per cent of the firm's sales revenue. Manipulative use of 'ethical marketing' is unquestionably an unethical business practice.

ethical trading: operating every aspect of a business with care for the impact upon people and the environment. This might be carried out as a consequence of the ethical principles of key staff, or because of careful consideration of the best interests of the business, e.g. avoiding bad publicity.

ethics are the moral principles that should underpin decision-making. A decision made on ethics might reject the most profitable solution in favour of one of greater benefit to society as well as the firm. Typical ethical dilemmas in business include:

- should an advertising agency accept an alcopops producer as a client?
- should a firm in a *takeover* battle hire a private detective to investigate the private lives of the rival executives?
- should a producer of chemicals sell to an overseas buyer it suspects will be using the goods to produce chemical weapons?

If public opinion and media pressure force firms to take the publicity impact of their decisions into account, this may change the decisions made. This would not mean, however, that the firm was becoming more ethically minded. An ethical decision means doing what is morally right; it is not a matter of scientific calculation of costs and benefits.

EU: see *European Union (EU)*

EU competition policy: the European Commission has the power to investigate any instance of monopoly. Mostly it works on mergers and cartels that affect more than one member country. However, all members are required to bring their competition policies into line with EU Treaty obligations. This is part of the level playing field that is a key element in the way the EU operates. The EU was a key player in the case against Microsoft, which sought to prevent competitors from getting the information they needed to make their products compatible.

EU enlargement: increasing the number of countries belonging to the EU from 15 to 27 in 2007. The new countries are: Hungary, Poland, Czech Republic, Slovakia, Slovenia, Estonia, Latvia, Lithuania, Malta, Cyprus, Bulgaria and Romania.

euro: the single European currency which has been used for all transactions in the *euro zone* since June 2002. The euro was introduced at the start of 1999 by 11 member countries: Austria, Belgium, Finland, France, Germany, Luxembourg, Ireland, Italy, the Netherlands, Portugal and Spain. Greece joined later; since EU enlargement, Cyprus, Malta, Slovenia and Slovakia have joined. Several others may be ready to join soon. Of the long- standing members, the EU 15, only the UK, Denmark and Sweden are outside the *euro zone*.

Member countries have to be confident that they can cope with a one-size-fits-all monetary policy. (See also *European Central Bank (ECB)*.) The euro has far-reaching implications for member countries:

- Firms in the euro zone find it very easy to trade with one another. There are none of the uncertainties arising from having different exchange rates. Transactions costs are reduced.
- Prices across the euro zone are much more transparent. It is easy for buyers to see who is charging the least and to buy from them. This has probably led to increased competition and lower prices for consumers.
- Within the euro zone, there is a single *monetary policy*, determined by the ECB. There can be difficulties if the ECB *interest rate* which is appropriate for the euro zone as a whole is too high or too low for an individual country. Adjusting the level of economic activity in that economy so that it is similar to that of the rest of the euro zone could be difficult.

European Central Bank (ECB): the *central bank* established to control the workings and monetary policy within the *single currency* (euro) area. Founded in June 1998, the Bank is based in Frankfurt, Germany but controlled collectively by the member countries of the single currency. The Bank's primary objective is to keep inflation below 2.2 per cent per annum in Europe. Its main tasks are:

- to set interest rates throughout the *euro* area
- to determine monetary policy
- to provide a monthly report on the *euro zone* economy.

Within the euro zone, there is a single *monetary policy*, determined by the ECB. There can be difficulties if the ECB *interest rate* which is appropriate for the euro zone as a whole is too high or too low for an individual country. This can mean that low interest rates will cause expansion in some economies, leading to inflation, instability and a loss of competitiveness.

European Commission: the civil service of the *European Union (EU)*, but with one important difference from the UK's civil service in that the Commission actually proposes legislation. Proposals for any new EU regulations and directives pass from the Commission to the *European Parliament* for debate and possible modification before going to the *Council of Ministers* for approval or rejection.

European Court of Justice is the supreme court of the European Union's legal system. The court makes judgements on European law and treaties when they are in dispute. The court has the power to fine firms, but it can only apply moral pressure on governments. This has often resulted in the slow implementation of European law by some member states.

European Economic Area: the agreement signed in 1991 between the members of the *European Union (EU)* and the *European Free Trade Association (EFTA)*. It allows for free trade to take place between EU countries and Norway, Iceland and Liechtenstein.

European Free Trade Association (EFTA): set up as a *free trade* rival to the *European Union (EU)*, this economic area has reduced in importance as key members have left to join the EU. Since February 2003, it has consisted of just four members: Iceland, Liechtenstein, Norway and Switzerland.

European Monetary System (EMS): the attempt at harmonising the financial arrangements of the member states of the *European Union (EU)* in the late 1980s. It was the first phase of the movement that led to European monetary union in January 1999. A key element of the EMS was tightening the bands of the exchange rate mechanism, to lock European currencies closer together. This proved successful, even though Britain and Italy both suffered currency collapses in 1992 which forced them to withdraw from the mechanism.

European Parliament: the elected chamber of the *European Union (EU)*. The members debate and amend proposals put forward by the *European Commission* (the European civil service) before they are passed to the *Council of Ministers* for approval or rejection. The Parliament is quite restricted in its powers. As the only directly elected European institution, the Parliament feels it ought to be given more powers, and indeed it is slowly having greater influence.

European Union (EU): The EU was formed in November 1993, following the *Maastricht* Treaty. It replaced the European Community, which in turn had replaced the European Economic Community. It currently consists of the following 27 members: France, Germany, the Netherlands, Belgium, Luxembourg, Italy (the first six members), the UK, Denmark, Ireland (joined 1973), Greece (1981), Portugal, Spain (1986), Sweden, Finland, Austria (1995), Hungary, Poland, Czech Republic, Slovakia, Slovenia, Estonia, Latvia, Lithuania, Malta and Cyprus (2004), and Romania and Bulgaria (2007). The EU was established under the Treaty of Rome in 1957 with the objective of removing all trade barriers between member states. The background to this was the desire to form a political and economic union which would prevent the possibility of another war in Europe.

The countries of the EU enjoyed strong economic growth until the 1980s. This led to calls for further integration, leading to the Single European Act of 1987 and the abolition of all trade and other restrictions. The Act came into effect in 1993, forming the single European market, which harmonised regulations aimed at creating a level playing field for business. The Maastricht Treaty, enacted later in 1993, laid the foundations for even greater unity, and was seen by some as a move towards a federal Europe. This fear of closer political as well as economic ties persuaded the populations of both Norway and Switzerland to vote against joining the EU when referendums were held in 1994.

For some countries, however, the attraction of membership remains very strong. Turkey has consistently made overtures, but has so far been turned down because of its record on human rights. The addition of 12 new members in recent years pushed the population of the EU to nearly 500 million people. Some of these countries, especially Poland, have large agricultural sectors, which could add to the problems of the *Common Agricultural Policy (CAP)*.

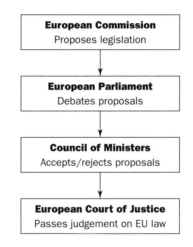

The institutions of the EU

PROS: • it offers a huge market with possibilities of *economies of scale*. The combined strength of the EU creates a potentially powerful trade bloc

• by creating competition it reduces costs and increases efficiency as well as encouraging innovation

• investment is encouraged, especially inward investment from non-EU countries like Japan that are seeking to produce within the EU's boundaries

• it offers the possibility of income and wealth redistribution within Europe and offers more career choices for EU citizens

CONS: • the budget has not always been wisely spent. In particular, the **Common Agricultural Policy (CAP)** has distorted spending in favour of agriculture, which has led to over-production in certain areas and fostered corruption

• the bureaucracy of some elements of European law making has made some people think that law making should be delegated to member states. This is the idea of **subsidiarity**

• countries outside the EU bloc, especially those in the developing world, see the Union as another conspiracy by the rich Western economies to keep them poor (by trade advantages for EU members over non-members)

• individual members still tend to put national interests before those of the wider community. Often, although laws have been passed, they have not always been applied with equal force.

euro zone: a journalistic phrase for the countries linked by their single currency, the **euro**. It has also been called euroland or the euro area. EU enlargement means that it is steadily growing.

exceptional item: an entry in an **income statement** which arises from ordinary trading, but is so large or unusual as to risk distorting the company's trading account. Therefore it is listed separately as an exceptional item. An example would be unusually large **bad debt** charges.

excess aggregate demand means that the quantity of goods and services demanded in the economy as a whole is greater than the amount which can be produced, given the available resources (**full-capacity output**). The consequence is likely to be accelerating **inflation**. It will be possible to raise prices and still sell the product. Firms will bid up the price of **labour** as they compete for the few available employees, especially if they have scarce skills. This will raise costs and prices will rise further. Expectations of inflation may set in and influence pay negotiations. The diagram below shows that if the economy is producing at or near full-capacity output, rising aggregate demand will lead to excess demand and a rising price level. The solution will be to reduce aggregate demand using **fiscal policies** and **monetary policies**.

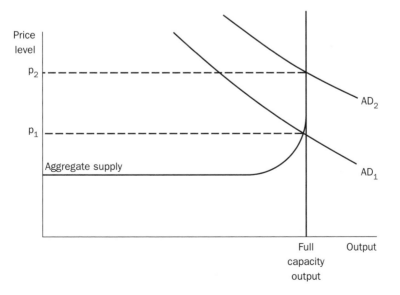

103

Excess aggregate demand will usually be associated with the boom phase of the *economic cycle*. Prospects of economic growth will make firms optimistic about investing and consumers will have increasing incomes, leading to higher consumption. *Aggregate demand* will grow faster than the capacity of the economy to produce. This situation is unsustainable because it will lead to inflation and probably to *contractionary policies*.

excess capacity means having more storage or production potential than is likely to be used in the foreseeable future. Therefore the *capacity utilisation* will be low and the *fixed costs per unit* of output will be relatively high. Firms faced with excess capacity might rationalise by closing down one production site or renting out spare space to another firm. For the whole economy, excess capacity means that resources are underutilised. There is likely to be unemployment and many firms may contract or close down because of low levels of *aggregate demand*. The economy is therefore producing less than it could and some resources are being wasted.

excess demand occurs when the quantity demanded outstrips the quantity supplied, as in the diagram below. This shows disequilibrium in the market, which fails to clear. Excess demand can be seen when there are large numbers of people wishing to buy an item which has just become fashionable and shops have difficulty in obtaining adequate stocks. This situation will not usually last long as either prices will rise or supplies will increase.

One market in which excess demand can persist for quite a while is the housing market. If incomes are rising, demand for housing will rise in many areas. However, in the short run the supply of housing is fixed (i.e. perfectly inelastic). It will take time to acquire land with planning permissions and add to the stock of housing by building more. In this situation, houses will sell very quickly, reflecting their scarcity on the market. Prices will usually rise, perhaps very sharply.

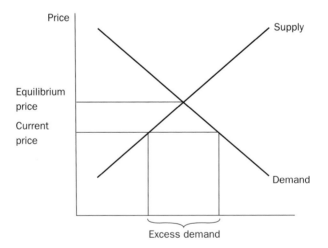

excess supply occurs when the quantity supplied is greater than the quantity demanded. On the microeconomic level, it means that the price is higher than its equilibrium level and gives producers an incentive to supply more of the product. At the same time the high price discourages buyers and the result is seen in stocks of unsold goods. (For diagram of excess supply, see *disequilibrium*.)

Excess supply will usually come to an end if sellers cut prices. However, in some markets this may take quite a while. You can see excess supply in the housing market if there are a great many 'for sale' signs, relatively few buyers looking around and people making offers well below the advertised price.

On the macroeconomic level, excess supply would imply that firms were producing more than consumers wanted to buy, there would be stocks of unsold goods and in time firms would adjust production downwards. This could happen at the onset of a *recession* when there would be falling aggregate demand.

exchange is the process by which people trade with each other, offering goods and services they have produced for goods and services they need or want. Exchange is crucial to economic life, making it possible for people to specialise in the type of production in which they have an advantage. This *specialisation* allows people to produce much more than they can if they have to be self-sufficient.

exchange controls are limits set by law on the dealings in gold and foreign currency which a country's citizens can make. In effect, they prevent a country's *exchange rate* from settling at a market-determined price, because they are a way of fixing the market. Exchange controls were abandoned by the UK in 1979, and by all the member states of the *European Union (EU)* in 1993.

PROS: • can counter a *balance of payments* deficit by limiting the value of imports to the value of export earnings
- allow the internal price level to be established by the workings of the internal economy rather than external factors such as the exchange rate

CONS: • discourage international trade
- may encourage other countries to follow suit

exchange rate: the rate at which one currency can be exchanged for another. Effectively, it is a price for the currency, expressed in terms of other currencies. If it is said that the pound fell against the US dollar, it means that the pound is now worth fewer dollars.

The exchange rate influences the prices of imports and exports and the ease with which producers in different countries can compete with each other. A rise in the exchange rate (*appreciation*) means that export prices will be higher and import prices will be lower. All producers who compete with overseas producers will lose competitiveness. (See also *exchange rate depreciation*.)

exchange rate depreciation: if market forces cause the exchange rate to fall, exports become cheaper and imports dearer in terms of the domestic currency. This may happen because the demand for exports has been falling or because capital inflows have diminished. Either way, demand for the currency will fall and with it the equilibrium exchange rate, as shown in the diagram overleaf.

The same outcome will occur if there has been an increase in demand for imports or a capital outflow. In this case there will be an increase in the supply of the currency by people who want to buy foreign currency on the foreign exchange markets, leading again to a fall in the exchange rate.

Appreciation leads to the reverse situation in which the exchange rate rises, imports become cheaper and exports become dearer.

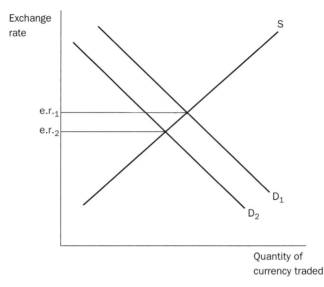

Depreciation following falling demand for the currency

Exchange rate depreciation can have a very favourable effect on the level of economic activity. It makes potential exporters more competitive. Equally it helps firms that compete with imports on the domestic market. Both are likely to find their products bringing in more profit. The UK benefited from this flexibility while outside the euro zone.

exchange rate index: a measure of change in the exchange rate which takes a weighted average of the changes across a number of currencies. Currencies are selected according to their importance in the trade pattern of the country concerned. For the UK, these will be first the euro, then the US dollar and the yen. These will be given the largest weights, with other currencies having smaller weightings. The resulting index number is sometimes called the *effective exchange rate*. It provides a useful measure of changes in competitiveness due to exchange rate variations (see table).

UK effective exchange rate, January 2005 = 100

2000	101.2
2001	99.5
2002	99.5
2003	95.8
2004	102.4
2005	101.1
2006	101.6
2007	104.1
2008	92.9

Source: Bank of England

exchange rate policy: the UK government's strategy regarding the international value of the pound. There are three different approaches the government can take:

- a freely floating exchange rate where the Bank of England does not intervene at all
- a managed rate where the Bank of England intervenes by buying when market pressures are forcing the pound down, and sells pounds when it is concerned the price is getting too high
- a fixed rate, in which the government commits the currency to be fixed in value to other currencies. This would effectively happen if Britain joined the European single currency, the *euro*.

excise taxes are levied by HM Customs and Excise on goods produced for home consumption, as opposed to customs duties which are levied on imports. Excise taxes are paid on a wide range of goods, the best known being alcohol, tobacco and petrol.

executive summary: a précis of a report's main findings and conclusions to enable busy managers to gain a quick understanding and to decide which parts are worth reading in full.

exit: the way in which businesses may leave the market, or close down altogether, if their product has begun to make losses or just become less profitable. Easy exit is very important in ensuring efficiency, because without it the allocation of resources cannot adjust to changes in the pattern of consumer demand. Exit can be difficult in state-owned enterprises and may be affected by employment protection legislation.

expansionary policies may be used by governments which wish to reduce *unemployment* and achieve higher rates of *economic growth*. *Fiscal policies*, e.g. tax cuts and increases in expenditure, and a *monetary policy* of reduced interest rates will all tend to increase aggregate demand and encourage firms to take on more *labour* and expand output. Care must be taken not to overdo expansionary policies, lest growth leads to pressure on resources and accelerating inflation. Expansionary policies will not help in the long run to reduce *structural unemployment*.

expectations are what people believe will happen in the future. Economists and business leaders place great importance on expectations because they assume that they influence people's behaviour. If, for example, people believe that house prices will rise sharply, they may rush to buy before the price rise occurs. The extra *demand* will pull prices up, making it a self-fulfilling prophecy.

expenditure simply means spending. Consumer expenditure and government expenditure are commonly used terms.

expenditure taxes tax spending rather than income. They include VAT and the *excise taxes*. Expenditure taxes are important as sources of government revenue but are sometimes considered *regressive* in their effect, i.e. they have more impact on poorer people than on richer people.

expense: a payment for something of immediate benefit to a business. It causes a debit on the accounts and is charged to the current *profit and loss account*. Maintenance costs and wages are expenses; these are also known as revenue expenditure.

exploitation means taking advantage of a situation or resource for one's own gain. The term implies that the gain will be at the expense of others. Exploitation could be used to describe the employment of labour at very low wages, or the profitable extraction of a scarce mineral from a developing country.

Export Credit Guarantee Department (ECGD) is a government department offering a service by guaranteeing that if foreign importers of UK-produced goods fail to pay, then it will step in and pay instead. It is a way of insuring UK exporters against *bad debts* overseas. By offering such a service, exports are encouraged. As with any insurance policy, fees are charged, and critics of the British government have pointed out that ECGD charges much higher premiums to British exporters than the governments of France, Germany and Japan do to their own companies. In this way, the competitiveness of British exports is hindered. In 1991, the ECGD's short-term export credit insurance business was privatised. In 2008, the ECGD insured around £2 billion of exports in sums ranging from £25 000 to £300 million.

export-led growth occurs when there is rapid growth of exports which then has a *multiplier* effect on the rest of the economy. China has experienced this type of rapid growth, leading to improvements in the standard of living there. An *undervalued exchange rate* may be helpful in achieving this.

export marketing: devising a strategy for developing and sustaining profitable sales overseas. Although largely the same as UK marketing, selling overseas has certain points of difference:
- gaining *distribution* is likely to be harder and far more expensive, so most firms use a local *agent* who already knows and has access to the local distribution channels
- the exporter must decide whether to keep the product the same in all markets (benefiting from *economies of scale*), or to tailor-make it for differing local tastes; the latter should generate higher sales, but the former will keep unit costs down and therefore might be more profitable
- brand names may have different meanings in different languages and should therefore be researched (the German soft drink Pschitt was tested in the UK but failed).

exports: goods and services sold for foreign currency. Goods are described as visible exports while services such as tourism or insurance are invisible exports. (See also *pattern of trade*.)

extension strategy: a medium- to long-term plan for lengthening the *product life cycle*. It is likely to be implemented during the maturity or early decline stages of the product or brand. Extension strategies can be either defensive or offensive.

Defensive: a plan designed to postpone the obsolescence of a product by a year or two, perhaps to keep sales going until a replacement can be launched. Examples include car manufacturers' 'special editions', which usually offer different paintwork, slightly different equipment and a bouncy name.

Offensive: a plan to revitalise or reposition a product to give it a wholly new, long-term market. Johnson and Johnson's repositioning of its baby powder and baby oil to appeal to women instead of just the babycare market provides an example.

Types of extension strategy include:
- redesigning or reformulating the product ('New improved!')
- adding an extra feature ('Now with…!')
- repositioning a product's price and image (usually downmarket)
- changing the packaging and advertising imagery to appeal to a new or additional market sector.

Note that sales promotions or extra advertising spending alone would not be regarded as extension strategies. They are ways of boosting sales that could work equally well at any stage of the life cycle.

external balance: a situation in which exports and imports are roughly the same in value.

external benefits accrue to third parties, not just the producer or the consumer. They may arise from production or consumption. An external benefit of consumption occurs when the consumption process benefits third parties who are not themselves involved in buying the product. Users of public transport benefit anyone else who wants to travel and does so faster because of reduced congestion. (See also *externalities*.) With external benefits there will be *underconsumption*.

external constraint: a factor outside the control of an enterprise that restricts it from meeting its objectives. Main types of external constraint include:
- changing consumer tastes
- competitors' actions
- economic circumstances (especially the level of interest rates, the value of the pound, consumer and business confidence, and the level of *aggregate demand*)
- legal constraints
- social attitudes and *pressure group* activity.

external costs are negative consequences of activities that are paid for by people or organisations other than the originator of those costs. For example, the sulphur emissions from power stations cause acid rain that damages forests; the cost of this is borne by the owners of the forests, not the electricity companies. As external costs do not affect the *profit and loss account* of the firm causing the costs, the firm has no direct incentive to minimise the pollution. This is why government intervention is required to force the polluter to pay (or stop). (See *cost–benefit analysis*.)

external diseconomies of scale are cost increases that affect all firms in the industry as output increases. These are likely to be local in effect and result from increased pollution and congestion or from pressure on resources generally. Expansion may drive up wage rates for specific skills.

external economies of scale: see *economies of scale*

external environment: the circumstances within which firms operate that are outside their control. (See *external constraint*.)

external financing means obtaining capital resources from outside the firm's resources or accounts. This can only be done in one of three ways: debt, *share capital* or *grant*.

Debt can be obtained for day-to-day (short-term) transactions or for longer-term capital needs. Among the ways of borrowing for the short term are: bank *overdraft*, *trade credit* and credit factoring; for the longer term: bank loans, commercial mortgages and *debentures*.

Share capital can be obtained via a *rights issue*, the issue of *preference shares*, or by a *flotation* of the company's shares on the *Stock Exchange*.

Grants could come from the *European Union (EU)*, the government's *regional policy* or from a local enterprise board. It should be remembered, however, that grants provide only a tiny fraction of the capital needs of business.

external growth comes from outside the firm, such as by acquiring or merging with another firm. This is the easiest way to grow rapidly, but results in a huge number of managerial problems based on the difficulty of integrating a new business, management and *culture*. *Internal growth* is a far safer way of expanding, though it may be too slow to allow the firm to capitalise on exciting short-term prospects.

external recruitment means appointing someone from outside the business, i.e. a person new to the business. Inevitably they could bring in some fresh thinking, but they may never fit successfully into the business culture. Those appointed from outside are much more likely to quit their new job within six months.

externalities are those costs or benefits which occur as a result of the main operation of a business but which are not part of the firm's *profit and loss account*. Examples include *pollution* and congestion – costs that are the result of production but which are borne by the community, not the business. There are moves for some *external costs* to be passed back to organisations, such as by legislation that forces firms to pay for any smoke emissions from their factories. Where it is possible to 'make the polluters pay', firms have an incentive to minimise their costs by minimising the pollution. (See also *emissions trading schemes* and *social efficiency.*)

External benefits can arise through the effect on local service and supply industries of new firms opening up in an area, or from the spill-over effect of new technology, such as in defence or related industries. An example of an external benefit from the development of space exploration was Teflon, which was used to produce non-stick saucepans.

An attempt to account fully for external as well as internal costs and benefits is made through *cost–benefit analysis*.

extraordinary general meeting (EGM): a shareholders' meeting called in addition to the normal *annual general meeting (AGM)*. This might be to gain approval for a *rights issue* or for a vote of confidence in the *chairman (or chairperson)*.

extrapolation: in forecasting the near future it can be assumed the recent past will be a good guide. This is known as extrapolating from the past to the future. When *trend* values have been established, they can be plotted on a graph and extrapolation by eye or by mathematical means can be undertaken.

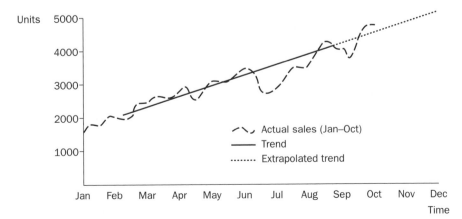

Extrapolation of a sales trend

factor markets: where *demand* and *supply* interact to determine the prices of *factors of production*, namely land, labour and capital.

factors of production include land, labour, capital and enterprise. Enterprise is not considered to be a specfic factor of production by some economists because they regard an *entrepreneur* as someone who, whilst having special skills, is nonetheless just a part of labour. Others argue that without entrepreneurship the other factors would not be combined in order to produce profit, and hence increase living standards. The factors are rewarded as follows:

- land receives rent
- labour receives wages
- capital receives interest
- entrepreneurship (or enterprise) receives profit.

factory farming: the use of *production line* techniques to ensure maximum *output* from farm livestock with the minimum of inputs. This usually means that the animals live in isolation in very confined spaces, and are fattened up with the aid of hormones. It is a good example of where *profit maximisation* could be thought to conflict with *ethics*.

factory gate prices are the prices charged by producers for output sold to wholesalers. They provide a helpful *leading indicator* of possible future consumer price changes.

fair trade means buying imported products from developing countries at prices which give a fair return to the producers. It is an attempt to avoid buying products which depend upon very cheap *labour*, implying that the producers get a very poor return for their efforts. The Fairtrade Foundation certifies firms which are engaged in fair trade so that consumers have some guarantee that producer incomes will benefit if they buy the product.

Family Expenditure Survey: carried out by the Office for National Statistics, this provides the information needed to construct the *retail prices index (RPI)* and the *consumer prices index (CPI)*, which measure the rate of inflation.

family-friendly policies: a term used in connection with the Employment Relations Act 1999, reflecting the focus upon longer time off for mothers and fathers at the birth of a child or later if a child becomes ill.

Fayol, Henri (1841–1925) was a French management pioneer who focused on the problems of organisational structure within large firms at the turn of the century. Whereas his American contemporary, *F W Taylor*, concentrated on the efficiency of shop-floor labour, Fayol looked at senior management. He was largely responsible for introducing the concepts of *chain of command*, the *organisational chart* and *span of control*.

FDI: see *foreign direct investment (FDI)*

Federal Reserve Bank (known as the 'Fed') includes the Federal Reserve Board and 12 regional reserve banks. The governor is appointed by the President with Senate approval and presides over the Federal Open Market Committee which decides all matters of *monetary policy*. The Fed is independent of the US government.

feedback is response to a piece of communication. Without it the communicator cannot know whether the communication has been received effectively. Not only could this cause operational problems (such as stocks not being reordered), it may also undermine *motivation*. This is because communicators have a psychological need for response to their efforts. For instance, if homework goes unmarked students will soon lose the impetus to produce more, and any that is done will be of poor quality.

fertility rate: the number of births per thousand women between the ages of 15 and 45. It provides a useful way of predicting population changes.

field trials: testing a new or improved product on consumers within your target market. For example, 400 households might be asked to use a new detergent for a month, then be interviewed on its qualities compared with their regular brands. If the brand name of the product is kept hidden from the households, this is known as a *blind product test*.

fieldwork is the process of carrying out field research. An example would be a *market research* survey, which could be conducted through face-to-face interviews in the street, or via a postal or telephone survey.

finance: a term covering sources of funds which may be borrowed to pay for investment or consumption.

financial accounting is largely concerned with the reporting and production of financial accounts according to the requirements of the Companies Act 2006 so that users of accounts have an accurate view of a firm's financial position.

financial assets include cash, bank and building society balances, bills, *bonds*, *shares*, pension entitlements and *derivatives*.

financial economies: see *internal economies of scale*

Financial Reporting Standards (FRS): accounting standards issued under the authority of the *Accounting Standards Board*. The first standard was issued in 1991 and aimed to improve the reporting on *cash flow* in published company accounts.

Financial Services and Markets Act 2000: this legislation established the Financial Services Authority (FSA) as the sole regulator of the financial services industry. Before then, the Bank of England had always been important, with its ability to have a quiet word with banks it considered to be acting too riskily. The importance of the Act became clear when the *credit crunch* hit in 2007. As banks such as Northern Rock collapsed, many questions were asked about banking regulation. It became clear that the FSA had struggled to regulate a finance sector that was expanding rapidly with the enthusiastic backing of Labour and Conservative politicians. The FSA's weakness can be traced back to the legislation passed in 2000.

Financial Services Authority: the organisation which supervises the operations of the financial system. It was set up in 1997 to create a new, overarching system which supervises banks as well as other financial intermediaries, such as insurance companies. It is likely to be reformed soon. Supervision is important; properly carried out it can, for instance, prevent banks from making imprudent loans and financial advisers from misleading the public. (See also *Financial Services and Markets Act 2000*.)

financial year: the UK financial year runs from 6 April to 5 April and so income tax changes apply accordingly. Each individual person or company may make up their accounts annually to any date. The essence of a financial year is simply to create a consistent reporting period.

financing requirements: the capital a firm needs to carry out its plans for the coming trading periods. If this cannot be achieved through *internal financing*, it will be found from external sources such as share issues, loans or grants. The length of time the financing requirements are needed is important. At some future point the plans should become self-financing.

finite resources are resources which are fixed in supply and cannot be renewed. They are also referred to as *depletable resources*. Oil is one example, along with many other mineral products. Others include tropical timber and fish stocks which are not being exploited in a sustainable way.

firm: a collection of factors of production brought together by an entrepreneur for the purpose of producing goods or services. The term is often used when theory is being employed to analyse a particular situation, in contrast to the term business, which is used in a more practical context.

firm-specific skills are those skills which are acquired on the job and relate to that particular employer. A business will try hard not to make redundant a person with firm-specific skills because a replacement will have to be trained all over again. Their wages may be viewed as a fixed cost for this reason.

fiscal policy is government policy towards its raising of revenue and its level of (public) spending. The task of setting fiscal policy is undertaken by the *Chancellor of the Exchequer*. It is arrived at in the following order:

1 establish government economic objectives
2 decide on the correct balance between government revenue and government spending (known as the fiscal or budgetary balance)
3 make the individual decisions that are compatible with 1 and 2 and maximise political advantage. Such decisions may include increasing the tax on petrol or cutting government spending on the National Health Service.

In the *circular flow of national income*, taxes represent a withdrawal that is balanced by government expenditure on such items as pensions, unemployment benefit and so on. If the government takes in more than it spends, consumer spending power is reduced and *demand* falls, thus slowing down the economy. If it spends more than it takes in, then it increases demand and therefore increases economic activity. Because of the impact on demand, fiscal policy is often called 'demand management', as opposed to *monetary policy*, which attempts to control the economy through the money supply and interest rates. From a government's point of view, fiscal policy has the following advantages and disadvantages:

PROS:
- government spending injected into the economy has a **multiplier** effect as it moves through the economy. For instance, if an unemployed person gets a job helping to build a new road, some of his or her wages will be spent on things which previously could not be afforded, such as new clothes. This creates demand in the clothing industry, so more people are employed to make clothes, which creates more income and so on. If the clothes are made abroad, however, it is the overseas economy and workforce that benefits
- revenue can be raised either through direct taxation, e.g. **income tax** and **corporation tax**, or through indirect taxation, e.g. **VAT**. Governments can alter the mix of the two for policy reasons, such as reducing direct taxation, which some believe has an important impact upon people's incentives to work

CONS:
- the timing of government intervention is crucial, yet extremely difficult to judge
- many large-scale projects take a long time to have any effect on the economy. For instance, if a new motorway is to be built, it may take years of planning before the first contractor moves on to the site, by which time the economy may have recovered
- some economists believe that government spending has a 'crowding out' effect, meaning that any boost to the economy from the **public sector** is at the cost of the **private sector**. There is no hard evidence to support this view.

fiscal rules: while Chancellor of the Exchequer, Gordon Brown said that the government would adhere to the golden rule. There were two elements in this:
- Over the course of the **economic cycle**, the government would balance the budget. This left some scope for counter-cyclical policy, with deficit spending in a recession to be balanced by a surplus in times of recovery.
- There would be no borrowing to finance consumption, although there would be borrowing to finance investment that had a reasonable prospect of generating funds for repayment over the long run.

In October 2008, Chancellor Alistair Darling signalled a change of policy so that the government could borrow very large amounts to provide a greater stimulus to the economy and limit the damage caused by the recession.

Fisher Equation: see *equation of exchange*

fixed assets: items of a monetary value which have a long-term function and can be used repeatedly. These determine the scale of a firm's operations. Examples are land, buildings, equipment and machinery. Fixed assets are not only useful in the running of the firm, but can also provide **collateral** for securing additional **loan capital**.

fixed costs are the expenses that do not alter in relation to changes in demand or output (in the short term). They have to be paid whether the business trades or not. Examples are rent, **depreciation** and interest charges. Part of the wage and salary bill may be a fixed cost when the people concerned are not directly involved in the production process.

fixed costs per unit (also known as **average fixed costs**) are total **fixed costs** divided by the units of output produced. While total fixed costs cannot be changed by definition in the short run, fixed costs per unit continually fall as output or activity is increased up to the *capacity* level.

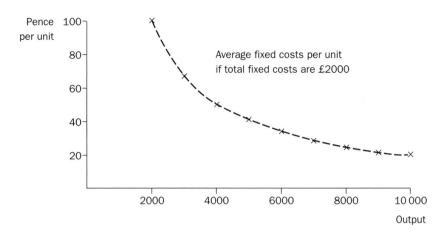

Fixed costs per unit

fixed exchange rates are currency rates which are not permitted to respond to changes in the demand for currencies. In a free market, there is always some movement, but the rate is controlled by **central bank** intervention. If the pound came under selling pressure, the market reaction would be a fall in the exchange rate. On 1 January 1999, the **euro** became the first truly fixed exchange rate regime, by locking the European currencies together.

fixed factors of production are the resource inputs to a production process, the quantity of which cannot be altered in the short run. In other words, the quantity of the factor employed does not change with the level of output. For example, capital equipment is a fixed factor because it takes time to arrange to have more or less of it. **Labour** will be a fixed factor if there are difficulties about increasing or decreasing the quantity of it as output changes, as in the case of managers.

fixed overheads: see *overheads*

fixed rate loan: a loan on which the interest rate payable is determined at the outset and does not vary with the market rate of interest.

PROS: • enables interest costs to be budgeted accurately
  • the firm is protected from the potentially serious impact on **overheads** of sharp rises in interest rates

CONS: • fixed rate loans are inflexible, as they are taken out for specific time periods (such as five years)
  • timing must be right; it is easy to become tied to a high fixed interest payment just before market rates fall

flat organisation (or hierarchy): a management structure based on a wide *span of control*, therefore requiring relatively few *layers of hierarchy*. This results in:
- good *vertical communication* as there are few management layers between the bottom and top of the company
- the need to delegate a high proportion of the tasks and decisions
- higher motivation potential, given the greater responsibility delegated to junior managers and staff.

flexibility in business usually means the ability and willingness to change methods of working. This relies on a workforce that is multi-skilled and is not too resistant to *change*. A flexible worker would be capable of doing many different jobs, perhaps when filling in for an absentee.

flexible labour markets occur where employers are able to take on new employees on a full-time or a part-time basis, temporarily or permanently, and are able to make employees redundant without great expense. *Labour flexibility* can be further enhanced if there are few rigid *demarcation* lines so that employees are willing to do a range of different tasks and acquire new skills, i.e. *multi-skilling*. It is generally thought that there is less unemployment in a flexible labour market. The US labour market is believed to be more flexible than the UK labour market. Within the EU, the UK and the Netherlands are thought to have more flexible labour markets than France and Germany. (See also *labour market flexibility*.)

flexible specialisation: a manufacturing theory stating that because modern markets are broken down into small niches, yet customer tastes are always changing, the successful firm must be able to produce specialised products flexibly. This requires machinery that can quickly be reprogrammed, instead of conveyor-belt driven plants designed to mass-produce a single item. Flexible specialisation implies a move back to *batch production* and places a premium upon a multi-skilled, adaptable workforce.

flexible working: the acceptance by staff and management that rigid *demarcation* lines lead to inefficiency, and therefore that *labour flexibility* is preferable for long-term success. The same term is also used to describe a staffing pattern that is not dependent upon full-time, permanent jobs. In this context, flexible working means a willingness to work on a temporary or part-time basis.

floating exchange rate: a currency which responds to supply and demand on the foreign exchange markets without *central bank* intervention.

PROS: • requires no gold or foreign currency reserves
   • responds to the automatic discipline of the market
   • accepts that 'you can't buck the market' (to use Margaret Thatcher's phrase)

CONS: • firms cannot predict future rates, adding to the uncertainties involved in business decision-making, which might restrict trade
   • leaves the international competitiveness of a country's goods to a market that is often affected by speculative money flows; these may have little to do with the underlying state of the economy and its *balance of payments*

(See also *exchange rate* and *exchange rate depreciation*.)

flotation: the term given to the launch of a company on to the *stock market* by the offer of its shares to the public.

flow production is the manufacture of an item in a continually moving process. Each stage is linked with the next by a conveyor belt or in liquid form, so that the production time is minimised and production efficiency is maximised. The diagram below shows a continuous system in which sub-components are being fed into the main production line just as streams flow into a river. In order to operate effectively, a flow system needs high capacity utilisation, as the highly mechanised line is likely to be expensive to purchase, install and maintain. Therefore high demand levels are needed to spread the *fixed costs* over many units of output.

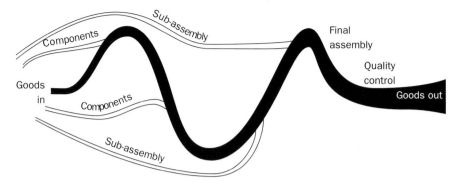

Flow production

focus upon the core of a business represents the opposite corporate strategy to *diversification*. Focus might be achieved by selling off fringe activities or by the decision to stop developing new products outside the core market.

focus groups: an American term for *group discussions*, i.e. small-scale, in-depth research into the reasons behind consumers' habits and attitudes.

food miles: how many miles the contents of a pack of food have travelled to reach the shop shelf. For a smoothie, the banana would have travelled 3 200 km to get to the Netherlands, then – after processing – another few hundred kilometres to get to your local Tesco.

Food Safety Act 1990 is a wide-ranging law which strengthens and updates *consumer protection* in the food sector. The Act brought food sources, and by implication farmers and growers, specifically under food safety legislation for the first time. It made it an offence to sell food which is not of the 'nature or substance or quality' demanded by the purchaser. Other key features include:
- premises selling food must register with the local authority
- those handling food must receive appropriate training
- enforcement officers can issue an improvement notice or, in extreme cases, an emergency prohibition notice
- the harmonisation of UK laws and standards with those of Europe.

The 1990 Act was given more teeth when the General Food Regulations 2004 made offenders liable for up to 2 years' imprisonment.

footloose industries are able to locate in a wide range of places because their costs do not vary much between one place and another. Traditional industries are often tied to a location for historical reasons, such as past raw material or energy availability. Recently developed industries such as electronics are likely to be footloose. The term is most often used in relation to *multinational* organisations.

Footsie (FTSE 100): a widely quoted index denoting shifts in the average share price level among 100 of the largest public companies in the UK. The market prices are plotted regularly through each working day and their *weighted average* is the basis of the index. A rise in the index indicates greater confidence in the financial community about UK economic prospects generally, so the Footsie is considered an important *leading indicator*. The term stands for the *Financial Times* Stock Exchange 100, though it is usually referred to as the Footsie.

Fordism: the application of Henry Ford's faith in *mass production* run by autocratic management. This implies high *division of labour* and little workplace democracy, but with the consolation of high wages.

forecasting has two meanings. In the context of a business, it means estimating future outcomes such as next year's sales figures. Although forecasts can only be guesses of the future, the aim is to base the guesswork on the best possible information. There are three main sources for this:

- projecting an established trend forward (*extrapolation*)
- *market research* into consumers' buying intentions
- consulting experts with proven ability at anticipating trends.

In the macroeconomic context, forecasting means using sophisticated models to predict changes in the economy as a whole. Output, investment, inflation, employment and unemployment might all be the subject of forecasts.

foreign aid may be offered to developing countries with a low per capita income in order to help them invest. It may also be available to countries with serious famine problems. It may be bilateral aid, given by one government to another. Or it may be multilateral, given through an international organisation, often the World Bank or the European Development Fund. There have been strenuous efforts over the years to persuade the developed countries to give more foreign aid, almost always unsuccessful. A target of the 1960s and 1970s, that 1 per cent of GDP should be given by each developed country, never came near to being reached and since then aid has tended to diminish rather than to grow.

Not all aid has been well used; some has been spent on prestige projects and military objectives which have not benefited poor people. There has been some evidence of corruption in the disbursement of aid and its usefulness has been further compromised by the tying of aid payments to a commitment to buy goods from the donor country. In some cases aid has been tied to the purchase of military goods.

foreign competition: refers to the imports from abroad that compete with firms in their home markets, and the goods and services produced abroad that compete with them in their export markets. Often businesses will be competing with the same foreign firms in both their domestic and their export markets. This can be confusing because many businesses that export are actually foreign owned. Think about Nissan.

foreign direct investment (FDI): the sums invested directly into an economy by foreign people, firms or governments. For example, the US computer giant IBM might invest £50 million in building a new factory in Scunthorpe, or Cadbury might buy an established chocolate producer in China.

foreign exchange may mean foreign currency, the medium of exchange of another country.

foreign exchange market (FOREX) is the market where dealers buy and sell currencies either 'spot', i.e. for immediate exchange, or 'forward', i.e. at a rate agreed today for some future time, such as in three months' time. Currencies are bought and sold depending on the demands of international trade but also for reasons of speculation. The major world trading markets are in London, New York and Tokyo.

foreign exchange reserves: the stocks of foreign currency held by the central bank and available if the exchange rate needs to be maintained at its existing level at a time when market forces are tending to push it downwards, i.e. to bring about a depreciation. The level of the reserves is important if there is either a *fixed exchange rate* or a *managed exchange rate*. Even if the exchange rate is floating, if it threatens to depreciate very rapidly, the central bank may want to try to stabilise its value by buying it, using the foreign exchange reserves.

foreign investment may take place in two ways:
- *foreign direct investment (FDI)* means spending in another country which will create production or distribution facilities
- *portfolio investment* means buying shares in companies based abroad or bonds issued by other countries' governments or moving money to bank accounts abroad.

formal communication takes place within the official channels, i.e. the lines of communication approved by senior management. An example would be a marketing manager talking to the marketing director: his or her immediate boss. Within that channel any form of communication is regarded as formal. Beware of muddling formal communication with written and informal communication with oral. (See also *informal communication* and *direct communication*.)

formal economy: that part of the economy which is recorded in official statistics. So it includes all legally organised business and all government activity but excludes the use of resources which are not paid for such as voluntary and domestic work and work done for cash which is not declared for tax purposes. Some of the latter will be legal but some will not.

forward buying means contracting to buy a certain quantity of goods or foreign currency at a price agreed today, for delivery at a specific future date. This can act as insurance against unforeseen problems that may damage the profitability of an export order, such as a sudden jump in oil prices due to war breaking out in the Middle East.

forward integration means creating a business which takes care of further processing and/or distribution and marketing of the final product, as well as its manufacture. It means that producers of intermediate goods may expand their business by taking the production process a stage further. Makers of computer chips might actually start to manufacture computers. The more likely route would be to buy or merge with an established business which has some expertise in the next stage of the process.

forward markets are the markets in which it is possible to buy a certain quantity of goods or foreign currency at a price agreed today, for delivery at a specific future date.
This can act as insurance against unforeseen problems that may damage the profitability of an export order, such as a sudden jump in oil prices due to war breaking out in the Middle East. Contracts made in the forward market are known as *futures*.

franchise: a business based upon the name, *logo* and trading method of an existing, successful business. To obtain a franchise requires the payment of an initial fee and the signing of a contract that places tight restrictions upon the *franchisee*, including:
- limitation on the area of operation
- design of premises to be exactly as laid down by the *franchisor*
- all supplies to be purchased from the franchisor
- an annual payment to the franchisor based upon a percentage of the franchisee's turnover

Despite these costs and constraints, business start-ups based upon franchising have a far lower failure rate than independent firms. This is due to the following advantages of franchising:

- the niche, trading strategy and methods have been tried and tested elsewhere, reducing many of the risks associated with business start-ups
- the name and logo may have wide customer recognition and loyalty, ensuring high demand from day one
- part of the annual payment goes into an advertising fund that finances much larger advertising campaigns than could be afforded by an independent; television advertising has played a major part in the success of franchise businesses such as McDonald's and Pizza Hut.

Despite these considerable advantages, potential franchisees should never forget that running any business is very demanding and involves significant risk. Franchising has attracted some would-be *entrepreneurs* who lack the experience or the personality to lead a company.

franchisee: a person or company who has bought the local rights to use the name, *logo* and training method of another company (the *franchisor*).

franchisor: the holder of the *franchise* who will sell the local rights to suitable *franchisees*. From the franchisor's point of view, this can be a far better way to expand the company than via the traditional route of opening up more managed branches or outlets.

free enterprise: a system by which individuals are allowed to set up in business without interference from governments, whether local or national. Free enterprise is commonly regarded as a good thing and it often is where there is strong *competition*. It can lead to there being lively and innovative producers who strive to meet real consumer needs and wants. If on the other hand producers acquire market power through monopolies or *cartels*, they may be able to charge unnecessarily high prices. Or they may sell poor-quality goods against which the consumer has little protection. Regulation may be needed to protect consumers.

free entry refers to the situation in which entry is very easy for firms which seek to break into a new market. Where the market has a large number of small businesses, e.g. hairdressers, antique shops, accountants and so on, entry is usually fairly free. Manufacturing industries in which large potential *economies of scale* create barriers to entry illustrate the reverse situation. Free entry is used as a theoretical concept which helps to define *perfect competition*. Easy entry will always make for a more competitive market.

Free entry is important in that it is necessary in order to ensure that resources can be reallocated to adapt to changes in the pattern of consumer demand. Easy *exit* is also important in this respect, because it frees the resources needed by growing industries.

free goods are goods which have no price and no property rights associated with them and require no factors of production for their enjoyment. It is rather hard to find satisfactory examples because, increasingly, it has become apparent that the traditional examples such as fresh air and sunshine are not free at all. Hence the saying, 'there is no such thing as a free lunch'.

freehold: the right to own a piece of land and/or property for evermore. A freehold can become a substantial, long-term *asset* with a strong impact on the *balance sheet*.

Freeholds can provide the security (*collateral*) that banks want before lending money, or be the basis of raising cash via a sale-and-leaseback contract.

freelance: a self-employed person who expects to earn a living by providing a service to different clients at irregular intervals. As they are not employed on a permanent basis, freelancers need to work especially hard at keeping their clients satisfied.

free market: a marketplace where there are many buyers, each free to choose who to buy from, and many sellers, each free to supply without government intervention. This *laissez-faire* ideal ignores business realities such as *market power* and *collusion*.

free movement of capital is an important aspect of creating the *single European market*, and important worldwide in facilitating growth and *globalisation*. It allows firms to invest in the locations where production will be most efficient and can lead to lower prices for consumers. They then have higher real incomes. Both they and the employees who find work in new locations get improved standards of living.

free movement of people: an important element in the underlying framework of the *European Union (EU)*. (The other two pillars of the system are free movement of goods and services and free movement of capital.) All EU citizens have the right to live and work anywhere in the EU and moves have been made to recognise qualifications across all member countries. This increases the international *mobility of labour*.

free rider problem: where there is a *public good*, no one can be excluded from benefiting from it and so no one has an incentive to pay for its installation or upkeep. Street lighting is a standard example; because of the free rider problem no individual will pay for it. All will wait for someone else to provide it, knowing that they will have the use of it without paying. This is why public goods must be provided by governments which have the legal right to tax people to pay for them.

free trade exists when trade between countries is not restricted in any way by *tariffs*, *quotas* or other barriers. It is based on the theory of *comparative advantage*, which argues that every country will be better off if it specialises in producing goods at which it is comparatively more efficient. The *World Trade Organization (WTO)* accepts the notion that more trade benefits everyone, and through successive 'rounds' has sought to reduce trade barriers around the world. In effect, the opposite of free trade is *protectionism*, which often emerges in countries suffering from *recession*.

frequency distribution: where events occur many times, the values they have on each occasion can be recorded to see the frequency with which each value occurs. Examples might be daily sales of a chocolate bar, or the precise length of a bolt to be used in car production. Distributions can be presented as *histograms* or as line graphs.

frictional unemployment occurs in the time delay between losing one job and finding another. By its nature it is temporary, as opposed to *structural unemployment* which is more fundamental and therefore longer term. If a government wished to reduce frictional unemployment it could improve the quality of service in Job Centres, so that the newly unemployed are able to find work more quickly.

Friedman, Milton (1912–2006) was an American economist whose views on *monetarism* had a great influence on Conservative governments during the 1980s. His work at Chicago University helped give rise to the 'Chicago School' of economists. Their view of governments' responsibility for poor economic growth due to *interventionist policies* and overtaxing made them recommend a *laissez-faire* approach.

friendly societies: non-profit-making savings organisations similar to building societies. To encourage their continued use, successive governments have allowed every household to save a limited amount tax free with a friendly society.

fringe benefits: any benefit received by employees in addition to their wages or salary. Common fringe benefits are a company pension scheme, a company car, discounts when buying the firm's products and the provision of sports facilities. All add to the cost of employing labour, but are expected to pay for themselves by their contribution to staff loyalty and therefore the reduction of *labour turnover*.

FRS: see *Financial Reporting Standards (FRS)*

fuel tax: excise taxes which raise the market price of petrol, diesel and heating oil. Initially the purpose of the taxes was to raise revenue. In the case of petrol and diesel, this was partly intended to cover the cost of building and maintaining roads. In the past fuel taxes have been raised to discourage consumption of fuels which generate greenhouse gases, but recently public opinion has tended to turn against this. The Department of Transport has estimated that a 10 per cent increase in the real price of fuel will reduce quantity demanded by 3 per cent, but governments have shied away from creating strong incentives to cut energy use for fear of losing popularity.

fuel tax escalator: the system by which fuel taxes were raised by more than the rate of inflation at each budget, so that the proportion of the price which was tax rose steadily. This was abandoned in the 2000 Budget due to its unpopularity with road users. This may have had some impact on greenhouse gas emissions.

full-capacity output: the highest level of output which can be achieved in the economy as a whole, given the type of resources available and their existing location. *Aggregate demand* for goods and services in excess of this level of output will lead to accelerating inflation. However, there may at this level of output still be some *structural unemployment*. This will occur if the unemployed people do not have the skills which are required by employers or if they are located in areas other than the ones in which employers are recruiting. In other words, if they are *occupationally immobile* or *geographically immobile*, they may be unable to contribute to production.

full cost pricing: another term for *cost-plus pricing*.

full employment is the level of employment that provides jobs for all those who wish to work apart from those *frictionally unemployed*. It implies that the capital stock of the country is fully utilised. *LFS unemployment* reached its lowest rate for more than 20 years at 4.8 per cent in 2004, having been around 5 per cent since 2000. This might represent full employment in the UK. By late 2009 unemployment had risen above 8 per cent as recession set in.

full line forcing: a (trade) *restrictive practice* whereby a retailer wanting to buy one brand or product from a supplier is told that unless it stocks the full product range it can have nothing. As in-store space is limited, if the retailer accepts this manufacturer's full range it may not be worthwhile to stock any rival products. This is a way in which producers can attempt to achieve monopoly distribution in retail outlets (especially smaller ones). The manufacturers of ice-cream and of batteries have been accused of full line forcing in the past. Retailers wanting to fight against it could make a complaint to the **Office of Fair Trading (OFT)**, but they would be worried that a powerful manufacturing firm might stop supplying them with the key brands demanded by customers.

function: an individual's job role, defined broadly within headings such as marketing, production, personnel or finance. Therefore a business structured by function is organised into departments such as the above. This contrasts with businesses structured by product or by **matrix management**.

functional organisation is based on a hierarchy in which each department operates separately under the leadership of those at the top of the pyramid. **Coordination** stems from the top, but may be hard to achieve at the lower management layers due to the separation of job functions into the different departments. This form of structure can be contrasted with the more flexible **matrix management** organisation.

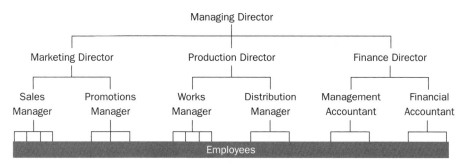

A functional organisation

functional strategy: the medium to long-term plan to help meet the objective of a business function/department, e.g. the marketing strategy.

futures trading is when a **commodity** or financial asset is bought or sold at some time in the future at an agreed price. In London such trading in financial assets occurs on the floor of the **London International Financial Futures Exchange (LIFFE)**. Commodities such as wheat, oil, wool and many other products can also be bought or sold 'forward'. This can be purely speculative, but it can also be vital for a business to protect itself against possible exchange rate or commodity price fluctuations (see **hedging**).

3G: abbreviation for third generation mobile phones. This new, much more powerful type of phone was launched nationally in 2003. These phones offer picture messaging, speedy internet access and access to serious computing power. The licences for the UK 3G networks were auctioned in April 2000 for an astonishing £22.5 billion. This was paid to the government by Vodafone, Orange, O_2, T Mobile and Hutchison.

4G: abbreviation for fourth generation mobile phones. These are expected to be launched in 2013–2015 and will provide instant wireless downloads of video in high definition.

G8: see *Group of Eight (G8)*

gains from trade: the benefits arising from trade which result in increased output from a given quantity of real resources. The theory of *comparative advantage* shows that trade allows countries to specialise in the goods and services which they produce most efficiently. By increasing efficiency, gains are made overall.

Galbraith, J K (1908–2006): a Canadian-born economist who popularised the works of *Keynes* and contributed to an understanding of the workings of large corporations and the motives of firms and politicians. His writings were sceptical of *free enterprise*, as in his criticisms of the idea that the free market satisfies people's needs. In his book *The Affluent Society* (4th edn, Deutsch, 1985) he spoke out strongly against the persuasive power of advertising:

'As a society becomes increasingly affluent, wants are increasingly created by the process by which they are satisfied.'

Galbraith's *The Great Crash, 1929* (3rd ed., Penguin, 1988) is one of the most readable insights into that dramatic event. The book enjoyed a new sales boom after the 2007 *credit crunch*.

game theory applies when the bodies which are competing in the marketplace exhibit interdependent behaviour (see *interdependence between firms*). This means that for each one, the actions of the other will have an impact on the decisions taken. For example, if one business decides to cut prices, its competitor may follow suit. Game theory can be applied in a range of oligopoly situations, whether the businesses are competing or colluding with each other. There may be gainers and losers or all may gain together.

gap (in the market): an identifiable market opportunity that has not yet been exploited. The term might be used in relation to:
- market segments, such as an age group that has not been catered for
- products, such as a flavour of fruit juice that has not yet been marketed
- distribution, such as a new, *impulse purchase* product that is not yet being distributed to garages, cinemas and other non-standard outlets.

GATT: see *General Agreement on Tariffs and Trade (GATT)*

GDP: see *gross domestic product (GDP)*

gearing measures the proportion of *capital employed* that is provided by long-term lenders. The gearing ratio is:

$$FORMULA: \quad \frac{\text{non-current liabilities}}{\text{capital employed}} \times 100$$

If loans represent more than 50 per cent of capital employed, a company is said to be highly geared. Such a company has to pay interest on its borrowing before it can pay *dividends* to shareholders or reinvest profits in new equipment. Therefore the higher the gearing, the higher the risk. Note that capital employed is found by adding total equity and non-current liabilities.

gee whiz graph: a graph drawn to a scale that exaggerates a trend (to produce the effect: 'gee whiz!'). This is achieved by starting one of the axes (usually the vertical one) at above zero. It is useful to remember that examiners prefer axes to start at zero, in order to prevent the deception implied by the gee whiz graph.

General Agreement on Tariffs and Trade (GATT) was established after the Second World War to encourage the growth of international trade by removing or reducing *tariff* and non-tariff barriers. In 1995 GATT was succeeded by the *World Trade Organization (WTO)*.

general union: an organisation founded to represent the collective interests of employees from within any industry and with no specified skills. General unions tend to attract unskilled or semi-skilled workers.

generic brands are those that are so totally associated with the product that customers treat the brand name as if it was a product category. Examples include Hoover (vacuum cleaner) and Bacardi (white rum). This could be said to be the ultimate marketing achievement.

genetically modified (GM) foods: these products of the biotechnology industry burst onto the consciousness of the consumer when the US firm Monsanto ran an advertising campaign in 1998 to persuade public opinion of their worth. The campaign backfired, leaving a widespread consumer image of GM foods as 'Frankenstein foods', of doubtful origin and with doubtful consequences for consumer and environmental welfare.

geographical immobility occurs when people who have been made redundant are unable to move to areas in which jobs are available and thus remain unemployed. It is made worse when there is a lack of housing for rent at reasonable prices in the areas where jobs exist. Also differences in house prices, such that areas with high unemployment have low prices, make it hard for people without jobs to move to areas with jobs. Improved transport facilities can reduce geographical immobility.

gilt-edged securities are a type of *government security*. They are used by governments to borrow the sums needed to cover a *budget deficit*. Originally such stock certificates were literally edged with gold leaf, hence the name. This is no longer true, but it is the case that gilts are a totally safe form of investment because no government would refuse to pay up when the gilt matures.

Gini coefficient: a measurement of inequality in the distribution of income. It is the ratio of the area between the diagonal and the *Lorenz curve* to the total area under the diagonal. It measures the extent to which the distribution of income diverges from precise equality. Latin America has the greatest inequality with a Gini coefficient around 0.5. Developed countries typically have a Gini coefficient of around 0.3. In the UK, the Gini coefficient rose from 0.25 in the early 1980s to 0.37 in 2000, since when it has been fairly stable.

glass ceiling: the invisible barrier of discrimination that prevents women or non-whites from getting promoted to the top of organisations. In many businesses and professions, women form the majority of the workforce, yet hold a tiny minority of the senior posts. *Equal opportunities* legislation was supposed to break through the ceiling, but discriminatory attitudes have proved very hard to overcome.

global brands are branded products that have been marketed successfully worldwide. Examples include McDonald's and Bacardi. Although there may be a degree of tailoring to local tastes (such as more salads at McDonald's located in hotter countries), the key to global brands is standardisation. In other words, a Big Mac should taste the same in Tokyo as in Manchester. As so many global brands are American in origin, some critics worry that different national traditions are being swept aside in a shift towards the American way of life.

global imbalances: gradually, over many years, first Germany and Japan, and then China, developed large *balance of payments* surpluses. These had their roots in two factors – high levels of saving and at times, very low exchange rates, in the countries concerned. In 2007, their current account surpluses were respectively $253bn, $211bn and $372bn. For many years these surpluses were used to fund large loans to the deficit countries, the largest of which are the UK and the USA, both of which imported large quantities of the surplus countries' exports. Thus serious imbalances developed. So long as all countries were experiencing robust economic growth it was possible for their governments to ignore the potential problems. By 2009, however, it was clear that these imbalances had had a major role in the development of the financial crisis. The deficit countries need to cut spending so that they live within their incomes. However, this means much reduced demand for the surplus countries' products and the necessary adjustment could be very painful. The Chinese government recognises that it would be wise to encourage the Chinese people to consume more of their own products, but if they experience serious job cuts due to lack of demand, they may not be able to afford to. China is still a relatively poor country. At the time of writing the UK exchange rate is low and this may help UK exporters, which will reduce the external deficit.

This is a very complex story but at A-level you should be aware of the problem of global imbalances and the fact that long-term changes will be needed to prevent them from leading to further instability.

global industries: in many industries, producers market their products in a number of different countries. They compete with other companies that are also multinational in scope. Easy international communication ensures that they are able to keep in touch with their markets and they may actually produce within the market where they are selling. For example Unilever is active in selling household and food products in almost every country; its products may be manufactured within the country where they are selling or they may be imported.

global localisation means tailoring an international product to the local consumer tastes. Subtle differentiations can make a product acceptable in a local market where a *global brand* might not sell so well. For example, McDonald's sell beer in their French outlets.

global market niches: where there are small market segments with similar tastes and preferences in a range of different countries, profitable market *niches* can be identified. This applies to luxury goods, for which high prices are part of the marketing strategy. The price identifies the product as exclusive but the widespread recognition of its luxury qualities ensures that there is a small market for it in most countries. Louis Vuitton products provide an obvious example. The manufacturer is actually able to get the benefits of *mass production* although *market research*, *product development* and distribution costs will be very high. Alternatively, there may be global niches among *subcultures*. (See also *Ansoff's matrix*.)

global marketing means devising marketing strategies that can be used worldwide. This has potential marketing *economies of scale*. But it may fail to connect with buyers in some markets, especially in relation to advertising.

global sourcing means buying inputs wherever they can be obtained most efficiently. This may mean choosing a location with low labour costs but it can also mean buying from the producer with access to superior technologies. Decisions may be made on price or quality.

global trends can refer to any variable, e.g. output or inflation. In the past changes often happened at different times, so that one country might be in recession while others were not. This meant that firms in a country experiencing low aggregate demand could benefit from finding new export markets. Globalisation has made this rather less likely as individual economies are to some degree interdependent.

globalisation refers to the process by which there is both an increasing world market in goods and services and increasing integration in world capital markets. This means that governments need to consult with their trading partners in order to co-ordinate their *macroeconomic policies* and to avoid destabilising *capital movements*. Otherwise the success of their policies is likely to be compromised.

Globalisation has been associated with the rapid growth in world trade and has encouraged *economic growth*. It has improved standards of living for many people. It may also have increased the power of the *multinationals*. Some of the growth in trade has evolved as a result of efforts to make trade easier through the trade negotiations of the *World Trade Organization (WTO)*.

Globalisation has also made all economies more vulnerable to *shocks* elsewhere. The financial crisis of 2007–09 originated in the financial systems of the developed countries but had a serious effect on the developing countries, especially in Africa, because the fall in demand for manufactures and commodities reduced overall demand for their exports. Sharp falls in commodity prices were particularly difficult for poorer countries to deal with.

There is a view that globalisation is encouraging, even forcing, every country and every people to become increasingly similar. Extreme critics would suggest that globalisation effectively means Americanisation, with McDonald's, Coca-Cola and the dollar reigning supreme. Economists would not doubt that it is becoming increasingly difficult for any government to pursue economic policies outside the worldwide consensus. Business experts also suggest that local tastes are being swept aside by McDonald's in France, pizza in India and many other indications that the *transnational corporation* is king. (See also *global imbalances*.)

GM foods: see *genetically modified (GM) foods*

GNP: see *gross national product (GNP)*

goals are targets that act as a focus for decision-making and effort, and as a yardstick against which success or failure can be measured. The word 'goals' is used interchangeably with *objectives*.

going rate: the prevailing percentage wage rise being received by employees during a *pay round*. Its level is likely to be determined by the rate of price inflation and the degree of demand for labour. If the going rate is 6 per cent, workers will see that level of pay rise as the least they can expect.

golden rule: the idea that government budgets should balance over the course of the *economic cycle*, with borrowing used only to finance investment. During recession, incomes are falling and tax revenue will fall too. Unemployment is rising and benefit payments increase. The result will be an increasing *budget deficit*. As the economy recovers this process goes into reverse and it will be possible to generate a surplus which offsets the earlier deficit. Any borrowing which is additional to this should be spent on investment projects which have the potential to increase incomes in the future. This rule was important to the 1997 Labour government but by 2006 it appeared to be maintainable only by a changing interpretation of the data. (See also *fiscal rules*.)

good governance: all countries have institutions that exercise power and take decisions. Good governance implies that:
- there is *transparency* and openness so that information is freely available
- the *rule of law* is applied in a fair and consistent way
- governments both local and national respond to public opinion
- bribery and *corruption* do not have a significant impact on the decisions that are taken.

Where these conditions are not met, there may be a serious impact on standards of living generally and power-hungry individuals may be able to appropriate resources for their own use on a scale that most people would regard as unacceptable. In recent years the World Bank and other agencies have sought to impose requirements relating to good governance when agreeing to aid packages. However few governments are without fault.

goods are tangible products, in contrast to services. Goods are physical objects.

goodwill arises when a business is sold for more than the *balance sheet* value of its assets. A purchaser is prepared to pay more than this for the business as a going concern because it may have an established name and reputation as well as a favourable location. Goodwill is then shown in the purchaser's balance sheet as an *intangible asset*. Goodwill is a technical accounting term which should not be confused with the everyday use of the word.

Google: the incredibly successful internet search engine founded in 1998 by Californians Larry Page and Sergey Brin. It can sift through billions of pieces of data within seconds, and is now worth $billions, since its 2004 stock market flotation.

go-slow: a form of *industrial action* in which employees keep working, but at the minimum pace allowable under their terms of employment.

government borrowing is used whenever the revenue from taxation is less than total government expenditure. It can include sales of *bonds* (long-term borrowing), sales of Treasury bills (short-term borrowing) and the use of National Savings. (See also *bonds* and *budget deficit*.)

government economic objectives are the goals laid down by the political party in government. It was long thought that all governments pursued a mix of objectives including: steady *economic growth*, low *inflation*, low unemployment and a modest *balance of payments* surplus. There have been periods, however, when the pursuit of low inflation has been the primary economic objective. This has come into conflict with other aspects of policy, such as low unemployment. Other objectives may include *income redistribution* and the provision of *public goods* and *merit goods*.

government expenditure: the sum total of all spending by both local and national government. The Labour government was committed to keeping this under 40 per cent of GDP, but in recent years has obscured the reality by the use of *public private partnerships (PPPs)*. Support for the banking system after the 2007–09 financial crisis and the effects of recession are bound to raise the percentage considerably. The figures in the pie chart are based on the 2009 Budget Statement but will change in response to circumstances. (See also *budget*.)

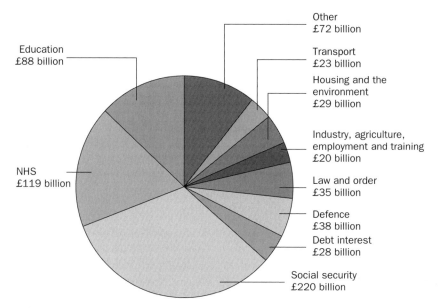

Government expenditure. (Source: UK Treasury.)

government failure occurs when governments act to deal with *market failure*, but in the process create further *distortions* in the market. Very broadly, government failure may be said to occur when government intervention makes the situation worse rather than better. For example, *National Insurance charges (NICs)* raise revenue which can be used to pay benefits, but they also make it more expensive for employers to take on more *labour*. They thus tend to discourage job creation.

government intervention is a loosely used term which usually refers to some way of influencing market forces and bringing about changes in production or consumption decisions. For example, the landfill tax is designed to give businesses an incentive to produce less waste and to use alternative forms of waste management, such as recycling. *Regulation*, tax incentives and government support for industry are all varieties of intervention.

government securities are sold by governments as a form of borrowing from households or firms. It is a way of making up for a shortfall in money raised through taxation, i.e. a *budget deficit*. The most common forms are Treasury bills and *gilt-edged securities*. (See also *public sector net borrowing*.)

grant: a government or charitable subsidy of a business investment or activity.

grapevine: the network of informal communication contained within every organisation. It will spread rumours that may undermine the public statements of senior management, but only if those statements are incorrect or incomplete. In firms with an *authoritarian leadership style*, the grapevine may be condemned for spreading gossip, whereas a person exercising *democratic leadership* might see it as a useful line of communication.

Great Depression: the term used to describe the period following the *Wall Street Crash* of 1929. In the years afterwards, unemployment hit 20 per cent in Britain and 33 per cent in America and Germany. The most important lessons that can be learnt from it are:
- the impact of the economy on political life (in Germany, mass unemployment brought Adolf Hitler to power)
- the dangers of allowing the banking system to collapse
- that positive government action to bring about recovery can be successful.

greenfield site: a site for a new factory that has no history of the manufacture of the product in question. Despite the implication of the countryside, the same term would be used for an urban site. Among the firms that have succeeded on greenfield sites are Nissan UK and Toyota UK; a well-known failure was De Lorean motors in Northern Ireland.

PROS: • the site can be chosen on modern not historic criteria
       • traditional restrictive labour practices will not hinder productivity

CONS: • no pool of local labour with the right skills or temperament
       • local infrastructure not geared towards the product

greenhouse effect: the theory that global warming is taking place as a consequence of a build-up of carbon dioxide preventing heat from the sun leaving the earth's atmosphere. Carbon dioxide is thought to be increasing due to deforestation, industrial pollution and excessive use of petrol-driven cars. Worldwide concern about the greenhouse effect put many industrial companies under pressure to reduce air pollution emissions from *pressure groups* such as Friends of the Earth.

grey market: an unofficial market where buyers and sellers can trade legally (as opposed to the black market where trade is illegal). A grey market can develop when public interest in a new share issue is so high that people want to buy shares before the day official dealings start. More importantly, it is the grey market in goods that limits the effectiveness of price discrimination. When Fisher-Price was selling its 'Activity Centres' at a markedly higher price in Britain than in Germany, Tesco stores started buying grey market supplies from Germany and undercutting the prices charged by its competitors. Fisher-Price was furious and tried to stop this unofficial distribution channel, but had no legal power to do so.

gross domestic product (GDP) is the value of everything produced in the economy for the year. It is the most frequently used measure of national income and is used to provide economic growth rates and other important data. It is usually given 'at basic prices', which means that it is valued in terms of the costs of all inputs. Gross means total; domestic means it applies to everything produced within the economy, regardless of whether the producer is a foreign-owned business or locally owned, and product means output.

gross investment: the total of all investment in buildings, plant, machinery and vehicles and infrastructure, including both replacement investment and new productive capacity. (See also *net investment*.)

gross margin is the percentage of *sales revenue* which is *gross profit*.

$$FORMULA: \quad \frac{\text{gross profit}}{\text{sales revenue}} \times 100$$

gross national product (GNP) is calculated by adding the value of all the production of a country plus the net income from abroad. Net income from abroad is the income earned on overseas investments less the income earned by foreigners investing in the domestic economy.

gross profit is sales revenue minus *cost of sales* in the accounting period under review. Gross profit has not yet had overheads, interest and depreciation deducted from it and must not, therefore, be confused with trading profit. For a more detailed account, see *cost of sales*. (See also *profit margin*.)

group discussion: a form of *qualitative research* in which a psychologist stimulates discussion among six to eight consumers chosen to represent the *target market*. The aim is partly to probe for the motives behind people's purchasing decisions (consumer psychology) and partly to use the group as a sounding board for new ideas.

Group of Eight (G8): the collective term given to eight major countries brought together to debate future world economic policy. The political nature of this process is revealed by the fact that Russia, not China, was invited to join the traditional top seven economies: the USA, Japan, Germany, Britain, France, Canada and Italy.

Group of Twenty (G20) was set up in 1999 in recognition of the need to bring together important industrialised and emerging economies to discuss and co-ordinate their economic policies. The group has no administrative body but it provides for finance ministers and central bank governors to meet every year. The member countries are Argentina, Australia, Brazil, Canada, China, France, Germany, India, Indonesia, Italy, Japan, Mexico, Russia, Saudi Arabia, South Africa, South Korea, Turkey, the UK and the USA. In addition, the heads of the IMF and World Bank attend. Leaders' Summits were held in the UK in April 2009 to discuss the measures relating to the financial crisis.

growth: see *economic growth*

guesstimate: an estimate based largely on guesswork or intuition. Although firms want to make decisions on the basis of sound data (such as *market research* findings), there may be occasions when there is no time to collect it. For example, if Galaxy announced a two-month promotion offering 20 per cent extra free, Cadbury would have to decide immediately what effect this might have upon their chocolate sales, and decide whether to match Galaxy's offer. A sales guesstimate would be needed. *Scientific decision-making* takes time.

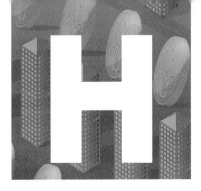

Handy, Charles: the author of many business books, notably *Understanding Organisations* and *Inside Organisations* (1990, BBC Books). Formerly an executive with BP Oil, Charles Handy has become a leading theorist about the future of organisations. He forecast the recent rise in contracted out and flexible work and the decline in the numbers employed securely as core workers. (See *shamrock organisation*.)

hard currency includes a number of currencies which are easily convertible and widely accepted in payment everywhere. The US dollar, the euro, the pound and the yen are examples. Indian rupees and Chinese renminbi (yuan) would usually be less acceptable because they are not fully convertible.

harmonisation within the European Union means making all member countries' businesses subject to the same legal framework, i.e. harmonising laws and regulations. In this way the EU tries to create a 'level playing field' so that all firms compete on equal terms within the *single European market*. Harmonisation of the regulations governing actual products allows firms to standardise their production process and make one version of the product for the whole of the EU. This can lead to *economies of scale* and lower costs and prices.

Hawthorne effect: the beneficial impact on staff workrate and morale of an active, personal interest being shown by management. The term derives from *Mayo*'s researches into workplace behaviour at a factory at Hawthorne, USA between 1927 and 1932.

Mayo was a follower of *F W Taylor*'s methods and was attempting to measure the impact on productivity of improving the lighting conditions within the factory. He followed Taylor's scientific principles by testing the changes against a control, a section of the factory with unchanged lighting. Although productivity rose where the lighting was improved, Mayo was surprised to find a similar benefit where no physical changes had taken place.

This led him to conduct a series of further experiments which cast serious doubts on Taylor's assumptions about the absolute importance of money in motivation. The phrase 'the Hawthorne effect' remains in use worldwide as an example of the importance of *human relations* in business.

HDI: see *Human Development Index (HDI)*

headhunter: a recruitment consultant who hunts actively for the right person for a job, instead of waiting for responses to an advertisement. The main benefit of this approach is that the headhunter may contact someone who is ideal for the job but who is not currently looking for work (and would therefore not notice an advertisement).

headline inflation is inflation as measured by the *retail prices index (RPI)*. This includes some price changes which may be strictly temporary in their impact on the economy, such as mortgage interest payments.

headline unemployment is the total number of registered unemployed, as measured by the claimant count. This covers all those who registered as unemployed, i.e. those eligible for benefits. It will obviously exclude *disguised unemployment*. The figure for *LFS unemployment* will usually be higher.

health and safety legislation has gradually improved employees' working conditions over many years. This raises the costs of production but reduces the risks associated with accidents and industrial health problems. The laws are enforced by the Health and Safety Executive, a government-financed organisation which employs inspectors to investigate conditions in the workplace. Safety at work is now governed by the Social Chapter of the *Maastricht* Treaty, part of the 'level playing field' of the *single market* within the EU.

heavy industry: a rather loose term denoting the producers of large, heavy products usually from large-scale factories. Examples include the production of steel, lorries, cars and bulk chemicals.

heavy user: a regular customer who uses large quantities of a product or brand. For example, whereas the average consumer of Bounty chocolate bars may buy no more than one a month, the heavy user may buy three a week. It is widely accepted in marketing that, for most products, around 20 per cent of customers consume 80 per cent of sales (this is known as the 80/20 rule). Therefore a great deal of *market research* effort goes into identifying who the heavy users are, what they like about the product, and how best to reach them through advertising.

hedge funds are pooled investments based on a very active approach to risk. If the fund manager believes that the price of a share, a commodity or a currency is about to fall, he or she can sell it short. This means selling it today with the intention of buying it back in a week or two when the price is lower. Hedge fund managers claim that their freedom of action enables them to make higher returns for investors. Critics say that their awful performance during 2007 and 2008 proves that hedge funds are no more successful (and may be riskier) than other types of investment.

hedging is a way to minimise risks. Commodities or currencies can be bought now for delivery on a date in the future at an agreed price which removes some uncertainty. The importer who will need foreign currency at a date in the future will have it available at a known price. Similarly commodities which are known to be becoming available in the future can be sold in the future at a price which is agreed now. The alternative is to trade in the *spot market* at the current spot price and carry the risk that the price may change.

Herzberg, F (1923–2000): an American psychologist whose researches in the 1950s led him to develop the *two-factor theory* of job satisfaction. Although many have criticised him for drawing conclusions about workers as a whole from a sample drawn solely from accountants and engineers, Herzberg's theory has proved very robust. Many firms have put his methods into practice, often with considerable success. Part of the reason for the interest shown by business leaders is because Herzberg offered a practical approach to improving motivation through *job enrichment*. This, he stressed, should not be confused with *job rotation*.

Herzberg's stress on redesigning workplaces and work systems to provide more fulfilling jobs was a major move away from the ideas of Ford and **Taylor**. Despite this, Herzberg could be criticised for making too little of the role of groups and teams at work. His focus on the job made him lose sight of the motivational power of team spirit.

hierarchical structure: where each person within an organisation has clear roles and responsibilities, which he or she cannot exceed. It is likely to be a **tall hierarchy**, in other words have many management layers, each with a narrow **span of control**.

hierarchy: the management structure of an organisation, sometimes presented as a diagram showing who is accountable to whom. (See also **layers of hierarchy** and **organisational chart**.)

hierarchy of needs: **Maslow**'s theory that all humans have the same type of needs which can be classified into a single hierarchy. They span from the lower order, physical needs through social needs towards the higher order, psychological needs. Maslow believed that each need has to be fulfilled totally before the next becomes important. By the time all needs have been catered for, the individual will be motivated by self-actualisation, in other words psychological growth and development. Yet if the threat of **redundancy** occurs, the individual's focus will return to the basic needs, such as security.

Maslow's five categories of need:
1 Physical, the requirement to eat and sleep (and therefore earn an income).
2 Safety, the need for security.
3 Social, the desire for friendship, love and a sense of belonging.
4 Esteem, the need to have respect from others and, more importantly, self-respect.
5 Self-actualisation, to fulfil one's potential through actions and achievements. Note that Maslow did not believe that this could be satisfied fully; in other words, people will always strive to develop further and achieve more. Hence the funnel at the top of the pyramid diagram.

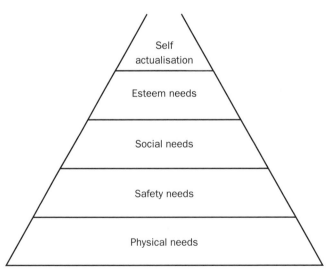

Maslow's hierarchy of needs

hierarchy of objectives: a diagram to show the logical order in which a firm should determine its *objectives*. First the *aims* must be agreed, then the medium- to long-term objectives, and finally the *strategies* for achieving the objectives. Although these elements can be determined in advance at board level, changing daily circumstances may force short-term, tactical objectives to be set that might not be fully in harmony with the overall aims. (See *corporate objectives*.)

higher order needs: see *hierarchy of needs*

hire purchase: a system of obtaining *credit* for the purchase of an *asset* whereby the purchaser puts down a proportion of the price as a deposit and pays the balance in equal instalments over an agreed repayment period. The purchaser becomes owner when the last instalment is paid. The hire purchaser pays a fixed monthly sum that is likely to amount to a far higher total than for outright purchase. In the short term, however, the firm may be pleased to obtain a vital asset without a large outflow of cash.

histogram: a diagrammatic way of representing a *frequency distribution* in which the area of the block is proportional to the value of the variable measured. A histogram differs from a *bar chart* because the width of the bars can vary as well as the height.

hit-and-run competition comes from firms which enter the market expecting to make immediate profits and then make a rapid exit from the market. This works only if the fixed costs of entry are relatively low. A fashion for the product may attract hit-and-run competition. Profits for the stable producer who has been in the market for a long time may be much reduced by this.

holding company is one which holds a majority of the shares of other companies and thus controls them without direct involvement in their running. The degree of influence can vary depending on the management style of the holding company. It can operate as little more than an industrial bank, with the head office staff simply deciding on the most profitable uses of the company's funds.

homeworking: earning an income from work undertaken at home. Traditionally, homeworkers have completed labour-intensive, very low-paid jobs such as hand-sewing or packing. Modern technology offers the possibility that more professional employees could work from home, armed with communication links such as e-mail, fax and telephone.

homogeneous products are identical. It is impossible to know whether the product came from one firm or another. A homogeneous product is an important feature of the model of *perfect competition*. The more homogeneous the products are, the stronger the competition is likely to be in the marketplace. Examples include many agricultural products, e.g. wheat, and many mineral products, e.g. iron ore.

In contrast, many businesses spend a great deal of time and money trying to persuade consumers that their products are different from others; theirs are *differentiated products*, the opposite of homogeneous.

horizontal communications represent the passage of information between people on the same hierarchical level within an organisation, e.g. between section heads.

horizontal integration occurs where a firm takes over or merges with another firm at the same stage of production. The production process starts with raw materials being processed, then moves through manufacture and assembly to be sold to wholesalers and then retailers. Horizontal integration can occur at any of these stages. The merger of two breweries would be an example of horizontal integration, and would have the following advantages and disadvantages:

PROS: • increases market power over the next or the previous link in the process
• enables greater *economies of scale* to occur

CONS: • may restrict customer choice
• unequal market influence may increase costs overall by the exercise of monopoly power, and may thus attract the attention of the *Competition Commission*

horizontal promotion: the Japanese idea that as those at the top of an organisation need to have a thorough grounding in every aspect of the business. To be invited to transfer to a different department represents an effective promotion. Improved status, salary and career prospects go hand in hand with a new challenge, even though the individual has not moved up to a higher rung on the hierarchical ladder.

host country: one that receives foreign investment from a *multinational* company. This provides advantages and disadvantages to the host:

PROS: • provides income and employment
• helps the *balance of payments* initially by providing a demand for the host country's currency, and then by providing exports of finished goods
• may provide new training and skills to the workforce
• may encourage the growth of other domestic industries, and industrialisation in general

CONS: • agriculture may be changed from being based on long-term self-sufficiency to reliance on cash crops; these crops may receive high prices in the short term, but end up ruining the soil
• once income and wage levels have been raised, the multinational may move on to the next source of cheap labour and/or raw materials
• the multinational may not adhere to the highest standards of safety and responsibility that it would be required to follow in other, more developed countries

hostile takeover bid: this is where a *predator* company wishes to acquire a target company and its actions are unwelcome. The predator offers a price for the shares of the target and, as soon as it has acquired a majority, it has management control. It can vote in its own directors at a general meeting. According to the takeover rules, the predator has a time-limit to persuade shareholders to accept the offer and during this period the two companies may publish their campaigns. By contrast, some companies agree terms and carry out an agreed *merger*.

hot money: a phrase that describes speculative flows on foreign exchange markets. Whilst foreign exchange is necessary for trade to occur, it is also possible to hold cash in order to gamble on changes in rates. This 'gambling' cash can be called hot money.

household: the basic economic decision-taking unit. Economists tend to talk about households rather than individuals because their consumption patterns have more in common than, say, those of a teenager living at home and a single person living alone.

human capital is the degree of skill and training embodied in labour as a *factor of production*. As in financial capital, its value can be increased by investment, in this case in education. Investing in human capital makes people more productive and can increase their earnings, provided there is a demand for their particular skills and knowledge. It is an important element in the process of *economic growth*. Some skills and knowledge are firm-specific and of particular importance to the relevant employer.

Human Development Index (HDI): a measure of the quality of life constructed by the United Nations Development Programme. It takes into account not just income but also a range of other criteria such as literacy, life expectancy, clean water, inequality and gender issues. Canada and the Scandinavian countries usually rank among the highest.

human relations is the aspect of management that Elton *Mayo*'s work highlighted. The Human Relations School promoted the benefits to morale and productivity of a *paternalistic leadership style* in which the worker was to be seen more as a member of the family than as a mere *factor of production*. Among the policy outcomes were:

- a move to more social facilities surrounding work (sports teams, social clubs, etc.)
- the appointment of personnel or welfare officers whose function was to look after the well-being of the labour force
- a move to greater communication and *consultation* between the management and the factory floor.

human resource management (HRM): the responsibility of using and developing an organisation's personnel in the most productive way. This appears to be little more than restating the role of the personnel department, but HRM has some distinctive features:

- its spur has been the success of the Japanese at managing people, even though their firms rarely have personnel departments; so HRM represents a rethink by personnel professionals
- it places greater emphasis on development through training and career planning
- it has the potential to persuade *all* managers that the development of their human resources (subordinates) is *their* job, not the personnel department's.

Human Rights Act 1998: from 2 October 2000, all courts and tribunals were required to act in accordance with the European Convention on Human Rights.

hunch: the intuition that can lead a decision maker to go against the obvious or statistically proven route. This may prove a stroke of genius or a source of great embarrassment.

hygiene factors: elements of working life that have the potential to cause dissatisfaction, such as salary, working conditions, status and over-supervision. (See *Herzberg, F.*)

hyperinflation: a situation where the value of money decreases so fast that it loses some, or all of its functions. Consequently, people resort to *barter* or to the use of some other commodity which has intrinsic value or to the use of a foreign currency. The exact level of inflation which turns into hyperinflation is not precise since it will be determined by psychological factors. The best-known example of hyperinflation occurred in Germany in the 1920s, but in more recent times Zimbabwe has suffered the most.

hypothesis: a theory about how to explain or solve a problem. A manager would want to test a hypothesis by a numerate technique such as *quantitative research*.

IBRD: see *International Bank for Reconstruction and Development (IBRD)*, commonly known as the World Bank.

idle time is the amount of time a work station is not operational. A work station can be a machine waiting to be used in a production process or a booking clerk in a railway station.

IFRS: see *International Financial Reporting Standards (IFRS)*

ILO: see *International Labour Organisation (ILO)*

imbalances: see *global imbalances*

IMF: see *International Monetary Fund (IMF)*

immobilities occur when people are unable to take up a job which is available because they are living in another area (*geographical immobility*) or because they do not have the right skills for the job (*occupational immobility*). Immobilities impede the process of reallocating resources in response to changes in consumer demand.

imperfect competition occurs when there are a number of competing firms, but the market lacks some or all of the features of *perfect competition*. Broadly there are three types of imperfect competition: *oligopoly*, *monopolistic competition* and *monopoly*.

imperfect information is a market imperfection as a result of which competition is impaired by lack of easily available information. The consumer who does not know where to find a product at the cheapest price will pay more, and this protects the producer from the competition which might exist if information were fuller. Similarly, the firm which does not know where to find the cheapest inputs will have costs higher than necessary, which reduces efficiency.

imperfections occur in an imperfect market, and include *immobilities*, *imperfect information*, *government intervention*, *barriers to entry*, small numbers of buyers or sellers and any other source of distortions which may interfere with the operation of competitive market forces.

imperfect market occurs when there are *imperfections*, i.e. distortions in the market such that competition is not as forceful as it might be. An imperfect market departs in one or more ways from the conditions of *perfect competition*. It will generally not achieve *productive efficiency* and *allocative efficiency*. For example, firms which have a degree of monopoly within their markets may not be forced to seek the most efficient methods of producing and, as a result, prices may be higher than they need be.

import: the purchase of a product or service from overseas.

import controls are *tariffs* or *quotas* designed to limit the number of overseas goods entering the domestic market. In extreme cases, some goods are prevented from entering at all, which is called an **embargo**. Other forms of import controls are collectively called *non-tariff barriers*, which discriminate against imported goods in a more subtle way. For example, quality requirements may be used to exclude unwanted imports. Import controls have been generally reduced over the years by WTO negotiations. Import controls are not allowed within the EU.

import penetration: a measurement of the share of the home market taken by importers. Twenty-five per cent penetration means, therefore, that imports account for a quarter of sales within a market.

import tariff: a tax levied on an imported item at the point of entry to the country.

impulse purchase: an unplanned decision to buy a product or brand. Certain types of product are especially prone to impulse purchase, such as confectionery and snacks. This makes it worthwhile for retailers to display the items prominently (such as by the checkout), as impulse purchase products generate extra takings. If a manufacturer knows that its products are mainly bought on impulse it is likely to:
- increase spending on packaging design and display materials at the point of sale
- offer high retail profit margins in order to maximise distribution and give the shops a strong incentive to display the product in an eye-catching position.

incentives: financial and other rewards which can influence the decisions of firms and individuals. Favourable tax treatment of **investment** spending can induce firms to invest more. Increased taxes on tobacco give smokers an incentive to give up. On a wider level, the term may be used in connection with groups of people who, for example, lack the incentive to work because they are in the **poverty trap**.

Incentives can be vital in ensuring that the **allocation of resources** reflects the pattern of consumer demand. People may need an incentive to move from one kind of production to another; this could be a pay differential which encourages them to switch jobs.

income is a flow of money which acts as a reward for the services of a **factor of production**. Wages and salaries are a reward to **labour** and are described as earned income. Unearned income includes rent, interest and profit: rent is a reward for the owner of land or property. Profit gives a return on capital invested and also rewards the efforts of **entrepreneurs**. Interest is a return on a capital sum which is loaned to someone else.

For firms, income comes from sales revenue plus the return on any investments. For the economy as a whole, income is the total income derived from all activities and is measured most often using GDP.

income and expenditure account: the equivalent of a **profit and loss account** that records the year's trading for a **non-profit-making organisation** such as a charity or club.

income elasticity measures the way in which demand changes when consumers' real incomes change.

$$FORMULA: \quad \frac{\text{percentage change in demand}}{\text{percentage change in real incomes}} = \text{income elasticity}$$

There are two main elements in a product's income elasticity:

1 Is the income elasticity a positive or negative figure? Most goods have positive income elasticity, meaning that people buy more of them when they are better off. The term *'normal goods'* is given to these.

Products with negative income elasticity include sausages and supermarket own-label goods. When consumers feel better off they switch from these cheaper foods to more luxurious ones. For example, if the demand for sausages fell by 2 per cent in a year when real incomes rose 5 per cent, the income elasticity of sausages would be –2% ÷ 5% = –0.4. A product with negative income elasticity is known as an *'inferior good'*.

2 What is the degree of elasticity? As with price elasticity, a value of more than one indicates an elastic demand, while less than one means inelastic demand. Luxury items will tend to be highly income elastic: in other words, quite a small drop in the living standards of consumers can lead to a substantial fall in demand for expensive sports cars, perfumes or whiskies. Necessities such as toothpaste and detergents are income inelastic.

Worked example: Market research reveals that following an increase in disposable income of 10 per cent, the demand for aftershave rises by 22 per cent. What is the income elasticity of demand for aftershave?

FORMULA: Income elasticity of demand $= \dfrac{\text{percentage change in demand}}{\text{percentage change in income}}$

so in this example $: = \dfrac{22\%}{10\%} + 2.2$

---

income redistribution means taxing high incomes much more than low incomes and providing benefits for those with little or no income of their own. The objective is to achieve a more equal distribution of income across society as a whole. ***Progressive taxes*** will achieve the first outcome. Providing more generous unemployment benefits, disability and child allowances and income support will achieve the second. ***Means-tested benefits*** may be used to ensure that the greatest help is given to the most needy.

Some income redistribution measures have been challenged on the grounds that they reduce the incentive to work. Where most benefits are means tested, there can be a *poverty trap* which is very difficult to escape. Recent policies on benefits have sought to ensure that everyone is actually better off working. The ***Working Families Tax Credit*** addresses this. (See also ***income tax***.)

income statement: the document within a public company's annual report that shows the revenue, costs and profits made from operating a business. Up until the switch to international accounting standards in 2005, this was known as a profit and loss account. Here is an example of an income statement for the financial year ending 31 December 201X:

Income statement for the year ending 31 December 201X

	(£000s)
Revenue	47 000
Cost of sales	(43 000)
Gross profit	**4 000**
Expenses	1 000
Operating profit	**3 000**
Finance income	100
Finance costs	(600)
Profit before tax	**2 500**
Taxation	(800)
Profit for the year	**1 700**

income tax is a *direct tax* levied on the incomes of individuals. There is a personal allowance, which is tax free. Tax rates are announced annually in the Budget by the Chancellor of the Exchequer. The following example uses the bands and the tax rates set in the 2009 Budget.

Income between	Tax rate (%)
0–£6475	0
£6476–£37 400	20 (basic rate)
£37 401 upwards	40 (higher rate)

Worked example

Income between	James earns £15 000 per year		Jane earns £50 000 per year	
	Tax %	Tax due	Tax %	Tax due
0–£6475	0	0	0	0
£6476–£37 400	20	£1705	20	£6185
£37 401 upwards	40	0	40	£5040
Total tax		£1705		£11 225
As a percentage of income		11.4%		22.4%

Income tax is a **progressive tax**, which means that it takes a higher proportion of a higher income and a lower proportion of a lower income. (**Regressive taxes** do the reverse, while proportional taxes are neutral in this respect.) Income tax thus has a major role to play in **income redistribution**.

If tax rates are kept constant, tax revenues will vary with incomes and will fluctuate over the course of the **economic cycle**. Income tax plays a part in the operation of **automatic stabilisers**, which help to reduce fluctuations in the level of aggregate demand.

High marginal income tax rates are usually resented by those who have to pay them. It is sometimes said that they create a disincentive to work hard. There is no statistical evidence for this. Scandinavian countries have high tax rates and good economic growth rates over the long run. Income tax is an important revenue raiser for the government, contributing roughly a quarter of total tax revenue at the present time.

incomes policy: an attempt by government to control inflation by restricting increases in wages and salaries. Governments used to try to control the rate of increase in incomes throughout the economy. Now they tend only to focus upon their own employees: nurses, teachers, civil servants and so on. By limiting pay rises in the public sector it is hoped that private sector employers will be influenced to keep pay rises down.

incorporation: the process of becoming a corporate body, that is establishing a business as a separate legal entity. Before incorporation, the owners of a business are liable personally for all of its debts. Becoming incorporated requires these steps:
- preparing a memorandum of association
- preparing *articles of association*
- sending these to the *Registrar of Companies* and applying for a certificate of incorporation.

indexing: see *index-linked*

index-linked: a value linked to the changes in the *retail prices index (RPI)* – the standard measure of inflation in the UK. Thus pensions or some forms of savings may be indexed or index-linked so that their real value is preserved. Index-linking protects the receiver from the loss in the real value of money caused by inflation.

index numbers can be created for any time series so that comparisons can be made more easily. A reference year is required and the value for this year becomes 100. In each subsequent year, the percentage change from the reference year is added to 100. There are many important indices.
- The *retail prices index (RPI)* gives a measure of average price rises. It is built up from a large number of price changes for products which are frequently bought. These are made into a *weighted average* to ensure that the products which figure largest in the average shopper's buys are given the most importance in the index.
- The *consumer prices index (CPI)* is very similar to the RPI but constructed in line with international rules so that it can be used for comparisons with other countries.
- Stock Exchange indices such as the *Footsie (FTSE 100)* are also weighted averages, where the most frequently traded shares are given the largest weights.
- The *sterling exchange rate index* is a weighted average of exchange rate changes. The currencies of the UK's most important trading partners are given the largest weights.

These and other index numbers put a lot of complex information into a single series. They can be more easily interpreted than raw data. They can be used within an individual business to track trends, e.g. in staffing levels.

indicators help to show what is happening in the economy. *Leading indicators* foreshadow changes to come: an increase in machine tool production might indicate that an increase in output is likely. The level of vacancies would show a sharp rise if skill shortages were developing in the *labour* market.

indirect taxes are taxes paid on goods and services, as opposed to *direct taxes* which are paid on income and profits. Examples of indirect taxation include VAT and excise duty. Indirect taxes are usually *regressive*, that is to say they take a higher proportion of a poor person's income than a rich person's.

individual bargaining occurs when a firm negotiates with each employee in turn over salary levels and terms of employment. This takes place either when there is no *trade union* to undertake *collective bargaining*, or when individuals believe they can do better than the generally negotiated terms.

indivisibility is the machine utilisation problem that some equipment may be built to a large scale and not be divisible into smaller units. If all a firm needs is 600 units a week, but the smallest machine produces 1500, it will have to accept operating permanently at only 40 per cent of capacity. This will push up *fixed costs per unit* and put a small producer at a considerable cost disadvantage. In this situation, expanding output would lead to *economies of scale*.

industrial action: measures taken by the workforce that will halt or slow output, in order to put pressure on management during an *industrial dispute*. Types of industrial action include: strike, work-to-rule, *overtime ban* and *go-slow*.

industrial democracy means the attempt to provide a workforce with channels through which the decision-making powers of the organisation can be influenced. *Trade unions* tend to be sceptical of the motives behind management initiatives in this area, suspecting either that the intention is to undermine the role of the union, or that the channels provided will only give a facade of democracy. Nevertheless, when used in the right spirit, industrial democracy can be very successful. (See also *worker participation*.)

industrial dispute: a disagreement between management and the *trade union* representatives of the workforce that is serious enough for *industrial action* to be considered. The dispute might be resolved by successful *conciliation* or *arbitration*. Otherwise the union will consider balloting its members on whether to take industrial action. British Airways and the Royal Mail provide examples.

industrial espionage means using the semi-legal or even illegal techniques of spies to gain information about a competitor or customer. Although this sounds far-fetched, there have been several past cases where major firms have used private detectives in this way. What this demonstrates is the enormous importance placed on information. Just as in a war, finding out the enemy's battle plans is invaluable, so in a *takeover* battle businesses have gone to extraordinary lengths to find out their rival's next move.

industrial inertia is used to describe the situation when a firm or an industry stays in its original location after the reasons for its being there in the first place have disappeared. Reasons for industrial inertia include:
- the costs of upheaval may be too great to justify a move
- there may be external *economies of scale* which justify an organisation staying where it is, such as local colleges which specialise in training the precise skills needed in the industry
- there may be marketing advantages which derive from a traditional location, such as Sheffield steel or Scotch whisky.

industrial location: the decision taken on the geographical placing of firms and industries. The location of *heavy industry* was often based on the notion of **bulk increasing goods** or **bulk decreasing goods**. This meant that if the industrial process gained weight it would be located as near to the consumer as possible, whereas if it lost weight in the process it would be placed as near to the raw material source as possible. The soft drinks industry gains weight by adding water and so, for instance, Coca-Cola was originally sold to retailers in the form of a syrup to which soda was added at the point of sale. Even when Coke was sold in bottles, the syrup was sent to local bottling plants so that the relatively heavy product did not need to be transported very far. On the other hand, the steel industry is a considerable weight loser, and so it is located as close to its main raw materials – coal, iron ore and limestone – as possible. Today the bulk increasing/bulk reducing theory applies less because transport costs are a smaller proportion of total costs than they were. Communication links are better and the growth of the service sector has inevitably spread locations towards the consumer.

In recent years it has been argued that profit-maximising behaviour is not always followed by some managers, who locate in an area which is pleasant enough to suit their employees or themselves. Often, firms start up in a location close to the proprietor's home. This site may be clung to for many years after it has ceased to be economic to stay there (see *industrial inertia*). Also, governments have affected some location decisions by offering **grants** and other incentives (see *regional policy*). This has affected the decisions of **multinationals** who are able to locate in whichever country minimises their costs.

industrial policy: the government's strategy for boosting economic growth by improving industrial competitiveness. This might mean making fiscal, monetary and foreign currency decisions on the basis of business needs, including:
- increasing government spending on transport and communication infrastructure
- keeping interest rates relatively low
- keeping the pound at a competitive level on the foreign exchange markets.

industrial relations: the atmosphere prevailing between a management and its workforce representatives, the *trade unions*. Anything that damages the relationship between the two sides might destroy the element of trust that is the key to good industrial relations.

industrial union: an organisation founded to look after the collective interests of all types of employee within a specific industry, e.g. the National Union of Mineworkers (NUM). Whereas most unions represent workers with a particular type of skill from many different industries (e.g. electricians), an industrial union would have clerical, skilled and unskilled members, all working in the same industry.

inefficiency: failing to maximise the value of output from a given quantity of inputs. If the quantity of output is less than it could be, *productive efficiency* is compromised. If the value of the output is less than it could be, the problem is with *allocative efficiency*. The problem then is that the output is not actually what consumers most want.

inelastic demand means that a given percentage change in price leads to a proportionately smaller change in demand. It is the situation of a product that has low price sensitivity because consumers need it or think they need it. Examples of goods with inelastic demand are necessities like fuel and heavily branded items such as Levi's. If the price of Levi's rises by 10 per cent then demand might only fall by 5 per cent. In this case, the numerical value of its price elasticity would be: 5% ÷ 10% = 0.5.

Any good having inelastic demand would have a lower number at the top (the numerator) than at the bottom (the denominator), and therefore the final value will always be less than one but greater than zero. The minus sign is sometimes ignored, but it should of course be a part of the equation since as one factor goes up (+), the other must go down (–), and vice versa. An inelastic demand curve will slope fairly steeply down to the left.

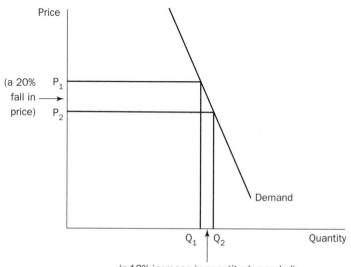

(a 20% fall in price) P$_1$ P$_2$

Q$_1$ Q$_2$

Demand

Price

Quantity

(a 12% increase in quantity demanded)

A 20% fall in price leads to a 12% increase in quantity demanded

There are two main reasons for inelastic demand.
• The product has few, if any, substitutes. When the price rises, people carry on buying the product because they cannot find a satisfactory substitute and they do not feel they can do without it. This would apply to bread, workclothes, rail travel for commuters, and many other products.
• The product takes a small part of total income. This might apply to chocolates.

(See also **price elasticity**.)

inequality: a situation in which there are large differences in incomes and wealth within a society. Most developed countries in Europe have a lower level of inequality than the USA does. Inequality has tended to increase everywhere in recent years. Inequality can be reduced by **progressive taxes** and social security benefits. (See also **equity**.)

infant industries: very new firms, starting up in an industry which previously did not exist in that country, may take some time to become competitive. They will not at first be able to reap the *economies of scale* which are a feature of production in countries where the industry is well established. If they are to survive they will need to be protected from competition from imports, by means of *tariffs* or other *import controls*. This argument is most often used in relation to new industries in *developing economies*. However, there are drawbacks to using import controls to protect domestic industries. There may be considerable difficulty in deciding when the industry no longer needs protection; in the meantime consumers will be paying more for the product than they would for imports. The cost of protection to consumers may be very high.

inferior good: a product for which demand rises when real incomes fall. This happens because the item is bought as a cheap substitute for a product thought more desirable. Examples include supermarket *own-label* brands, to which people turn when trying to economise. Inferior goods come into their own during a *recession*, when falling standards of living force consumers to switch to more economical products. A manufacturer that produces a range of products, half of which are inferior goods, would be in an excellent position to cope with the *economic cycle*.

inflation is an increase in prices generally. Money loses some of its value because its purchasing power falls. If the process accelerates to very high levels, there is said to be *hyperinflation*.

The causes of inflation are complex. Until the 20th century, inflation was very infrequent and the price level was as likely to fall as to rise. Until the late 1960s, inflation remained at a relatively low level in most developed countries, most of the time. Then it became much more volatile, until the mid-1990s, when it settled at low levels until 2008, when it began to rise again (see graph opposite).

The precipitating cause of accelerating inflation is *excess demand* in the economy as a whole. This occurs when *aggregate demand* is growing faster than the capacity of the economy to supply. At first there will be evidence of *skill shortages* and it will become clear that sellers can raise prices and still sell the goods. Firms will raise wages to attract the scarce skills they need to increase output. Trade unions and individuals will find it easier to negotiate pay rises.

Once inflation is accelerating it will tend to continue because of people's *expectations*. All employees will try to protect their real earnings by negotiating an increase equal to what they expect inflation to be. (See also *inflationary expectations* and *inflationary spiral*.)

The *monetarist* view of inflation holds that it is caused by excessive increases in the money supply. As bank lending increases, borrowers are able to increase spending, leading to the excess demand already described.

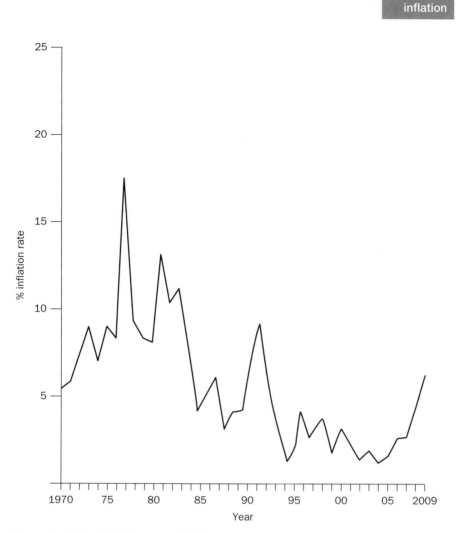

Inflation rate, 1970–2009. (Source: ONS.)

Inflation has numerous consequences:

- *Borrowers gain.* So for firms and households which have borrowed substantially, inflation makes the debt smaller in real terms. Incomes and sales revenue rise in line with inflation, while debt repayments stay the same, becoming more affordable. At various times during the past 30 years, home-owners typically made large capital gains as the value of their homes rose while the scale of their debt fell.
- *Creditors and savers lose.* When the money they have lent is paid back, it will have lost some of its value. The purchasing power of money held in the bank will be reduced. Interest rates may be too low to compensate for this (as in 2009).
- *Inflation increases uncertainty.* While a stable rate of inflation may appear predictable, in practice, the higher the rate of inflation, the more volatile it has proved to be. This makes planning difficult for firms and individuals.

Contractionary policies may be used to control inflation. Strict control of the growth of the money supply reduces aggregate demand and pressures in the labour market. In

147

time, people's expectations of inflation will fall and they will accept lower pay increases. However, this process in the early 1980s and 1990s proved to be slow and to entail a considerable rise in unemployment.

At the time of writing, inflation was subdued by the recession but may accelerate if it turns out that there has been too much *quantitative easing*, or if commodity prices rise again. The low exchange rate could have an impact. The *Monetary Policy Committee* of the Bank of England comments on this regularly.

inflation accounting is the attempt to eliminate the distorting effects of price rises from the underlying financial position of a firm. The most common method is current cost accounting (CCA), which values assets and profits on the basis of current replacement cost instead of historic cost. The complexities of this procedure have prevented it from being adopted widely by the accounting profession.

inflationary expectations are the views of the general public as to what will happen to the rate of *inflation* in the future. Usually, people anticipate that a period of rising inflation will continue into the future. For example, if the rate of inflation has risen from 3 per cent a year ago to 5 per cent today, people are likely to expect inflation to be 7 per cent by the same time next year. Therefore they might negotiate a pay rise of 7 per cent now in anticipation of that future level. By so doing, they add to costs and help to bring about that new level, so that their prophecy becomes self-fulfilling. (See *inflationary spiral*.)

inflationary spiral: the way in which price rises in one sector of the economy cause price increases in another, so that they spiral ever upwards. If *monetary policy* is too loose, so that the *demand* for goods and services exceeds *supply*, prices rise and people will react by negotiating pay increases. One person's pay increase becomes another's price increase and so the spiral continues.

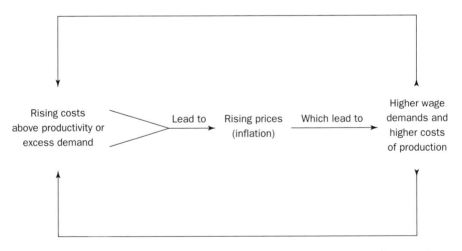

inflation target: the *Monetary Policy Committee* is required by the government to keep inflation within 1 per cent of the target rate, which is 2 per cent. It adjusts interest rates to ensure that there is neither deflation, nor accelerating inflation.

informal communication means passing information outside the official channels. In a firm run on *authoritarian leadership style* lines this might be regarded as a serious breach of company discipline, especially if the message contained embarrassing information (such as details of a dangerous leak at a chemical plant). In a democratically run organisation, however, the management should not be attempting to keep secrets from the workforce, so informal communication should be accepted, even encouraged. After all, **direct communication** is often the quickest and most effective method, so why rely on the **layers of hierarchy** within the official channels?

informal economy: that part of economic activity which is not recorded in official statistics. This includes all kinds of voluntary and domestic work and work done for cash payments which are not declared for tax purposes. Some of this is legal but some consists of tax evasion or leads to fraudulent benefit claims. The amount of income which is not declared is difficult to determine and estimates vary within the range of 5–10 per cent of GDP. The value of voluntary work is impossible to quantify.

informal group: a group of employees who influence each other's behaviour and attitudes, either for or against the company's best interests. It was a key discovery of **Elton Mayo** that such groups were common, especially in organisations with weak **human relations**. He found that such groups often had unofficial leaders who wielded more effective power than the department head, especially in the setting of group norms regarding the work-rate considered acceptable.

information failure can lead to a type of **market failure**. The **allocation of resources** may be less than optimal because people lack full information. Consumers may simply choose a selection of goods and services which omits items which would make them better off and includes items which make them worse off, because there are some things that they do not know about these products. For example, they may choose to curtail their education, not realising by how much it might increase future income. Or they may go on smoking because they underestimate the health effects. The allocation of resources can be improved if education is provided free as a **merit good** and if tobacco is taxed as a **demerit good**.

information technology (IT) includes the use of three electronic technologies: computing, telecommunications and microelectronics, and the way they gather, store, process and distribute information. The use of IT within an organisation tends to reflect the prevailing management style. Supermarket chains tend to concentrate on its potential for collecting vast quantities of data at shop-floor level and then transmitting it for head office analysis. So those at the top of the management hierarchy are pulling information up and then passing decisions back down to local branches. A leadership with a more democratic approach would use computer networks to allow information to flow more freely throughout the staff. This would provide an **empowered** workforce with the information needed for sound decision-making.

informative advertising: paid-for communication that provides messages based on facts rather than images. An extreme example is 'Car Boot Sale, Saturday 2.00, Town Hall'. The key issue about informative advertising is that it is unarguably in the public interest to be provided with useful facts. Information about the prices and product ranges offered by different shops helps competition by encouraging people to shop around. When advertising is under attack from critics of its persuasive powers, the defence is often to point to the benefits of the information it provides.

infrastructure is the name given to the road, rail and air links, sewerage and telephone systems and other basic utilities which provide a network that benefits business and the community. One of the main advantages which industrialised countries have over less-developed ones is the existence of an efficient infrastructure. Building up such a system is very expensive, requiring a great deal of **capital** to be set aside, capital which poorer countries find difficult to afford. Successive British governments have been criticised for allowing the UK's transport infrastructure to fall behind that of its main European competitors.

inheritance tax is currently levied on estates of more than £325 000 at a rate of 40 per cent (2009–10 figures). It thus works to create a more equal distribution of wealth. Where the estate is owned by a couple, the tax is payable after the surviving spouse dies.

injections are items adding to the **circular flow of national income** and consist of government expenditure, exports and investment spending. They are 'matched' by **withdrawals** from the circular flow: taxes, imports and savings.

innovation means bringing a new idea into being within the marketplace (product innovation) or workplace (process innovation). It is a major source of **competitive advantage** for individual firms.

- Product innovation is of major competitive significance because consumers tend to fall into patterns of purchasing behaviour that change little over time. Therefore the **market shares** of the rival products may be quite static. Product innovation can change that, to the considerable advantage of the innovator. The sources of the innovation may be based on new technology, new design or a wholly new **invention**. In recent years, James Dyson has been among Britain's leading innovators, with his cyclone floor cleaner a huge, worldwide success.
- Process innovation is also of great significance as it can lead to major cost advantages over competitors. When the British firm Pilkington PLC invented a new way of making glass more cheaply and to a far higher quality standard (the float glass process), it provided not only a direct **competitive advantage**, but also earned considerable sums in licensing fees from overseas manufacturers.

inorganic growth can help a firm to grow larger by merging with or taking over other companies. The objective is to expand without having to undertake complex and costly investment projects.

inputs are the elements which go into producing a good or service, such as the workforce, raw materials, components and capital.

insider dealing or trading: profiting personally from the use of information gained from the privilege of working within an organisation. For example, if a manager knew that his or her firm was about to make a **takeover bid** of £1.40 for a firm whose shares are currently £1, a guaranteed overnight profit of 40 per cent is there for the taking. Some say this is a victimless crime, because no one loses money directly. In fact, the manager has taken advantage of the shareholder who unwittingly sold at too low a price (£1). Insider dealing is illegal, but it has proved very hard to convict those caught doing it.

insolvency occurs when a firm's external **liabilities** are greater than its **assets**. In practice, this is likely to be revealed through the inability to meet financial obligations, e.g. the inability to raise the necessary cash through ordinary operations, asset sales or borrowing so as to make payments as they fall due. A business which continues to trade when insolvent is operating illegally.

Insolvency Act 1986: the legislation that sets out the possible ways of dealing with an insolvent company. The options include:

- a voluntary agreement between the company and its creditors for *recapitalising* the business
- putting the company into *administration* to try to reorganise the company in the best interests of shareholders and *creditors*
- *winding up* the company if there appears no way of saving it; this might be conducted by the administrator or by the appointment of a *receiver*.

institutional investors are those who manage the portfolios of the *pension funds*, insurance companies and *unit trust* groups which, between them, own a majority of the shares listed on the *Stock Exchange*. The influence of these financial institutions has given rise to a heated and important debate. Critics say that because the portfolio managers' performance is measured every year, they focus too much upon the short-term share price performance of the firms they have invested in. This, in turn, makes them put too much pressure on companies to produce high short-term profits and *dividend* pay-outs. Few doubt that *short-termism* is a major competitive weakness of British industry; institutional investors may be one of its causes.

insurance is the principle by which risks are shared between all those who wish to protect themselves from unforeseen eventualities. To insure against a risk, a premium is paid. The insurance company then pays compensation if the risky event happens. The premiums paid provide the necessary funds for compensation, together with an amount which covers the insurance companies' administrative costs.

intangible assets: assets are intangible when they do not have a physical existence, i.e. cannot be 'touched'. Whereas *plant* and equipment are tangible, *goodwill* (the value of brand names) is intangible. This is the most common example as it frequently arises when business assets are sold. Other intangibles include *patents*, *trade marks* and *copyrights*.

integration is a term used in two ways. It may refer to the bringing together of two or more companies, either by takeover or merger. (See also *forward integration*, *vertical integration*, *horizontal integration* and *conglomerate*.)

Alternatively it may refer to the way in which the economies of different nation states become *interdependent*. For example, the EU is a powerful force for integration within Europe.

intellectual property derives from the invention or ownership of a *patent*, *trade mark*, *logo* or any other *copyright* material. If it can be given a monetary value it can be listed on a firm's *balance sheet* as an *intangible asset*. In theory, intellectual property rights are protected by law but in practice, breaches are common, for example in the music industry. (See also *property rights*.)

inter-bank market is the wholesale money market where banks lend to each other on a very short-term basis, to cover temporary deficits in their payments to each other. This market froze up during the financial crisis in 2008. Many such assets turned out to be much riskier than the banks had earlier supposed, so they became unwilling to buy them.

interdependence refers to the way in which the economies of nation states have become increasingly reliant on one another in recent years, through the growth of trade and capital movements. This integration means that they are more vulnerable to adverse events in the economies of their trading partners but they are also more likely to gain from positive trends. For example, as the US economy shrank in 2008–09, businesses in many countries experienced falling demand because the US is an important market for their exports.

interdependence between firms describes the way businesses in an *oligopoly* will each take decisions in the light of the behaviour, or the expected reactions, of the other firms in the industry. For example, if one firm cuts prices, others may follow suit because if they do not, they will lose market share.

interest is the return on *capital* which has been lent. The terms of a loan will usually specify a fixed percentage rate or they may provide for the rate to rise and fall with interest rates generally. Similarly, interest provides savers with the incentive to make their funds available to others. If they lend it (or deposit it in a bank which will lend it) they will be rewarded with interest payments.

interest rates represent the cost of borrowing money or, to put it the other way, the return for lending funds or for parting with *liquidity*. Interest rates also measure *opportunity cost* in that individuals give up the interest on their money by spending it on consumer goods rather than saving and receiving interest. Firms considering an investment project do so on the basis of whether the return from the project will exceed the interest paid if they borrow, or be foregone if they use their own funds (opportunity cost).

Interest rates can also be a key weapon of economic policy. If the Bank of England pushes interest rates up, consumer and business spending is likely to fall. High interest rates can also be used to support the exchange rate by attracting flows of short-term currency into the country.

intermediate goods are purchased by producers and include such products as materials and components (for short-term usage) or machinery and equipment for the long term.

intermediate technology can be used in situations where high-technology methods of production are not appropriate. For example, in developing countries where wages are low it is often not cost effective to use capital-intensive approaches. In addition, such an approach may worsen poverty by creating job losses. Intermediate technology uses imaginative ways of making people more productive but does not require expensive imported equipment. A wheelbarrow may be an improvement, for moving soil, on the traditional Indian method of a basket carried on the head. It does not reduce employment in the way that a JCB might.

internal audit: measuring the effectiveness of a firm's organisation and functions, to help identify internal weaknesses. This may be carried out by the firm's own managers or by external consultants. The results would rarely be published. Just such a procedure might have helped banks such as HBOS realise the excessive risks they were taking in the lead-up to the *credit crunch*.

internal costs are those expenditures that affect a firm's own accounts, such as wages and materials. In contrast, *external costs* are the ones which are paid for by third parties. So internal costs cover *labour* and capital costs and the cost of inputs. The external costs arise from any pollution or congestion caused by the production process and any other costs to the community.

internal customers: people within an organisation who are supplied with goods or services, for example a shop assistant being delivered stocks from the storeroom. Internal customers should be treated in as efficient and businesslike a way as external ones, for all the workings of a business are part of a chain that leads to the marketplace. Delays or sloppiness at any point can break the links in the chain. This issue becomes of crucial importance within a *just in time (JIT)* production system, as there are no buffer stocks to mask inefficiency.

internal economies of scale: see *economies of scale*

internal financing: the generation of cash from within a company's resources/accounts. This can be obtained from:
- *retained profit* (plus *depreciation*)
- *working capital* (by cutting stocks or *debtors*)
- the sale of *fixed assets* or under-performing divisions (for example, Grand Metropolitan financed the purchase of Burger King by selling off its hotels division).

internal growth arises from within a company, through increasing sales of existing products and/or the launch of new ones. This is likely to be a slower, steadier process than the alternative of buying up other firms (*external growth*). Even internal growth can be risky, however, if it is financed by debt. The ideal is expansion based upon reinvested profit. Internal growth is also known as *organic growth*.

internal markets can be created in large organisations such as the National Health Service in order to foster a spirit of competition and thereby encourage greater efficiency. The process requires that instead of just handing work over to the department that has always undertaken it, the job be given to whichever department can offer the lowest 'price'. In this way, less efficient departments will lose work and may therefore be forced to lose staff.

internalising externalities means finding a way to turn an *external cost* into an internal cost. For example, if a firm has been emitting harmful products through chimneys into the air, it can be required by law to clean up its emissions. It will have to install new equipment capable of doing this job and this will add to its costs of production – its internal, private costs. Meanwhile the people who suffered from the air pollution will no longer be experiencing the external cost. This is an example of the operation of the *polluter pays principle*.

International Bank for Reconstruction and Development (IBRD) is the proper name of the World Bank. It borrows funds on Western capital markets and lends them to developing countries for projects of many kinds including infrastructure, agriculture, industry, education and health. It charges commercial interest rates, but lends for purposes and in countries which banks might usually find too risky. Loans are often conditional on the adoption of particular policies, which may be unpopular. However, this does mean that governments can shift the blame for necessary but unpalatable policies onto the World Bank.

international competitiveness measures the ability of firms to sell abroad and to compete with imports. It is determined by a number of factors, including price, quality, delivery and *after-sales service*. Such competitiveness will often be affected by the level of the foreign exchange rate, though successful exporting countries can succeed despite high and rising exchange rates. This shows that the price of goods is often not the main determinant of competitiveness. Germany and Japan, for instance, have thrived through well-designed, high-quality products such as BMWs and Sony Playstations, for which consumers are willing to pay a price premium.

International Financial Reporting Standards (IFRS): the standards adopted in 2005 as the only way public companies are allowed to present their published accounts. Using common standards should make it easier to decide whether to invest in a British, German or Hungarian producer. This should lead to increased economic efficiency within Europe.

International Labour Organization (ILO): a member organisation of the United Nations, the ILO exists to help improve working conditions throughout the world. It maintains relationships with trade unions as well as governments and seeks to promote social justice in the workplace.

international marketing: planning and executing a strategy for marketing products or services throughout the world. This might be done through product localisation (in effect, niche marketing) or by a global approach, sometimes known as pan-continental or *pan-European marketing*. When trying to break into a new market, most businesses will have limited knowledge on which to base their strategies. This increases the risks and emphasises the need for in-depth market research. Many companies have used their existing approaches and failed because they did not understand local cultures. Products may need to be modified and promotion strategies adapted. (See *Ansoff's matrix*, *market development* and *product development*.)

International Monetary Fund (IMF): the banker to the world's *central banks*. In other words, if a country requires to borrow money (inevitably it would be foreign currency), it can apply for a loan from the IMF. It is then likely that the IMF would send a team of inspectors to the country who would advise on the conditions to be tied to the loan. Usually these conditions include cuts in government spending. The IMF played an important part in planning the international response to the financial crisis in 2008–09. Many emerging economies needed loans to help with balance of payments deficits. At the G20 meeting in April 2009 the IMF agreed to provide US$250 billion in new Special Drawing Rights (SDRs) for this purpose.

International Standards Organisation (ISO) 9000/9002 is a worldwide quality certification procedure of exact equivalence to *British Standard 7750*.

international trade consists of exports and imports between countries. Through the principle of *comparative advantage*, international trade should cause an improvement in people's living standards and, in the long run, there is a very clear link between international trade and *economic growth*. (See bar chart opposite. The dip in 2001 shows the impact of the Asian financial crisis.)

Being able to buy a cheap imported substitute for a dearer domestic product can increase many people's purchasing power, giving them higher real incomes. However, in the short run, some people may lose out as growing international competition forces the less competitive firms out of business and makes their employees redundant. This can lead to *protectionism*, a movement to reduce trade through import controls.

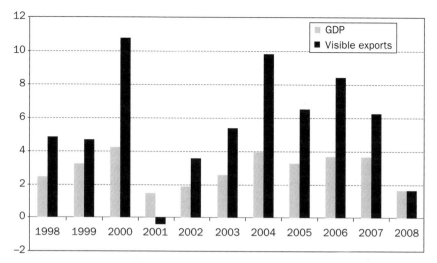

Growth in visible exports and GDP, 1998–2008, annual % change. (Source: WTO.)

internet shopping: purchasing items on-line from a website, using a credit or debit card. Potential benefits of internet shopping include:

- ease of price comparison, enabling the customer to identify the cheapest (and have access to it)
- convenience, especially for those in rural areas or parents with small children
- low transaction cost may allow internet retailers to charge lower prices.

intervention (in foreign currency markets) occurs when a ***central bank*** steps in to buy or sell a currency in order to stabilise its exchange rate.

interventionist: an individual who believes that government intervention can help to make markets more efficient, and protect individuals from socially irresponsible business behaviour. Such a person is also likely to promote an active economic policy by government, as opposed to a ***laissez-faire*** approach.

interventionist policies are pursued by governments that believe it is their duty to exert a strong influence over the running of a country's economy. They might include 'rescue packages' to help out large firms which have got into financial trouble, ***fiscal policies*** and ***monetary policies***, and laws to provide stronger protection to consumers or workers. Many interventionist policies were derived from ***Keynesian*** beliefs that the state could help to iron out the extremes of the ***economic cycle***. Other interventionist policies include competition and environmental regulation and many ***supply-side policies***.

interviewing is the process of obtaining information through questioning conducted face to face or over the telephone. There are two main business circumstances in which interviewing is used: as part of a job selection process and as part of a ***market research*** study. In either case, the interview can use ***closed questions*** to obtain specific (and quantifiable) information, or ***open questions*** that allow attitudes and ideas to emerge.

intranet: links between computers within a company to provide the same facilities to browse information and send e-mails that exist worldwide on the internet. The advantage of an internal internet (intranet) is that information confidential to the company can be published internally without outsiders having access. GlaxoSmithKline, for example, uses an intranet to keep its research scientists up to date with discoveries made throughout the business.

invention: the creation of a new product or process. If it represents a scientific or technical first, an invention can have a *patent* to ensure that any user of the idea must pay royalties to the inventor. Britain has an impressive record at invention (including penicillin and the hovercraft), but a far poorer record at achieving the crucial next stage: *innovation*, i.e. bringing new ideas to the marketplace.

inventory: another term for *stock*.

investment means doing without consumption today in order to use *capital* to generate future returns. To an economist, investment means the purchase of capital equipment such as *plant* and machinery. On the *stock market*, investment means buying shares. In accounting terminology, investment might be in *fixed assets* or *working capital*. It is also possible to invest in *human capital*, through education or training.

investment appraisal: the process of deciding whether a proposed investment will actually be worthwhile. For big projects, there are various ways of estimating the future income stream which can be expected. This must be compared with the *interest* payments which will be needed where loan finance is involved. Even where *internal financing* is being used care is needed to see that the returns are at least equal to the *opportunity cost* of the capital invested.

investment banks: the term used in the USA to describe *merchant banks*.

investment trust: a company formed to invest in the shares of a wide range of other companies. Investment trusts are a long-established way for the small investor to invest in the *stock market*.

invisible export: the sale of a service to an overseas customer. As well as services such as banking, airline travel and insurance, visits by foreign tourists are counted as invisible exports, since they bring income in from overseas.

invisible hand: *Adam Smith*'s famous term for how the free market successfully and efficiently brings together willing sellers and willing buyers (through the *price mechanism*). If the product loses popularity, the lack of *demand* will force the price down until the buyers return, so the marketplace will invisibly secure a balance between *supply* and demand. Adam Smith believed that people acting entirely out of self-interest unwittingly serve the community as a whole through the operation of this 'invisible hand'. Consequently, he saw no need for government intervention in the workings of business.

invisible import: the purchase of a service from an overseas supplier.

invisible trade consists of imports and exports of services. They include financial services such as banking and insurance, as well as tourism and shipping. Invisibles account for approximately a quarter of world trade. Traditionally, the UK has enjoyed a surplus on invisibles, which has helped to pay for the long-standing deficit on *visible trade*.

inward investment: the capital attracted to a region or country from beyond its boundaries. An example of such investment is a Japanese car manufacturer opening an assembly plant in the UK. Inward investment can provide employment, perhaps in areas where *structural unemployment* is a problem, and should have a beneficial *multiplier* effect upon the economic health of local manufacturing and service businesses.

IP: see *intellectual property*

ISO 9000/9002: see *International Standards Organisation (ISO) 9000/9002*

issued share capital: the amount of a firm's *authorised share capital* that has actually been issued (sold) to investors. The memorandum of association states the authorised share capital of a company, but not all the shares need be issued at once. Thus, under *shareholders' funds* in the *balance sheet*, both the authorised and issued share capital may be listed. Shareholders can see whether further shares can be issued, which would raise further funds but also dilute the ownership.

IT: see *information technology (IT)*

Aiming for a grade A*?

Don't forget to log on to **www.philipallan.co.uk/a-zonline** for advice.

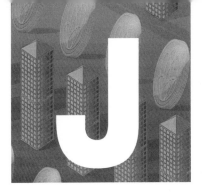

Japanese way: a term summarising the Japanese approach to management. Although there is a danger in over-simplifying, the Japanese way comprises three main elements:

- a strategic focus on the long term, in which the goal of a strong market position is more important than short-term profit
- a highly educated, highly trained workforce that is given a key role in improving production methods and quality; the *kaizen* (continuous improvement) group and the *quality circle* are ways of achieving this
- *lean production*, eliminating wastage of materials and time; hence *just in time (JIT)* production and *stock control* and the reduction in product development time that enables Toyota to get a new product idea to the marketplace in half the time taken in the West.

Japanisation: the process by which Western firms have attempted to follow the *Japanese way*.

jargon: the terms used among specialist employees that form a language which may mean little to outsiders. This may, indeed, be the motive behind its use.

JIT: see *just in time (JIT)*

job design: deciding how the tasks required within a production process should be subdivided or grouped into specific job functions. The key decisions are between:

- high *division of labour* and a complete unit of work
- close supervision and self-checking.

The role of job design is crucial in *job enrichment* and in *motivation* generally.

job enlargement: increasing the number of tasks and possibly responsibilities involved in a job. Examples of job enlargement are *job rotation* and *job enrichment*.

job enrichment: the attempt to motivate by giving employees the opportunity to use their abilities. This definition is closely based upon Professor *Herzberg*'s work, as job enrichment was the main policy recommendation that stemmed from his theories. Herzberg suggested that an enriched job should ideally contain:

- a range of tasks and challenges at different ability levels, some of which should be beyond the employee's experience to date
- a *complete unit of work*, in other words a meaningful task rather than a repetitive fragment
- direct *feedback*, by which the employee could know immediately how well he or she was performing.

job flexibility: see *flexible working*

job production means producing a one-off item that has been tailor-made to suit a specific customer. Although most of this type of production is undertaken by small firms (because there are no *economies of scale*), shipbuilding may operate on the same job basis. Also very common among smaller firms is a combination between batch and job methods. A baker might bake a dozen celebration fruit cakes. Some are then tailor-made into wedding cakes while others are decorated for birthday cakes.

job rotation: widening the activities of a worker by switching him or her around a number of work tasks. For example, a shop worker might spend two hours on the checkout, two filling shelves and another two in the warehouse. This is intended to relieve the tedium of the work, but has the useful side-effect of ensuring that if one person is absent, others can cover the job without difficulty.

job satisfaction: the degree to which an employee feels positively towards his or her present job function. Many writers have pointed out that the term is not only hard to define but also to measure. Indeed several believe it to be virtually irrelevant to managers, as it has not been possible to prove that higher job satisfaction results in higher job performance. Despite these reservations, the huge research effort and the management time spent considering the problems and opportunities involved suggests that job satisfaction is of great importance. Most clearly, job dissatisfaction can lead to *absenteeism*, high *labour turnover* and poor *industrial relations*. (See *Herzberg, F* and *job enrichment*.)

job security: the extent to which a job is, or seems to be, guaranteed for the foreseeable future. Although lack of job security would prevent a worker's *lower order needs* from being satisfied, it is possible that the implied threat would stimulate greater effort.

job sharing: when employees agree to divide the working week on a job in two, so that they each do half of the one job. This can be very useful for parents with young children, and may provide the employer with the bonus of having two, fresher minds on the one task.

job specification: a statement or listing of the characteristics required to do a job successfully. So whereas the job description describes the job, the job specification specifies the person. Drawing up a 'job spec' is one of the first stages in the recruitment process. It provides a yardstick against which the job applicants can be measured. Typical elements in a job specification include: educational qualifications, experience, impact on others and special aptitudes (such as speed of thought).

joint demand occurs when two items are consumed together, i.e. are complements. Examples might be shoes and shoe laces or CDs and CD players. An increase in sales of one may lead to an increase in sales of the other.

joint-stock company: the traditional term for describing a limited company, i.e. a separate legal entity financed and owned by individual shareholders. Joint-stock companies may be *private limited companies* (Ltd) or *public limited companies (PLC)*.

joint supply occurs when the production of one good also entails the production of another. This often happens in the chemical industry where one chemical may be produced as a by-product of another. Meat and leather provide another example. A fall in the market price of one may affect the quantity supplied of the other.

joint venture: when two or more firms set up a business division that will be operated jointly. This method avoids the need for a complete *merger*, with all the managerial problems that can entail. The potential problem with a joint venture is that the common interests that brought the firms together may shift, leaving the possibility of a messy divorce.

junk bond: a fixed interest loan offering higher annual *dividends* than most bonds, but with far less security. The issuing of junk bonds was a major factor in the huge credit boom in the USA in the 1980s. It resulted in American firms becoming very highly geared, thereby turning the early 1990s recession into the longest for 60 years. In 2005, worries about the financial health of the USA's giant General Motors led to its borrowings being downgraded to junk status. By 2009 General Motors required government assistance to survive.

just in time (JIT): a manufacturing system which is designed to minimise the costs of holding *stocks* of raw materials, components, *work in progress (WIP)* and finished goods by very carefully planned scheduling and flow of resources through the production process. It requires a very efficient ordering system and delivery reliability. It is usually implemented in conjunction with a shift from *mass production* to *cell production*.

JIT also has enormous implications for managing the workforce. High stock levels act as a cushion against workforce indiscipline, be it absenteeism or strike action. Without them, it is essential that managers encourage cooperation instead of confrontation. Factory workers need to be treated as valued members of a complete team – trusted, trained and consulted.

As a result, JIT can lead firms to rethink their approach to factory work. The traditional approach of splitting work into repetitive fragments results in an uncooperative workforce, so firms organise the workforce into teams, working together on large units of work instead of working in isolation on the same boring task.

From its origins in Japan, the JIT approach has spread widely throughout the West. In Britain, Rolls Royce divided its car plant into 16 zones, each acting as a business within a business, responsible for purchasing, cost, quality and delivery. Rolls Royce's new approach halved the break-even level from 2800 cars per year to 1400.

A–Z Online

Log on to A–Z Online to search the database of terms, print revision lists and much more. Go to **www.philipallan.co.uk/a-zonline** to get started.

k: a common abbreviation of thousands (of pounds).

kaizen: a Japanese term meaning continuous improvement. Tesco has enjoyed huge success by adopting kaizen within the slogan 'every little helps'. The importance of this element in the *Japanese way* has often been overlooked. When General Motors realised how far their efficiency had slipped behind the Japanese car firms, they invested billions of pounds in brand-new, highly automated production lines. Yet in the period it took to design, install and test the plant, the Japanese firms had moved the productivity goalposts by their continuous improvement policy. Furthermore, the Japanese improvements cost relatively little, as they were just shop-floor ideas on how to complete tasks more efficiently. Most were generated by kaizen groups that met regularly to discuss problems and solutions.

The diagram below shows the kaizen effect on productivity growth as compared with the traditional Western approach of large, technology-based leaps forward. Note that whereas the Western version would probably entail large-scale *redundancies*, steady productivity improvements are more likely to be accommodated by rising demand or by *natural wastage*.

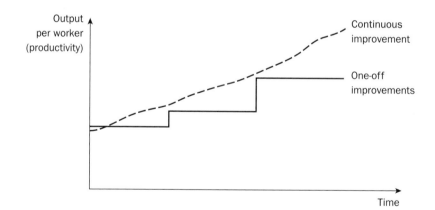

Kaizen: continuous improvement

kanban: the Japanese system of order cards that pull component supplies through a factory. This is the practical basis of the *just in time (JIT)* production system. It often operates on the simple basis of two component bins. When one is empty, it is wheeled to the component production section with its kanban order card. That triggers production of the component that must be completed just in time before the other bin runs out of supplies.

This approach minimises the amount of semi-completed stock within the factory, focusing minds on the need to avoid production hiccups that could quickly bring the factory to a halt.

keiretsu: a Japanese term for a group of companies that have interlocking minority shareholdings in each other. This encourages them to consult closely on long-term planning. Well-known keiretsu include Mitsui and Mitsubishi.

Keynes, J M (1883–1946): unarguably the most important British economist of the twentieth century. His most important works included *The Economic Consequences of the Peace* (first published 1919), and *The General Theory of Employment, Interest and Money* (first published 1936). Keynes was a major influence on Britain's successful handling of its wartime economy 1939–1945, and his ideas were adopted worldwide in the long period of economic growth between 1945 and 1970. (See *Keynesian*.)

Keynesian: a person whose economic ideas can be traced to those of J M *Keynes*. At the risk of over-simplification, these include:
- scepticism that the economy tends to stabilise at full employment; Keynes believed that government action might be needed to push an economy out of *recession* (for example extra spending on road-building)
- conviction about the desirability of a *counter-cyclical policy* by government
- the belief that allowing people to suffer (through unemployment, for example) while waiting for the free market to bring the economy into balance is morally and socially unacceptable.

kitemark: the symbol that shows that a consumer product has met the standards laid down by the *British Standards Institute (BSI)*.

knowledge economy: an economy in which the business of acquiring and transmitting knowledge is a substantial part of total output.

Kondratieff cycle: the theory that in addition to the 5–10 year *economic cycle*, there exists a 50-year cycle of economic upturn and downturn. This theory was put forward by the Russian economist Kondratieff in the early twentieth century. It was dismissed by many economists until the great depressions of the 1880s and 1930s were duly followed (50 years later) by the frequent and severe *recessions* of the period from 1975 to 1992. The most widely accepted explanation for the Kondratieff cycle is that the introduction of a new technology causes disruption, but once established it forms the basis for many new products and jobs. In the 1930s the car was displacing rail, while in the 1980s the microchip was replacing mechanical technology.

Kyoto Protocol: an international agreement that sets targets for the reduction of emissions of greenhouse gases, signed in 1997. It was never ratified by the USA; powerful forces within the US were profoundly sceptical about the connection between climate change and the use of fossil fuels. Developing countries were reluctant to prejudice their chances of income growth while still suffering from widespread poverty. Developed countries were mostly reluctant to attack the problem energetically unless the developing countries also made progress. Only Denmark, Germany, Russia and the UK have actually reduced greenhouse gas emissions since the Protocol was agreed; other EU member countries have made progress. China, India and the USA have not. Negotiations for a new Kyoto agreement are continuing.

labour: the factor of production which involves people working to produce goods and services. Labour involves both doing and thinking. Labour is often referred to as if it were a single type of resource. In practice there are many different categories of labour, depending on their respective capabilities, which are referred to as human capital. This can be increased through education and training. (See also *labour, demand for* and *labour market*.)

labour, demand for: the demand for *labour* reflects the demand for the product and is thus a *derived demand*. There will be a demand schedule for labour just as there is a demand schedule for the product and the numbers employed will depend partly on the going wage rate. At any given wage, more labour will be demanded if the price of the product rises or if more can be sold.

If labour *productivity* rises, there are a number of possible outcomes. Costs will fall, so prices may be cut, sales may rise and more labour will be demanded. Alternatively, the increased productivity may make it possible to pay higher wages but in that case costs will not fall.

The demand for labour is thus closely related to the product market and changes in the pattern of demand work their way through the labour market into the overall allocation of resources. There is also a close relationship between the demand for labour and the price of capital. If wages rise relative to the price of labour-saving capital equipment, employers will tend to substitute capital for labour and the quantity of labour demanded will fall.

labour flexibility: the ease with which a firm can change the jobs carried out by its staff. This is an important element in a firm's ability to cope with change within its marketplace. The main factors determining labour flexibility are:
- workforce attitudes, including any resistance to change
- traditional labour practices, which may be restrictive and entrenched, such as rigid job *demarcation*
- the general skills of the labour force (have workers been encouraged to take general training courses or do they only know their specialist function?)
- the strength and attitude of the local *trade union*.

labour force: the number of people available for work. This can be influenced by:
- birth rates in the past
- the number of people in education
- the retirement age
- the social security system and the extent to which poverty traps create disincentives
- the availability of child care.

When jobs are being created, discouraged workers and women who were not previously seeking work may rejoin the *labour* force.

Labour Force Survey: the quarterly government survey of employment and *unemployment*. It uses sample surveys to measure the number of people unemployed and actively seeking work and also the number of people who are not actively seeking a job but would like to work. It is thought to provide a more accurate measure of unemployment than the claimant count, which gives us the headline total for unemployment on a monthly basis, derived from the numbers claiming benefits.

labour intensive: a work process in which labour represents a high proportion of total costs. Such a situation is most likely to exist in the service sector, in a small firm, or in a firm operating on a *job production* or *batch production* system. This contrasts with firms that are *capital intensive*.

labour market is the supply of labour (i.e. all those offering themselves for work) and the demand for labour (i.e. employers in both the *private sector* and the *public sector*), which together determine wage rates. Talking of a single market for this *factor of production* is quite misleading because it is made up of a vast number of smaller markets which have quite different characteristics: road repairers, brain surgeons and pop stars for instance.

labour market failure refers to any imperfection in the *labour* market which impedes the movement of people away from the products with declining demand towards products with growing demand. The most important of these are *occupational immobility* and *geographical immobility*. Because they lack appropriate skills or live in a place where there is no demand for their services, people made redundant from a declining industry may be unable to find alternative work. Lack of information may also create imperfections.

labour market flexibility refers to the ease with which people are able to change jobs or adapt to changed circumstances in other ways. There are a number of examples:

- the trend towards greater *labour* market flexibility in recent years means that some people now have part-time contracts which allow the employer to vary the number and the timing of the hours worked
- improved education and training generally make individuals more flexible, so that they are relatively easily able to move to an alternative occupation
- any measure which improves *labour mobility* will be likely to increase flexibility. The US labour market is usually thought to be more flexible than the UK labour market. Within the EU, the UK and the Netherlands are thought to have the most flexible labour markets, but all are becoming more flexible.

Lack of flexibility can be due to *employment protection* law which may make it difficult for employers to make people redundant when demand for the product is falling.

labour mobility is the extent to which labour moves around in search of jobs, called geographical mobility, or the extent to which labour moves between jobs, which is known as occupational mobility. It is an indicator of a dynamic economy if such mobility is high. Geographical mobility depends on such things as available housing, costs of moving, communications and the importance of family ties, whilst occupational mobility depends on training facilities and a willingness to learn.

labour turnover: a measurement of the rate at which employees are leaving an organisation.

High labour turnover may be caused by:
- pay levels falling below comparable rates locally
- low morale, perhaps due to ineffective leadership or an **authoritarian leadership style**
- an economic upturn creating many other job opportunities.

The main effects of high labour turnover are:
- heavy overheads due to the costs of recruiting and training replacement staff frequently
- productivity reductions as new staff acclimatise
- the difficulties of building teamwork with an ever-changing team.

lagging indicator is a term used to describe a signal which lags behind the true state of economic activity. Unemployment figures often lag behind in this way because, as an economy moves out of **recession**, firms experience an increase in their order books and respond by increasing output, initially by working overtime rather than by taking on more staff. Only when firms are convinced that the recovery is well under way will they employ more people. Therefore, unemployment tends to fall some time after the economy has begun to grow.

lags may occur whenever a change in one variable has an impact on another, but after a lapse of time. It is usual for decision takers to take time to adjust to new circumstances. A change in prices will usually lead to a change in the quantity demanded but only after existing contracts have been completed.

laissez-faire is a political and economic philosophy which believes that governments should avoid interfering in the running of business or any other part of the economy. A laissez-faire economist places faith in the ability of the free market to maximise business efficiency and consumer satisfaction. **Interventionists** note that the theory of laissez-faire was devised in the eighteenth century when small firms did compete freely. Today, many markets are dominated by a few large firms, so the theory of laissez-faire is less persuasive.

laissez-faire leadership occurs where the leader has minimal input, leaving the running of the business to the staff. **Delegation** would lack focus and coordination, making it hard for employees to feel a sense of common purpose. This style can stem from a leader's inability to provide the framework necessary for a successful democratic approach. Or it may be a conscious and brave policy decision to give staff the maximum scope for showing their capabilities. Some people will love the freedom provided, and produce highly creative work. Others will hate their unstructured job with its low input from the leader. (See also **democratic leadership**, **authoritarian leadership style** and **paternalistic leadership style**.)

landfill waste tax: a tax imposed per tonne of waste dumped in landfill sites. Starting in October 1996, this tax is intended to make the polluter pay. This should provide an incentive for companies to minimise the waste they dump and maximise their efforts at recycling. The rate of tax rose to £32 per tonne in 2008 and the government announced the rate would rise by £8 per year from 2009 onwards.

lateral communication: another term for **horizontal communications**.

lateral thinking: the ability when faced with an apparently unsolvable problem to think creatively and either find a radical solution or realise the situation can be sidestepped altogether. This kind of creative thinking can pay especially handsome dividends in product development and in marketing, where originality can lead to exciting **innovation**.

launch: the programme of stockpiling, distribution, advertising and publicity required to thrust a new product onto its **target market**. The launch may be national or regional, depending upon the firm's confidence in the product, its available production capacity and any known regional taste differences. Once sufficient stocks of the product are ready, the launch is likely to consist of three phases:

1 *Trade advertising* plus aggressive salesforce activity to get wholesalers and retailers to stock the product.
2 A *merchandising* campaign to achieve high visibility at the point of sale, e.g. display stands near the shop checkouts.
3 A consumer advertising campaign, perhaps of TV commercials plus posters.

layers of hierarchy means the number of ranks within an organisational structure, i.e. the number of different supervisory and management layers between the shop-floor and the chief executive.

leadership style: the manner and approach of the head of an organisation or department towards the staff. The leader's manner affects the personal relationships involved. Will the leader inspire loyalty, affection, respect, trust? The style includes the use of *delegation* and *consultation*, plus the degree to which the leader gets involved personally in the daily problems of the business. Both aspects will be handled differently by different leaders, but there are four categories of leadership style that are used widely for purposes of analysis: see *democratic leadership*, *paternalistic leadership style*, *authoritarian leadership style* (or dictatorial) and *laissez-faire leadership*.

leading indicator is a term used to describe a signal which predates or predicts the true state of economic activity, such as the level of orders for machine tools. The *stock market* often leads in this way. For example, growing confidence that signs of a recovery are under way is often translated into rising share prices, as investors predict improving profits in the next year to eighteen months. The opposite also holds, with sharp falls in share prices indicating a falling off of activity in advance of the reality. Such leading indicators can be predictors of what is likely to happen to the 'real economy'.

lead time: the length of time a firm needs between receiving an order and delivering the finished product or service. Efforts by management at reducing lead times could result in considerable benefits in terms of customer satisfaction and faster turnover. Nevertheless, many customers would rather have a 100 per cent reliable delivery date than an apparently faster but actually less reliable service.

leakages occur when money is taken out of the *circular flow of national income*. They consist of taxes, imports and savings. In each case, the leakage leads to a lower level of aggregate demand for domestic output, i.e. it reduces spending power. A fall in leakages will lead to an increase in spending, as with a tax cut. Leakages are sometimes called withdrawals.

lean production: a term used to describe the range of waste-saving measures inspired by Japanese manufacturing firms. These include *just in time (JIT)*, shorter product development times and *flexible specialisation*. To the authors of *The Machine that Changed the World* (Womack, Jones & Roos, Macmillan, 1990), lean production has replaced mass production as the world's most efficient system. Its efficiency stems from the focus upon minimising the waste of any resource that does not add value to the product or service. Time spent re-checking and reworking the output of others is time wasted, therefore focus on getting the work right first time. However, time spent discussing how to improve the product or process can add value to the product, therefore improvement (*kaizen*) groups are encouraged. (See also the *Japanese way*.)

learning curve: the process of gaining experience and knowledge that depends on learning from your mistakes. New employees and firms new to a market both go through the same learning process. The successful ones will be those that move up the learning curve as rapidly as possible, probably through a combination of good research and a willingness to experiment.

learning organisation: an enterprise that makes *continuous improvement* a central theme of its management approach. Therefore it is always willing to listen to new ideas and make the necessary changes – however radical. For this to be successful there needs to be an open style of management, excellent internal communications and a sense of common purpose amongst managers and staff alike.

lease: a way of acquiring property for a restricted period of time; after the lease runs out, ownership returns to the freeholder. As it has value for the years of its life, a lease is recorded as a *fixed asset* on a firm's *balance sheet*.

leasing: a method of acquiring non-property *assets* without the need for the initial cash outlays implied by purchasing. This can also be done by renting or hiring equipment, though leasing is cheaper per month because the firm must contract to lease the assets for a period of two or more years. Compared with purchasing, leasing has various advantages and disadvantages:

PROS: • avoids the damage to *cash flow* caused by purchasing
      • releases *capital* for other, perhaps more profitable uses

CONS: • in order to provide the leasing company with a profit, it is inevitable that in the long run most leasing arrangements will prove more expensive than outright purchase
      • when a firm leases a machine it does not own it; therefore it does not appear as an asset on the *balance sheet*; so if a firm leased all its equipment, its accounts may look worryingly short of assets

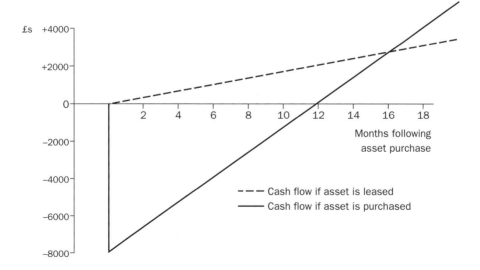

Leasing compared with purchasing an asset costing £8000

least developed countries: the 49 countries identified by the UN as having the lowest per capita incomes. Thirty-three of the countries are in Africa south of the Sahara. Examples include Sudan, the Democratic Republic of Congo, Myanmar and Laos. The criteria for inclusion are:
- per capita incomes average less than US$750 per annum
- they are close to the bottom of the *Human Development Index (HDI)*
- they are economically vulnerable in being prone to natural disasters, dependent on a narrow range of commodities with unstable prices and having few non-traditional sources of income.

legal liabilities: the responsibility firms have to obey relevant laws, such as those concerning health and safety, *equal opportunities*, paternity and maternity rights and so on.

legislation: laws passed by Acts of Parliament.

lender of last resort: an important function of the Bank of England (and other central banks), which guarantees to lend to banks which find themselves temporarily unable to meet their customers' requests for withdrawals. This process was much in evidence during the financial crisis, especially in 2007–08 when Northern Rock, Lloyds TSB, Royal Bank of Scotland (RBS) and others needed to be recapitalised due to massive losses. In fact the system-wide crisis was so severe then that only the government could rescue the banks by taking a large share of ownership.

This does not mean that a central bank will bail out any bank at any time; a bank which has been mismanaged or involved in fraud may still fail or be sold, as happened with Barings in 1995, or with the US bank Lehmans, in 2008. But central banks will try to ensure the stability of the banking system as a whole.

level playing field: a phrase that sums up the need within a *market economy* for all firms to be competing on the same terms. If one national government is subsidising its steel producers, for example, they will have an unfair advantage over those from a country like Britain, which offers no State aid to steel. The *single European market* is an attempt to provide a level playing field in relation to laws and regulations governing traded goods within the *European Union (EU)*. If product and factory regulations could be made the same throughout the EU, the trading field would have been levelled out.

leverage: the American term for *gearing* (i.e. the level of borrowing).

LFS unemployment refers to the measurement of unemployment based on the *Labour Force Survey*. (Headline unemployment is based on the claimant count.)

liabilities: a legal obligation to pay debts. Liabilities appear in the accounts of banks and companies. They imply the existence of some form of loan or responsibility to cover debts in the future. (See also *limited liability*.)

liberalisation (of trade) is a term used to describe the freeing up of international trade from barriers such as *tariffs* and *quotas*. The General Agreement on Tariffs and Trade (GATT) was established in 1974 to negotiate reduced barriers under a succession of so-called 'rounds'. This work is now carried out by the *World Trade Organization (WTO)*.

licensing: when the holder of a *patent* or *copyright* allows other firms to use his or her creation in return for a *royalty*. The royalty might be an agreed percentage of the value of the sales made by the licensee, or a fee per unit sold. The holders of the Star Wars name and *logo* might, for example, charge licensees £1 per Star Wars T-shirt and 10p per Star Wars pencil.

168

LIFFE: see *London International Financial Futures Exchange (LIFFE)*

limited company: a firm that enjoys *limited liability*. In other words, the owners (shareholders) are risking only the amount they have invested in the company rather than their personal wealth.

limited liability is the idea that the owners (shareholders) are financially responsible only for the amount they have invested in the company rather than their personal wealth. Thus if a firm becomes insolvent, the maximum *creditors* can receive is the shareholders' original investment. In order to protect and inform creditors, the word 'Ltd' (standing for Limited) or 'PLC' (standing for public limited company) appears after the company's name. The importance of limiting the amount of a shareholder's liability is that it encourages people to invest with relatively little risk.

limit pricing involves selecting a price below the profit-maximising price. A company may choose to do this if it seems likely to discourage *new entrants* to the industry. This may help to preserve its competitive position. High profits could attract new entrants who would compete strongly. It is likely that this is an element in the pricing strategies of many firms producing consumer durables. The limit price will be lowest when entry is easy, indicating a *contestable market*. It will be higher if there are substantial *economies of scale* in the industry.

line extension: adding a new flavour or model type to a product line. For example, once Wall's had launched 'Magnum' successfully, 'White Magnum' soon followed.

PROS:
- a line extension can offer more variety to regular customers, encouraging higher levels of *repeat purchase*
- it can also be used to segment a market, as, for example, a plain chocolate choc-ice will appeal more to adults than to children
- most importantly, a line extension can protect a successful product from competition; once the success of 'Magnum' had become clear, competitors would look for ways of getting into this market sector; the easiest way would be to offer a 'Magnum' imitation (*me-too product*) with a point of differentiation; if Walls had not offered 'Magnum White', a rival would have done so

CONS:
- line extensions can cannibalise your existing products, in other words much of the demand for 'Magnum White' may have come from buyers of 'Magnum'. By spreading sales among more products, each one's chance of gaining high retail distribution is reduced

line management: managers who have been delegated specific authority over people, decisions and results within the management hierarchy.

liquid assets are either money or something that can very quickly be sold for money at a price which involves little or no loss. In the case of a bank, liquid assets would include cash and any kind of very short-term loan.

liquidation means turning assets into cash. The term is usually used in the context of a firm ceasing to trade in its current form, probably due to *insolvency*. The closure may be the result of *creditors* taking the firm to court to seek compulsory liquidation due to non-payment of debts. In this case a *receiver* will be appointed to attempt to raise the cash

169

to satisfy the creditors. If the firm has sufficient assets, or a fundamentally strong trading position, it may well be that the receiver is able to find a buyer for the firm or to keep it going. More common is **voluntary liquidation**, in which the firm's directors decide that they wish to stop the firm continuing to trade as at present. This might be because an elderly proprietor wants to retire and can find no buyer for the firm. The main alternatives to liquidation are **administration** and financial restructuring.

liquidity: the ability of a firm to meet its short-term debts. As bills can only be paid with cash, liquidity can also be understood as the availability of cash or **liquid assets**.

liquidity crisis: a loss of confidence in a firm's ability to meet its short-term debts. This may encourage bankers or **creditors** to demand payment before others get at the firm's money. Inability to meet those payments might lead to **liquidation**.

listed company: a firm that has its shares listed on the main London **Stock Exchange**. In order for this to be possible, the firm must be a **public limited company (PLC)**.

listing refers to those public **joint-stock companies** (PLCs) which appear on the **Stock Exchange** list.

living standards refer to the well-being of the population but the term does not have a precise meaning. A serious attempt to assess progress in this area requires inspection of a wide range of data, including:

- measures of real income such as GDP at **constant prices**, to assess the economic component of the standard of living
- per capita income, if population growth is rapid
- measures of social welfare such as mortality rates, life expectancy, participation in education, access to health care, clean water and so on
- in some cases, data for the **distribution of income** would add detail to the picture. The presence or absence of a **social security** system may also be relevant.

International comparisons of the standard of living can be confused by exchange rate variations. The World Bank produces data based on **purchasing power parity (PPP)** which gives a clearer picture. The UN's **Human Development Index (HDI)** also provides useful data.

Lloyd's insurance market is one of the world's main centres for obtaining insurance cover on anything from a car to an oil rig. Lloyd's members underwrite risks from throughout the world, earning Britain considerable sums of foreign currency, and thereby making insurance one of Britain's main **invisible exports**.

loan capital: medium- to long-term finance, either from banks or from **debenture** holders. Loan capital plus **shareholders' funds** represent a firm's **capital employed**. When raising extra loan capital, a firm should consider its **gearing** level, i.e. the extent to which it is reliant on borrowed money. If loans represent more than 50 per cent of capital employed, the firm is considered over-geared.

Loan Guarantee Scheme (LGS): a government-backed loan insurance scheme which guarantees bankers that up to 80 per cent of the money they lend to a business will be guaranteed by the **Treasury**. This was introduced in 1980 as a way of encouraging banks to lend to small and medium-sized companies thought too risky to justify a conventional loan. In return for its financial risks, the government charges a fee. The precise terms of the LGS are often changed in the annual *Budget*, but would easily be available from the *Department for Business, Innovation and Skills (BIS)* or from any high-street bank.

lobbying: putting your viewpoint across directly to a person in a position of power and influence. The term comes from the central lobby of the Houses of Parliament, which is where members of the public go to put their case to their Member of Parliament. Although intended as an aid to the democratic process, lobbying has become tainted by the number of MPs who are paid to represent special interests such as the tobacco industry. (See *pressure group*.)

local content: the proportion of the value of output that is produced within the country where a product is assembled. This is an important issue within the *European Union (EU)*, because products imported directly from the Far East are subject to restrictions and taxes, whereas free trade exists for products made within the EU. Yet that opens the possibility that a Japanese firm might set up in Britain, import all components from Japan, and simply bolt them together in the UK. Other European countries are keen to ensure that a product with such a low local content is treated as if it were a direct import from Japan.

local government is responsible in the UK for most school education, social services, local roads, planning and a range of other services. Changes in local government, and the trend towards unitary authorities (single authorities responsible for all locally provided services), may affect the way these services are organised.

localised industry: where one area has a particular advantage for an industry, that industry will tend to develop there rather than in other locations. In the past the existence of coal often created an industrial area involving steel making and engineering. *Industrial inertia* may mean that these industries have continued to be located in the same place. Other possible local advantages include a supply of appropriately skilled *labour* with a tradition in the industry concerned. Localised industries that decline may create a significant unemployment problem.

local multiplier: when spending in one particular area increases, then a local multiplier effect will be observed. Extra spending will generate employment: if a new bridge is being built, people will be employed to do the building. These people will then spend some of their earnings locally, thus creating further demand and increased employment in the immediate area.

location of industry: see *industrial location*

lock-out: when an employer decides to bring an *industrial dispute* to a head by preventing the workforce from getting in to work.

logistics is the process of ensuring the right supplies and products are in the right place at the right time, at a competitive cost. The main functions covered are:
- materials ordering and handling
- *stock control*
- *distribution* and delivery.

logo: a visual symbol of an organisation or brand. It might be the design of the brand name, such as the Coca-Cola signature, or pure creation, such as the 'golden arches' yellow M that symbolises McDonald's.

London Derivatives Exchange: the financial exchange formed from the 1990 merger of the Traded Options Market with the *London International Financial Futures Exchange (LIFFE)*.

London International Financial Futures Exchange (LIFFE): pronounced 'life', LIFFE is the financial market where companies can obtain forward currency or hedge their

171

future currency commitments (see **hedging**). In 1990, LIFFE was merged with the Traded Options Market to form the **London Derivatives Exchange**.

long run: the period of time in which all factors of production can be varied. For example, it is possible to invest in new capital equipment and build new factories. Similarly, some businesses may enter or exit from the marketplace, so changing the size of the industry.

long-run trend rate of growth: the rate of growth of output which can realistically be achieved over a long period. In the UK this has historically been about 2.2 per cent per year. It is a moving average of growth rates over a period of time, typically the 30 years shown in the diagram. It represents the average rate of growth of productive capacity for the whole economy. It is influenced by:

- the level of investment
- improvements in education and training
- increased technical knowledge
- innovation generally.

Improved management techniques can also have some impact. Shocks to the economy such as oil price changes or serious loss of business confidence, which lead to falling aggregate demand and recession on a serious scale, will tend to reduce the long-term trend growth rate. Counter-inflation policies can have the same effect. It follows that **macroeconomic stability** can help to raise long-term growth rates.

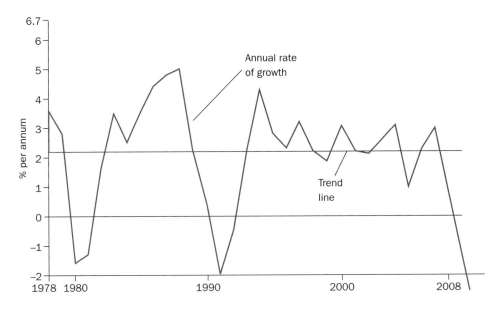

Long-run trend rate of growth in the UK. (Source: ONS.)

long tail refers to the way in which e-commerce has made it possible for suppliers to provide for a wide range of niche markets. By searching the internet people with minority tastes can find exactly what they want. The cost to retailers of supplying small markets has fallen significantly. Sales of conventional, popular, products are likely to fall while sales of niche products increase. The product range becomes larger and more diverse – this is the long tail.

long-term unemployed are people who have been unemployed for more than a year. The number or proportion of long-term unemployed has policy implications:

- they may become discouraged and cease to make active efforts to find work
- they may become deskilled or lose their work habits
- as a result, they may for practical purposes have dropped out of the *labour* market.

To the extent that these consequences have followed upon long-term unemployment, governments have to consider retraining or policies to reduce *geographical immobility*.

loose economic policy is the relaxation of fiscal and monetary measures to allow greater consumer spending, cheaper loans and lower taxes. The result is an increase in the rate of economic activity, leading to higher levels of employment, output and expenditure. It is a policy likely to be pursued when an economy is emerging from *recession*. It suffers from the potential danger of sucking in more imports if there is no spare productive capacity. This can lead to a *balance of payments* crisis, and/or to rising rates of inflation, especially if demand for goods and services increases too fast in certain sectors of the economy for output to rise to match it.

Lorenz curve: a graphical representation showing inequality. In the diagram, the Lorenz curve will run along the 45° line if the range of percentages of the population are the same as the share of total income which they receive. The more unequal the distribution of income, the more the Lorenz curve will be bowed out below the 45° line. For example, at point A, 24 per cent of the population have 10 per cent of the total income. So the closer the curve is to the 45° line, the greater is the degree of equality and vice versa. Lorenz curves can be used to compare other frequency distributions which are not equal, such as the number of firms and cumulative market shares. The *Gini coefficient* is the area between the Lorenz curve and the 45° line and gives a measure of inequality.

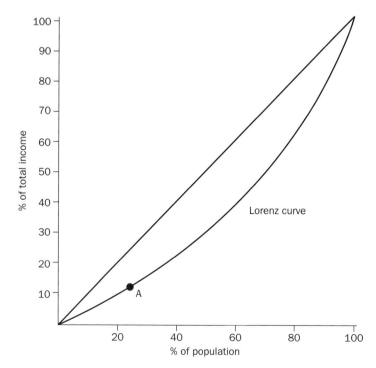

Lorenz curve

loss: the difference between total costs and sales revenue. Loss indicates that demand for the product is declining. The *profit-signalling mechanism* is working in reverse, indicating that resources should be reallocated away from the product in question. The product may have gone out of fashion or there may be a competing producer who can create and sell it at a lower price. The firm in question may cut production or it may exit from the marketplace. It may then switch to a more profitable product or go out of business altogether.

loss leaders: products sold at or below cost in the hope of generating other, profitable sales. The method is most commonly used in retailing, where a shop may advertise a loss leader heavily, enticing in customers who will probably buy other, full-priced items as well. The same term can also be used to describe a manufacturer who prices a lead item cheaply, knowing that usage of the item requires further, full-priced purchases. For example, publishers of sticker collections may charge only 50p for a large, glossy album, but 30p per pack for the cheaply produced stickers that go inside.

lower order needs: see *hierarchy of needs*

lower turning point is the lowest point in the *economic cycle*, where the economy moves out of *recession* or *depression*. During the downswing of a recession, economists and politicians attempt to forecast when the lower turning point is to be reached. In fact it is often only six to nine months afterwards that it becomes clear when it happened.

Ltd: see *limited liability*

Do you need revision help and advice ?

Go to pages 324–35 for a range of revision appendices that include plenty of exam advice and tips.

Maastricht is the name of a city in the Netherlands where the Treaty on European Union was signed by all the member states in December 1991. The Treaty envisaged the introduction of a single currency by 1999 and formulated a number of areas for combined policy action, including industrial and social policy, health and education. The Maastricht Treaty attempted to push the pace of European unity forward, but perhaps too quickly for countries such as Denmark and the UK. Nevertheless the success of Maastricht can be seen in its achievements:

- the *euro* currency area began on time in January 1999
- important social protection measures were introduced, such as the European Working Time Directive, tighter legal protection for part-time workers and the legal right to paternity leave
- important measures were introduced to support workplace democracy, such as the European *works council*.

McGregor, D (1906–1964): an American psychologist whose book *The Human Side of Enterprise* (first published 1960; Penguin, 1987) popularised his view that managers can be grouped into two types: *Theory X* and *Theory Y*. McGregor had researched into the attitudes of managers towards their employees. He found that the majority of managers assumed that their workers were work-shy and motivated primarily by money; he termed this type of manager Theory X. The alternative, minority, view was that workers look to gain satisfaction from employment, and therefore evidence of low achievement levels should make managers question whether they were providing the right work environment. In other words, the Theory Y manager's first assumption should be that the blame for poor workforce performance lies with management rather than with the workers themselves.

The Theory X manager assumes:
- workers are motivated by money
- unless supervised closely, workers will under-perform
- that workers will only respect a tough, decisive boss
- that workers have no wish or ability to help make decisions.

The Theory Y manager assumes:
- workers seek job satisfaction no less than managers
- that, if trusted, workers will behave responsibly
- that low performance is due to dull work or poor management
- staff have a desire and the right to contribute to decisions.

McGregor's use of the easily memorable X and Y has made his work widely used in management training. This is despite the fact that it is largely derived from other theories. Theory X is derived from the work of *F W Taylor* and from *Adam Smith*'s notion of 'economic man'. Theory Y stems clearly from **Mayo**'s human relations approach and **Maslow**'s work on human needs. Nevertheless, just the introduction to *The Human Side of Enterprise* will give the reader a clear understanding that McGregor's writing has much more to contribute than just the memorable theories X and Y.

machine tools: the capital equipment needed to make the machines used in manufacturing. In other words, not the robot welder on the car **production line**, but the machinery to make robot welders.

macroeconomic: a term indicating the study of a whole economy and the way it interacts (macro means 'large'). The main elements within the macroeconomy are firms, consumers, the government and other countries, which depend on each other in a way described as the **circular flow of national income**. The macroeconomy is the sum or aggregate of all the elements within it. Thus the **sales revenue** of an individual firm is a part of the microeconomy; by adding up the sales revenue of all producers (their aggregate income), the size of the macroeconomy can be measured. The study of the macroeconomy leads on to consideration of macroeconomic policy. As there are areas of macroeconomics that are still poorly understood, policy prescriptions are often controversial.

macroeconomic policy aims to bring about desirable outcomes by influencing the economy as a whole. The objective might be to raise the rate of economic growth or to make the economy more stable, by making adjustments in the level of **aggregate demand**. This could be done by making changes in:

- *fiscal policy*, using tax changes or government expenditure changes. Reducing taxes and increasing expenditure will increase aggregate demand and tend to stimulate the economy. Provided there are some unemployed resources, output will increase
- *monetary policy*, using interest rate changes to influence levels of spending on investment and consumer goods, will also affect aggregate demand and activity in the economy as a whole
- *exchange rate policy* may also be used because a falling exchange rate may stimulate demand for exports and discourage imports. Alternatively, a rising exchange rate may make imports cheaper and tend to reduce inflationary pressures.

In all macroeconomic policy decisions, it is important to consider how close the economy is to **full-capacity output**. **Expansionary policies** used when the economy is close to full-capacity output and there are supply constraints will encourage inflation to accelerate. Equally, if **unemployment** is largely structural in nature, expansionary policies will not help. They may defeat the objectives which the government is aiming for. In these circumstances **supply-side policies** may provide a more appropriate strategy.

macroeconomic stabilisation: market economies experience **economic cycles**, in which output fluctuates and unemployment and falling incomes can become a problem. Governments use macroeconomic policies to stabilise the economy, attempting to avoid sharp fluctuations. Two types of policy can be identified:

- *Automatic stabilisers* may be in operation. As incomes rise, tax revenues rise, reducing the growth of aggregate demand in the upswing of the economic cycle. Similarly, unemployment will be falling and government expenditure on benefits will fall too.
- *Discretionary policies* allow governments to make an explicit decision to raise or lower tax rates or government expenditure. During a recession, they may choose to cut taxes and raise spending levels, as the Conservative government did in 1991.

The main difficulty with stabilisation policies is that it is not always easy for governments or central banks to gauge the precise amount of change which will have the desired effect. Statistical errors and time lags in the operation of policies make for uncertainty.

maintenance factors: another term for *hygiene factors*.

make-or-buy decision: the management choice between buying in components or making them in-house.

managed exchange rate: a floating exchange rate may still be managed to ensure that day-to-day fluctuations are kept to a minimum. The central bank buys when the exchange rate is falling and sells when it is rising, so as to keep the exchange rate from deviating too far from its current market level. (See also *fixed exchange rate*.)

management buy-out (MBO): when the managers of a business buy out the shareholders, thereby buying ownership and control of the firm. It is hoped that this will give the management the incentive it needs to maximise the productiveness of the organisation. Many MBOs involve buying a single business unit from a large parent company. This gives the added benefit of separating the firm from its potentially *bureaucratic* (and therefore high overhead) parent.

However, some MBOs have been financed in a risky manner, with high debt levels. If the business is successful, the managers stand to make millions as the value of their shareholding soars. Failure, however, may lose not only the managers' investment but also the workforce's livelihood. So whereas the managers are taking a risk which may pay them handsomely, the workforce stands to gain nothing, but may lose everything.

management by objectives (MBO): a method of coordinating and motivating a workforce by dividing the company's overall goal into specific targets for each division, department, manager and possibly employee. Peter Drucker, in his book *The Practice of Management* (Heinemann, 1955), put forward the view that management by objectives is the only effective way of delegating authority in a large firm. He urged that targets should be agreed after discussion, not imposed from above. A *Theory Y* management would be expected to take the former approach; *Theory X* managers would impose targets from above.

management consultant: an individual or firm which specialises in giving independent advice to companies. The advice may relate to internal management issues such as *delayering* or *restructuring*, or on divisional issues such as obtaining better production technology or tackling a marketing problem. Management consultants are expected to have greater breadth of experience than the company's own management, since they are likely to have tackled the same problems before at a different firm. No less important is that the consultant has no *vested interest* in ensuring that one department triumphs over another in a reorganisation.

management information system (MIS): computer software that gathers financial, production, stock and other numerical data to provide an up-to-date record of a firm's current position.

management succession: the issue of who will take over the key positions in a company when the current directors retire. This can be a very important issue for family businesses, should there be no obvious successor. It can also worry the shareholders in a large *public limited company (PLC)* that has been dominated by one or two people. Such worries might lead to a flagging share price that would leave the firm vulnerable to a *takeover bid*.

M

manager: an employee with authority over a number of subordinates and the responsibility to plan and monitor short- and medium-term strategies.

managerial economies: see *internal economies of scale*

M and A: see *mergers and acquisitions (M and A)*

manual worker: an employee who works with his or her hands, usually in a factory context. Manual workers are often subdivided into three categories:
- skilled, e.g. welders and qualified electricians
- semi-skilled, e.g. van drivers and production line workers
- unskilled, e.g. cleaners and road sweepers.

manufacturing resource planning (MRP II) is a computer-driven, universal planning system for the whole of a company's production processes. It is designed to translate sales forecasts (or actual orders) into purchasing requirements for raw materials and components, factory production schedules, individual work instructions and completion deadlines. Complex as this sounds, it only underestimates the real task. Most firms will have many different product lines and many different orders from a variety of customers. The MRP II system must coordinate and schedule all of these in such a way as to maximise **capacity utilisation**. If it is impossible to produce all the orders within the desired delivery deadlines, the computer will show the overtime requirement, or warn that customers must be alerted to delivery delays.

mapping means selecting the key variables that differentiate the brands within a market and then plotting the position of each one. Usually this is done on a two-dimensional diagram as below. Here, ice-cream brands are plotted against the key criteria of customer age and product price. By contrast, the criteria for cider might be trendy or traditional and strong or standard (alcoholic strength). Brand mapping enables a firm to identify any gaps or niches in the market that are unfilled.

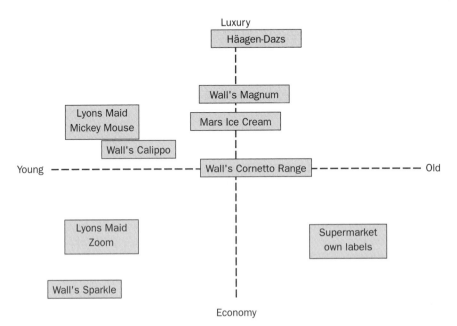

Brand mapping for ice cream (based on authors' estimates)

margin: a commonly used shorthand way of referring to a *profit margin*, i.e. the proportionate difference between revenue and cost.

margin of safety: see *safety margin*

marginal analysis: economic theory analyses decisions taken at the margin. That is to say, people usually decide not whether to do something at all but whether to do a little more or a little less. They may produce, or consume, more or less. Producing a little more will bring in marginal revenue and have a *marginal cost*. The profit-maximising producer will carry on producing up to the point where these two are equal. This is economically efficient because the price a consumer is prepared to pay for that last unit is exactly equal to the real resource cost of producing it.

marginal cost: the change in the total cost of a product or service which results from changing output by one unit more (or less). In the short run, only the *variable cost* can be altered, so marginal cost in the short run is entirely variable cost. Marginal costing is an alternative term for *contribution costing*.

marginal cost pricing: an item may be priced at its marginal cost, thus ensuring that the price is equal to the *opportunity cost* of the resources foregone in producing it. The drawback is that the price may fail to reflect some of the fixed costs of production and so lead to losses being made.

marginal propensity to consume (MPC): the proportion of an increase in income which will be spent on consumption. It is important within the Keynesian model of the macroeconomy because, along with the *marginal rate of tax* and the *marginal propensity to import* (i.e. the *marginal rate of leakage*), it helps to determine the size of the *multiplier*. The higher the marginal propensity to consume, the larger the multiplier will be.

marginal propensity to import: that proportion of an increase in income which is spent on imports.

marginal propensity to save: that proportion of an increase in income which is saved.

marginal rate of leakage: that proportion of an increase in income which leaks out of the circular flow of national income in the form of savings, taxes and imports. The marginal propensity to consume and the marginal rate of leakage together are equal to one by definition. So a high marginal rate of leakage will be associated with a small multiplier.

marginal rate of tax: the proportion of an increase in income which is taken in tax. This may be used as a macro- or a microeconomic concept.

marginal social benefit: includes all the extra benefits which result from an increase in the output of a particular product, whether they are felt by the person who bought the product or by some third party. It thus takes in any *positive externalities*. If you spend money on extra clothes, you get a marginal private benefit from feeling good in them. There is a marginal social benefit to anyone else who appreciates your appearance. The marginal social benefit of devoting additional land to sheep farming in mountain areas includes the private benefit of the meat and wool produced and also the benefit to people who like to see the countryside farmed in the traditional way. In the diagram overleaf, Q shows the social optimum equilibrium. The existence of social benefits indicates that the free market equilibrium would be at a lower level of output and sales. There would be *underconsumption* in the case of the extra clothes, and underproduction in the case of the meat and wool. (See also *welfare gain*.)

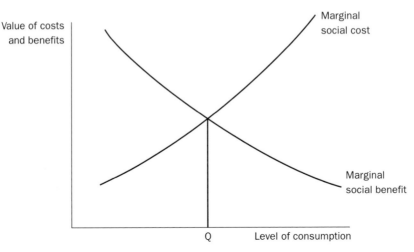

Marginal social benefit and cost

marginal social cost includes all the costs of producing one more unit of output, whether they be the costs of production incurred by the business or the **external costs**, which may be borne by third parties. So the marginal social cost of producing more electricity in coal-fired power stations includes the cost of the coal and other inputs and also the cost to people in the neighbourhood of the increased atmospheric pollution. This may show up in health problems or any other problem caused by pollution. Social cost will exceed private costs and there will be overproduction at the free-market equilibrium output level, which will be greater than Q in the diagram above.

Marginal social costs and benefits can be compared diagrammatically. If output is below the level Q, the marginal social benefits of extra consumption would outweigh the marginal social costs. From the point of view of society, it would make sense for output to be increased.

market: all the buyers and all the sellers of a product and the way in which they are able to interact. A market may be located in a particular place or it may merely have a way for buyers and sellers to communicate. The market will allocate resources among competing buyers. The interaction of buyers and sellers will lead to an **equilibrium price** at which **market clearing** will take place. Markets will be created wherever there are people who have a product which potential buyers want. In recent years markets have developed in internet banking and new kinds of recreational drugs. Some markets are generally left free to operate according to market forces, others are often regulated or controlled by governments. (Try making a list of markets in each category.)

When considering entering a market for the first time, a business must consider:

- the consumers
- the competitors
- the distribution outlets.

The main ways of measuring a market are by volume (the number of units sold) and by value (the money spent on all the goods sold).

market analysis: breaking down a market into its component parts to find out key information, such as:
- the consumer profile
- how the market can be segmented
- the growth sectors
- the key competitors.

market-based pricing: a collective term for pricing methods that are based on market rather than cost considerations. (See **pricing methods**.)

market capitalisation: the value placed on a company by the **stock market**. It is the number of shares issued multiplied by their market price. It is important to realise that this is only one way of valuing a company and there are others based on asset values. A **takeover bid** is another way.

market clearing: the process by which price changes until the amount which sellers wish to sell is exactly equal to the amount which buyers demand. If this process does not occur, then there is said to be market failure. The market clears at the equilibrium price, by definition. Situations in which the market does not clear are known as **excess demand** or **excess supply**, depending on the circumstances.

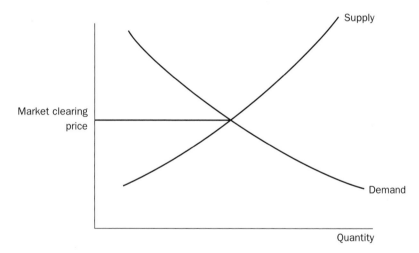

The market clears at the equilibrium price

market concentration: see **concentration ratio**

market conditions: the factors outside the control of an individual business that affect the size and competitiveness of the market in which it operates.

market demand: see **demand** and **demand curve**

market development: a marketing strategy based on launching existing products into new markets, e.g. Innocent Smoothies in China (see **Ansoff's matrix**). Attention to market development is particularly important in international markets because businesses will be exploring markets where brand recognition is limited. It is sometimes necessary to combine both market and product development in order to succeed. Extensive market research will be important.

market distortions occur whenever prices fail to reflect marginal social costs and benefits. They may be caused by *externalities*, taxes or monopoly. For example, when a firm with monopoly power restricts output and raises its prices, consumers choose to buy less of the product than they would if its price was roughly equal to the long-run average cost of producing it. Underconsumption results.

market dominance: the extent to which a business dominates sales, pricing and distribution within its market. This means that it will be a *price leader* and all other producers in the field will tend to adapt their decisions to the behaviour of the dominant firm. This is likely under *oligopoly* conditions, where the dominant firm has a large market share. Competition will be rather limited. This may be because of significant economies of scale, such that the market is not large enough to make more than a few producers profitable (as with wide-bodied aircraft). Or the firm may have important patents, as with the biggest pharmaceutical manufacturers. In order to continue to dominate the market, a firm may have to put a lot of resources into research so as to maintain its advantage. A highly dominant firm such as Wall's ice cream may be able to manipulate the market, perhaps by stifling product innovation or keeping prices unnecessarily high.

market economy is an economy which allows markets to determine the allocation of resources through *supply* and *demand*.

PROS:
- automatic: no need for regulation
- offers freedom of choice
- efficiently allocates resources; keeps costs down
- leads to greater economic growth

CONS:
- means those with the most money have greatest power
- leads to inequality of income
- the price of a good may not reflect its cost to society; these costs are called *externalities*
- monopolisation within marketplaces can lead to inefficiency and exploitation

The main advantage of relying on the *market mechanism* is that it leads to greater efficiency, encouraging *productive efficiency* and *allocative efficiency*. However, because markets possess disadvantages, in particular they tend to exploit the weakest members of society, they are always modified or regulated in some way by governments. The extent to which this regulation takes place is a political decision. (See also *mixed economy*.)

market failure occurs when market imperfections lead to an allocation of resources which is less efficient than it might be. For example:
- *Imperfect competition* can lead to firms not striving to minimise costs and prices, especially if buyers have imperfect information.
- Some goods may not be produced at all unless the government steps in – these are *public goods* such as the legal system.
- *Merit goods* such as education and health care may be consumed in smaller quantities than would be most effective from society's point of view, if available only through the market. (See *underconsumption*.)
- *Externalities* may lead to high *social costs* which affect third parties, who are not producers or consumers of the product.

- The market may fail to clear, as is the case where large numbers of people are unemployed; this may be partly due to labour immobilities.

Government intervention can correct market failures but does not always do so in the most efficient way due to *government failure*.

market forces are the forces of supply and demand in the marketplace. When demand is growing, other things being equal, the price will rise. If supply is rising but demand is constant, prices will tend to be pushed downwards. Market forces lead to price changes which reflect underlying changes in demand and supply. They influence the *allocation of resources* so that production is in line with consumer demand and reflects the real resource cost of production.

market imperfections come in many forms, each of which is a departure from the conditions of *perfect competition*. The main ones are:
- few firms in the market
- differentiated products
- imperfect information
- immobile factors of production.

marketing: the all-embracing function that links a company with customer tastes to get the right product to the right place at the right time. Marketing decisions are made through the *marketing model*, based on the findings of *market research*, and carried out through the *marketing mix*. At all stages in the marketing process, the firm needs to work closely with the production department and *research and development (R&D)*, to ensure that what is promised is delivered.

marketing activities are all the actions an organisation can take to achieve its marketing objectives. These would include *market research*, product *mapping*, *market positioning* and carrying out the different elements of the *marketing mix* – product, price, promotions and place. In the past, marketing activities were conducted differently among not-for-profit compared with profit-making organisations. For example, direct sales techniques might be used by double-glazing companies but not by charities. Today charities, *pressure groups* and even political parties use aggressive techniques such as telesales and direct mail because of their proven effectiveness.

marketing ethics concerns the rights and wrongs of marketing. Issues arise in relation to truth in advertising and the wisdom of promoting products that may be harmful. There are legal restrictions that ensure product safety and advertising standards to prevent deliberate lies. But is it right to advertise products that may be harmful, e.g. fatty processed foods? Some say that the primary concern for the business is profit. Others promote the ideas of *corporate responsibility* and *social responsibility*.

marketing functions: these are the main areas in which marketing activity helps to achieve the marketing objectives/principles, such as:
- managing changes in technology, competition and consumer taste
- coordinating marketing with production planning and control
- establishing a distinctive identity for a product (partly through *branding*) or company (through the *corporate identity*)
- planning, coordinating and monitoring the *marketing mix*.

M

marketing mix: the main variables through which a firm carries out its marketing strategy, often known as the four Ps:

- product (including range of pack sizes and/or flavours or colours)
- price (long-term *pricing strategy* and *pricing methods*)
- promotion (*branding*, *advertising*, *packaging* and *sales promotion*)
- place (choosing *distribution channels* and seeking shop distribution).

Textbooks tend to treat each of the elements of the mix as of equal importance. Few marketing companies would agree. The most important element of the mix is the product, which needs to be designed to meet the requirements of those within the *target market*. If this process has been achieved successfully (probably through extensive *market research*), the other three elements of the mix become clear. The price must be suited to the pockets of the target market and to the image of the product. The promotion will be through the media that they watch or read, while the place should be the shops visited by those types of people.

The only one of these elements that is outside the company's control is place, for obtaining shop distribution is a very difficult task in crowded modern marketplaces. No retailers have spare shelving, so in order for your product to gain distribution, another product will probably have to be removed from the shelves. Needless to say, every manufacturer is fighting hard to keep its distribution as high as possible, so it is never easy to gain or to keep hold of high distribution levels.

marketing model: a framework for making marketing decisions in a scientific manner. It is derived from *F W Taylor*'s method of basing decisions on scientifically gathered research evidence.

The model has five stages:

1 Set the marketing objective based on the company's *objectives*. For example, if the corporate *goal* is *diversification*, the specific marketing objective may be to launch a product into a new market that can achieve minimum sales of £5 million within 18 months.

2 Gather data: this will require the collection of *quantitative data* and *qualitative data* about the market's size, competitive structure, distribution pattern and consumer attitudes.

3 Form *hypotheses*, theories about how best to achieve the objective. For example, a producer of canned food might consider whether to:
- move into the frozen-food market
- move into the chilled-food market
- take the more radical route of moving into petfoods.

4 Test the hypotheses: this may be done solely through *market research* or, more thoroughly, by *test marketing* new product ideas. After the results are evaluated, a decision can be reached on how to proceed.

5 Control and review: making decisions is only one part of the marketing function; implementing them is no less important. The means of implementation will be via the *marketing mix*. The effectiveness of the distribution, pricing or promotion policies must be controlled, with careful conclusions drawn from the success or failure of the project.

The marketing model

Having completed the task, the managers must look towards new objectives. So the process begins again.

marketing objectives are the *goals* the marketing department must achieve in order to help a company achieve its overall objectives. Marketing objectives may include:

- halting a decline in market share
- making a brand's image younger
- boosting the awareness of a brand that has faded from consumers' memories.

marketing plan: a report detailing a firm's *marketing objectives* and *marketing strategy*, including: costings, forecast results and contingency plans. The stages of constructing a marketing plan are as follows:

1   Conduct a marketing audit to ensure full knowledge of the firm's marketing assets. This could be supplemented by a *SWOT analysis* (identifying the firm's marketing strengths, weaknesses, opportunities and threats).
2   Set clear objectives for the coming year based on *goals* for three to five years ahead. These might include targets for sales, *market share*, distribution levels and brand image ratings.
3   Devise a strategy for achieving the objectives that operates within a defined budget and covers: new product development, new product launches and going brands, and looking at a range of promotional stratagies.

marketing strategy: a medium- to long-term plan for meeting *marketing objectives*. The word 'strategy' suggests a carefully thought-out, integrated plan. It should set out the balance of marketing activity between new and existing products – with carefully costed budgets. The strategy is likely to be fully researched and then implemented through the *marketing mix* – the four Ps of product, price, place and promotion. A successful marketing strategy is one that achieves the objectives without going over budget. (See also *marketing plan*.)

market leadership refers to the way in which a dominant firm may be able to lead the market in setting prices and sometimes by determining the design and quality of the product. This is most likely to happen where there is an *oligopoly*, with one firm which has a particularly large *market share*.

market-led pricing: setting a price for your product based upon what the market can bear. This contrasts with producer-led pricing methods such as cost-plus. Market-led pricing will be particularly important in markets where **product differentiation** is low and therefore **price elasticity** is high.

market manipulation occurs when companies influence markets to make them less than perfectly competitive. Firms attempt to manipulate markets in a number of ways, for instance by **collusion** with other producers, or by cross-subsidising one market by another in order to force out the competition. Even **advertising** could be said to represent manipulation, if it makes consumers willing to pay a premium price for a good which is not really any different from one produced by other firms.

market mapping: see *mapping*

market mechanism: the operation of **demand** and **supply**, which together determine price. If the market mechanism works smoothly, it should allocate **factors of production** in the most efficient way to produce those goods which consumers want in the right amount and at the right time. In practice there is bound to be a degree of **market failure**, especially since there is a time lag between changes in demand and changes in supply.

market niche: a gap in the range of products or services offered within a market. Having identified that such a gap exists, a business must decide whether the niche is large enough to be profitable and, if so, how best to fill it. (See **niche marketing**.)

market orientation: the extent to which a firm's strategic thinking stems from looking outwards to consumer tastes and competitive pressures. The main alternative is **production orientation**, where the firm looks inward to its own production needs and limitations. For many years, British firms were criticised for their lack of market orientation. However, there is a danger that market orientation results in lost power and status for engineers and production managers, which might affect long-term technological competitiveness.

market penetration (1): a marketing strategy based on building on a firm's strength with its existing products in their existing market. (See **Ansoff's matrix**.)

market penetration (2): a pricing strategy for a new product based on a desire to achieve high sales volume and high **market share**, perhaps with the effect of discouraging competitors from entering the market. Penetration pricing would mean setting the price relatively low, thereby accepting low **gross profit** margins with the expectation that the high turnover will allow overheads to be covered.

PROS: • very useful if the market is one in which customers build up **brand loyalty** (prices can be pushed up later)

• sensible if you have only a small technological edge, because competitors will be arriving soon

CONS: • loses the opportunity to charge higher prices to those willing to pay them for being first or innovators

• once a low-price image has been established in the customers' mind, it is hard to shift and may always be associated with low quality

market period: the period of time in which the quantity supplied cannot be altered. For example, the quantity of a crop product such as potatoes cannot be altered until the next season. This means that supply is perfectly inelastic, i.e. the quantity is fixed. The length of the market period will vary from product to product. For some manufactured products it will barely exist.

market positioning: where a manufacturer positions a brand within a marketplace, in terms of image, pricing and distribution. *Up-market* or *down-market*? Young and trendy or old and established? For specialists or for the general public? Such a decision is fundamental to the long-term *marketing strategy* of a product. (See *mapping*.)

market power: a firm may have power over its market. This means that to some degree the seller is able to determine the price charged. Market power develops when:
- a seller is able to distinguish what is offered for sale from that which is on offer from other producers (*differentiated product*)
- there is little competition from other sellers
- there is a *monopsony* buyer which has more influence in the market than the seller does.

A person with scarce skills which are in strong demand will have some power in the *labour* market because buyers of those skills are competing to hire the few people who have them.

Marketing strategies can be used to increase market power and reduce the threat from competing products. Market power opens up the possibility of being able to determine the price at which the product sells and is a feature of *oligopoly*, where a small number of firms each have a significant *market share*. The *Competition Commission* exists to reduce market power wherever it threatens to work against the interests of the consumer.

Several sources of market power can be seen in the position of the large supermarket chains. Typically, they have market power in relation to suppliers because they can negotiate very favourable prices. Most of their suppliers will be operating in much more competitive markets, being relatively small-scale producers. They also have some market power in relation to consumers because many of the latter have only limited choices about where they can shop. Market power can develop wherever competing substitutes are hard to find.

market price is the one at which the demand for a product exactly matches its 'supply'. It is therefore also known as the 'market clearing' price (labelled MP on the diagram).

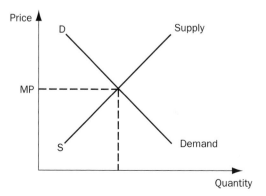

market research: the process of gathering **primary data** and **secondary data** on the buying habits, lifestyle, usage and attitudes of actual and potential customers. The intention is to gather evidence that can enable marketing and production decisions to be made in a more scientific way than would otherwise be possible. Most large consumer goods firms would agree with Sherlock Holmes (in *Scandal in Bohemia*), 'It is a capital mistake to theorise before one has data.'

Market research can be subdivided as follows:

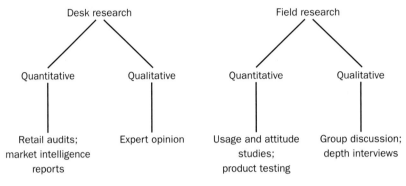

Market research process

market saturation occurs when all those who want a product already have one. If the product is a **durable** (such as a freezer), demand will dry up until wear and tear creates a replacement market. With **consumables**, market saturation should not result in falling sales, but will inevitably prevent sales growth.

market segmentation: analysing a market to identify the different types of consumer. By matching the consumer categories to the types of product on offer, an unfilled **market niche** may emerge. The potential profitability of filling such a gap can then be assessed. The main ways in which a market can be segmented are:

* demographically, e.g. by age, social class or sex
* psychographically (by attitudes and tastes), e.g. trendy versus staid, or home-loving versus adventurous
* geographically, by region.

market share: the percentage of all the sales within a market that are held by one brand or company. This can be measured by volume (units sold) or by value (the revenue generated). Analysing trends in market share is important for a firm because it shows its position in relation to the market as a whole. It may not be good enough, for example, to have a 5 per cent sales increase if the market is rising at 10 per cent, as market share is being lost. The 5 per cent sales increase may boost profits this year, but if the market becomes highly price competitive as it reaches **maturity**, the firm's products may not be strong enough to survive.

market share maximisation: a possible goal for firms, which in some cases may be more important than **profit maximisation**. Economists usually assume that all firms strive to maximise profits and in some cases this is undoubtedly broadly true. However, increased market share can bring many benefits:

* firms may improve their position relative to that of a particular competitor
* they may establish a reputation which is conducive to long-run profitability and survival

- they may increase their *market power*
- managers may relish the personal power and influence that comes with a substantial market share.

market-sharing agreement: a *restrictive practice* in which a number of firms in an industry agree to allow each a profitable part of the total market. This is known as *collusion* and is generally illegal as it means that price competition is being suspended (forcing consumers to pay excessive prices). A market-sharing agreement is only likely if supply is dominated by a small number of firms (an *oligopoly*), and if it is hard for new competitors to enter the market.

market size: the total sales of all the producers within a marketplace, measured either by volume (units sold) or by value (the revenue generated). This information is needed to:
- assess whether the market is big enough to be worth entering
- calculate the *market share* held by your own products and brands
- identify whether the market is expanding or contracting.

Markets grow when:
- new technologies are making it possible to reduce prices
- tastes are changing in favour of the product
- incomes are rising (if the product has income-elastic demand)
- competing substitutes are becoming more expensive.

market standing: the reputation of a firm amongst its suppliers, distributors and customers. If its market standing is high, a firm can feel confident that its new products will get *product trial*.

market structure refers to the number of competing firms in the market. There may be:
- *perfect competition* or something resembling it in many respects, as with many farm products
- *monopolistic competition*, for example hairdressers
- *oligopoly*, as with supermarkets
- *monopoly*, as with water supply.

These are theoretical structures and in practice, a much fuzzier picture emerges. For example, it is possible to argue about whether the computer hardware industry is an oligopoly or whether it really has important elements of monopolistic competition.

market system: the form of market organisation in which the decisions of firms and households are made on the basis of the market forces of supply and demand. A *market economy* will allocate resources largely on this basis, although some government intervention and regulation will also be important and will influence market conditions.

market testing is an investigation by a *public sector* business of the price that *private sector* firms would charge to supply a service. As a consequence, it might contract private companies to supply services such as accounting (and, by implication, make its own accountants redundant).

market value is the price determined by *supply* and *demand*. Sellers often say things like, 'My motorbike is worth £1000', but when they come to sell it the bike realises only £400, which is its true 'value'. In the harsh world of economics, goods have no intrinsic value; in other words it makes no difference how much it costs to produce them, their true value (market value) has to be related to the amount people are willing to pay for them.

Marx, K (1818–1883) perceived capitalism as one stage in economic development, because it would lead to revolution and the collective ownership of the means of production. Workers would be paid according to their needs rather than their market power and capitalists (owners of capital) would no longer be able to exploit their employees by paying them less than the value of what they produced.

The development of communism in Russia (from 1917) and later in Eastern Europe and China (from 1948) was based on Marx's thinking. In all cases communist revolutions created much more egalitarian societies than those which preceded them. But they also experienced rather slow economic growth rates. Since 1989 only China, Cuba, North Korea and Vietnam retained communist governments and even they are becoming far more market oriented.

Maslow, A (1908–1970): an American psychologist whose work on human needs has had great impact upon management theorists. Best known for his work on the *hierarchy of needs*.

mass marketing targets a firm's advertising and promotional spending at the whole market, not at a particular segment. This might be because the whole audience has to be addressed, e.g. with government road safety advertising. Most firms prefer *niche marketing*.

mass production: the system devised by Henry Ford that turned raw materials into finished product in a continuously moving, highly mechanised process. Mass production's great strength was its high *productivity*, but this relied on manufacturing vast numbers of an identical product. This was epitomised in Henry Ford's famous phrase about his Model T, 'You can have any colour you want… as long as it's black.' As modern markets have become increasingly segmented, mass production has given way to *lean production* or *flexible specialisation*.

matrix management: the willingness to organise the management of a task along lines that cut across normal departmental boundaries. A new product development team might be formed from an engineer, a research chemist, a marketing manager and a designer. This means that each team member can end up with two bosses: their department boss and the project leader. This has the potential to cause problems, though the Japanese seem to use this system effectively.

PROS: • ensures that projects are better coordinated than with four departments meeting occasionally
• if many different project teams are organised, it gives more people an opportunity to use their abilities

CONS: • individuals may suffer if both bosses make heavy demands on them
• there is a failure to provide the clear line of accountability that is present when everyone has just one boss

mature economies are those which have been fully industrialised for some time and are now experiencing a shift of resources into the service sector. The USA and the UK are examples of economies where the manufacturing sector has tended to shrink while a number of services have shown above-average growth rates. Financial services, tourism, health care and a variety of personal and professional services have all been growing over the long term. (See also *deindustrialisation*.)

maturity is the peak sales period of the **product life cycle**. It is likely to be a phase of fierce competition from new producers attracted to the market during the growth stage. This may cause a shake-out in which the less successful withdraw in the face of heavy losses. The survivors could then enjoy a highly profitable decline stage. Alternatively, mature products may be relaunched in an **extension strategy** designed to rejuvenate and thereby postpone sales decline.

Mayo, E (1880–1949): Elton Mayo was a follower of **F W Taylor**, whose experiments led him to conclude that scientific management could not explain key aspects of people's behaviour at work. Many of his findings derived from his direction of research studies at a factory at Hawthorne, USA, from which stemmed the phrase the **Hawthorne effect**.

MBO: see either **management buy-out (MBO)** or **management by objectives (MBO)**

mean: see **arithmetic average (mean)**

means-tested benefits are social security payments which are available only to those whose incomes are below a certain level; for example income support.

measure of central tendency: an attempt to describe a **frequency distribution** in a single measure. There are three main measures: **mean**, **median** and **mode**.

media advertising: paying for advertising space or time in national, regional or local media. Media advertising aimed at consumers is known as above-the-line marketing.

median: a **measure of central tendency** which divides the distribution into two equal parts. If the items in the distribution are ranked in ascending order, the **median** is the middle item. One advantage of the median is that it is not affected by extreme values. A disadvantage is that it gives findings that are biased towards the most numerous and (perhaps) away from the most important.

media planning: the process of selecting media to advertise to your target market as cost-effectively as possible. This function is usually carried out by an advertising agency. It involves gathering research data, deciding between television, newspapers, magazines, cinema, radio, posters or the internet and selecting cost-effective approaches.

mediation: another term for **conciliation**.

mentor: an experienced and trusted adviser to a new recruit; in effect, an appointed father-figure. This is a modern development of **human relations** theory that ensures that all recruits have a senior figure they can turn to for advice. The mentor will keep any comments or complaints confidential, and could therefore be a more effective adviser than the recruit's boss.

merchandising: visiting retail outlets to ensure that a company's products are displayed in as attractive and prominent a way as possible. Merchandisers might offer special display stands or shelves to retailers.

merchant bank: a form of specialised commercial bank that performs a variety of banking functions, although rarely those directly concerned with the public. Their most important functions today are as issuing houses, and as advisers to businesses, particularly on matters concerned with **mergers** and **takeovers**. As issuing houses, they advise firms on the right time and how to raise capital on the **Stock Exchange** or the **Alternative Investment Market (AIM)**. They also act as underwriters to the issue by guaranteeing to buy stock which is not immediately sold at the time of issue. In recent years, many merchant banks have become part of larger banking **conglomerates**, but their names live on. Employees of Hambros, Rothschilds, Lazards and Schroders are often seen on television offering expert advice on economic and financial matters. Unfortunately, many merchant banks proved guilty of incompetence and greed in the run-up to the 2007 **credit crunch**.

merger: an agreement between the managements and shareholders of two companies of approximately equal size to bring both firms together under a common board of directors. (See also **takeover** and **takeover bid**.)

mergers and acquisitions (M and A) is a collective term used by American-influenced City institutions to denote the general area of corporate **mergers** and **takeovers**. Many **merchant banks** have M and A departments that can charge substantial fees for advising companies on how to win or to defend against **takeover bids**.

merit goods are provided by the government for those who are deemed to need them. Examples include health care, education and social services. The logic for government provision is that there is likely to be **market failure** in that there will be underproduction and **underconsumption** of these goods and services if decisions are based on market forces. Many of the people who would benefit from health care and education would have insufficient income to buy the services for themselves. Yet it is in the interests of society as a whole that the population have good health and education. Government provision ensures that everyone likely to benefit does so.

merit pay: a form of bonus payment received by employees considered to have performed at a high standard during a year or half-year. To evaluate who deserves a merit pay award, **performance appraisal** is often used.

PROS: • merit pay is a reward system that can apply to all employees (whereas com-mission, for example, will only be received by those involved in direct selling)

CONS: • often involves tiny sums: a 5 per cent bonus may seem poor reward for out-standing work
• offers scope for mistrust and misunderstanding if some workers suspect there has been favouritism in the allocation of the bonuses

me-too product: a new brand that is largely an imitation of a successful existing one. Usually me-toos struggle to get distribution in shops and are looked down on by customers, so they can only gain sales if they sell at an unprofitably large discount to the price of the original product. Occasionally, though, a firm with an exceptionally wide and powerful distribution network can make me-toos more successful than the original. Wall's Cornetto was a me-too of Lyon's Maid's King Cone, and Magnum a me-too of the Häagen-Dazs Stick Bar. In both cases, consumers became so familiar with the Wall's product that its origin was soon forgotten.

mezzanine debt is a source of business finance that is halfway between debt and equity. Like a loan, mezzanine finance pays a fixed interest rate. Unlike most loans, however, mezzanine finance is not secured to asset-backed collateral. Therefore it represents a high-risk loan. When sold on to the **Stock Exchange**, such a debt is often called a **junk bond**.

microeconomics is the study of how markets work. It provides a theoretical framework for the way firms and *factors of production* operate. Taken together, the workings of small-scale (micro) markets lead to the macroeconomy.

micromarketing means focusing on the variations between *market segments* and niches so as to communicate with individual consumers more effectively. Mass advertising, e.g. using TV, reaches large audiences but cannot adapt its approach to fit market variations. There are various ways of targeting small markets and focusing on individual consumer needs and preferences:

- customised pricing policies allow individual retail outlets within a large retail chain to adapt to local market conditions
- new communication and distribution technologies enable retailers to cater for smaller niche markets through direct sales
- new store formats, e.g. specialist outlets, enable retailers to focus on specific markets.

(See also *long tail* and *niche markets*.)

middleman: the *agent* or wholesaler who brings together buyers and sellers. It is often assumed that middlemen serve little function, but merely add to the retail prices of items they deal in. Some middlemen could be regarded as parasitic (such as arms dealers), but most are fulfilling the normal *wholesaling* function of breaking bulk.

milking a product: maximising the profit from a brand, usually by pushing its price up as far as possible without forcing regular purchasers to switch to another brand. This high price level is likely to discourage new users from starting to buy the product, therefore the brand's *product life cycle* will be shortened. So milking a product implies short-term profit maximisation, even at the cost of the brand's long-term prospects.

The *Boston matrix* shows the situation in which a firm might milk a product. If the firm has two brands with a high *market share*, one in a growth sector and another in a declining sector, the correct strategy would be to milk the *cash cow* and use the funds to support the 'rising star'.

minimising waste means keeping production costs down as much as possible. This could mean, literally, ensuring that the quantity of inputs used is kept to the lowest possible level but it can also mean organising production in ways that save time. Or it can mean finding the lowest cost suppliers of inputs. *Lean production* minimises waste by ensuring that stocks of inputs are kept down, saving storage costs.

minimum efficient scale (MES): the lowest level of output at which costs can be kept at their minimum. In the diagram overleaf this is the lowest output at which average total cost is minimised. For most goods, efficient production is possible across a range of output levels, so the average total cost has a flat-bottomed U-shape and the minimum efficient scale is on the extreme left of the bottom of the curve.

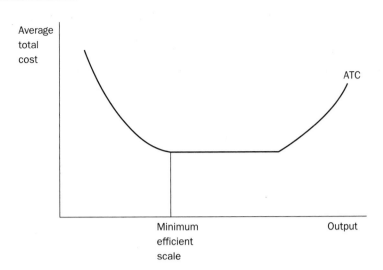

Minimum efficient scale

minimum wage: the minimum rate of pay per hour which must by law be paid by employers. This was introduced in 1999 at £3.60, rising to £5.80 in 2009. The rate for those aged 18–21 is £4.83 and for those aged 16–17, £3.57.

The impact of the minimum wage varies greatly from one region to another. Few employers will be able to hire even unskilled people in London at the minimum wage anyway but it may have more impact in less prosperous regions. The objective is to prevent employers from paying very low wages.

Some economists have argued that a minimum wage will reduce employment, possibly leading to an excess supply of labour (see diagram). However, there is no evidence yet that the introduction of the minimum wage in the UK has significantly reduced employment. It may give employers an incentive to provide better training.

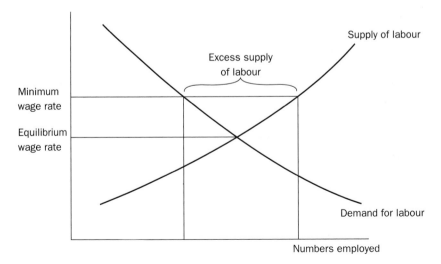

Minimum wage rate may reduce employment

Mintel, standing for Marketing Intelligence, is one of the leading sources of secondary marketing information. Every month, Mintel analyses the consumers, producers, advertising and distribution within a range of markets.

misallocation of resources occurs when the composition of output is not the optimum in terms of prevailing supply and demand conditions. This may be because of *market failure*, or *government failure*. There may be people who would be willing to pay for certain products at a price reflecting the true costs of the resources needed to produce them, but find that they are not available. Normally the price would then rise and firms would have an incentive to produce them. Or there may be a glut of a product that no one wants to buy at the price being charged. A wide variety of measures could be used to restore *allocative efficiency*.

mission: an aim that can be tackled with passion, such as 'to free the world from cancer'. In its early days, staff at McDonald's were passionate about bringing cheap, clean, fast food to the world. It is hard to maintain a sense of mission once a business has grown to a size where it becomes an impersonal corporation. (See *mission statement*.)

mission statement: a document detailing the aims that should provide the sense of common purpose to direct and stimulate an organisation. Their purpose is set out by Sir John Harvey-Jones in his book *All Together Now* (Heinemann, 1994): 'Ultimately the businesses that win are those where all the people have the same aim and give freely in their commitment to it.' Advocates of mission statements believe that their focus on goals, such as high quality and customer service, are far easier for employees to relate to than profit. Critics suggest that the statements are little more than public relations exercises.

Examples of mission statements include:

- James Dyson: 'Long-term business success based on newly invented, innovatively designed products.'
- Body Shop: 'Tirelessly work to narrow the gap between principle and practice, whilst making fun, passion and care part of our daily lives.'

mixed economy: one which combines a *market economy* with centrally planned or state-run enterprises. A wholly market-led economy has certain disadvantages, the most important of which is the exploitation of certain members of society, usually those who are economically the weakest. Consequently, governments regulate the workings of the market either through laws, or by running parts of the economy through state enterprises. This is known as a mixed economy. In the UK, those industries run indirectly by government have included coal, steel, gas and electricity production, and services such as British Rail and the Post Office. Since 1979, there has been extensive *privatisation*, which has resulted in a greater influence of the market.

Centrally planned economy	Mixed economy	Market economy
Production organised and run by the state	Some production state-run, e.g. large-scale services such as NHS	Production market-driven
Prices of goods and services controlled	Some prices determined by government, e.g for prescriptions	Prices determined by supply and demand

mobility of labour: the ability and willingness of workers to move from one job to another. This is an important issue because economic change is so rapid that unless people are able and willing to change jobs they may become permanently unemployed if their type of job becomes obsolete. There are two parts to this mobility: *geographical* and *occupational*. In practice, however, they are closely connected, since it is often necessary to change geographical location if a worker's occupation changes. Because of social, cultural and economic ties, mobility can be improved but not eliminated.

mode: the most frequently occurring result within a set of data. This is a *measure of central tendency*.

model: a representation of reality designed to provide insights into how and why an event has occurred or is expected to occur. Usually models are presented in a graphical form (such as a *break-even chart*), though they may be stored as a series of equations within a computer program (as with the Treasury model of the macroeconomy).

modern apprenticeships are structured programmes that combine work with continued education and training. The training is largely on-the-job and will be part of the Qualifications and Credit Framework (QCF). At Foundation level, the programme takes at least 12 months; the Advanced level apprenticeships last a minimum of 24 months. The whole programme is part of the government's attempt to improve the technical skills of the majority of the workforce that does not go to university.

monetarism: an approach to the analysis of macroeconomic trends which emphasises the link between the money supply and the rate of inflation. It suggests a very direct relationship between the two. The strongest proponent of monetarism was the American economist *Milton Friedman*.

In practical terms, strict adherence to monetarism involves very careful control of the money supply. This requires willingness to raise *interest rates* very sharply if inflation threatens to accelerate. High interest rates will discourage spending and reduce aggregate demand and may lead to *recession*. This will reduce expectations of inflation: the threat of unemployment frightens employees into accepting lower pay increases. This feeds through into lower costs and prices but the cost in terms of lost income and output may be very high.

monetary policy uses changes in *interest rates* to control the demand for money and hence the rate of increase of bank lending. This in turn will influence the level of demand in the economy as a whole. High interest rates discourage borrowing for consumption, *investment* and house purchase, which helps to damp down *inflation*. If the economy is in *recession*, low interest rates can be expected to stimulate borrowing and reduce the impact of falling *aggregate demand*. However, there are always time lags between interest rate changes and their effect on the economy. It can take two years for monetary policy to take effect.

In 1997 the Chancellor of the Exchequer gave the Bank of England responsibility for monetary policy. This means that although the Treasury keeps in close touch with the Bank, the actual decisions about interest rates are taken by the Bank's *Monetary Policy Committee.* The *bank rate* is set on a monthly basis and that determines the general level of interest rates throughout the financial system. In 2006 inflation was gathering pace and interest rates were increased. Then in 2007/08 the financial crisis led the MPC to cut interest rates drastically (see graph opposite), in order to try to stimulate spending and contain the loss of output and the increase in unemployment that followed.

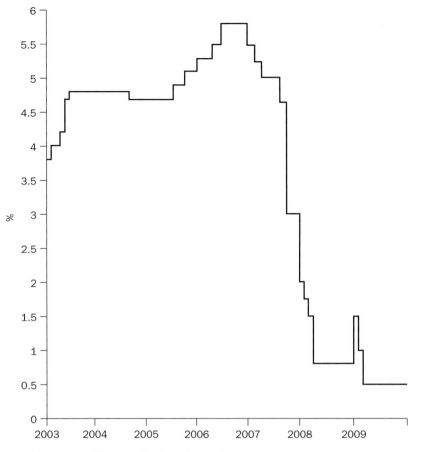

Changes in bank rate. (Source: Bank of England.)

When the recession came on fast, the Bank of England began to use an additional policy tool, **quantitative easing**. This allows the Bank of England to lend extra funds to the banks to encourage them to lend more to businesses and individuals. This was expected to provide an additional stimulus to the economy. The Bank of England kept in close touch with other central banks in order to try to co-ordinate the response to the global recession.

Monetary Policy Committee: the group of nine Bank of England officials and independent experts which decides **monetary policy**. The committee meets monthly to agree any change to interest rates. The idea is to ensure that monetary policy can be decided without political interference. The MPC's target for the underlying rate of the inflation is currently 2 per cent.

monetary system: the structure which provides the money needed to make the economy function effectively. The component parts of the system are:

- the banking system
- the central bank
- the body which supervises the banking system, which in the UK is the Financial Services Authority (FSA), although this may change.

monetary union: see *Economic and Monetary Union (EMU)*

money: anything which is generally acceptable as a means of payment. Money is usually defined according to its functions. These are: a medium of exchange, a unit of account, a store of value and a standard of deferred payments. Keep in mind that these functions may be affected when money loses its value during a period of rapid *inflation*.

money income is the measure of a person's income without taking price levels into account. So, if your money income was £10 000 this year and it rises to £20 000 next, you are twice as well off in money terms. If prices have doubled during the same period (ignoring taxes, etc.), *real incomes* will not have changed at all.

money laundering occurs when people who acquired money in an illegal way want to disguise its origins. Drug dealing, tax evasion and other crimes lead people to move money around until it appears to have been generated by a legitimate activity.

money market: where buyers and sellers of financial securities and loans come together at an agreed price, usually a rate of interest called the discount rate. There is no single physical marketplace, since transactions are usually conducted over the phone, through on-line computer links or through faxes. The 2007 *credit crunch* began when banks stopped trading with each other on the money market.

money supply means the amount of money available to the general public and the banking system. This is an important macroeconomic variable because it can affect the capacity of firms and individuals to spend. The money supply must be allowed to grow in line with output. The figures must be interpreted with caution because they can be affected by a wide range of events and, in the short term, there is often considerable uncertainty about their true meaning. This makes monetary policy difficult at times.

monopolistic competition occurs when there are many firms in the industry, each selling a slightly *differentiated product*. The market is easy to enter and exit, so small businesses can easily be set up and there is strong competition between them. Yet each has a small degree of monopoly power because the differentiated product allows consumers to choose to buy from a particular producer. This usually results from the development of brand names strong enough to prevent competition being purely on the basis of price. Restaurants, hairdressers, estate agents, potteries and many others illustrate situations of monopolistic competition. It merges into oligopoly if there are relatively few producers or a few large ones and many smaller ones. Building societies provide an example of the latter situation.

monopoly is in theory a single producer within a market. This represents one end of a spectrum of competition, at the other end of which is *perfect competition* (see diagram opposite).

In practice such dominant producers rarely exist, especially as the definition of the market widens. The potential danger of monopolies is that they will exploit the *consumer*, either by charging excessive prices, or by offering a poor service, or they will simply waste scarce resources by being inefficient. In some cases, monopolies exhibit all these characteristics, and hence governments exercise legal or voluntary restraints on their activities. In the UK monopolies can be investigated by the *Competition Commission*. The former nationalised utilities such as gas, electricity and water each have a *regulator* appointed to control them.

Monopoly — — — — — · Oligopoly — — — — — — · Monopolistic — — — — — — — Perfect
competition   competition

Increasing number of firms in the market
increasing competition

Market dominance

monopsony means a single buyer, as opposed to a *monopoly*, which is a single seller. A
single buyer is in a strong position to exploit the supplier of the good or service required. This
can be done by forcing the supplier to lower the price, by delaying payment, or by imposing
quality standards which might otherwise not be possible. It is sometimes said that large
Japanese corporations act as monopsonists, pushing stock holding requirements onto their
suppliers and forcing each to compete very strongly for business. Large employers in areas
where there is not much choice of jobs may exert monopoly power over their employees. This
may enable them to hire people at lower wage rates than they could in other locations.

morale is a measurement of the confidence and pride of a workforce. High morale should
lead to good quality work and a commitment to participate in problem-solving and decision-
making. For a manager, few challenges are more daunting than the attempt to transform a
group with very low morale into one with far higher self-confidence and pride.

morality (in business): the willingness to make decisions on the basis of principle rather
than profit, self-interest, or convenience. This may be easier to achieve for the proprietors of a
family business than for the directors of a *public limited company (PLC)*. The former run the
business they own, whereas the latter are answerable to shareholders for whom *profit* may
be an overriding consideration.

mortgage: a form of commercial loan, secured against a specific property asset. It may or
may not be at a fixed rate of interest.

motivation: as defined by Professor *Herzberg*, is the will to work due to enjoyment of
the work itself. He urged that it should be distinguished from 'movement'. According to the
Professor, 'If you do a good job because you want to do a good job, that's motivation. If you do
it because you want a house or a Jaguar, that's movement' (*Jumping for the Jellybeans*, BBC
Books, 1973). Many other writers and business people use the term motivation differently, to
mean anything that causes people to achieve more than they would otherwise do.

motivational research: see *qualitative research*

motivators are the aspects of a job that can lead to positive job satisfaction on the part of
the employee (see *Herzberg*). They include:
- achievement
- recognition for achievement
- meaningful, interesting work
- psychological growth and advancement at work (such as learning new skills or learning
  more about yourself).

M

movement: Professor *Herzberg* distinguished between movement (seen as short-term or temporary motivation — when someone does something for a specific purpose or because he or she has to) and *motivation* (when someone wants to do something for its own sake).

movement along the demand curve: a change in price which leads to a change in quantity demanded but does not alter the position of the *demand curve*. A likely cause of this would be when the producer is able to cut costs, for example by investing in new technologies. This will shift the supply curve to the right (from S_1 to S_2 in the diagram) but the general conditions of demand and the demand curve itself will remain unchanged.

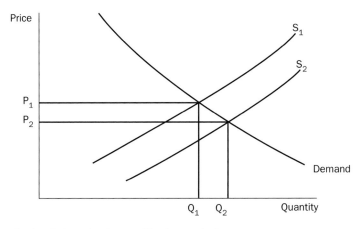

The fall in price leads to a rise in quantity demanded

movement along the supply curve occurs when the demand curve shifts to the right or left, showing changing levels of demand for the product at any given price. Supply conditions are unchanged but costs may rise if the equilibrium quantity rises, just because the supplier has to find more resources to meet the demand.

moving average: a calculation of the trend that exists within a series of data over time. It enables erratic and seasonal factors within the data to be smoothed out so that the underlying trend can be identified.

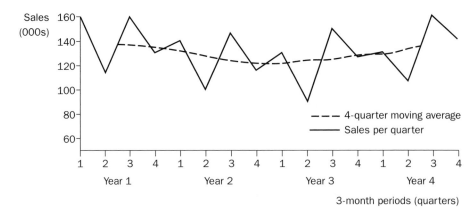

Using a moving average to show the underlying trend

To calculate a moving average:

1 Decide on an appropriate number of time periods for calculating the average; usually this will be to cover a full year, e.g. four quarters.
2 Add up the values over the first available time period and average them, e.g. year 1 quarters 1, 2, 3 and 4 (divided by 4).
3 Repeat the process for the next time period, e.g. year 1 quarters 2, 3 and 4 plus year 2 quarter 1 (divided by 4). Carry this process through until the last four quarters within the data series.

MPC: see *marginal propensity to consume (MPC)*

multilateral negotiations or agreements involve a number of governments. Trading blocs such as the EU or the *North American Free Trade Agreement (NAFTA)* require multilateral negotiation as do the rules of the *World Trade Organization (WTO)*.

multilateral trade involves trade, which need not be reciprocal, between a number of countries. For example, if China buys office equipment from the UK, while the USA buys toys from China and the UK buys computers from the USA, multilateral trade has taken place.

multinational: a firm which has its headquarters in one country, but with bases, manufacturing or assembly plants in others. Developing countries are often delighted to welcome multinational companies, but there are two sides to the argument:

PROS: • they provide employment and income and therefore better living standards
      • they may improve the level of expertise of the local workforce and suppliers
      • they improve the country's *balance of payments* because imports are reduced and exports increase

CONS: • the jobs provided may only require low-level skills
      • they may export all the profits back to the 'home' country
      • they may cut corners on health and safety or pollution, which they could not do in their 'home' country
      • they have been known to exert excessive political muscle

multiple (retailer): a store chain which has a number of shops that run on similar, head-office dominated lines. Their size provides the opportunity for tough negotiation over the unit prices of the stocks being purchased.

multiplier: the concept that an increase in *injections* to the *circular flow of national income* will be multiplied as it goes through the economy, raising incomes as it goes, although by smaller increments. For instance, if the government decides to build a new rail link it will inject, say, £100 million into the economy by paying for wages, raw materials and so on. The money will go to the workers and shareholders of the companies concerned, and they will in turn spend more on goods and services, raising wages and profits in consumer-orientated industries. Steadily, then, beneficial knock-on effects are spread through the economy.

A decrease in *leakages* will have the same effect. Similarly, increased leakages or reduced injections will lead to a downward multiplier effect, with a cumulative fall in income. The size of the multiplier will depend on the extent to which increasing incomes leak away into savings, taxation or imports. (See flowchart overleaf.)

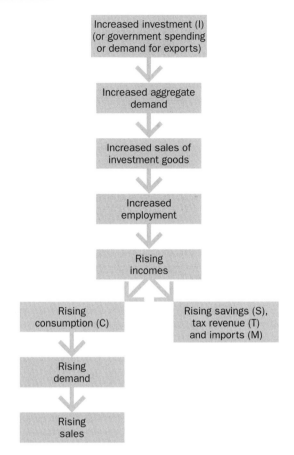

The multiplier effect

multi-site locations: when a business produces at many different sites. It may use specialisation, whereby one site concentrates on, say, engines, where another focuses on gearboxes. This could enable the business to maximise its *economies of scale*.

multi-skilling means training a workforce to be able to work effectively across a wide range of tasks. This is necessary if *demarcation* barriers are to be broken down and the scope of jobs is to be enlarged. Multi-skilling has many short- and long-term benefits:

SHORT-TERM:
- staff can cover for absent colleagues
- trained staff can spot maintenance or other problems before they become serious
- faults can be corrected without the need to wait for a series of different tradespeople

LONG-TERM:
- staff promoted from the shop-floor will have a far wider knowledge and understanding of the process they are now managing
- changes to working practices or to products will be far easier to achieve with a multi-skilled workforce
- wider responsibilities and expertise may help to improve motivation

municipal services: council-run facilities such as leisure centres, community centres, refuse collection and street cleaning. Many of these have been contracted out in recent years, meaning that they have been taken out of local authority direct control.

NAFTA: see *North American Free Trade Agreement (NAFTA)*

national bargaining occurs when *trade unions* negotiate with employers on behalf of members throughout the country. This has become far less common as firms have looked towards plant (local) bargaining or rejected *collective bargaining* totally, in preference for individual contracts.

National Debt: the sum total of all past debt accumulated by the UK government. It has tended over the long run to rise sharply during times of war. In relation to national income, it has fallen during periods of rapid inflation. It is currently rising, due in part to increased spending on health and education during the period 2002–06, and significantly due to *recapitalisation* of banks in 2007–09. It is still low by international standards. However, it is set to rise much further, to an estimated 78 per cent. The ONS argues that three banks, Northern Rock, Lloyds TSB and Royal Bank of Scotland (RBS), should be classified as public sector organisations; their debts would then be part of the National Debt.

Country	Year	National debt as % of GDP
UK	1946	150
UK	2002	30
UK	2007	37
UK	end 2008	48
Japan	end 2008	194
USA	end 2008	74

Source: UK Treasury

national income is the sum of all incomes within an economy after allowing for depreciation. Through the *circular flow of national income* it will necessarily equal the value of annual national output. It includes wages, salaries, profits (whether distributed to shareholders or not), rents, and net income from abroad.

National Insurance is the social framework established in the UK after the Second World War whereby all employers, employees and the self-employed make contributions which provide a number of benefits. These include a safety net in the event of illness or unemployment, pensions beyond retirement age, child and maternity benefits, and various other grants. The increasing cost of state benefits, especially as the population ages into the twenty-first century, has become a matter of concern and some debate since a smaller working population will have to support an ever-growing number of dependents.

National Insurance charges (NICs): the payments made by employees and employers as their contributions to the funds needed to cover benefit payments. Employers' contributions raise the cost of employing *labour*. They may create some disincentive to employ people and thus contribute to unemployment so some attempts have been made to make them less onerous to employers. The employee's contribution effectively raises the marginal rate of tax: a pay increase will lead to higher tax payments and a higher NIC.

nationalisation: the transfer of firms or services to the *public sector* from the *private sector*. The Labour government of 1945–51 nationalised a number of industries, including the railways, steelmaking, coalmining, British Airways and BP. In time it became apparent that civil servants were not necessarily best placed to make the necessary business decisions. After 1979 the then Conservative government began a programme of *privatisation* which returned most of the nationalised industries to the private sector, but not the BBC or the Post Office (yet). In 2008, the government nationalised Northern Rock bank — the first to collapse during the period known as the *credit crunch*.

national minimum wage: see *minimum wage*

National Savings is a form of government borrowing which encourages people to save by offering not only a reasonable interest rate free of tax but also, perhaps more importantly, offering absolute security for the money itself. From the government's point of view, National Savings provide a reasonably cheap source of finance.

National Vocational Qualification (NVQ): a government initiative to provide young people and employees with a widely accepted, job-focused qualification at a variety of different skill levels. It is being replaced by the Qualifications and Credit Framework (QCF).

natural monopolies exist where the supply infrastructure required makes it uneconomic to have several suppliers, for example gas supply, water supply, railways and landline telephones. To have competing gas mains running side by side to every house in Britain would be completely uneconomic. For this reason, many analysts believe that natural monopolies should be in the *public sector*, i.e. state-owned. When privatised, there is a severe risk that *monopoly* power will encourage the supplier to charge high prices for poor services (exactly as happens with many train-operating companies). Nevertheless, it is possible that the profit motive might prove such an incentive to increase efficiency that customers will still be served better than when a natural monopoly is left in the hands of the government. All the natural monopolies have regulatory bodies, e.g. *OFWAT*, that are charged with preventing their acting like monopolists.

natural resources: include land and supplies of basic raw materials such as oil reserves. They may also include sites with development potential, which may for example be turned into deep water ports or hydro-electric schemes.

natural wastage: the process of natural labour turnover as employees retire, leave to have children, or leave for other jobs, i.e. for any reason other than *redundancy* or *dismissal*. The rate of natural wastage will differ depending upon demographic factors such as the number of older workers and the proportion of young women. If the rate is relatively high (for instance 12 per cent per annum), then it is possible for the company to reduce its workforce rapidly without needing to resort to redundancies.

needs and wants: the preferences for particular consumer goods and services that people use as their basis for making the decisions that create a demand for various products. They figure in the process of choice which is necessary because people have unlimited needs and wants but a limited income with which to buy them. This is the fundamental feature of scarcity, with which economics as a subject is deeply concerned.

negative cash flow occurs when the *cash flow* entering a company is less than that leaving it, i.e. cash outflow is greater than cash inflow. This may be perfectly normal for a firm in its off-season, but if negative cash flow persists it will drain the business of its *liquidity*.

negative equity can be found when people have borrowed to finance a house purchase, only to find that house prices subsequently fall. The size of their loan may then be greater than the value of the property.

negative externalities occur when an economic activity affects third parties, i.e. people other than the producers or the consumers, in some way which reduces their quality of life. For example, a polluting factory creates a negative externality for people living in the area affected by the pollution. They may encounter health problems which are a cost to the community. This cost is not borne by the producers or the consumers. The price of the product to the consumer is lower than it would be if it covered all of its *social costs* and the producer's profits may be higher than they would be if the social cost were included in the costs of production. (See also *externalities*.) It is difficult to put a money value on some negative externalities, especially when they relate to health or personal well-being.

negative income tax: a unified tax and benefits system, such that people could be taxed or receive benefits according to a single set of rules. Its attraction is that it could be used to eliminate the *poverty trap* which sometimes means that people lose money by taking a job. Although the UK does not at present have a unified system, it is moving in that direction with the *Working Families Tax Credit* which reduces the impact of the poverty trap.

negligence is a legal term implying that an individual or company has failed in its duty to have regard for the interests of others. The injured party may be able to sue for *damages*.

negotiation is a method of joint decision-making involving bargaining between different firms or between workforce and management representatives within a firm. The *objective* is to arrive at mutually acceptable terms. A distinction can be made between negotiation and *consultation*, as the former term implies competitive rivalry between conflicting interests.

neo-Keynesians: those economists who have generally followed the teaching of *J M Keynes* and sought to develop his ideas in the context of recent economic conditions.

net assets: the value of a firm's assets minus its external liabilities. This means that net assets are the same as net worth and will always balance with the firm's 'total equity', also known as shareholders' funds. When looking at a balance sheet, there are two possible ways to calculate net assets:

1 non-current (fixed) assets + net current assets – long-term liabilities

2 (non-current + current assets) – (current + non-current liabilities)

net current assets, also called *working capital*, comprise *current assets* minus *current liabilities*. It is the finance available for the day-to-day running of the business.

FORMULA: current assets – current liabilities = net current assets

205

net foreign assets means all assets held overseas by UK residents less all assets held in the UK by people living abroad. These assets include bank balances, shares, factories, retail outlets and any other production facilities. In many cases the owners will be companies rather than individuals. For example, the Japanese company Nissan has a big factory in Sunderland while the UK company BP has extensive oil production facilities in Alaska.

net investment is gross (i.e. total) investment less *replacement investment* (also known as *capital consumption*). Net investment thus represents the value of the addition to total productive capacity which has taken place over the year. It gives a good indication of the extent to which the economy is able to increase *aggregate supply* in the future.

net margin is the percentage of sales revenue which is *net profit*. Unlike the *gross margin*, fixed *overheads* have been taken into account within this ratio. Therefore it is of far greater business significance.

$$FORMULA: \frac{\text{net (operating) profit}}{\text{sales revenue}} \times 100 = \text{net margin}$$

net profit is *gross profit* minus expenses such as *overhead* costs. In other words, it is sales revenue minus all the operating costs of a business. It can therefore also be termed *operating profit*.

networking: the establishment of business contacts and communication links by socialising, attending professional meetings or by belonging to the right clubs. People do this in the belief that 'it's not what you know, it's who you know'.

networking (IT): interlinking computer hardware to enable users to have access to information, applications software and computer resources without knowing where any of them are located. As many schools and colleges are aware, computer networks sound excellent in theory, but can be a disappointment due to their unreliability.

New Deal: a second chance for adults to find work-related training or a job in a government-funded initiative. Although focused originally on 18–24-year-olds, it is now open to those over 25 and those with disabilities. It is a key part of the government's welfare to work strategy – an attempt to stop the benefit system from trapping people into a 'culture of dependency'. Critics of the programme consider it an expensive way of forcing people off benefits.

new entrants: firms which set up in business in a particular industry for the first time. Usually they will be attracted by potential profits. These may arise because there has been an increase in demand for the product. This is part of the *price mechanism*, which creates incentives for firms to produce goods and services for which there is a demand. New entrants may be new businesses or well-established businesses venturing into a market which is new for them.

newly industrialised economy (NIE): one which has moved from having a dominant *primary sector* (agriculture and mining) to a fast-growing and substantial *secondary sector* (manufacturing). The best known examples are countries around the Pacific Rim such as Singapore and Taiwan. They experienced rapid growth, often through attracting *multinationals*, especially while wage rates remained far behind those of developed economies such as Japan and the United States.

new product development (NPD) implies all the functions required to identify, develop and market new product opportunities. This requires close cooperation between *research and development (R&D)*, *market research* and general marketing functions. A great deal of new product development is based on *qualitative research*, in which psychologists probe for the reasons behind consumer attitudes and actions. This is because radical new products are rarely the result of scientifically conducted research; they stem from insight into the minds of the customer.

new technology: rapid changes in communications, production methods and control mechanisms. The innovations resulting from the use of new technology can be split into three main types:
- by process, that is advancements in manufacturing technology and automation
- by product, that is new product opportunities such as electronic games and new medicines
- by communication links, that is *information technology (IT)*.

NGOs: see *non-governmental organisations (NGOs)*

niche marketing: a corporate strategy based on identifying and filling relatively small market segments. This can enable small firms to operate profitably in markets dominated by large corporations. It can also be a strategy pursued by a large firm that prefers to have five brands selling 50 000 units in each of five niches, rather than one brand selling 250 000 in the mass market.

PROS: • the first company to identify a niche market can often secure a solid market position as consumers see the original product as superior
 • consumers are willing to pay a price premium for a more exclusive product

CONS: • lack of *economies of scale* may make costs too high to achieve satisfactory profit margins
 • the firm's production system must be flexible enough to cope with relatively small quantities of several products (see *flexible specialisation*)

Nikkei Index is Japan's Stock Exchange Index, equivalent to London's *Financial Times* Stock Exchange index (see *Footsie (FTSE 100)*).

NIMBY: see *not in my back yard (NIMBY)*

NINJA mortgages: bank loans to buy property given to those with No Income, No Jobs or Assets. These were the sub-prime mortgages at the heart of the US housing boom then bust in the period 2004–2009.

noise: factors that can distract from the accurate reception of a piece of communication. These include communication overload, i.e. when too many points are being communicated simultaneously to the same person; and a poor or faulty transmission mechanism.

nominal GDP means *gross domestic product (GDP)* at current prices. This means that no allowance has been made for *inflation*.

nominal value means a face value, not a *market value*. No allowance is made for *inflation*. Nominal wages will increase over time. Some of this increase will be nominal, reflecting the current rate of inflation. The rest of the increase will be a *real* increase, reflecting an increase in the purchasing power of the wage. It also applies in the case of financial securities or shares where the value written on the face of the certificate is not related to its market price. In other words, a £1 share may currently have a market price of £3 because the firm is prospering. The term nominal value is sometimes used when something is sold at a trivial or merely nominal price.

non-collusive oligopoly: a situation in which there is a small number of producers competing strongly with one another and making no attempt at collaboration or at *tacit collusion*. The market will exhibit interdependent behaviour in that each producer will be observing and reacting to the strategies of the other producers.

non-discriminatory legislation: Acts of Parliament that make it illegal to discriminate against an employee on grounds of sex, race or disabilities when selecting staff for recruitment, training or promotion and outlaws men and women receiving different pay levels for work of equal value. The Equality Act 2006 updated all past laws against discrimination.

non-excludability: a feature of *public goods*, the consumption of which by one person does not exclude consumption by others. The security provided by the police force is one example. Provided there is a police force, all will benefit regardless of whether they have contributed to its financing.

non-executive director: a part-time director of a company who has no day-to-day involvement or executive powers. The function of a non-executive director is to supply unbiased advice and specialist expertise and to act as a control on the executives. Often a non-executive director may represent a large shareholder such as a pension fund.

non-governmental organisations (NGOs) are bodies which are associated neither with governments nor with firms in the private sector. For the most part they are charities or *pressure groups* which are non-profit making. Oxfam is a well-known example. They can be big spenders worldwide, although their local projects tend to be small scale. They are a significant presence at some meetings of international organisations such as the UN and the *World Trade Organization (WTO)*, where they will normally have observer status.

non-price competition is all forms of competitive action other than through the price mechanism. Examples include advertising, sales promotions, packaging, branding, point-of-sale activity and sponsorship as marketing tools and design and reliability as product features. Non-price competition is particularly significant in market structures that fit the pattern of *oligopoly*.

non-profit motives: reasons for business activity that are not based on financial gain. There may be social or environmental motives, e.g. to start an organic farm even if its profit prospects were poorer than a farm that uses chemicals. Or the motives may be morally based, e.g. to tackle poverty in Africa by providing free, clean drinking water. (See also *satisficing*.)

non-profit-making organisations are run without profit as an objective, although they may try hard to cover all their costs. They include charities, some schools and a range of other organisations designed to operate in the public interest.

non-renewable resources: see *finite resources*

non-rivalry refers to *public goods* which can be consumed by an unlimited number of people because the presence of one consumer does not exclude the enjoyment of the product by another. Public parks provide an example: people are generally not in competition with one another in order to consume their benefits. A number of people can enjoy them at the same time.

non-tariff barriers are restrictions on trade that do not involve taxing imports. Many of them are contrary to either the spirit or the letter of the **World Trade Organization (WTO)**'s international regulations. **Quotas** involve an upper limit on the level of imports of specific products. Occasionally, quotas are negotiated with the exporting country's government and are then called voluntary export restraints.

There are also some hidden barriers to trade which are imposed when governments wish to restrict imports without being seen to do so. These include:

- technical regulations which force exporters to make specific changes to the product so that it is acceptable in that particular market. This raises costs for the exporter
- forcing importers to use specified points of entry where documentation is dealt with only slowly
- regulations which favour domestic producers, e.g. packaging, and labels which conform to local language requirements.

Because barriers to trade tend to reduce the level of trade, they also reduce the real incomes of the countries which employ them, by depriving consumers of cheap substitutes for domestically produced goods. They may be popular with voters, though, because they are thought to protect the jobs of domestic producers.

non-tradables are products which will not normally figure in international trade. They include some sorts of services which are unlikely to be consumed much by tourists and some very heavy construction materials. Usually, the markets for non-tradables are rather less competitive than those for tradable goods and services. Prices may be rather higher because there are fewer substitutes.

normal curve: the bell-shaped curve of the **normal distribution** as shown below.

normal distribution: a *frequency distribution* which is bell-shaped so that half of the variables lie to the left of the *mean* and half to the right. Due to the symmetry of the curve, the mean, *median* and *mode* all coincide at the same value. If data is collected on an event that occurs many times over, variations in the result will tend to form a pattern that is known as normal distribution. This means that the results will tend to be clustered around the average, and will be split equally between results above and below the average (see the diagram below). Normal distributions can be standardised so that the width of the distribution is about six standard deviations. The areas within each standard deviation can be very useful in statistical analysis, for example in significance testing.

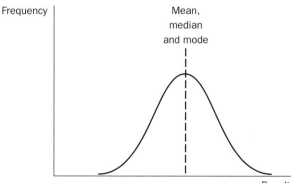

Normal distribution

normal goods are those for which demand will increase when incomes increase. In other words, the *income elasticity* of demand for them is positive. They include a huge range of products, such as hairdressing, furniture, foreign holidays, restaurant meals, theatre visits, golf clubs and so on. All luxury goods fall into the category of normal, as do the majority of everyday items. In contrast, *inferior goods* experience falling demand when income rises. Examples include maincrop potatoes, basic models of consumer durables and so on.

normal profit: that level of profit which is just sufficient to keep the resources employed in making a particular product from being used for some other purpose. Any profit in excess of that amount, termed *supernormal profit*, will tend to attract additional resources into the industry; in other words there will be entry into the industry by new firms. If less than normal profit is earned, some resources will leave the industry to exploit more profitable opportunities producing other things. Normal profit is an important feature of *perfect competition*. The theory predicts that under perfectly competitive conditions, only normal profit will be earned in the long run, because the entry of new competitors will force prices back down to the level which just covers the costs of all resources used in production. (See also *profit-signalling mechanism*.)

North American Free Trade Area (NAFTA), whose members consist of the United States of America, Canada and Mexico, is an attempt to create the equivalent of the *single European market* within the North American continent. It may become a *trading bloc* with an even more protectionist outlook than the *European Union (EU)*. This would create the risk of a serious *trade war*.

no-strike agreement: a contract signed as part of a firm's negotiation and *disputes procedure* that bars the *trade union* signatories from calling or encouraging a strike.

not-for-profit organisation: see *non-profit-making organisations*

not in my back yard (NIMBY) is applied in a number of areas of economic life. It generally applies in situations where everyone agrees that something has to be built for the good of all, but no one wants it near their own home. The most common example is motorways, which everyone agrees are extremely useful and which most people use, but which cause uproar and extreme resistance from those immediately affected by their construction. The same thing happens with potentially dirty or hazardous production processes. This is why both motorways and these factories are often located in areas where residents are poor, lack access to the media and are therefore unable to resist effectively.

NPD: see *new product development (NPD)*

NVQ: see *National Vocational Qualification (NVQ)*

objectives are the medium- to long-term targets that can give a sense of direction to a manager, department or whole organisation. If a team can be given a sense of common purpose, it becomes much easier to coordinate actions and to create a team spirit. For maximum effect, objectives should be measurable and have an explicit timescale, for example to boost *market share* from 8 per cent to 10 per cent within the next three years. They must also be realistic, as an objective that seems unattainable can be demotivating. Consequently, it is desirable for objectives to be agreed rather than set.

Objectives form the basis for decisions on strategy, i.e. the plan for the achievement of your *goals*. Therefore questions about business strategy should not be answered until the individual or company's objectives have been considered fully. (See *aims, corporate objectives* and *strategy*.)

obsolescence occurs when a product, service or machine has been overtaken by a new idea that provides the same function in a better or more attractive way. Obsolescence may occur as a result of *new technology*, or due to changing lifestyles or fashions. The threat of obsolescence encourages firms to update their products regularly and to look for new products to replace declining ones. Some firms look to gain financial advantage from two specific types of obsolescence: built-in and planned.

- Built-in obsolescence means designing and building failure into a product, in order that the user needs to buy a replacement. This is a way of overcoming the effect of *market saturation* upon the sales of a *durable* item. In other words, if everyone who wants a lawnmower has one, sales will fall to zero. This tempts manufacturers to build the products so that they wear out after three or four years. The customer must then go and buy a new one.
- Planned obsolescence is the creation of a feeling on the part of customers that they should replace items that are in fact still usable. This is largely done through restyling or adding new features. For example, although your Liverpool shirt may look as good as new, you want to get the new season's styling.

Environmentalists would regard both built-in and planned obsolescence as equally undesirable ways of encouraging wastage of the earth's resources.

occupational immobility occurs when people have been trained in a skill which is no longer in demand and have difficulty in retraining in a skill which is in demand. This may result in their being unemployed. This type of unemployment is known as *structural unemployment*. Policies to deal with it include projects such as the *New Deal*, which gives help in finding work as well as additional training.

OECD: see *Organisation for Economic Cooperation and Development (OECD)*

OFCOM is the regulator for UK communications industries. It has been instrumental in opening up the telecommunications market to many competing suppliers. By creating much stronger competition it has helped to bring down the cost of phone calls. It covers radio, television, telecommunications and wireless communication services. It set price controls for BT until 2006 but this is no longer necessary. (See also *regulatory capture*.)

off-balance-sheet financing is 'the creative accounting trick which improves companies' balance sheets' (Roger Cowe, *The Guardian*). It is a device by which a business's debts can be removed from the *balance sheet*. This shrinks the firm's stated *gearing* and therefore apparent risk level. The most common method is by the creation of a *subsidiary* company, which the firm controls, but does not consolidate into its accounts. This subsidiary may have obtained the loans essential for running the entire business, but these may not need to be listed on the firm's consolidated accounts. The *Accounting Standards Board* is trying to ban off-balance-sheet financing.

Office of Fair Trading (OFT) was set up in 1973 to oversee all of the UK's competition policy. It operates in a range of areas. It:
- monitors changes in *market structures*, collecting data and investigating merger activity generally
- decides whether to refer takeovers to the *Competition Commission* for further investigation before approval can be given
- responds to complaints about anti-competitive activities (which usually come from competing firms)
- takes care of many aspects of *consumer protection*, including trades description.

The OFT was greatly strengthened by the 1998 Competition Act, giving it the power to stage a *dawn raid* if a firm might try to obscure important evidence. Also, it gave firms immunity from fines if they inform on other members of a *cartel*. The Enterprise Act of 2002 made forming a cartel a criminal act and allows the OFT to fine firms which collude up to 10 per cent of their UK turnover for up to three years.

The OFT first used its power to bring criminal charges in 2007 against a cartel of British, Swedish and US producers of marine hoses. The operation was carefully co-ordinated with the EU Competition Commission and the US Department of Justice. Eight people from the three companies involved were arrested in the US, in order to avoid extradition problems. They were accused of rigging bids, fixing prices and allocating markets. A Japanese competitor was the whistle blower.

off-shoring: moving production (and therefore jobs) to an overseas, usually low-wage, country, or setting up a company in a foreign country or tax haven in order to take advantage of low tax rates or light touch regulation. An offshore investment fund is based in an offshore centre for tax or other reasons.

OFGEM, the Office of Gas and Electricity Markets, is the *regulator* for the gas and electricity industries. The industry has been regulated since *privatisation* in the late 1980s. OFGEM regulates the extent to which gas and electricity prices can be raised and also the value-for-money which customers get. It can require suppliers to restrain their activities in order to ensure that the market remains competitive. Because both industries are to some extent *natural monopolies*, regulation is needed to protect the interests of consumers.

Since 1999, neither British Gas nor the electricity suppliers have had a monopoly position; consumers can choose where to buy. *Regulation* has at times brought OFGEM into dispute with shareholders. To the extent that suppliers' profits may be reduced, shareholders sometimes object when prices cannot be raised.

OFT: see *Office of Fair Trading (OFT)*

OFWAT is the regulator for the water industry, set up at the time of privatisation in 1989. In spite of its efforts to hold down price increases, many people think that the water companies continue to act like monopolies. Water remains a true *natural monopoly* in that it is not usually possible to choose between competing suppliers and the need for a pipe network makes duplication of facilities wasteful and inefficient. In fact, prices have risen in part because of the need for extensive investment in improved water supplies. It is hard to tell how effective regulation has been in this case.

oil crisis: a situation in which supplies of oil are threatened and prices rise as it becomes more scarce. The precipitating cause could be war in the Middle East, as in 1973. *OPEC* has in the past been able to restrict production with a view to raising prices. Protesters have at times succeeded in blocking supplies by picketing the refineries, when attempts were made to raise taxes to discourage greenhouse gas production.

Because demand for oil is very inelastic, a relatively small fall in production can bring about a much larger increase in prices. Shortages are likely to disrupt economic activity because of the crucial role of oil in industry and distribution.

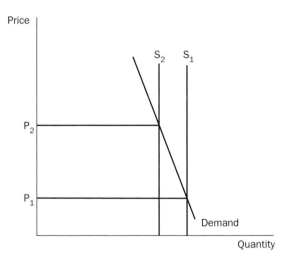

A small fall in quantity supplied leads to a large increase in price if demand is inelastic

oil price: the price of oil in the wholesale market, which is a significant indicator of future pressures on production costs and sometimes of impending *inflation*. The price is usually quoted in US dollars.

oligopoly: a market in which there are a few large firms competing with one another. It is characterised by:

- *differentiated products*, sometimes with well-known and easily distinguished brand names
- *barriers to entry*, such that it may be difficult or impossible for *new entrants* to come into the market
- the fact that firms may make *supernormal profits* in the long run, because of the barriers to entry
- the relatively small number of competing firms, which is likely to include *price makers* and *price takers*. The former will tend to set prices and the latter will tend to follow.

Oligopolies can have very stable prices, because firms will often favour *non-price competition*. They may seek to expand their market share on the strength of design or advertising. There may be *tacit collusion*, with no price cuts but intense efforts to promote products in other ways.

Occasionally, though, a price war may break out, in which one firm begins aggressive price-cutting strategies and others follow, each trying to undercut the other in a bid for increased market share. This is good for consumers in the short run but may lead to the least profitable firm going out of business. Then competition is reduced and a return to tacit collusion is likely. Petrol provides occasional examples of price wars.

Interdependent behaviour is an important feature of oligopoly, because the small number of competing firms watch each other closely, devising strategies which take into account the likely reaction of the others.

Some oligopolies have a number of large competitors, as with Coca-Cola and other major soft drink suppliers, together with a large number of comparatively small suppliers which are price takers. (See also *concentration ratios*, *anti-competitive activities*.)

on-line: the linking of computer terminals so that information can be passed instantaneously. A common example is the electronic checkout at supermarkets that can provide on-line information to head office or even to suppliers about the numbers of each item being sold.

OPEC: see *Organization of Petroleum Exporting Countries (OPEC)*

open economy: an economy in which foreign trade is important. Exports contribute significantly to aggregate demand and imports are a significant proportion of total purchases. For example, the UK economy is a more open economy than the US. Luxembourg, along with many other small countries, is even more so.

open questions are those that invite a wide-ranging, reflective or imaginative response. On a questionnaire, they are questions that do not have specific answers to be ticked. In an interview, they are the (harder) questions that demand more than just a factual answer. An example of an open question would be, 'Tell me a bit more about yourself.' The term may also be used more generally to mean a questions that has no right or wrong answer, on which disagreement must be expected.

operating profit: the measure of profit which an organisation earns on its normal operations. This is total sales revenue less all operating costs, i.e. both cost of sales and overheads. It excludes any extraordinary or *exceptional items*, which might distort a true appreciation of its usual business. Therefore, clear comparisons with previous years or with similar firms may be made.

operating profit margin shows operating profit as a percentage of turnover. (See also *net margin*.)

operational research (OR): a set of multi-disciplinary techniques which are an aid to organising and planning operations such as production, scheduling and resource allocation. An *optimum* is usually sought, subject to a set of *constraints*. The distinctive approach is to develop a mathematical model of the system under investigation, including measurement of factors such as chance and risk. This model can then be used to predict and compare the outcomes of alternative decisions, strategies or controls. Devised at the time of the Second World War, OR techniques predated modern computers, yet are ideally suited to them.

operations management: the modern term for production management. It suggests a wider brief than just factory management. For example, it allows for service industries to be seen as requiring management of their operations, as has always been acknowledged in manufacturing.

opportunity cost measures cost in terms of the next best or highest-valued alternative foregone. It may be measured in money terms or not. The cost of an evening of studying might be the missed opportunity of seeing a film. The idea of opportunity cost may be applied in any situation where choices are being made. For example, consumers' decisions involve choices between items; one will be chosen and the one foregone is the opportunity cost. Similarly *labour* market decisions may involve choices between work and education or between two possible jobs. And the government may find that the opportunity cost of, say, more money for the NHS is less money for roads or social services.

Opportunity cost is also important in considering alternative investments. Even if the firm is using its own *retained profits* to fund the investment, it must allow for the interest which could have been earned if this money had been left in the bank. This is the opportunity cost of investing in, say, a new machine or office furniture. An investment which cannot equal the rate of return on a bank deposit is not a good use of funds.

optimise: to aim for the most favourable point or circumstances. For example, the optimum strategy might be one that is profitable, but not so much as to attract *me-too products*.

optimum means the best possible outcome, e.g. maximising *capacity utilisation* or minimising cost while still meeting quality standards.

optimum allocation of resources will provide a combination of goods and services that most closely matches consumer preferences. (See also *profit-signalling mechanism* and *consumer sovereignty*.)

option: the right to buy or sell an item at a price agreed in advance.

order book: the total number of orders taken from customers, usually expressed in terms of time. Thus an order book of three months means that the factory has that amount of work on order.

ordinary share or equity represents part ownership in a *joint-stock company*. Ordinary shareholders receive *dividends* on the capital they invest, but only after *debenture* holders, *preference shareholders*, long-term debt holders and the government (through taxes) have been paid. If the company goes into *liquidation*, ordinary shareholders are the last group of people to receive any return, after all other *creditors*. In return for these potentially high risks, ordinary shareholders enjoy the chance to benefit fully from their company's successes. Rising profits will lead to higher annual dividend payments and an increase in the market value of the shares they hold.

ordinary share capital is an important source of finance for businesses because it provides funds for long-term investment and if at any time profits are low, they need not pay a *dividend* until the situation improves.

organic food: produce made with the minimum of chemical and other additives. The organic label could add 20 per cent to the price of produce in 2004–2007, but this added value disappeared during the 2008/09 recession.

organic growth means expansion from within the firm, i.e. not as a result of acquisitions. It also implies that the finance for the expansion has come from internal sources rather than from shareholders or loans. As a result, organic growth is likely to be steady, even slow, but very secure.

organisational chart: a diagram showing the lines of authority and *layers of hierarchy* within an organisation. To be effective, the *chain of command* should be clear, with no one answerable to two people. An organisational chart should show:
- the different business functions and divisions
- who is answerable to whom
- the *span of control* in each division
- the official channels of communication.

organisational structure: the way in which management is organised, both horizontally (*layers of hierarchy*) and vertically (by function, by operation or by matrix). The traditional approach was to divide an organisation into functional areas such as marketing, production and finance. Each had many layers of hierarchy, leading to many rungs on the career ladder. Today, many companies have reduced the number of management layers and have reorganised away from functions towards operations (e.g. Wall's Ice Cream structures its organisation towards: impulse purchase products; take-home products; and the catering market). Within each operation, marketing, production and other staff would work together on the same projects.

Organisation for Economic Cooperation and Development (OECD) was set up in 1961 and aims to coordinate international aid for developing countries as well as providing a forum for discussion on economic growth and trade. Its members are mainly drawn from the developed world, but some of its most effective work has been in the collection and publication of worldwide economic and social data, standardised so that inter-country comparisons are possible.

organised labour means the trade unions and their membership. In contrast, employees who choose not to join a union and negotiate independently or accept the going wage are not part of organised labour.

Organization of Petroleum Exporting Countries (OPEC) is the name of the *cartel* which sets output quotas in order to control crude oil prices. The members of OPEC are countries of the Middle East, South America and Africa, but not the United States, Russian or European producers. OPEC wielded great power in the 1970s when it controlled 90 per cent of the world's supply of crude oil exports.

OTC market: see *over-the-counter (OTC) market*

output is the finished product coming from a production process. It can be measured by volume or by value (volume times price). The level of output should not be confused with output per worker (*productivity*).

output gap: the difference between actual output and the potential output of the economy when it is working at full capacity. By looking at real GDP over time and comparing it with the *long-run trend rate of growth*, it is possible to see when there is a divergence. In 2007 the UK economy grew by 3 per cent. The long-run trend rate of growth in the UK is about 2.2 per cent, so real GDP was above its underlying trend and the output gap was positive. With a growth rate in 2008 of –1.9 per cent, there was clearly a negative output gap. For 2009 this gap was estimated to be 9 per cent for the USA and probably no less for the UK.

The diagram below shows a negative output gap. The level of expenditure is less than the capacity of the economy to produce. There will be a deflationary situation with a significant amount of unemployment and idle capital equipment – i.e. a *slump* or *depression*. This may be eliminated by using expansionary fiscal and monetary policies.

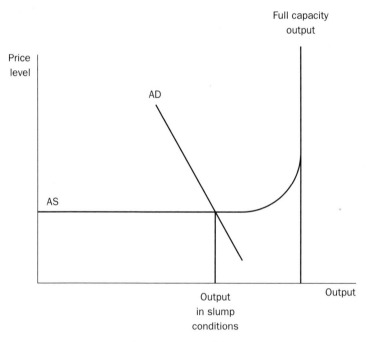

A negative output gap: aggregate demand is insufficient to buy all that the economy can produce

outsourcing means finding an outside person or organisation to carry out part of your work process. The motive is usually to cut costs or to obtain a better service. Typical examples would be to outsource the office cleaning instead of hiring cleaners who are your own employees. Other services, such as accounting, computing or *after-sales service*, are often outsourced.

overcapacity exists in a market where the maximum capacity of all the producers is significantly above current and anticipated demand. This threatens each producer with the possibility that demand will fall below the *break-even point*. The likely consequences of overcapacity are:

- that the weakest producers will sell out or go into *liquidation*
- that all producers will try to cut their fixed *overheads* by *rationalisation*
- that prices will fall as producers try to utilise their own capacity by boosting demand.

217

There is currently world overcapacity in the car industry; this started well before recession set in. In the US, the process started with the import of Japanese cars that were smaller, more fuel efficient and more reliable. US manufacturers carried on producing big cars and SUVs, which in time became less fashionable. For some years, Ford, GM and Chrysler tried without much success to rationalise production so that they might become profitable again and meet consumer demand effectively. In the UK, Ford Dagenham closed down in 2007. The US car companies finally took their medicine as a condition of getting some support from the US government, but the actual outcome remains uncertain.

overconsumption occurs when the price of the product does not reflect the full costs of the product. Prices may not include *external costs*. For example, it can be argued that cigarettes are overconsumed because buyers do not take full account of the health effects of smoking and the price does not fully reflect the health care costs of tobacco-related illnesses. Taxes go some way towards this, of course. We may be overconsuming petrol because we are not allowing for the long-term environmental effects of our behaviour. Overconsumption can be associated with *information failure* and also with *demerit goods*.

overdraft: a facility that enables a firm to borrow up to an agreed maximum for any period of time that it wishes. An overdraft is a very flexible way of raising credit in that it need not even be drawn at all and the amount borrowed may fluctuate daily. Banks may offer overdrafts without security, though for larger sums they will take security by a floating charge on all the assets of the business. The actual sum borrowed through an overdraft facility at the end of the financial year is recorded as a *current liability* on the *balance sheet*.

overheads are costs that are not generated directly by the production process. The term is often used interchangeably with indirect cost or even *fixed costs*. In fact overheads can be fixed or variable, though the overwhelming proportion are fixed.

Examples of fixed overheads: salaries, rent, heating and lighting. Examples of variable overheads: sales force commission, postage (for a mail-order company), advertising (for a direct marketing company).

overheating occurs when *aggregate demand* exceeds *aggregate supply*. The *excess demand* which results reflects the fact that *supply constraints* are preventing producers from increasing output. There will be a tendency for *inflation* to accelerate and for imports to rise as the pressure of demand increases.

over-the-counter (OTC) market exists to buy and sell stocks and shares outside the *Stock Exchange*, usually through banks.

overtime ban: a form of *industrial action* that attempts to disrupt the employer while keeping employees' basic wages unaffected. It can only be effective if a significant proportion of work in a key section is done on overtime. This is only likely to occur in seasonal production peaks.

overtrading occurs when a firm expands without securing the necessary long-term finance, thereby placing too great a strain on *working capital*. Increased demand creates the need for more cash to finance extra raw material stocks and *work in progress (WIP)*. In the absence of extra long-term funds, the firm is forced to apply pressure to *debtors* and *creditors*. If a creditor demands early payment, there is a severe danger of being forced into *liquidation*.

Overtrading is a particular problem for small firms in high growth sectors, but is also difficult for many firms when the economy moves out of **recession**. Rising demand during the recovery encourages overtrading which, in turn, can result in company failure.

overvalued currency: one which is trading on the foreign exchange markets at a price which makes the country's exports uncompetitive, and imports very desirable. The balance of payments will have a current account deficit.

In time, the resulting low level of demand for the currency, and high level of supply, will tend to push the exchange rate down again if it is floating fairly freely. Market forces will create downward pressure. The pound was probably overvalued in 2007. (See **exchange rate index**.)

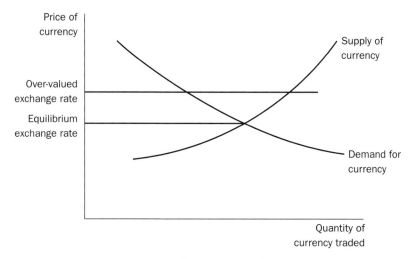

The overvalued exchange rate is above its long-run equilibrium level

own-label (own-brand) products are branded with the retailer's own name, or with a name invented by the retailer. Such products are made by manufacturers to the recipe or specification laid down by retailer. The products are usually made with a particular price level in mind, often around 10 per cent below the price of the **brand leader**. From the retailer's point of view, the advantages and disadvantages of own-label products are:

PROS: • can build a brand identity for your own shop (e.g. Next) and thereby add value

• gives a much stronger bargaining position than when dealing with the owners of powerful brand names, therefore buy supplies more cheaply

CONS: • unless your own brand has a good name, the shop's image will be cheapened

• requires backroom staff to check quality of own-brand produce, adding to **overheads**

packaging: all the design and cost elements involved in the physical protection and presentation of a product. Packaging has been referred to as the 'silent salesman'. An eye-catching pack design that conveys the right image and information about the product can be a highly effective promotional tool. It is a key element in the *marketing mix* for any consumer good, and important in *non-price competition*.

P and L account stands for profit and loss account, now replaced by *income statement*.

pan-European marketing means treating Europe as a single market by selling the same products in the same way throughout Europe. This strategy is used by *multinational* companies such as Levi's, Kellogg's and Ford. It reduces marketing staff costs in each country and can help ensure a consistent image. Most commentators believe that pan-European marketing will spread rapidly, especially within the *euro* currency area.

parallel imports are goods brought into a country by *entrepreneurs* working outside the official *distribution* network of the manufacturer. If cans of Coca-Cola were being sold for 80p per can in France and 60p in Britain, it would be profitable for a parallel importer to bring container loads of the drink in from Britain to distribute in France. Producers try any legal way they can to stop parallel imports, as they interfere with the pricing differentials that enable profits to be maximised. (See *price discrimination*.)

Pareto efficiency, or Pareto optimality, refers to a situation in which it is impossible to make anyone better off without making someone else worse off. This means that there must be an optimal *allocation of resources*, such that inputs are used in the most efficient way (*productive efficiency*) and output yields the maximum possible satisfaction to consumers (*allocative efficiency*).

Parkinson's Law is that, 'Work expands so as to fill the time available for its completion' (C Northcote Parkinson, *Parkinson's Law*, Penguin Books, 1965). This golden rule points to the danger of assuming that, because managers look busy, they must necessarily be doing useful work. Parkinson's Law is a warning against bureaucracy.

participation rate: the proportion of the population which is either in work or registered unemployed. It is thus a measure of the size of the total workforce available and the extent to which the population is economically active. This in turn depends on the age at which people cease full-time education, the retirement age and the extent to which parents take time out from employment to look after children.

partnership: a legal form of business organisation where two or more people trade together under the Partnership Act of 1890. It is usual for partnerships to have *unlimited liability*, which means each partner is liable for the debts of the other partners, including their tax liability. Because this requires a high degree of trust, partnerships are most common in the professions, such as in medicine and the law. Forming a partnership allows more capital to be used in the business than is the case with a **sole trader**, and some of the strain of decision-making is taken off the shoulders of individuals. It also allows partners more personal freedom. For example, they can take holidays when they like. However, unlike private or public companies, they retain major responsibilities for the success of the organisation, and their ability to raise finance remains somewhat limited.

par value: see *nominal value*

patent: the right to be the sole user or producer of the *invention* of a new process or product. To register a patent, the inventor must:
- provide full drawings of the invention for the *Patent Office*
- demonstrate that the ideas have original features
- promise that the ideas are his or her own.

Under the Copyright, Designs and Patents Act 1988, patent holders have the monopoly right to use, make, license or sell the invention for up to 20 years after it has been registered. Although this grants the inventor rights that can be very valuable, there is no agency for enforcing patents. Therefore the holder has to be willing to take to court those that infringe the patent. An individual inventor is very unlikely to be able to afford the legal costs, so new patents are often sold on to larger firms.

Patent Office: the only authority with the right to grant *patents* or *trade marks* within the UK.

paternalistic leadership style is reminiscent of the way fathers treat their children, i.e. deciding what is best for them. The paternalistic approach is an *autocratic leadership style*, though decisions are intended to be in the best interests of the workforce. The leader is likely to explain the reasons for his or her decisions and may even have consulted staff before making them, but *delegation* is more unlikely. The paternal company treats its workforce as family, taking care of its social and leisure needs. Its emphasis is on *human relations* (see *Mayo, E*) and social needs (see *Maslow, A*).

P

pattern of trade: the way in which an economy trades with different parts of the world and in different products. The UK pattern of trade features: increasing trade with the EU; the US and Germany as its two single most important trading partners; a high proportion of exports consisting of services, particularly financial services.

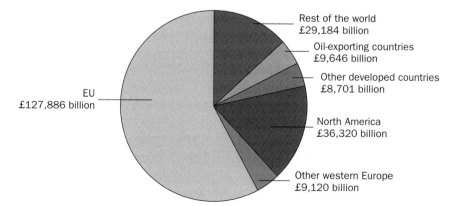

EU
£127,886 billion

Rest of the world
£29,184 billion

Oil-exporting countries
£9,646 billion

Other developed countries
£8,701 billion

North America
£36,320 billion

Other western Europe
£9,120 billion

Exports from the UK by destination, 2007, £ million. (Source: ONS, Annual Abstract of Statistics, 2008.)

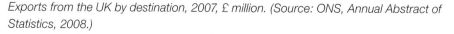

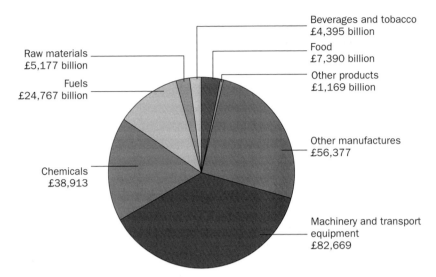

UK visible exports, by commodity, 2007, £ million. (Source: ONS, Annual Abstract of Statistics, 2008.)

PAYE stands for 'pay-as-you-earn', which is a system of *income tax* payment allowing employees to have their tax assessed for the year and then divided into 12 if they are paid monthly, or 52 if they are paid weekly. It avoids people receiving a large income tax bill at the end of the year, and so discourages *tax avoidance*.

pay round: the annual process by which employers and *trade unions* negotiate pay rises to compensate for price inflation and perhaps achieve an increase in real living standards. At times of low inflation the pay round is barely noticeable. It should not be forgotten, though, that pay expectations are affected not only by inflation but also the rises achieved by staff whose negotiations came earlier in the pay round.

penetration pricing: setting a price low enough to gain sufficient market share to achieve customer brand recognition within that market. (See *market penetration (2)*.)

pension funds are investment institutions that gather the pension contributions made monthly by employees and employers and invest them for long-term growth. The money is invested in well-spread portfolios of *shares*, property and *government securities*, with the intention that the growth achieved will enable the contributors to receive generous pensions when they retire. Pension funds, together with insurance companies and *unit trust* firms, are the main institutional shareholders that own the majority of shares in most of Britain's *public limited companies (PLC)*.

per capita means 'per head', and is often used in data where an individual measure is required, such as income per capita as opposed to total income.

perfect competition exists when a market exhibits the following characteristics:
- a large number of small buyers and sellers, none of whom can influence price on their own
- *homogeneous products*, i.e. all the rival products are identical
- perfect knowledge, i.e. all consumers know the prevailing price

- perfect freedom of entry into, and exit from, the market
- all the firms in the market are profit maximisers
- in the long run, only **normal profit** can be earned.

These unrealistic conditions mean that perfect competition is simply a model which has some use as the starting point to analyse the behaviour of firms in the real world, but which cannot be a true representation. It does show how both short- and long-run efficiency can be achieved, however, if at least some of the conditions prevail.

Productive efficiency can be achieved under perfect competition because there will always be many sellers competing, and they will need to keep costs to a minimum in order to survive. *Allocative efficiency* can be achieved because *free entry* to the market means that there will always be a producer seeking to meet consumer demand at a price that reflects the costs of production.

perfect knowledge is a condition of *perfect competition* implying that both consumers and producers are fully informed about the conditions in the market and about the best ways of producing. Consumers know all about the prices and availability of the products they may purchase and producers are all able to use the best technology available at the time.

perfect mobility is a condition of *perfect competition* and means that both *labour* and capital can move from one use to another. People will be able to move from one occupation to another without difficulty and also move to a different geographical area. Funds for investment will be able to move out of a less profitable use and into a more profitable activity.

performance appraisal is the process of judging the effectiveness of an employee's contribution over a period of time. It might be conducted every quarter, every six months or, most commonly, every year. The appraisal is carried out by a fellow employee, often the immediate superior, though it is usually based more on discussion than inspection. A performance appraisal might follow these stages:

- at the start of the year, discuss the appraisee's personal objectives, i.e. hoped-for achievements and developments
- towards the end of the period, ask the employee to complete a self-appraisal form
- use the latter as the basis for discussion of the employee's achievements, strengths, weaknesses, training needs, career intentions and future objectives.

The process is intended to provide employees with *feedback* on their performance and therefore be motivating. However, it can be stressful if the appraisal is used to judge *performance-related pay (PRP)* awards.

performance indicators are ways of measuring achievement in relation to *objectives*. The form of measurement is likely to be quantitative, such as sales figures, speed of response or the quality reject rate. Schemes such as *performance appraisal* need an element of numerate data, so performance indicators are often devised as a way of making appraisal more meaningful.

performance ratios are measures of managerial or asset efficiency such as *return on capital employed (ROCE)*. It is important to compare like with like: different types of business have different ratios so comparisons over time may be more meaningful than comparisons with different businesses.

performance-related pay (PRP) is a bonus or salary increase awarded in line with an employee's achievements over a range of criteria. For a receptionist the criteria might include helpfulness, efficiency, appearance and attendance. An employee performing well above average might get an 8 per cent pay rise while average achievers get only 3 per cent.

peripheral (workforce or business) means business elements or activities that do not form part of the core. As a result they are the most vulnerable to an economic downturn or a change of corporate strategy. *Handy* has suggested that, in the future, organisations will have a core of lifelong, highly rewarded and highly skilled employees supplemented by peripheral workers who are hired and fired as seasonal, cyclical or market changes dictate.

peripheral workers are those on the edges of an organisation's labour force. They may be employed part-time, on temporary contracts or on zero hours contracts. Unlike the salaried, core workforce, these people are used flexibly, allowing the firm to avoid fixed costs that prove a burden during periods of low demand. If the firm employs too high a proportion of peripheral workers, there is a risk that communication, teamwork and efficiency may be harmed. (See also *core staff*.)

personal allowance: the amount of an individual's income which is free of income tax. This amount is usually raised in line with inflation in the *Budget*, unless the Chancellor wants to increase the real level of tax revenue.

personal disposable income is the income which remains to individuals to spend as they wish, after all direct taxes have been deducted.

personal loan: a loan taken out by an individual, which could be used to fund consumption but could also be used to fund a business start-up or expansion. The individual is personally responsible for ensuring that the loan is repaid. On the other hand, a loan to a *private limited company* means that the owners of the business do not have to repay the loan out of their own personal funds because they have *limited liability*.

persuasive advertising is communication to customers designed to appeal to the emotions. Favourable or distinctive images are used to encourage the target market to identify with the product or service being promoted. A long-running example of persuasive advertising is 'Bounty – a taste of paradise'. The power of the moving image makes television and cinema advertising the favourite media for persuasive advertising campaigns.

Some pressure groups criticise the power of persuasive advertising to press people to buy – or long to buy – products that may have little merit (such as expensive children's toys) or actually be harmful, such as fatty foods or alcohol. *Informative advertising* rarely attracts such criticism.

PEST analysis (political, economic, social and technological analysis): a systematic means of analysing the external factors that may present opportunities or threats to a business.

Peter Principle: that 'in any hierarchy, an employee tends to rise to his level of incompetence, and that's where he stays'. This idea of Dr Laurence Peter became one of the best-known critiques of the modern corporation. He quoted examples of excellent motor mechanics being promoted to become second-rate foremen and of fine teachers becoming incompetent school heads. Dr Peter pointed out that the main criterion for gaining promotion is success, so competence is rewarded with promotion until the individual rises to a hierarchy level where he or she can no longer cope. On arriving at this level of incompetence, the overpromoted employee would be subject to frustration and stress, and be at risk of an identity crisis.

Phillips curve is named after A W H Phillips (1914–1975) who studied the data on increases in money income and levels of unemployment between 1851 and 1957, and showed that as unemployment rose, the rate of increase of wages and hence prices (*inflation*) declined. This conclusion appears obvious, since higher levels of unemployment mean that workers are in a less-powerful position to bargain for wage increases, and so the pressures on inflation are reduced. From a government policy point of view, it did have important implications, however, because a low-inflation policy became inconsistent with full employment, and vice versa. In the period 1995–2007, unemployment fell without inflation accelerating. It is likely that there is still a trade-off between unemployment and inflation but probably at a lower level of unemployment than previously.

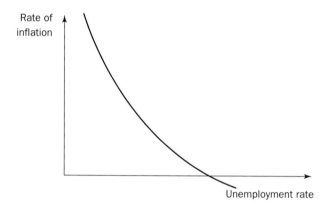

Phillips curve

physiological needs are the physical needs of human beings, such as food, warmth and the avoidance of pain. They form the lowest level of Maslow's *hierarchy of needs* and are therefore often referred to as *lower order needs*.

picketing occurs when strikers stand at entrances to the venue of an *industrial dispute* in the attempt to persuade others not to cross the picket line, thereby breaking the strike action. Employment legislation limits the number of pickets to six. This makes illegal the use of mass picketing, which can intimidate those thinking of going in to work.

pilot study: a preliminary stage in *market research* in which a small number of interviews are conducted to see whether the questionnaire achieves the research *objectives*. Any unclear questions can be rewritten before the full survey is undertaken.

place: the term given to *distribution*. The key marketing questions regarding place are:
- which types of outlet do we want to be distributed in? (newsagent, supermarket or Harrods?)
- what level of distribution should we seek to achieve?
- how are we to achieve that level?

Of far lesser significance is the choice of *distribution channels* by which the goods change hands between the producer and the customer.

planned economy: an economy in which all the resource allocation decisions are taken by government departments. So decisions about what is to be produced, and how, and how it will be distributed, all become a matter for the bureaucracy. Of the remaining centrally planned economies, China and Vietnam have large private sectors and North Korea and Cuba are opening up some areas of their economies to market forces. Many countries' governments still plan some parts of economic activity centrally, e.g. the NHS in the UK.

planned obsolescence: see *obsolescence*

planning permission (or planning consent) is required from a local authority before new construction can be started. This applies to shop signs, house extensions and change of use, as much as to house, factory and office construction. It is designed to protect the environment from haphazard development.

plant is the *infrastructure* of a factory, especially the buildings and services (such as ventilation).

PLC: see *public limited company (PLC)*

ploughed-back profit is another term for *retained profit*. It signifies the profit left after all deductions that is reinvested into the business to finance renewal and expansion.

poaching employees means attracting workers from a rival firm that have already been trained in the skills you need. This saves you the cost of the training process and means that your competitor has wasted its resources. If done widely within an economy, employers would stop (or cut down on) training new employees since it would become a pointless exercise. This would damage the skill level and therefore competitiveness of the workforce. Poaching can be seen as an example of *market failure*.

poison pill: a defence to a *takeover bid* by which the company under threat signs an agreement or buys out another firm that would represent a long-term drain on the resources of the bidder. As a consequence, the bidder should decide against swallowing up the poisoned pill (company), and give up their bid. An example of a poison pill is giving staff *employment contracts* with a three-year notice of termination clause. This would add greatly to the cost of taking over and reorganising the firm.

policy: another term for *strategy*. In other words, a plan for meeting *objectives*.

policy conflict: it is frequently the case that policies conflict with one another in that the effect of one policy is to make another policy harder to achieve. For example, policies which are likely to reduce inflation are also likely to increase unemployment. Policies to persuade more firms and individuals to use the railways are likely to entail raising the cost of road use. This conflicts with the objective of keeping road use costs at a level acceptable to public opinion. There are many other examples. As Abraham Lincoln said, you can't please all the people all the time. (See also *macroeconomic policy*.)

policy package: some economic problems cannot be solved with a single policy. Supposing the government wanted to reduce air pollution by 50 per cent. The causes of air pollution are quite varied so a range of policies would be required to deal with ozone, carbon monoxide, particulates and so on. The broader the policy objective, the more likely it is to require a policy package. Poverty, for example, has to be tackled in a whole range of ways.

political and legal system: the means by which rules and regulations are created to protect society from the excesses of human aspiration. The right to own and keep private property and the requirement to pay debts protect businesses. Consumer and employment law protects individuals from businesses making unreasonable demands. Environmental laws protect the environment (up to a point). These and other laws provide the stable framework for society which allows the economy to develop in positive ways.

To some extent the political and legal system imposes constraints on businesses and individuals. These have to be balanced against the protection, stability and reliability that it gives.

poll: a *quantitative research* survey, into either political or consumer opinions.

poll tax: a fixed amount of tax which must be paid by each person as an individual.

polluter pays principle is the idea that polluting emissions should be taxed so that the businesses which create the pollution carry the full cost, i.e. both the private and the *social cost*, of the pollution they create. This involves internalising an external cost.

pollution: impurities which are allowed to escape into the environment. Air pollution comes from vehicles, power stations and industries. Water pollution comes from farms, sewage and industries. Efforts are being made to ensure that polluters clean up more effectively. *Business responsibility* is often now described as entailing a commitment not to pollute or to control the level of pollution. In practice there is still much to be done.

pollution charges can be used to discourage pollution. Usually, such charges will be taxes on polluters, levied in proportion to the scale of their emissions. The climate levy in the UK forces firms to pay escalating amounts as pollution rises above set levels. This gives them an incentive to install equipment which will reduce the amount of pollution.

pollution permit: a licence given by the government which allows a firm to emit polluting substances up to a certain level. By allowing less than the amount of pollution currently occurring, the government can reduce pollution overall. Over time, levels allowed by the licences can be reduced. (See also *tradable permits*.)

population: has two meanings:

- All the people within a defined area or group. Most commonly it refers to countries or regions, but it can be used to refer to a more closely defined group, e.g. car owners or NHS users.
- A statistical term meaning all the people within the criteria chosen for a *market research* exercise. For example, it might be all lager drinkers, in which case a sample would be drawn from the lager-drinking population.

population growth: the rate at which the population increases. This may come from immigration or from a rising birth rate or a falling death rate.

Porter, Michael (1947–): the writer whose work on strategy and competitiveness has been influential worldwide. His analysis of generic strategies is very powerful, as is his five forces analysis of the main factors affecting a firm's competitiveness.

portfolio: a spread of assets or interests to provide *diversification*. A share portfolio would be spread among large and small, UK and overseas companies. A brand portfolio should have a mix of products: see *inferior goods*, *normal goods*, *price elastic* and *price inelastic*. In this way, it would be extraordinary for circumstances to arise in which the firm cannot succeed.

portfolio analysis is the examination of all the brands held by a firm to identify their strength and potential. A useful method is the *Boston matrix*, which analyses products in terms of their **market share** and market growth. This helps a firm allocate its resources, usually away from brands in declining markets and towards those with growth prospects.

positional goods are things which by their nature are fixed in supply and therefore, ultimately, accessible only to those who can afford to pay rising prices if demand increases. Examples include quiet beaches and unrestricted rural views. As population pressures and economic growth continue, demand for such things increases while supply diminishes, pushing the price up and limiting access to the relatively few people who can buy themselves a privileged position. Another example might be a seat on the centre court at Wimbledon or any other item the desirability of which is increased by its scarcity.

positive externalities are the external benefits that may result from a course of action. Sometimes they are called spillover effects because they bring some benefit to a third party, someone who is neither a producer nor a consumer of the product. The firm which builds an office block of some architectural merit improves the appearance of the neighbourhood. In this way it benefits anyone who appreciates the improvement. (See also **externalities**.)

positive skew is **bias** within a distribution towards high values. In other words, the majority of the values are above the average. For example, the diagram below shows the frequency with which people take driving tests, analysed by age.

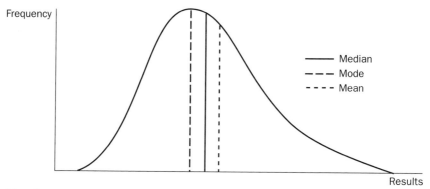

Positive skew

positive statements can be checked against the facts in order to decide whether they are true. They contrast with normative statements, which involve value judgements and will reflect personal opinions.

post-tax profit: profit after the deduction of **corporation tax**. This is the profit that is available for distribution to shareholders. It is also known as 'earnings' which, when divided among the number of shares issued by the firm, provides the ratio **earnings per share (EPS)**.

poverty is a situation in which people's **standard of living** is low. It may be measured in either absolute or relative terms. **Absolute poverty** means that a person's basic human needs for food, clothing and shelter are not being met and a poor standard of health may also result. This applies to people suffering from malnutrition or without homes. **Relative poverty** depends on the standards being applied and implies that within a particular society a given standard of living is unacceptably low. So people may be described as living in relative poverty if they are unable to participate in activities which are considered normal in that society, even though they have enough to eat and somewhere to live. Thus poverty may mean having basic needs satisfied but being unable to go to a football match or spend a short time at the pub or pay for children's books or outings.

There is some evidence that poverty is on the increase because income distribution has widened in the past 15 years, worldwide, under the impact of market forces.

poverty trap: a situation in which a person may be worse off working than living on *means-tested benefits* because the marginal rate of taxation and the rate at which benefits are lost in combination remove the incentive effects of the earnings. This results from low *tax thresholds* combined with a sharp tapering off of means-tested benefits as income rises. Incentives have increased with the introduction of the *Working Families Tax Credit*.

PPP: see *purchasing power parity (PPP)*

PPPs: see *public private partnerships (PPPs)*

PR: see *public relations (PR)*

predator: a company attempting to buy up another firm in a hostile *takeover bid*.

predatory pricing: setting a price low enough to drive competitors out of the market, or out of business. This anti-competitive practice is hard to prove, though the pest control firm Rentokil has been warned by the *Office of Fair Trading (OFT)* to stop doing it. Their tactic had been to target small but successful local competitors; whilst keeping their national prices high (thereby remaining profitable), they cut their local prices in a predatory manner. Once the competitor had withdrawn from the market, Rentokil's prices were pushed back up. Carried out on a rolling basis around the country, this enabled the firm to keep overall prices high, yet maintain their high *market share*. Predatory pricing can be a feature of *price wars*.

preference share: a share paying a fixed *dividend* that offers greater security than an *ordinary share*. It is like a compromise between an ordinary share and loan capital (*debenture*). If the company goes into *liquidation*, preference shareholders would be repaid in full before ordinary shareholders receive anything. This is also true of dividends, which are paid to them after loan repayments have been made, but before ordinary shareholders receive theirs. From the investor's point of view, the preference share carries less risk than an ordinary share, but no right to a share of the firm's profitability.

press release: a *public relations (PR)* statement issued to the media in the hope of obtaining favourable editorial publicity. Successful press releases will offer stories that can either be treated as news items or form the humorous items and pictures that press media and television like to use.

pressure group: an organisation formed by people with a common interest who get together in order to further that interest. Pressure groups exist in a wide variety of forms, such as the Licensed Victuallers Association, who pressure the government in the interests of the brewing trade; Greenpeace, who fight for environmental issues; and *trade unions*, who look after the interests of their members.

pre-tax profit: profit before the deduction of *corporation tax*.

preventive maintenance means building into a production schedule the maintenance programme for equipment and machinery. In this way, mechanics can work to prevent faults rather than cure them. This is essential to ensure that a production schedule can be relied upon 100 per cent, without which a *just in time (JIT)* production system cannot operate efficiently.

price: the money value of anything which is bought and sold in the marketplace, including goods, services, assets and factors of production. In competitive markets price is determined by market forces, i.e. supply and demand. Businesses with some monopoly power may be able to decide prices within limits. In some cases prices are decided by governments, e.g. prescription prices in the UK. Mostly, prices are displayed and known in advance. In some cases, they may be negotiated, depending on the quantity bought or the means of payment, or there may be a haggling process in which the price emerges as a compromise.

price competition means the rivalry between firms which use price as a way of attracting consumers. It contrasts with non-price competition, which involves other ways of attracting consumers, e.g. through advertising.

price controls can be used to prevent prices from rising. However, they are seldom used because they tend to lead to excess demand which cannot be satisfied because there is no incentive for firms to increase output.

price discrimination means charging different prices to different people for what is essentially the same product. This is done in order to maximise revenue by charging more to those that can afford, and are willing to pay, more. Price discrimination is a response to the recognition by a firm that different types of people may have different *price elasticities* of demand for a product. For example, under-16s get half-price entrance to cinemas and football grounds because the owners know that higher prices will cut demand substantially. In this case, as in all considerations of price discrimination, it is essential that there should be the minimum of crossover between market segments. In other words, if many adults could get in for half-price, the point of the discrimination would be lost.

price : earnings ratio (PE ratio): a measurement of how highly a firm's shares are valued in the *stock market*. The ratio divides the stock market value of the shares by the firm's earnings (profit after tax). The higher the PE figure, the higher the company's share price in relation to its profit.

$$FORMULA: \quad \frac{\text{market share price}}{\text{earning per share}} = \text{PE ratio}$$

Worked example: PE ratio

$$\frac{£1.50p}{10p} = 15 \text{ times}$$

Conclusion: the stock market rates the share at 15 times earnings; this means it would take 15 years of this year's profit level to justify the current share price. Is this realistic? If the firm is Tesco, one could feel confident of sustained profits. If it is a small computer software firm, however, 15 years of profitability cannot be guaranteed. Therefore the share may be overpriced.

price elastic: a product for which a proportionate increase or decrease in price leads to a proportionately greater increase or decrease in the quantity sold, i.e. its elasticity is greater than one. (See *price elasticity*.)

price elasticity is a measure of the way the *demand* for a good responds to a change in its price. In order to avoid the problems with absolute numbers, it is always measured in proportionate or percentage terms, thus:

FORMULA: $\dfrac{\text{percentage change in quantity demanded}}{\text{percentage change in price}}$

So if the price of a good rises by 10 per cent, and its demand falls by 20 per cent as a result, the value of price elasticity is:

$-20\% \div 10\% = -2$

A value greater than one is called **price elastic**, whilst a value of between zero and one is called **price inelastic**. In mathematical terms, the value of price elasticity is negative, since an increase in price will cut demand, and a fall in price will increase demand. Since this is always true, the minus sign is sometimes (wrongly) ignored.

There are two important determining factors for price elasticity:

- Most important in deciding elasticity of demand is whether **substitutes** are available. If there are, people will shop around and if the price rises, they will switch to an alternative. If there are no good substitutes, the demand will be inelastic. Often the elasticity depends on how tightly defined the product happens to be. The demand for toothpaste is inelastic because there are no acceptable substitutes so far as most people are concerned. But the demand for Colgate toothpaste may be quite elastic because a price rise may lead people to choose another brand.
- A second factor of relevance in determining price elasticity is the amount spent on the product in question. Where the price is low relative to the income available, demand is likely to be inelastic. Demand for a packet of crisps or a box of matches is usually inelastic.

There is a link between price elasticity of demand and sales revenue. If demand is elastic and prices rise, the greater-than-proportionate fall in quantity sold will mean that sales revenue will fall and vice versa. In the diagram, the box showing lost revenue is larger than the box showing gained revenue. With inelastic demand, a price increase will result in a rise in sales revenue. In the diagram below, the box representing revenue gained is larger than the box representing revenue lost.

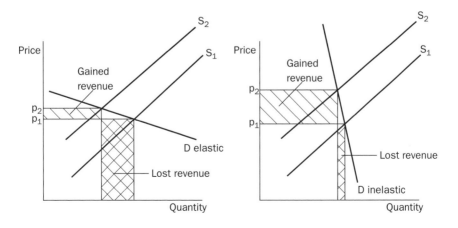

- Price elasticity of demand can affect decisions about price. Raising the price of an item which has elastic demand may not help to cover rising costs. Also price elasticity affects the impact of certain indirect taxes, e.g. those on petrol, alcohol and tobacco and of *tariffs* and *quotas* on imports.

price fixing occurs when two or more firms agree to charge a minimum price. This is defined as an *anti-competitive activity*. It is generally illegal under competition law but occurs if businesses in a *cartel* are trying to reduce the impact of competition on each other. So long as they all stick to the agreement, they will be acting collectively like a *monopoly* and will be able to keep quantities sold lower and prices higher than they would be if there were strong competition. A participant in a price agreement can go to the OFT with information so that it faces lower fines than the rest of the group if the OFT decides to prosecute.

price index: a way of measuring changes in the general level of prices using index numbers. The *retail prices index (RPI)* measures inflation generally. The wholesale price index measures changes in wholesale prices and provides a useful leading indicator of inflation. The *consumer prices index (CPI)* measures inflation in a way that allows international comparisons.

price inelastic: where a proportionate change in a product's price leads to a proportionately smaller change in the quantity sold, i.e. elasticity is greater than zero but less than one. Such goods tend to have high *product differentiation*, meaning that consumers perceive them as having no acceptable substitutes. This may primarily be due to the effectiveness of their *branding* and *advertising*, e.g. Levi's. For the manufacturer, the advantage of a price-inelastic product is that if its costs rise, it can pass them on to its customers with minimal effect on demand.

price leader: a brand that is in such a powerful position within its marketplace that it can largely dictate the prevailing price level. The managers of rival brands know that consumers see the price leader as *the* salad cream, baked beans, coconut chocolate bar or whatever. Therefore the price set by the rivals has to be in relation to the leader. For instance, HP baked beans has to be priced at least 2–3p below Heinz (the price leader), otherwise its market share will dwindle. If HP's costs rise, it may be unable to risk putting its price up until Heinz decides on a price increase. Therefore being second-best in a market with a price leader can be a dangerous position.

price maker: another term for *price leader*.

price mechanism: the interaction of *demand* and *supply* which determines prices, and hence the allocation of scarce resources. Price rations the available resources among competing buyers. It causes prices to rise when demand exceeds supply, and vice versa, so ensuring that prices send signals to producers about the nature of changes in consumer demand. This in turn enables the *allocation of resources* to change in response to consumers, thus preserving *consumer sovereignty*.

prices and incomes policy: a way of controlling *inflation* by government restrictions on increases in prices, wages and salaries. The difficulties of controlling wages and salaries are bad enough (see *incomes policy*), but they are nothing compared with attempting to control prices. This is because it is almost impossible to police price increases because of their number, and because they respond to market signals. If these signals are ignored, markets become distorted. For example, firms might stop producing items for which the price is being kept too low to be profitable. Governments can try to control prices in the *public sector*, but again this leads to distortions if the *private sector* is not also constrained.

price sensitive refers to a good whose demand will react very strongly to a change in its price. For instance, a small increase in price will result in a large reduction in quantity sold. Therefore price sensitive means the same as *price elastic*.

price system: the mechanism which causes prices to rise when demand exceeds supply, and vice versa, so ensuring that prices send signals to producers about the nature of changes in consumer demand. This in turn enables the *allocation of resources* to change in response to consumers, thus preserving *consumer sovereignty*.

price taker: a firm with products that are insufficiently distinctive to stand out amongst the competition. As their *price elasticity* is high, these products must be priced at or below rival brands. This *competitive pricing* is the only way to ensure satisfactory sales levels.

price theory: the area of economics which is concerned with the determination of price, through the study of demand and supply and their interaction. The focus of price theory is on *equilibrium* and disequilibrium prices and it seeks to predict the outcome of a variety of possible changes in the marketplace.

price war: a clash between rival companies in which prices are being cut in a cycle of thrust and counter-thrust. The situation in which a price war is most likely to start is when there is oversupply, i.e. *capacity utilisation* is low. So firms attempt to keep their *overheads* covered by boosting their *market share*. If only one firm cuts prices to boost market share, it could benefit. When a price war breaks out, however, no company benefits, only the consumer. Even that is only in the short term, however, because many price wars end when one firm withdraws from the market. In the longer term, that may enable the remaining producers to push up their prices sharply. (See also *predatory pricing*.)

pricing methods are the different ways in which a firm can decide on the price level to set for its products. The methods can be split into two: *cost-based pricing* and *market-based pricing*. In either case, however, psychological factors can and should be taken into account (see *pricing psychology*).

COST-BASED:
- mark-up pricing, as used by most small firms, means adding a standard profit proportion to the variable costs; clothes shops, for instance, tend to work on a 100 per cent mark-up, so a dress bought for £40 will be priced at £80
- *cost-plus pricing* is similar, except that a profit is added to the full cost of the good or service; in other words, an allowance for *overheads* is added to the *variable cost* and then a profit percentage added to the total

MARKET-BASED:
- *competitive pricing* means taking your price level from the prices set by others within the marketplace; a new petrol station, for example, would have to charge prices in line with local competitors; too high a price would mean inadequate sales volume
- *contribution pricing* takes advantage of the fact that different prices can be charged in different circumstances for the same product (as long as all prices exceed the *variable cost*)
- *profit-maximising pricing* is achieved by researching to find the likely level of demand at different prices, then calculating which is the most profitable

p

In addition to the above, firms may price tactically, in other words to achieve short-term *goals*. Examples of pricing tactics include using a *loss leader* and *predatory pricing*.

pricing psychology is of importance because consumer perceptions and images of products have a major impact on demand. In particular, price cutting will boost demand in the short term, but may undermine the long-term image. Consumers do not want 'cheap' Mercedes or Chanel. (See *psychological pricing*.)

pricing strategy is the medium- to long-term plan of the price level that a firm wishes to set for a product. For a new product there are two fundamental strategies: *market penetration (2)* (pricing low to maximise sales) or *skimming the market* (pricing high to maximise profit margins). A further possibility for an existing product is *price leadership*. This is only feasible if the product in question has the dominant image within the mass market (examples would include Hellman's mayonnaise and L'Oréal hair products). There are many other ways in which a firm might determine the price of its products: see *pricing methods*. Because competition in international markets is likely to be strong, market-based pricing is likely to figure large in decisions about prices in different countries.

pricing tactics: ways of using price to take advantage of a short-term opportunity or threat, e.g. *loss leader*, *psychological pricing* or *predatory pricing*.

primary data: first-hand information that is related directly to a firm's needs. *Secondary data* may be useful, but is unlikely to provide the answers to the exact questions you are interested in. For example, secondary data might provide information about total consumer spending on soft drinks. To find out about consumer attitudes to 7-UP would require *primary research* to gather primary data.

primary research is the gathering of first-hand data that is tailor-made to a firm's own products, customers or markets. This is carried out by fieldwork, whereas *secondary data* (second-hand) is gathered by *desk research*.

primary sector is that part of an economy consisting of agriculture, fishing and the extractive industries such as oil exploration and mining.

Prince's Trust: set up by the Prince of Wales to provide *grants* for young people wishing to start up their own businesses.

private benefits are the benefits which accrue to the individual buyer and seller of a product. In contrast, the *external benefits* are those which accrue to third parties. For example, if a large new factory is built, shopkeepers close to the area where employees of the new factory live will probably find that their profits are rising because of the increase in incomes in the area.

private costs are the costs of production which are borne by the business which produces the product. For example, private costs will include wages and salaries, interest and the costs of raw materials and components, as well as any research and development costs. They do not include *external costs*, i.e. those which are borne by third parties. These might be the costs to health and welfare of pollution which results from the production process.

private enterprise includes all economic activities which are undertaken for *profit* within the *private sector*. The owners of the business will be individuals operating as sole traders or as shareholders or other private sector organisations. In contrast, *public enterprise* involves the government. Private enterprise is normally subject to market forces, with decisions being made according to conditions of demand and supply.

Private Finance Initiative (PFI): a strategy begun in 1992 to invest in UK *infrastructure* using a mixture of private and public sector funding. The objective was to modernise the infrastructure without being committed to a big increase in government spending. It has been used to encourage private sector approaches to increasing the efficiency of building programmes in health, education and transport. Projects are run by private sector contractors, using private sector funds. The public sector body concerned undertakes to pay an annual fee for a given length of time (sometimes 20 years) which covers the costs. The most controversial plan is to modernise the London Underground through a PFI. It is still too soon to say whether the costs of PFIs are worth the benefits. Some projects have delivered on time at reasonable cost while others have not. (See also *public private partnerships (PPPs)*.)

private label: a retailer's own brand, which often carries the company name (such as Sainsbury's) but may also be an invented name (such as John Lewis's 'Jonelle' brand). For the retailer, the great advantage of a strong private label is that instead of buying supplies from a powerful branded-goods manufacturer (at high prices), it can obtain supplies from whoever is willing to provide the right quality at a low price. Accordingly, private-label goods generate far higher profit margins for the retailer than branded goods. (See also *own-label*.)

private limited company: a small to medium-sized business that is usually run by the family that owns it. Within such a firm, the family can determine its own *objectives* without the pressures towards short-term profit that are so common with a *public limited company (PLC)*. It is private in that the shares cannot be bought or sold without the consent of all the existing shareholders and it cannot be listed on the *Stock Exchange*.

private sector is that part of an economy operated by firms that are owned by shareholders or private individuals. In Western economies it is the dominant sector; the remainder is called the *public sector*. Within the private sector, decisions are made on the basis of *market forces*, with businesses responding to the conditions of supply and demand so that changes in consumer demand will be reflected in decisions about what to produce.

privatisation: the process of returning firms or industries to the private sector after being run by the state. In the UK, the policy of privatisation was vigorously pursued by Conservative governments in the 1980s and 1990s. It became a model for many other countries where it was felt that the mix between state and private sector organisations had become unbalanced. The surprise to many was that the 1997 Labour government continued to part-privatise Air Traffic Control and the London Underground.

Privatisation has a variety of meanings, from the contracting out of refuse services within a local authority, to the deregulation of bus routes. It is as much a way of thinking as a closely defined programme. However, the majority of people when they talk of privatisation tend to mean the high profile transfers of nationalised industries into public limited companies, such as British Telecom (BT), British Airports Authority (BAA) and British Airways (BA).

Many of the nationalised industries were actually declining and privatisation made it somewhat easier to close down parts of them. Others were very profitable, e.g. BT, and their sale sparked off a big increase in the number of people who owned shares. On the whole the privatised industries have become more efficient when subjected to market forces.

There are still many controversial issues pertaining to privatisation. Much depends on the way in which the *regulators* operate. The Post Office may soon be part privatised but this is opposed by the workforce and the trade unions involved.

proactive: a decision or action that initiates rather than responds to the initiatives of others. For example, if a *recession* occurred, the proactive company might develop a range of new, lower-priced products. The reactive firm would copy that initiative.

probability is the likelihood of an outcome occurring, expressed as a numerical value. Most managers would tend to refer to probabilities in percentage form ('a 50/50 chance') or as a fraction ('the chances are only 1 in 10'). Statisticians use a third method, which is based on the fact that all the possible outcomes from an event must add up to 1. Therefore if the chances are 1 in 10, the statisticians describe that as a 0.1 chance.

The most important aspect of probability for business students is to recognise what is known as the gambler's fallacy. If a roulette player sees the ball land on red four times in a row, there is a tendency to think, 'Ah, well next time it's bound to be black.' In fact, every time the ball is put into play the chances of red and black are even. Therefore a firm that has launched two new product flops should not be kidding itself that, 'Our luck should turn.'

process innovation: improvements in the way a product is produced, arising from new technologies. This is a powerful way to cut costs and become more efficient for many businesses. It can lead to big increases in *productivity*.

procurement means the purchase of goods and services by governments. Very large contracts are involved, e.g. for aircraft for the defence forces. In the past it has been quite normal for governments to favour domestic producers, but procurement contracts are being gradually opened up to competition within the EU. The issues may be discussed further within the *World Trade Organization (WTO)*.

product: a term used by manufacturing and service businesses to indicate the goods or services they provide.

product awareness: the proportion of all those within a *target market* who are aware of a particular brand/product. *Brand leaders* such as Coca-Cola may have almost 100 per cent awareness, whereas only 60 per cent of soft drink buyers are aware of 7-UP. For companies, product awareness is a crucial first step towards product trial. High product awareness is usually a function of:
- heavy advertising or sales promotion
- gaining favourable *public relations (PR)* media coverage
- the age and past prominence of the product
- the level of distribution and display
- the distinctiveness/memorability of the product.

product development: fulfilling *marketing objectives* by developing new products or upgrading existing ones. This might be in order to boost sales/*market share* or to add value and therefore price. Successful product development relies upon excellence in *research and development (R&D)* and in design, plus the technical ability to turn good designs into well-engineered products or services. Product development can be through marginal changes (low risk, small reward) such as 'new, improved Ariel' or major innovations (high risk, high reward) such as Toyota's fuel-efficient Prius car. (See also **Ansoff's matrix**.)

product differentiation: see *differentiated product*

product innovation: creating new products or improving the design of existing ones. (See also *innovation* and *product life cycle*.)

production is the process of organising resources in order to meet a customer requirement. In a manufacturing context, production is the whole process from obtaining raw materials to goods inward inspection, to production processes, to assembly and finishing, to delivery. The term 'production' can also be applied to the supply of services.

production chain: the entire sequence of activities required to turn raw materials into a consumer purchase. The chain will include activities in the *primary sector*, *secondary sector* and *tertiary sector*, with the latter involved at every stage. A highly simplified example for beer production is shown in the diagram.

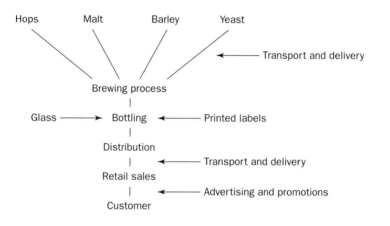

production line: the arrangement of a flow production system so that parts move systematically from one stage to the next. Within such a process, *division of labour* is likely to be high and production-line workers may feel threatened by the prospect of automation.

production orientation is a term used by many writers to indicate an old-fashioned business that ignores customer tastes and needs. The management is assumed to be inward-looking, focusing upon the convenience of producing the same old product in the same old way. This is contrasted with more thrusting, market-orientated companies that spot new trends and devise the products to meet them. Although there is truth in this, production orientation does have some important strengths:

- implies a commitment to focus on the firm's strengths rather than diversifying into unknown markets
- will often be associated with high quality, even to the point of producing an item that is stronger or better than the market thinks it needs (but that can boost long-term *corporate image*)
- may lead to longer-term planning for new capital investment than in a market-orientated firm.

productive capacity refers to the ability of the economy to produce. An increase in productive capacity, which might result from an increase in investment, implies that it will be possible to increase output.

productive efficiency: a production process is said to be productively efficient if the costs of production have been minimised by economising in the use of real resources. It is one element in *economic efficiency* and is achieved when average total cost is at its minimum point. Achieving productive efficiency involves using the lowest cost resource inputs in the most effective way, e.g. by avoiding wasted inputs and co-ordinating production to avoid wasting time. *Economies of scale* are often important in achieving productive efficiency.

productive potential: see *productive capacity*

productivity measures the efficiency with which resources are used. The most commonly used productivity measure is output per person employed. When people speak of productivity, this is usually what they mean. However, it is possible also to measure output per unit of capital employed – the productivity of capital. Productivity can be measured within the individual firm or for the economy as a whole.

On the international level, differing levels of productivity growth (efficiency) are important in explaining variations in industrial performance and rates of economic growth. These in turn have a major impact on standards of living. Productivity grows for a number of reasons including:

- increased capital investment, so that *labour* inputs are working with better quality or larger amounts of capital equipment
- technological change, so that production processes are more efficient
- improved management techniques, so that people work more effectively together. Examples of the possibilities would be *multi-skilling* and *teamwork*.

Rising productivity can cause unemployment, which may persist for a number of years, if demand does not rise as fast as the productivity gains. Despite this, it is difficult for an economy to grow healthily in the long run without productivity improvements. In the past, UK productivity grew very slowly compared to other developed countries, but since the early 1990s, productivity has much improved, though there is still concern in some industries.

Productivity increase, annual average growth, 2001–07

US	Japan	France	Germany	Italy	UK
2.0	2.1	1.7	1.3	−0.1	2.1

Source: OECD

productivity bonus: a financial *incentive* to encourage a workforce to work hard. Employees receive a basic wage supplemented by a bonus related to their output level. The bonus rate can be calculated on a group or individual basis. *Herzberg* would describe such a system as a way of achieving *movement*, not *motivation*.

productivity deal: an agreement between management and union representatives that the former will provide some financial or other benefits in exchange for higher output per worker. If a 5 per cent pay rise has been granted in exchange for 5 per cent higher *productivity*, this would leave labour costs per unit unchanged and therefore have no harmful effects upon competitiveness or *inflation*.

product life cycle: the theory that all products follow a similar life course of conception, birth, growth, maturity and decline (see diagram), although products pass through these stages at different speeds. The modern cigarette was born in 1873 and sales peaked in 1973 (implying a product life cycle of around 200 years), whereas the entire sales life span of Pokemon cards was three years.

Factors affecting the length of a product's life cycle:
- durability: if the item need be bought only once (such as a sandwich toaster) then *market saturation* can hit demand, as all those who want the item, have it
- fashion: if the item's sales grew because of fashion, it is likely that they will die quite quickly, for the same reason
- technological change can be very significant in turning the customer away from a product that now seems obsolete.

An important implication of the theory is that as every product will eventually decline and die, it is necessary for firms to carry out continuous *new product development (NPD)* programmes. Ideally, new products should be financed from the *cash flow* generated by mature brands, and should be launched before maturity turns to decline. The product life cycle relates to company cash flow in the following way:
- during the development phase there is substantial negative cash flow from the money spent on *research and development (R&D)*, *market research*, product design and setting up a *production line*
- if birth turns to growth, more cash must be ploughed into expanding factory capacity
- once sales have stabilised, the firm can reap the cash rewards from their success
- in the decline phase, brands with a high *market share* can provide the cash for the development of replacement products. (See *cash cow*.)

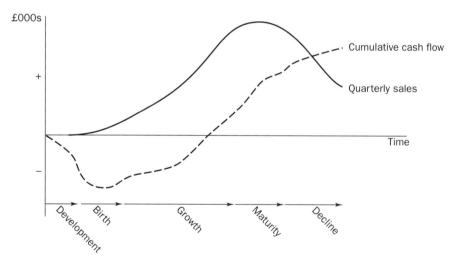

product mapping: see *mapping*

product placement occurs when a manufacturer gets a brand placed in a scene of a film or television programme. If the hero of a worldwide box-office hit insists on Bacardi and Coke several times in the film, it may be because the producers have paid for the product to be placed there. In effect this is a form of advertising.

product portfolio: the range of products or brands held by a company that provide it with diversified sources of income. Ideally this portfolio should range over different markets and different stages in the *product life cycle*. A well-known and very useful way of analysing a firm's product portfolio is through the *Boston matrix*.

product positioning means having a clear idea about the segment of the market that a product or service is targeted at. For example, everything about Primark is targeted at fashion-conscious but price-conscious shoppers.

product proliferation is the tendency for successful market sectors to become overcrowded by a large number of new product launches. This proliferation makes it hard for shopkeepers to find shelf space for all the products available, and can lead to confusion on the part of the customer.

product range: the full listing of the products offered by a firm.

product trial is the rate at which consumers in your *target market* buy or try your brand for the first time. It forms one of the three prime objectives for a firm launching a new product:
- distribution
- product trial
- repeat purchase.

Most firms set quantitative targets for each, such as to get a chocolate bar distributed in 80 per cent of sweetshops, tried by 50 per cent of chocolate buyers and repeat purchased by 12 per cent of trialists. In markets such as chocolate, product trial is heavily influenced by *packaging*, *promotion* and *advertising*. If the market is more fashion orientated, word of mouth is likely to be the main single influence upon the rate of trial.

profit: a simple definition of profit is what is left from sales revenue after costs have been deducted. Profit is also a return on capital invested: it compensates the owner of the capital for the loss of the capital for any other potential use. (See also *surplus*.)

Economists distinguish *normal profit* and *supernormal profit*. The former is that amount of profit which is just sufficient to keep the resources employed in their current use. The latter is profit in excess of this amount and indicates that buyers are prepared to pay a price above the costs of all the resources used in production. In time this will attract more resources into production and increase output in line with consumer demand. (See also *profit-signalling mechanism*.)

> *FORMULA:* revenue – costs = profit

profitability is the measure of an organisation's ability to earn revenues above its expenditures. Profitability is usually assessed in relation to some yardstick such as *sales revenue*. In a general sense it refers to how much profit can be made by an industry or a sector of the economy.

profitability ratios measure profit in proportion to a yardstick such as *net assets* (*return on capital employed (ROCE)*) or *sales revenue* (*profit margin* ratio).

profit and loss account: a statement recording all a firm's total *revenue* and costs within a past trading period. Although firms have a degree of leeway about how they present their 'P & L account', most adopt the format set out in the following example. To show how the calculations work, sample figures are included on the right-hand side. Public companies are now required to produce an *income statement*.

Worked example: profit and loss account

		£000	
	Revenue	940	
minus	Cost of sales	610	
equals	**Gross profit**	330	
minus	Overheads	180	
equals	**Trading/Operating profit**	150	
Plus	One-off items	(30)	(a £30 000 loss)
equals	**Pre-tax profits**	120	
minus	Tax	30	(25% of pre-tax)
equals	**Profit after tax**	90	
minus	Dividends	40	
equals	**Retained profit**	50	

profit centre: a division or department of a company that has been given the authority to run itself as a business within a business, with its own *profit and loss account*. Before the start of the year, a senior manager will discuss with the leader of the profit centre the likely *revenues* and costs for the forthcoming year.

PROS: • power delegated to the local level, which speeds up decision-making
• the local profit and loss account can form the basis of financial incentives for all the workforce at the centre

CONS: • hard to coordinate the activity of several different 'small firms', all wishing to grow rapidly, and competing with each other
• the performance of a profit centre may bear no relation to the effort and skill of its management; after all, a blazing summer would make high profits in the ice-cream market an inevitability

profit margin: *profit* as a proportion of *sales revenue*. It can be expressed as a total (the percentage of sales revenue which is profit), or it can be calculated on a unit basis (profit as a percentage of the selling price). Profit margins can be calculated using gross profit (*gross margin*) or operating profit (*net margin*).

Worked example: a sofa is bought by a furniture shop for £500 and sold for £625

Profit margin

$$\frac{profit}{selling\ price} \quad \frac{£125}{£625} \times 100 = \mathbf{20\%}$$

profit maximisation is often taken to be the reason why firms exist and to be their primary *corporate objective*. In practice, most firms have a hierarchy of objectives. When a firm's survival is threatened, it may profit-maximise in order to restore its financial health. Otherwise it is likely to pursue longer-term *objectives* such as *diversification*. Another possible strategy is *satisficing.*

profit-maximising pricing is achieved by researching to find the likely level of demand at different prices, then calculating which is the most profitable. If the product has a relatively low *price elasticity*, the price set through this method is likely to be quite high. That is likely to attract new competitors who may make serious inroads into your medium-term *market share*. Therefore profit-maximising pricing may benefit the firm's short-term performance at serious cost to its longer-term future.

profit motive: here the pursuit of profit is the governing force behind a person or organisation's decisions. This is most likely to be influential within the *private sector*, since shareholders require *dividends* large enough to justify the risks taken when investing. Economic analysis usually rests on an assumption that all entrepreneurs are motivated by profit. In fact, although it is important to make a profit to ensure long-term survival, many businesses have other motives as well.

profit quality refers to the likelihood of a profit source continuing into the future. If a profit has arisen from a one-off source (such as selling property at above its *book value*), its quality is said to be low. High-quality profit is trading profit that can be expected to be repeated in future years.

profit-related pay: a system of remuneration in which a proportion of each employee's salary varies in line with the firm's profit level. So, instead of being paid £20000 a year, an employee might be paid £15000 plus 0.01 per cent of the firm's trading profit. If the firm's profit last year was £60 million, then the employee can expect a salary of £15000 + (0.01% of £60m = £6000), i.e. £21000.

profit share: a bonus paid on top of employees' salaries to ensure that a proportion of the firm's profit is shared out among staff.

PROS: • could help to bridge any '*them and us*' divide between staff and management or shareholders

• provides staff with a personal *incentive* to keep costs down and *productivity* up (at John Lewis, for example, the profit share has amounted to over 20 per cent of annual salary)

CONS: • unless it amounts to a substantial sum, the profit share may be disregarded by staff, or even seen as insultingly low

• research evidence has shown that profit sharing, on its own, has little effect on performance, partly because individuals cannot believe that their own efforts will make a significant difference to the whole firm's profit level

profit-signalling mechanism: when demand for a product is increasing, prices will tend to rise and the product therefore becomes more profitable. This encourages entrepreneurs to expand output in profitable lines of production by moving resources into them. When losses are being made the reverse happens: resources will be moved out of the unprofitable lines. In this way profits signal the existence of unsatisfied consumer demand and ensure that the allocation of resources falls into line with the pattern of consumer demand. This link between the pattern of demand and the allocation of resources is an important element in the working of the *market system*.

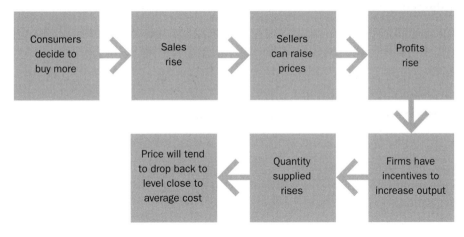

Profit-signalling mechanism

programmed trading is the use of computer programs that decide when to buy or sell shares or foreign currencies. The computer might be instructed, for example, to automatically sell any share that has fallen by 10 per cent or more (to prevent a client from losing everything).

progressive tax: one which takes in tax a higher proportion of high incomes than it does of low incomes. The most important example is *income tax*. Having a tax-free allowance means that people on lower incomes are taxed on a smaller proportion of their incomes than people on higher incomes.

promotion has two different meanings:
- being appointed to a more senior or more desirable job (though see *horizontal promotion*)
- the promotion of a product as part of the *marketing mix* by the use of *advertising*, *branding*, *sales promotion* and *public relations (PR)*.

promotional message: the impression gained from advertising, branding and other aspects of promotion. This requires particular attention in an international context. Cultural variations between markets make it all too easy for exporters to market their products in ways that offend the target market. (See also *export marketing*.)

property rights: all economic goods are associated with property rights and their owners have the right to decide how they may be used. Owners of *assets* have a right to charge people who want to make use of those assets. For example, owners of fishing rights may charge for the use of them by other people. The term is often used in connection with *intellectual property* rights such as copyright and patents. Extending property rights can be useful in correcting market failures. For example, if it is established that those who suffer from pollution (e.g. from a local chemical plant) have the right to be free of it, polluters can be required to pay compensation. (See also *intellectual property*.)

proportional tax: a tax which takes an equal proportion of income whatever the person's income level.

protectionism describes policies of erecting barriers to trade such as *quotas*, *tariffs* and *non-tariff barriers*. These will raise the price of the imports to which they apply, so reducing the threat to domestic producers.

Protectionism can reduce the benefits of free trade in terms of consumer access to cheap products and enhanced economic growth. It is therefore discouraged by *World Trade Organization (WTO)* agreements and has been reduced through international trade negotiations. (See also *comparative advantage*.)

The most notorious period of protectionism was during the *Great Depression*, when country after country put up barriers in the hope that unemployment would not increase. The barriers made unemployment worse: they reduced exports for all concerned. At international meetings in early 2009 world leaders said that they would not make this mistake again. On the whole, they have kept to this.

Despite the benefits of trade generally, people with vested interests in certain industries are sometimes able to bring pressure to bear on their MPs or Congressional representatives so that they will support protectionist measures. For example, anti-dumping measures can be used to exclude imports.

prototype: a sample product manufactured on an experimental basis to see if the engineering and design ideas work in practice. The prototype can be tested both from an engineering and from a *market research* perspective, before the firm decides whether to start full production.

psychological pricing means setting a price based on the expectations of the consumers within your *target market*. If, for example, a perfume producer has identified a *market niche* for a special occasion fragrance for mid-teenage girls, the price may be set above the level of the competition. This will help to reinforce the image set by the perfume's packaging and advertising messages. In this way, the price level becomes an integral part of the product's *marketing mix*.

public borrowing means borrowing by the government to finance current and capital expenditure. (See *public sector net borrowing*.)

public corporation: the technical name for a nationalised industry, i.e. an enterprise that is owned by the state but offers a product for sale to *public sector* and *private sector* customers. It should not be confused with a *public limited company (PLC)*, which is in the *private sector*.

public deficit: the amount by which government expenditure exceeds tax revenue. This must be financed by borrowing.

public enquiry: a way of judging a *planning permission* case that is thought to be of particular public interest. A typical example might be the building of a motorway through a site of outstanding natural beauty. The enquiry will hear evidence from the proposers and the protesters; it has the power to turn the planning application down.

public enterprise refers to state-owned organisations, i.e. *nationalised industries*, which produce for the market, for example the Post Office (for now).

public expenditure is spending by the government, for example on social security, defence, education and health. Public expenditure in recent years has been averaging around 42 per cent of GDP. (See also *fiscal policy* and *government expenditure*.)

public finance refers to government expenditure and the ways in which it is financed through taxation and *public sector borrowing*.

public goods are items which must be provided by society as a whole for two reasons. No one can be excluded from benefiting from them. (If provided by the private sector, *free riders* would benefit.) And their consumption by one person does not prevent their consumption by someone else, i.e. they are *non-rivalrous*. Examples include street lighting, defence and the police force. These are pure public goods.

public interest: the interests of society as a whole. The term is usually used in relation to the actions of the public sector, in particular of the remaining nationalised industries and the regulatory bodies set up to monitor the privatised industries (e.g. *OFGEM*). These are charged with acting in the public interest. This needs constant reinterpretation in the light of changing circumstances but can be loosely defined as protecting the consumer and the community from hidden or unnecessary costs.

public limited company (PLC): a *limited liability* business with over £50000 of share capital and a wide spread of shareholders. PLCs are the only type of company allowed to be quoted on the *Stock Exchange*. This provides them with relatively low-cost access to equity finance.

There are disadvantages, however. Changing from a private to a public limited company means moving from the control and support of a family firm to the profit-focus, the limelight and, perhaps, the short-termism of public shareholders, City analysts and the financial press. (See also *divorce of ownership and control*.)

public ownership refers to *nationalised industries*, which produce for the market but are owned by the government and are therefore part of the *public sector*.

public private partnerships (PPPs) can be used by governments to induce private sector companies to contribute to investment in the development of public services. For example, regeneration of run-down areas can involve government agencies in planning a variety of developments alongside private building projects. In return for planning permission or a share of the revenue, the government may persuade private sector firms to contribute new roads or other assets useful to the community. PPPs have also been used to fund school and hospital buildings and to develop public transport. (See also *Private Finance Initiative (PFI)*.)

public relations (PR) is the process of obtaining favourable publicity via the editorial columns of press media, or in television or radio broadcasts. The PR expert has the contacts within the media to ensure that the client's story or side to a dispute is reported sympathetically. Public relations can be a positive process such as organising interviews on Breakfast TV shows or setting up launch parties for new products. However, there have also been cases where PR personnel have spread negative stories about rival firms. This is legal but unethical.

The Institute of Public Relations explains that public relations involves:
- liaising with the media; writing press releases, answering press enquiries, setting up interviews
- producing and writing publications; newsletters, annual reports, leaflets and brochures
- organising events; exhibitions, conferences, product launches and opening events
- planning publicity campaigns and measuring results.

public sector: the organisations and activities that are owned and/or funded by national or local government, such as *public corporations* (nationalised industries, e.g. the BBC), *public services* (such as the National Health Service) and *municipal services* (such as local council-run leisure centres).

public sector borrowing: total borrowing by the *public sector*. *Public sector net borrowing* shows the amount of borrowing needed in the current year to cover the public deficit when expenditure exceeds taxation. The *National Debt* is the total loan outstanding, accumulated over many years. If there is a surplus of tax revenue over government expenditure, there will be a *public sector debt repayment (PSDR)*. This will reduce the National Debt.

public sector debt repayment (PSDR): if government expenditure is less than tax revenue, then the government will be able to pay off some of its debts. This occurred from 1987 to 1990, partly because the government was receiving large payments for shares in the privatised industries. It occurred again in 1999–2000 as the economy grew and tax revenues rose.

public sector net borrowing is the amount by which *government expenditure* exceeds revenue from taxation and other income. It varies from year to year, depending on government policies at the time and on the state of the *economic cycle*.

High levels of borrowing may necessitate high interest rates, in order to encourage people and organisations to buy Treasury *bonds*. Treasury bills may also be used to fund government expenditure; these provide short-term finance. Borrowing increases in times of *recession* as tax revenues tend to fall and expenditure on benefits increases. The reverse may happen in a boom.

Public sector net borrowing as % of GDP

2003	2004	2005	2006	2007	2008	2009 (est)	2010 (est)
3.0	3.4	3.0	2.3	2.4	8	10	9

Source: HM Treasury

The Budget of 2009 revealed a massive increase in public borrowing which will be very difficult to deal with. In order to borrow so heavily, interest rates on bonds will probably have to rise. The various rules which have been applied to levels of public borrowing are usually relaxed in times of recession.

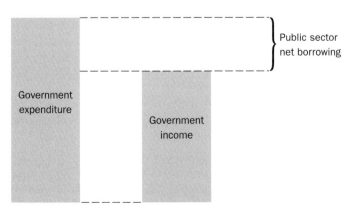

public services are services within the *tertiary sector* made available to all members of society. They include waste collection, street lighting, education and health services. They are often 'free at the point of delivery', i.e. when you receive the service, but of course they are not 'free' as such. For instance, householders do not have to pay the operator every time their refuse bins are emptied, but of course they do pay for this service indirectly through taxation.

public spending is the amount of expenditure which governments undertake with the revenue which they obtain from taxes and other sources. (See *government expenditure*.)

public utility: the suppliers of basic services to homes and businesses, including water, gas and electricity. These are *privatised* industries with *regulators* to protect consumers from the *market power* of the companies.

purchasing power: the real value of a given sum of money in terms of what it will buy. Inflation causes the purchasing power of the currency to fall.

purchasing power parity (PPP): an approach to international comparisons of standards of living which takes into account price levels in different countries. It uses exchange rates which have been adjusted to give accurate comparisons of purchasing power.

pyramid: this usually refers to the company hierarchy, in other words the formal management structure, including the numbers of management layers and the *span of control*.

pyramid selling is a clever (though generally illegal) way of encouraging inexperienced people to part with their cash in exchange for the right to sell a questionable product to others at high prices. Those at the top of the pyramid can benefit hugely from the commissions that those lower down pay on anything they sell. The nearer to the bottom you go, the more you encounter disillusioned people who realise that they have spent hundreds of pounds on items that most consumers do not want.

p

qualitative data: information that cannot easily be put into a numerical form, such as the opinions of a well-respected adviser.

qualitative research is in-depth research into the motivations behind consumer behaviour or attitudes. It is usually conducted by psychologists among small groups of people within the *target market* for a product (see *group discussion* or *focus groups*).

The idea behind qualitative research is that when people are asked direct questions (as in a *questionnaire*) they may give answers that make them sound sensible or rational. Yet many purchasing decisions are based on emotion, not logic. Consumers pay £20 extra for the 'right' pair of jeans. Qualitative researchers aim to find out consumers' real thought processes during a relaxed discussion that has no pre-set questions. It can therefore lead wherever the psychologist feels the truth lies.

PROS: • can reveal the motivations behind consumer decisions
- as discussion can range freely, it can discover the unexpected (whereas questionnaires can only consist of questions that were known beforehand to be significant)
- group discussion can provide ideas about how to solve a marketing problem from the most important people of all: the customers

CONS: • each interview or discussion is expensive, therefore few firms can afford to conduct many; this leads to possible concerns about whether the sample is representative
- the unstructured nature of the responses means that the data cannot be quantified

quality assurance: the attempt to ensure that quality standards are agreed and met throughout an organisation, to ensure customer satisfaction. Among the key factors that must be considered are:

- the time, effort and technology input into product design
- the quality of supplies of materials and components
- the commitment of the workforce
- the system of quality monitoring and control
- the ability to deliver on time
- the quality of advice and *after-sales service* provided.

quality circle: a discussion group that meets regularly to identify quality problems, consider alternative solutions and recommend a suitable outcome to management. The members are usually drawn from the factory floor, but may include an engineer, a quality inspector and a member of the sales team (to provide the customer angle). This method was first devised at the Toyota Motor Company in Japan in the 1950s. Its success as a form of *consultation* and *job enrichment* led to its wider adoption in Japan and then, in the 1980s, in the West. The two principles behind the quality circle are that:

- no manager or engineer can understand production problems as fully as the shop-floor workers, therefore their knowledge is a huge untapped asset for the firm
- workers appreciate the opportunity to show their knowledge and talents in a problem-solving environment.

quality control: the process of checking the accuracy of work bought in or completed. This is usually carried out by quality inspectors, though some modern factories encourage employees to check their own quality. This conforms to *Herzberg*'s view of the importance of personal responsibility and self-checking.

quantitative data: numerical data that can be stored and used in a form such as a spreadsheet or database.

quantitative easing: relaxing the controls on the money supply to inject more capital into the money markets. This term was used by the Bank of England at the time of the 2007/09 *credit crunch*. In effect, it meant printing more money and was a way to enable banks to lend more freely to businesses and individuals, at a time when loans were in exceptionally short supply.

quantitative research means research using pre-set questions among a large enough *sample size* to provide statistically valid data. In practical terms that means using a *questionnaire* to poll at least 200 consumers within each segment of a market. It is a way of discovering data such as:

- a product's *consumer profile*
- the way a market can be segmented
- probable sales at a given price level
- estimated sales of a new product
- the results of a *blind product test*.

Large firms tend to use group discussions (see *qualitative research*) to help understand customer views and then write a questionnaire based upon them. Interviewers can then be employed to conduct the survey upon a representative sample of the population. The three main ways of drawing a sample are by *random sample*, *quota sample* and *stratified sample*.

quantity theory of money: the theory which links the quantity of money in circulation with the rate of *inflation*. The simplest version of this is given by the *equation of exchange*.

This theory was important in economics in the early part of the 20th century but was superseded by the ideas of Keynes and other economists in the 1930s. *Monetarism* related money and prices in a more sophisticated way. It was developed primarily by *Milton Friedman*. His ideas were influential during the early 1980s and became associated with Margaret Thatcher's time as prime minister. The policy prescription which resulted from monetarism was one of strict monetary control which would bring down the rate of inflation.

quartile: the total accounted for by one quarter of a population. For instance, a computer might rank all of a firm's 1000 customers in order of sales value. The 250 biggest customers (the top quartile) could then have their sales totalled, which might reveal that they buy 80 per cent of the firm's *output*. The smallest 250 customers (the bottom quartile) might be worth less than 2 per cent of the firm's output. This information would help the company to make decisions on its sales and distribution strategies.

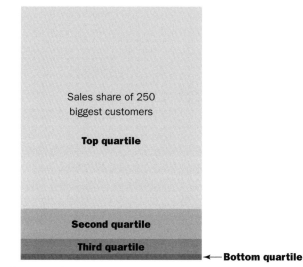

Analysing data into quartiles

questionnaire: a document containing a series of questions designed to discover the information required to meet a firm's research objectives. When writing questionnaires there are four main principles to bear in mind:
- each question should ask only one point
- questions should not contain *bias* (e.g. 'How much do you like cider?')
- the time, cost and ability to quantify the analysis of the answers depends on whether the questions are closed or open. The use of the *closed question* is far more common (e.g. 'Have you bought cider within the last week?' Yes ☐ No ☐)
- the questions must be asked in the right sequence, leaving personal details such as age, address and occupation until the end, and making sure that earlier questions do not bias the answers to later ones.

quotas: an *import control* which places a fixed limit on the quantity of the good which can be imported. The objective is usually to protect domestic producers. The supply of the imports will be reduced and the price will usually rise.

The more inelastic the demand for the imported product, the more the price is likely to rise. Above the level of the quota, the supply is fixed and the price is demand determined. (See diagram opposite).

Quotas are strongly discouraged by the *Wolrd Trade Organization (WTO)* but are nevertheless widespread in some product areas. This is because there has been support in recent years for protectionist policies on the grounds that they may save jobs. In reality it is likely that the loss of output caused by the restraint on trade is more serious for standards of living than the loss of jobs.

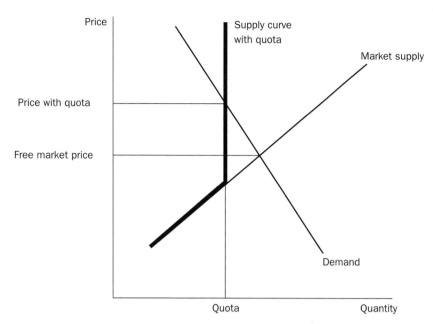

Price

Supply curve
with quota

Market supply

Price with quota

Free market price

Demand

Quota

Quantity

The effect of a quota

quota sample: the recruitment of respondents to a *market research* exercise in proportion to their known *demographic profile*. Therefore if you know that 25 per cent of your buyers are men, you would instruct interviewers to recruit one man for every three women within your sample. This is a far cheaper method of recruitment than *random sampling*.

Aiming for a grade A*?

Don't forget to log on to **www.philipallan.co.uk/a-zonline** for advice.

race relations legislation makes it illegal to discriminate against people at work on grounds of colour, race, ethnic or national origin. The *Equality and Human Rights Commission* can investigate and pursue employers or *trade unions* which are thought to discriminate.

racial discrimination means refusing a job or a promotion to someone on grounds of race. Although it is illegal, recent studies show that it is still occurring. It is sometimes difficult to prove in individual cases. Unemployment rates amongst different ethnic groups are too large to be explained entirely by differences in qualifications.

R&D: see *research and development (R&D)*

random sample: contacting survey respondents so that every member of the population has an equal chance of being interviewed. This sounds straightforward but is, in fact, both hard and expensive to achieve. The reason is that random must not be confused with haphazard. If all that an interviewer did was to stand outside Marks and Spencer one Tuesday afternoon and interview as many people as necessary, various distortions would occur in the sample:

- relatively few men would be interviewed
- few working women would be interviewed
- few hardworking students would be interviewed.

In other words, the sample would be biased towards pensioners, parents of preschool children and the unemployed.

In order to avoid these pitfalls, random samples are drawn from local electoral registers, and interviewees are contacted at home. The interviewer must call three times before giving up on an address. This adds to fieldwork costs, so although random sampling is common in social research, businesses tend to use the *quota sample*.

rate of interest: the amount which will have to be paid annually for the loan of funds. This will be higher for risky borrowers than it is for known, reputable borrowers. The lowest interest rates are those used by banks when they lend to each other. (See also *interest rates*.)

rating agencies are firms that specialise in assessing risks. Banks use them to provide risk ratings. They have been blamed for giving excessively favourable ratings to debts that turned out to be very risky indeed, during the run-up to the 2007/09 financial crisis. This meant that potential asset buyers were given very inaccurate information and made decisions to buy what became known as toxic assets, which, if fully informed, they might not have wanted to buy. The two biggest agencies involved are Moody's and Standard & Poor's. Many of the ratings were based on unrealistic assumptions, such as that house prices would continue to rise indefinitely.

ratio analysis: an examination of accounting data by relating one result to another. Users might be:

- internal managers, wanting to measure their own performance compared with previous years and with their rivals: they might use *return on capital employed (ROCE)*, *gross margin* and *net margin*
- shareholders or potential shareholders should start with key indicators such as return on capital employed and *gearing*
- the staff (perhaps through *trade union* representatives) would be interested in the financial security of the firm and its profitability: widening *profit margins* would make a substantial pay claim seem far more plausible.

rationalisation means reorganising to increase efficiency. The term is mainly used when cutbacks in costs of *overheads* are needed in order to reduce an organisation's *break-even point*. This may be achieved by:

- closing one of a company's factories and reallocating the production to the remaining sites
- closing an administrative department and delegating its tasks to the firm's operating divisions
- *delayering* (removing a layer of management).

Public relations officers often use the term rationalisation as a euphemism for *redundancy*.

rationing means imposing a physical limitation on individuals' consumption of a good or service. For instance, in time of war it might be necessary to limit each car driver to five litres of petrol per week. Rationing is often achieved through the *price mechanism*, in that only those who can afford a good will be able to have it.

At present the term appears most frequently in relation to the NHS, which is forced to ration certain health-care procedures because there is not enough money for everyone to have all the treatments from which they might possibly benefit. The rationing process requires careful investigation to determine which treatments give best value for money.

raw materials: *commodities* bought by a firm in a virtually unprocessed state. Examples would include sugar for making chocolate and sand for making glass.

real means that the item in question is being expressed in a way which removes the effects of inflation. (See also *real incomes*.) For example, real earnings show the actual change in the *purchasing power* of what people are earning. In contrast, *nominal values* are expressed in money terms, without allowance for inflation.

real disposable income: the amount of money that people have to spend after all taxes have been paid and any welfare benefits have been added.

real GDP means a figure for total output in the economy which has been adjusted to allow for *inflation*.

real incomes are money incomes adjusted to allow for inflation. For instance, if you earned £100 last year and £200 this, but in the meantime prices had doubled, your real income would remain the same. Money values can be deflated using a *price index*, which expresses the values in *constant prices*.

R

real interest rates are the rates above (or below) prevailing rates of *inflation*. For instance, if inflation is 5 per cent per annum and interest rates are 8 per cent, real rates are 3 per cent. During periods of rapid inflation, a seemingly attractive rate will often be negative. For instance, an attractive interest rate of 20 per cent will actually be minus 5 per cent, if inflation is 25 per cent per year.

reallocation of resources: when the pattern of consumer *demand* changes, resources are reallocated in line with the new pattern of demand, through the *price mechanism*. This process was first described by *Adam Smith*, who characterised it as the *invisible hand*. This process is not always easy. It may entail some *structural unemployment* as some industries decline while others grow. People take time to adjust to the new composition of output.

real resources are all the things which can be used to create products for which there is a demand. So they include the *factors of production*, land, *labour* and *capital*, *human capital* and *natural resources*.

real terms: a figure or series of figures presented after stripping out the effects of *inflation*. For example, a firm may boast that its revenue has grown by 6 per cent in the past year; but if inflation is running at 7 per cent, the firm's revenue has fallen by 1 per cent in real terms.

real values show changing values over time with the effects of *inflation* removed. This means they will be expressed in constant prices, using a base year.

recapitalising: injecting more *capital* into a business that has insufficient to trade effectively and safely. The alternative to recapitalisation is probably *liquidation*, though in this case existing or new shareholders believe it preferable to keep the business going.

receiver: the person appointed by creditors when a company has insufficient assets to cover its *liabilities*. The receiver's job is to try to sell the company to any other interested parties as a going concern so that those who are owed money can get it back. If the receiver fails to find a buyer, then the company will be sold off in parts, and will be liquidated.

recession is that part of the *economic cycle* characterised by falling levels of demand, very little investment, low business confidence and rising levels of unemployment. It is neither as long lasting nor as severe as a *depression*. The official definition of a recession is two successive declines in quarterly *gross domestic product (GDP)*.

reciprocity is the principle by which countries agree to grant the same trade concessions to their trading partners as they are receiving from them. When governments are negotiating trade arrangements through the *WTO* this principle is often important in securing agreement.

recognition: see *union recognition*

recommended retail price (RRP): the price the manufacturer suggests that the retailer should charge. With most products the manufacturer has no legal right to force retailers to sell at this price, so some charge more and some charge less.

recovery is the upswing phase of the *economic cycle*. At first *aggregate demand* and output will grow slowly. *Investment* will begin to recover from its previous very low level. There will be little inflation at this stage. For a while, *unemployment* may continue to rise because employers will be reluctant to take on more people until they are certain that the rise in demand will be sustained. (There is a time lag of 12–18 months between changes in output and changes in employment.) Later in the recovery, optimism returns and investment grows faster. There will be a *multiplier* effect.

recruitment is the process of identifying the need for a new employee, defining the job and the appropriate person for it, attracting a number of suitable candidates, then selecting the one best suited to the job.

recruitment procedure: the complete process of turning the need for a new employee into a successful appointment. This would include advertising the vacancy (see also *headhunter*), shortlisting, dealing with references, assessing candidates, deciding on the most suitable person and then debriefing the unsuccessful candidates. Throughout the process it is necessary to avoid discrimination by sex, race, disability or age. This not only avoids legal challenges to decisions, but also ensures that the best candidate is appointed to the job.

recycling means dismantling and/or sorting products so that they can be collected and reused. This reduces the need for more raw materials to be mined or grown. As the cost of *raw materials* increases, technology improves, and the legal, moral and ethical implications of polluting become more critical, firms will move into recycling more of their own and other firms' products.

redeployment means moving to a different job offered by the same employer. When *structural change* is under way and people are being made redundant, redeployment can reduce the number of actual *redundancies* required. It may happen as a result of *rationalisation* or of declining demand for one product when the firm has other products for which demand is stable or growing.

redistribution of income: see *income redistribution*

redistribution of wealth: see *wealth distribution*

redundancy occurs when a job function is no longer required. Therefore the employee holding the job becomes redundant through no fault of his or her own. If an organisation requires a large number of redundancies in order to reduce its *overheads*, it may ask for volunteers, offering financial inducements to those that accept. If insufficient numbers of the right types of employee apply to leave, compulsory redundancies may have to follow. The staff involved are legally entitled to the following minimum payments:

Age of employee	Payment per year of service
18–21 years	Half a week's pay
22–41 years	One week's pay
Over 41 years	One-and-a-half weeks' pay

These terms only apply to those with over one year of continuous employment.

refinancing means much the same as *recapitalising*, though the latter carries the implication of being based rather more on equity finance. A refinanced business might, therefore, have received a high proportion of its extra *capital* in the form of loans.

reflation means stimulating aggregate demand by using *expansionary policies* in order to increase the rate of economic growth and reduce unemployment. These could be *fiscal policies* such as tax cuts or increases in government spending or *monetary policies* such as reducing interest rates.

Regional Development Agencies (RDAs): the bodies responsible for implementing *regional policy*. Scotland, Wales and Northern Ireland have had them for some time; the nine English RDAs were set up in 1999. The objectives are to enhance competitiveness within each region and to create job opportunities in areas where they are scarce.

regional policies are designed to address inequalities between regions. Incomes and unemployment vary considerably. In particular, the policies aim to address the problems created by localised industries' decline. The policies are administered partly through the government's regional offices and partly through the *Regional Development Agencies (RDAs)*. The amount of money spent on regional assistance by the UK government has declined over the past 20 years. The decline in the UK budget reflects concerns about the costs and effectiveness of regional policies.

regional test: a form of test marketing in which a real experiment is undertaken within a whole marketing region. An example would be launching a new product within the North West. This would find out whether the product can achieve a high enough *market share* to be profitable if launched nationally. A regional test is a far more expensive experiment than *market research*, but should yield far more accurate information. (See also *test market*.)

regional trading blocs or regional trade agreements (RTAs) are groups of countries that negotiate to trade more freely with each other than with the rest of the world. NAFTA is the best known, uniting Mexico, the USA and Canada. There is also Mercosur, which includes Argentina, Brazil, Paraguay and Uruguay. These allow freer trade, achieved with less lengthy and painful negotiation than worldwide attempts at liberalisation. They may be a step towards freer world trade, or a source of difficulty in achieving it.

regional unemployment is one element of *structural unemployment*: It is associated with the decline of localised industries which have in the past been big employers and have experienced a fall in demand for their products. Shipbuilding, iron and steel and coal are the industries most affected; in all three cases production was concentrated in locations which had been very favourable in the past. Another example comes from Merseyside, where 100 000 jobs were lost on the docks between 1970 and 1990. Shipping traffic gradually shifted away from Liverpool towards air transport and towards the ports facing Europe rather than the US. The unemployment has persisted: it can take a long time for the local economy to adjust.

Register of Members' Interests: a document in which Members of Parliament specify any group with which they are associated which might influence the way they speak or vote in the House of Commons. By declaring such interests, it is allowable for MPs to advance the causes of those groups.

Registrar of Companies maintains a record of every *joint-stock company* in the UK, including for larger companies, their *annual report and accounts*. All the information held by the Registrar is available to the public at *Companies' House*.

regressive tax: a tax which takes a larger proportion of low incomes than it does of high incomes. Expenditure taxes are all broadly regressive. To the extent that people on lower incomes are likely to save less, poorer people will find that expenditure taxes take more of their total income. Everyone who smokes 100 cigarettes a week will pay the same tax; it will be a large proportion of a poor person's income, a smaller proportion the higher the income.

The regressiveness of *value added tax (VAT)* is greatly reduced by the fact that it does not apply to food prepared and eaten at home, housing and public transport.

regulation is one way in which companies are constrained by law, for instance on maximum pollution levels. Many firms complain that the existence of many consumer protection, employment and pollution regulations imposes excessive overhead costs upon business. For example, many staff are required to ensure that laws are being complied with. Furthermore, dislike of dealing with rules and regulations may put people off starting new businesses. In fact, regulation in the UK is lighter than in many similar countries.

When the credit and banking crisis led to bank failures in 2008 and 2009, many people asked why the banks had not been better regulated. In fact, for the previous 20 years in the USA and Britain, bankers had succeeded in persuading governments that tight regulation was unnecessary and undesirable.

regulator: an independent body set up by the government to ensure that privatised industries with an element of monopoly in their markets do not exploit consumers by overcharging and do make strenuous efforts to keep their costs down. Important elements in their approach have included the monitoring of prices, price caps and performance targets. For example, the Office of Rail Regulation (ORR) requires rail operators to comply with a huge range of conditions, relating to pricing, punctuality and safety. ORR is responsible for licensing train operators; these licences are reviewed regularly. National Express lost the right to run the east coast railway line in 2009. (See also *OFCOM*, *OFGEM*, *OFWAT*.)

regulatory capture: it is possible for regulators to be influenced by the firms they are supposed to regulate. This may make them prone to favour the interests of the industry rather than those of the consumer. It has been suggested that the US *Federal Reserve Bank* (central bank) has been subject to regulatory capture. Unlike the *Bank of England* or the *European Central Bank (ECB)*, it has responsibility for regulating the US banking system. It may have listened too carefully to the anxieties of the bankers and paid insufficient attention to the stability of the wider economy.

relative export prices: export prices compared to those of competitors or to world prices. Low relative export prices indicate a high degree of *competitiveness*.

relative inflation rates involve a comparison of *inflation* rates between countries. A high inflation rate relative to those of competing countries will mean that the exchange rate will become overvalued. As prices rise, exports will become dearer and are likely to fall while imports will become cheaper and may rise. *Depreciation* may follow.

relative interest rates involve a comparison of interest rates with those offered by other financial intermediaries or with those in other countries. Interest rates on very risky loans will always tend to be relatively high. Where one country has a higher interest rate than others, it will tend to attract deposits from abroad (provided its currency is one which the depositors are willing to hold). There are large amounts of capital which can be moved at short notice if an interest rate differential opens up, making the change worthwhile. (See also *capital movements*.)

relative poverty means lacking the income needed to lead a normal life in the society concerned. It reflects the variations in expectations between countries. In developing countries there may be large numbers of people who are living in *absolute poverty* and so do not have the basic necessities of life: nourishing food, clothing and shelter. In *developed economies* almost everyone has these basic necessities, but many people do not have opportunities for leisure pursuits or reading books; their housing may be damp or in an area where safety is questionable. In the UK it is estimated that one fifth of all children are living in relative poverty which will have an adverse effect on their opportunities as adults.

relative price: a price may stay the same in money terms but rise or fall in relation to that of another good if the price of the other good changes. Prices change in relation to one another because of market forces. For example, prices of British-grown flowers have tended to move with inflation, while prices of Dutch-grown flowers have stayed the same or gone down. This has reduced demand for British growers' flowers. A rise in wage rates (the price of labour) will make capital equipment look relatively cheap and businesses may decide to use more capital-intensive ways of producing.

renewable resources are natural resources which can be regenerated. For example, forests which are regularly replanted after felling has taken place are renewable and hydro-electric power is renewable because it is continuously available. In contrast, electricity from a gas- or coal-fired power station is not a renewable resource because fossil fuels which have been used are not replaceable – they have been taken from the earth's crust. Wind power is controversial. It is available whenever the wind is blowing so is theoretically renewable but wind farms do spoil the view, which is not so easy to renew.

rent is the payment made for temporary use of a property. Income from rent is the return on the capital invested in the property.

reorder level: the quantity of stock considered the minimum before more need be ordered from the supplier. To decide on the appropriate reorder level, a firm must take into account the following factors:
- how long suppliers take to deliver after an order has been placed (their **lead time**)
- the level of demand for the product
- the level of **buffer stock** set by a firm.

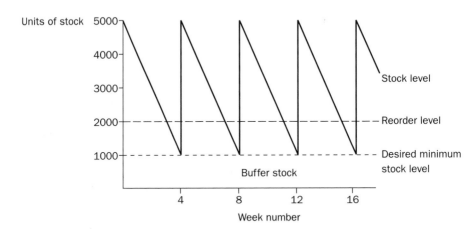

Stock reorder level

repeat purchase occurs when a first-time buyer purchases the same brand again. If this keeps happening, the process could be described as developing **brand loyalty**.

replacement investment: the level of investment needed to maintain the existing stock of capital equipment. This is sometimes known as **capital consumption**. **Gross investment** less replacement investment gives the level of net investment. This is the addition to the capital stock, which takes place each year.

research and development (R&D): scientific research followed up with the development of products or processes which are either new, better or cheaper. R&D is an important aspect of innovation and of the process of **economic growth**, leading to rising standards of living as quality products become more accessible. The UK has in the past spent relatively little on R&D, which may explain why **productivity** growth sometimes lagged behind that of competitor countries. Recently an R&D incentive scheme has made a difference.

Some economists argue that the firms most likely to spend on R&D are the ones in an **oligopoly** situation, where new product development can confer significant advantages. Some innovations can be protected by **patents** and this creates another type of incentive.

reserves are a company's accumulated, retained **profit**. When they were made, these profits represented an important source of long-term finance for the business. There is no reason to assume, however, that they are still held in the form of cash. Therefore it is a mistake to suggest that a firm can 'use its reserves' to finance investment; it can only use cash.

In the macroeconomic context, the term usually means reserves of foreign currencies held by the central bank, which may be used to manage fluctuations in the exchange rate.

resistance to change occurs as a result of: fear of the unknown; mistrust of the motives of those proposing change; and worries about loss of job security, income or status on the part of the staff concerned. Research has shown that in most organisations, middle managers are the staff most resistant to change. This is because middle managers have more to lose in any reorganisation than those below them in the hierarchy.

To reduce resistance to change, senior management needs to:
- have established in advance a sense of common purpose and of trust between the employees and management of the organisation
- explain and discuss the reasons for change in an attempt to achieve a consensus that it is essential
- if possible, guarantee staff that the changes will not result in compulsory **redundancy** or pay cuts
- consult fully on the options available for implementing the change, ensuring that employee views have a significant impact on the eventual strategy
- set a clear timetable for the entire process of change; this prevents rumours circulating about what may happen next.

resource allocation: see *allocation of resources*

resources: sources of inputs needed for the production process.

responsibility for decisions or results can be implied by **delegation**, but should remain with the directors, for they are ultimately responsible for the organisation's strategy and for the appointment of the staff involved. Nevertheless, there have been many occasions in business and in politics when the chief executive or government minister has refused to accept responsibility for actions taken by subordinates, in which case no one appears to be responsible for organisational errors or misdeeds.

responsibility to stakeholders: the idea that corporate social responsibility involves taking into consideration the interests of all **stakeholders**. These include customers, employees, shareholders, suppliers and the local community and its environment. Although this view is gaining ground, some businesses still see their primary responsibility as being to the shareholders.

responsible marketing: focusing the business not only on what customers want, but also on what is ethically or environmentally justifiable.

restrictive practice: a term used in two separate contexts.

Restrictive trade practices are active interferences by producers with the free working of markets. This reduces competition and is therefore likely to lead to higher consumer prices. Among the main restrictive trade practices are *full line forcing*, *market-sharing agreements* and the sharing of technological or marketing information. Practices such as the latter can be registered with the *Office of Fair Trading (OFT)* and would therefore be legal. Unregistered restrictive practices can result in prosecution.

Restrictive working practices are past agreements between producers and workers that limit the management's flexibility to decide who should work where and in what way. A common example is tight job *demarcation*, whereby a plumber may refuse to change a fuse because that is the job of an electrician. As the Japanese have demonstrated the benefits of workforce *flexibility*, British managements have tried to negotiate or to force through an end to job demarcation.

restructuring means reorganising with a view to improving efficiency. This may involve a restructuring of the management hierarchy (perhaps through the introduction of *profit centres*) or of the production capacity. Often, in fact, the word 'restructuring' is used as a euphemism or excuse for large-scale *redundancy*.

retail banks: the banks which cater for the needs of individuals and small businesses. They include the traditional banks, Barclays, Lloyds TSB and HSBC and a number of banks which used to be building societies, such as Birmingham Midshires (this eventually became part of Halifax and then Lloyds TSB). The remaining building societies also offer many retail banking services. In contrast, *merchant banks* deal mainly with the long-term needs of large businesses.

retail cooperatives are usually part of the national cooperative movement, which was established to provide consumers with goods at a fair price and with all the profits being paid back to the shoppers themselves.

retailer: a shop which sells goods to the general public.

retail margins: the percentage *profit* received by a shop on each item (or the average item) it sells. This is the retailer's *gross margin*, i.e. it does not allow for *overheads*. See the worked example below.

$$FORMULA: \quad \frac{\text{selling price} - \text{purchase price}}{\text{selling price}} \times 100 = \text{retail margin}$$

Worked example: if a furniture shop buys chairs from a manufacturer for £200 and sells them for £500, its retail margin is:

$$\frac{£300}{£500} \times 100 = 60\%$$

retail prices index (RPI): shows changes in the price of the average person's shopping basket. The RPI is a widely used measurement of *inflation* in the UK and is calculated through a *weighted average* of each month's price changes.

It starts with a study of people's spending patterns, to try to assess the average household's weekly expenditure. This is in order to provide the base weights. About 16 per cent of household spending is on transport; it therefore carries a weight of 0.16 within the RPI. So if transport prices rise by 10 per cent, this adds 1.6 per cent to the overall RPI (10% × 0.16). The bigger the proportion of household incomes spent on an item, the bigger the effect of any price change upon the overall inflation figure. The RPI is used to determine annual increases in welfare benefits.

The **consumer prices index (CPI)** is the measure of inflation that is used for international comparisons and the **inflation target**. It excludes housing costs, unlike the RPI.

retail selling price (RSP) is the actual price of an item charged to customers in a shop. This will differ from the wholesale price to a degree that depends on the price mark-up decided on by the retailer. In making calculations about manufacturers' revenues or profits, it is important to remember that they will not receive the RSP of the product. They will only receive the ex-factory price. This is shown in the table.

Event	Term
Manufacturer charges £4.20 to wholesaler	Ex-factory price
Wholesaler charges £5.40 to retailer	Wholesale price
Retailer charges £8.99 to customer	Retail selling price

retained profit is the profit left after all additions and deductions from sales revenue. These include trading costs, one-off profits or losses, taxation and **dividends**. Retained profit (the so-called 'bottom line') represents an important source of long-term, internal finance for the business. It adds to the **balance sheet** reserves, and therefore to **shareholders' funds**.

retraining: giving people who are part of the way through their working lives different or improved skills which are likely to be in demand in the future. Where people are **occupationally immobile**, this can enable them to take the jobs which are available.

return on capital employed (ROCE) is the percentage return a firm is able to generate on the long-term capital employed in the business. Its importance is illustrated by the fact that it is sometimes referred to as the primary efficiency ratio. A firm's ROC enables a judgement to be made on the financial effectiveness of all its policies. If, for example, it is unable to generate a higher ROC than the prevailing rate of interest, it could be argued that the firm should close down, sell off its **assets** and put the money in the bank. Apart from in times of **recession**, the average firm generates a return of around 20 per cent on its capital employed. Within its growth phase, however, Body Shop generated figures closer to 100 per cent, which meant that the firm was generating enough profit to double the size of the business each year.

FORMULA: $\dfrac{\text{operating profit}}{\text{capital employed}} \times 100 = \text{return on capital}$

Worked example: if a firm has an operating profit of £252 000 and capital employed of £2m, its ROC equals:

$\dfrac{£252000}{£2000000} \times 100 = 12.6\%$

returns to scale: the relationship between the level of output and the quantity of inputs needed to produce it. If there are possible *economies of scale*, there will be increasing returns to scale. A given increase in output will require a proportionately smaller quantity of inputs in order to produce it.

revenue is the total value of sales made within a trading period.

 FORMULA: price × quantity sold

revenue maximisation is one possible goal for a firm operating under imperfect *competition*. It may wish to expand its *market share* and therefore prefer revenue maximisation to profit maximisation.

revenue support grant: the block grant from central government to local authorities. It means that not all of local spending needs to be financed by local taxes (i.e. by *council tax* and the *Uniform Business Rate*). It also allows the government to provide extra money to those areas with the greatest needs. In recent years it has been reduced somewhat. (It used to be called the rate support grant.)

reverse takeover takes place when a smaller company takes over a larger one. This could be where the issued *share capital* of the victim is larger than that of the aggressor, in which case financing the reverse takeover involves raising more loan capital or issuing more shares. An example is Royal Bank of Scotland's February 2000 takeover of NatWest, a bank twice its size.

reward for risk: a way of evaluating profitability through comparison with the presumed risk-free investment of resources in a bank deposit account. The reward for risk is the amount by which the percentage rate of profit exceeds the prevailing interest rate. The higher the reward, the greater the risks it is worth taking.

Worked example: a new computer software firm is making a 10 per cent return on capital while interest rates are 7 per cent. Is this satisfactory?

Quantitative analysis: the reward for risk is 10% − 7% = 3%; if research shows that, each year, one in ten software firms goes into liquidation, the 3% reward would not justify the 10% risk.

Qualitative analysis: if the firm has a well-diversified product range, a wide spread of customers and management of proven quality, the level of reward may outweigh the low level of risk.

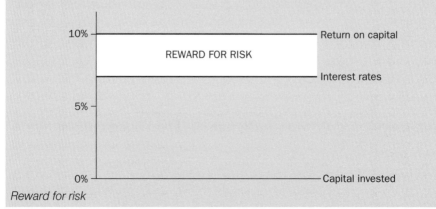

Reward for risk

262

rework is the extra labour and material cost involved in correcting manufacturing faults on a production line. Most modern procedures for improving quality (such as *total quality management (TQM)*, *quality circles* and *zero defects*) aim to eliminate rework altogether. This would cut costs and enable customer deliveries to be speeded up.

Ricardo, David (1772–1823): an economist whose most enduring contribution was the Theory of Comparative Advantage. This shows how each country will have a *comparative advantage* in producing different goods and services and if each specialises in the products in which it has the comparative advantage, it will be possible to increase total output, thus making everyone at least somewhat better off.

right first time describes a way of managing production that reduces the level of waste from faulty versions of the product that have to be scrapped. It is an element in *kaizen* and *quality assurance*.

rights issue: so called because it offers existing shareholders the right to buy more shares before anyone else. It occurs when a company wishes to raise more *capital* relatively cheaply. The company will ask its existing shareholders if they wish to buy more shares at what might seem an advantageous price, i.e. lower than the price at which the shares are currently trading. However, because the rights issue has the effect of supplying more shares to the market, the share price will fall after the rights issue has taken place. For the original shareholders who do not wish to take up the rights issue, their share value is protected because they are able to sell their rights to make up the difference.

risk: the possibility that events will not turn out exactly as expected. Risks are quantifiable, and probabilities can be assigned to them. Sometimes it is possible to insure against them, the insurers using the probability of their happening as a basis for setting the insurance premium. In contrast, uncertainty is not quantifiable. During the 2007/09 financial crisis it became clear that although risks are quantifiable, mistakes had been made in the way that risk was calculated.

risk aversion: many people are risk averse in that they do not want to be exposed to significant risks of any kind. They can be reassured by insuring against some common risks. They may however find that they are unsuited to entrepreneurial risks and the anxieties of running a business. Or they may be well able to handle a small business that has steady sales, but shy away from any risky expansion of activity.

risk-bearing economies of scale mean that risks are reduced for larger businesses compared to smaller ones. For example a larger business may have a diversified product range. If sales of one decrease, others may keep going so that total sales revenue is not drastically affected. Similarly a diversified market may reduce risks, as with a business that exports to a number of economies, not all of which are likely to go into recession at once or to an equal extent.

risk identification is the attempt to determine and then quantify any threats to the firm's continued operations. Identifiable risks may include:

- financial risks, arising from the firm's *liquidity* position (short-term ability to meet debts) or from its *gearing* level (its dependence on debt): these risks can be quantified using *ratio analysis*
- trading risks, stemming from the price sensitivity of the firm's products, the degree of competition, and whether producers are working at full capacity or far below it:

quantification could be achieved if the firm could discover the *price elasticities* of its products, their *market share* and the degree of *capacity utilisation*

- transactional risks, arising from reliance on large orders for materials that are subject to changes in market prices, or from reliance on foreign currency: substantial shifts in the price of materials or currencies may turn expected profits into heavy losses
- crises, such as when Coca-Cola became contaminated in 1999.

risk management is the attempt to identify and plan for threats to the firm's stability or profitability (see *risk identification*). Managers can apply a long-term strategy of risk minimisation by addressing each of the main areas of business risk:

- financial risks: avoid low *liquidity* and high *gearing*; ensure carefully prepared *cash flow forecast* and control
- trading risks: avoid over-reliance on one product or market; work at strengthening the product differentiation of your brands
- transactional risks: hedge your forward risks if they are substantial; consider buying on the forward market (giving a guaranteed price today for your needs in three, six or 12 months' time)
- crises: do *contingency planning*.

rivalrous marketing: where a small number of firms are competing fiercely, their marketing strategies may be quite clearly targeted at each other's products. Advertising may be designed to invite unfavourable comparisons. Products may be designed so that they compete directly. This type of behaviour is very typical of an *oligopoly*, where a small number of large firms compete on price and on a number of non-price features.

rivalry: a term used in two contexts:

- Competition between firms may lead to intense rivalry as each seeks to outdo the other in the marketplace. This is a likely outcome where there is an *oligopoly* or a *duopoly*, where each firm is using both price and *non-price competition* and is intensely preoccupied with increasing market share.
- Rivalry in consumption refers to the fact that private goods can only be used by the household that bought them. Other people are excluded from consuming them. In contrast, *public goods* such as defence or street lighting are not rivalrous in this way. Once they are provided, everyone can benefit from them.

road pricing: a system for ensuring that the costs of road use are paid for entirely by the road users. The technology for tracking road use now exists but it is unpopular with many motorists. Some cite potential invasion of privacy.

It has a number of advantages:

- Vehicle users would be paying for road use at a level closer to the full social cost. It can be argued that using roads free of charge leads to both overconsumption and overproduction.
- Prices could be set at a level which discouraged users from driving their cars in congested places unless the benefits to them outweighed the costs, so reducing the total amount of traffic.
- Congestion would be reduced and traffic would move faster, saving the economic costs of delay caused by congestion.
- Funds raised could be used to improve public transport.

The London Congestion Charge has reduced traffic jams but remains unpopular with many. Voters in Manchester rejected a similar scheme in 2008, despite serious congestion problems.

ROCE: see *return on capital employed (ROCE)*

role culture: in a long-established business, a management structure develops that has many formal, bureaucratic rules. The way individuals behave will be determined by their position within the business, rather than by their own personal qualities. Following the rules will work well so long as the business is on a stable footing with steady sales, but may be a disadvantage if there is a change in market conditions.

royalty: an agreed percentage of sales revenue paid to the owner of a *patent* or *copyright* for the use of the idea, process, name or work.

RPI: see *retail prices index (RPI)*

rule of law: where this prevails, business decisions are subject to much less uncertainty because *contracts* can be enforced if necessary and government actions are predictable. In the absence of *good governance*, business becomes much riskier. So some economic developments that make good sense will not happen.

A–Z Online

Log on to A–Z Online to search the database of terms, print revision lists and much more. Go to **www.philipallan.co.uk/a-zonline** to get started.

safety margin: the amount by which *demand* can fall before a firm incurs losses, i.e. how close the firm is to the *break-even point* level of output.

   FORMULA: demand – break-even output = safety margin

salesforce: the team of sales representatives employed to achieve high *distribution* in wholesale and retail outlets, or to sell direct to consumers. A national salesforce represents a major *overhead* cost to firms, as representatives will be required for every region. As a result, building up an effective salesforce is a major financial strain for new, small firms. Yet without a strong salesforce, a firm may find too few outlets to achieve a demand level above the *break-even point*.

sales forecast: estimating future demand for a new or existing product. Forecasting is necessary in order to estimate production capacity needs, and to make *cash flow forecasts*.

sale of assets: selling assets that are not needed can be a useful source of finance for investment if the business is already established. The proceeds will provide interest-free capital. Even if the assets are needed, it may be possible to organise a sale-and-leaseback arrangement. The assets are sold but immediately leased back from the finance company. This can be cheaper than simply taking out a loan.

sales maximisation: the highest output possible without making a loss. This can be an objective for the firm in certain circumstances, for example when it is striving to increase its *market share* by cutting prices.

sales promotion is the use of short-term incentives to purchase, such as free offers, *sampling and selling*, competitions and *self-liquidators*. The strategy behind the use of sales promotions may be aggressive or defensive. An example of the latter would be to defend the brand against a competitive attack by a new or existing product. An aggressive promotion would be attempting to gain sales and *market share*, and would therefore be targeted at purchasers of rival brands.

The main purposes of sales promotion are:
- to create the initial surge of demand to persuade shops to stock a newly launched product
- to attract new buyers who the firm hopes will become regular customers
- to lock customers in to buying your product when under threat from a new competitor.

sales revenue is the value of sales made within a trading period. For ordinary calculations, it is enough to realise that:

   FORMULA: quantity sold × price = revenue

This does require some explanation, however, in order to distinguish revenue from cash received. This is because a firm includes within revenue any sales made on credit. Therefore revenue comprises cash sales plus credit sales. This may sound a trivial matter, but because profit calculations are based on sales revenue, it follows that company accounts can present a healthy-looking profit position even though the firm is desperately short of cash.

sales turnover: another term for *sales revenue*.

sales volume is the quantity of goods sold, either by an individual firm or throughout a marketplace.

sample: a group of respondents to a *market research* exercise selected to be representative of the views of the *target market* as a whole. There are four main methods: *random sample*, *quota sample*, *stratified sample* and *cluster sample*. In consumer research, the quota sample is the one used most commonly.

sample size: the number of respondents to a research survey or to a specific question within the survey. The sample size is important as it needs to be large enough to make the data statistically valid. A sample of 20 people, for example, is so small that a different 20 could easily have quite separate views. When deciding on an appropriate sample size for a survey, a firm should bear in mind the following:
- the higher the sample size, the more expensive the research and the longer the *fieldwork* will take
- the lower the sample size, the greater the chance that random factors will make the results inaccurate
- if the research is to assist in a decision of great importance to the firm, it should invest the time and money into a large sample size (if affordable).

sampling and selling is a way of promoting product trial by using demonstrators to offer potential customers a free sample. While the customer is testing the product the demonstrator explains the product's key features and benefits. This is a useful way of tackling *consumer resistance* to, for example, an unusual foreign food. (See *sales promotion*.)

sampling methods: see *cluster sample*, *quota sample*, *random sample* and *stratified sample*

sanctions: rules made by international organisations or pressure groups which prohibit trade with countries which are behaving in ways which are considered unacceptable. The United Nations may place sanctions on a country which is considered to be behaving aggressively, as for a time with Serbia and later Iraq. South Africa was eventually forced by economic sanctions to abandon overtly racist policies in the early 1990s.

satisficing: a term used to describe the acceptance of what is satisfactory instead of pursuing the best or maximum result. There are two main circumstances in which this applies:
1 Setting a strategy based on a satisfactory compromise between objectives. For example, if two divisional directors are each attempting to persuade the firm to pursue a different strategy, the managing director might satisfice by deciding on a mixture of both.
2 Aiming for an achievement that is less than the maximum, perhaps because the firm does not want to draw attention to its powerful market position. For example, instead

of aiming for **profit maximisation**, a firm might pursue a profit level just high enough to finance its expansion plans. Many small businesses satisfice because their owners are happy with the business as it is.

saving: the amount of **disposable income** which is not spent on consumption but kept for the future. Saving is a **leakage** from the **circular flow of national income**. In the short run an increase in saving will reduce **aggregate demand**, other things being equal. Saving is normally measured by the **savings ratio**.

Saving can provide finance for investment. Over the long run this can be important in promoting economic growth. Japan, Taiwan and other Asian countries have high savings ratios which have contributed to high levels of investment.

savings ratio: that proportion of household income which is saved. The proportion can have a considerable impact on the development of an economy. Savings provide funds which can be used to invest in new **plant** and equipment, which clearly helps growth. On the other hand, if consumers save rather than spend then **demand** will be insufficient to sustain business confidence, and therefore growth. So, in the long term, the growth of an economy depends upon a high rate of saving, but in the short term a rise in the savings ratio would cut consumer spending and might lead to **recession**.

scale of production: a measure of a company's output level, usually in relation to competitors or to trends over time. So 'large-scale production' implies that the firm is one of the major producers in its marketplace; 'increased scale of production' may be from very small to quite small. As their scale of production increases, firms are likely to enjoy **economies of scale**. To a certain extent these will be counterbalanced by **diseconomies of scale**.

scarce resources: **factors of production** and **raw materials** which are scarce in relation to the scale of human needs and wants. The scarcer they are, the more the price will tend to rise as people compete to obtain what they want.

scarcity: the term used to describe the fact that people's wants and needs always exceed the resources available to satisfy them. In practice, choices must be made and those choices determine the **allocation of resources**.

scenario planning is the process of anticipating possible changes in a firm's situation and then devising ways of dealing with them. For example, a chocolate producer could ask itself:

'What if next summer brings a three-month heatwave? How will we cope with the collapse in demand for our products?'

Having conceived the scenario, the management could consider options such as providing special display cartons suitable for retailers' chilled cabinets, or even supplying their own chocolate chillers.

Schengen countries: most EU member countries have opted to eliminate border immigration controls on their internal frontiers. Only the UK, Ireland, Romania and Bulgaria have stayed outside this agreement. The fundamental principle of **free movement of people** wanting to live and work in other parts of the EU is not affected by this.

Schumacher, E F (1911–1977): a writer whose book *Small is Beautiful* (Vintage, 1993) began a serious rethink of the effectiveness of large business corporations, and of the environmental damage caused by modern business practices.

science park: an industrial estate placed next to a university or research centre with the intention that the businesspeople and the academics can get together to discuss practical applications of new developments or theories. Easy access to expert knowledge can provide *external economies of scale* for the firms in the science park.

scientific decision-making is the use of a formal procedure to ensure that decisions are arrived at in an objective manner. It attempts to eliminate *hunch* or *bias* by ensuring that decisions are based on factual, numerical evidence. The decision-making model shown in the diagram is widely used:

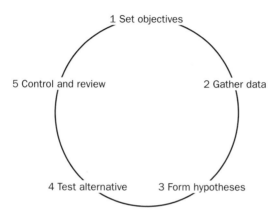

Scientific decision-making model

scientific management is the attempt to make business decisions on the basis of data that is researched and tested quantitatively. The principles were laid down by *F W Taylor* in *The Principles of Scientific Management* (Harper Collins, 1947). He considered it to be management's duty to identify ways in which costs could be accounted for precisely, so that efficiency could be improved. Although Taylor is remembered mainly for his advocacy of financial incentives and high *division of labour*, his most influential legacy has been his advocacy and part-invention of such tools of scientific management as cost accounting, work study and method study. (See also *scientific decision-making*.)

seasonal adjustment is a method for identifying and eliminating regular seasonal variations from a data series in order to identify the underlying trend. This statistical procedure is especially important for data that has a direct impact on decision-making. The monthly unemployment figures might affect government economic policy, and a poor month's sales might lead a firm to halt a 'failed' advertising campaign. Yet unless seasonal influences have been taken out of the figures, the data might look gloomy when the underlying trend is quite positive.

seasonal unemployment: unemployment which rises and falls according to a seasonal pattern. Wintry weather can lead to *unemployment* of construction workers or of people employed in tourism.

secondary action is *industrial action* at a place other than where a dispute originated. All such forms of action were made illegal by the 1990 Employment Act.

S

secondary data is information collected from second-hand sources such as reference books, government statistics or market intelligence reports. Such data can provide information on *market size* and market trends for most product categories. It may be accessible publicly and therefore free, but is in any case not as expensive to gather as *primary data*.

secondary picketing means setting up a picket line at a place other than where an *industrial dispute* originated. As with all other forms of *secondary action*, this is illegal.

secondary research involves collecting information and data from second-hand sources such as reference books, government statistics or market intelligence reports. Such data can provide information on *market size* and market trends for most product categories. It may be accessible publicly and therefore free, but is in any case not as expensive to gather as *primary data*. (See also *primary research*.)

secondary sector: the part of an economy concerned with the manufacture of products. *Primary sector* industry extracts materials from land or sea, while the *tertiary sector* provides business and consumer services. Although the secondary sector is Britain's most important supplier of exports, less than a fifth of the workforce is employed in manufacturing. It is a feature of developing economies that the secondary sector grows faster than primary industry. In developed economies such as Britain, however, the secondary (manufacturing) sector tends to grow less fast than service businesses.

secondment: a posting to another division of a firm or even to a different firm altogether, partly with a view to learning new methods and partly, perhaps, because there is not enough for the employee to do currently.

sector: the economy can be divided up into sectors, each of which consists of a group of decision takers with features in common. For example, one distinction is between the *private sector*, the *public sector* and the overseas sector. The economy can also be divided up into the personal sector, the corporate sector and the government sector. The personal sector consists of all individuals, the corporate sector of all businesses. (See also *primary*, *secondary* and *tertiary sectors*.)

secured loan: a loan made secure by the *collateral* put up by the borrower. This collateral (security) is usually land or property. A lender will be more willing to provide a loan if certain of repayment. Therefore secured loans are less expensive (carry a lower interest rate) than unsecured ones.

securities is a general term covering financial contracts such as *bonds*, *shares* and *derivatives*. In each case, a sum of money changes hands in return for an income stream which may be in the form of interest or dividends. Often, owners of securities take some risk as to possible changes in capital value, should they wish to sell them.

seedcorn capital is the initial *share capital* that enables a new business to be born. It might be invested by family or friends, or by a *venture capital* firm. It should provide sufficient funds for an *entrepreneur* to test out a business idea fully. Many business start-ups fail, therefore providing seedcorn capital is very risky. However, the occasional great success may make sufficient profit to more than cover the losses made on the failures.

segmentation: see *market segmentation*

self-actualisation is psychological self-fulfilment, i.e. feeling enriched or developed by what one has learned or achieved. *Maslow* considered this the highest need of human beings.

self-employed workers operate as their own bosses, either working *freelance* or with the permanent task of running their own business. Self-employment has various tax advantages over regular employment, especially in claiming expenses that can be offset against *income tax* bills. In 2004, it was estimated that 14 per cent (4 million) of the labour force was self-employed.

self-liquidators are a type of *sales promotion* designed to generate enough income to pay for themselves. An example would be a Smarties egg cup promoted at a price of 99p plus two Smarties tube lids. Consumers buy the product to collect the pack qualification, but in any case the promotion self-liquidates because the 99p covers the cost of the egg cup.

self-regulation occurs when an employers' organisation decides to issue codes of behaviour to encourage the firms in an industry to act more responsibly. Traditionally, such organisations have been founded when pressure for regulation from the public or parliament has become too great to ignore. The employers hope that the agreement to regulate themselves will pre-empt the need for government intervention.

sellers' market: a market in which there are more buyers than sellers, so that the sellers can raise the price and still sell. The term applies most often in a housing boom, when prices are rising steadily.

selling power: the extent to which a supplier has a hold over its customers. For example, when the iPhone launched in Britain, supplier Apple insisted on distributing the product through only one network: O_2. This helped ensure that Apple could keep prices (and profits) high for its brilliant new product.

selling short: see *shorting*

semi-variable costs are costs that vary with *output*, but not in direct proportion. Therefore, in order to calculate total costs at a specific level of output, a manager would have to work out the semi-variables especially. This makes them hard to deal with, notably in break-even analysis. Examples of semi-variables include maintenance expenditure and telephone bills. In the latter case, it is clear that although a doubling of customer demand would not necessarily double a firm's telephone calls or bills, it is reasonable to expect that they would increase. Therefore the telephone is neither a fixed nor a variable cost. (Note that if a cost such as a telephone bill comprises a fixed rental element plus a variable usage charge, a firm would split the cost up into its fixed and variable elements.)

separate legal entity occurs when a firm becomes incorporated as a *limited company*, in which the business becomes legally separated from the owners or shareholders. After that, if the company runs into debt or is sued for negligence, it is not the owner who is liable, but the company.

separation of ownership from control: see *divorce of ownership and control*

services: products which consist of something done, rather than a tangible object. They include retailing, hotels and catering, hairdressing, transport, technical services and financial services, among many others. The line between a good and a service can be blurred. As I write this book I am part of a long process in manufacturing it. It is a good and if someone throws it at you, it will hurt. But the Office for National Statistics would probably think I am offering professional services to the publisher. (See also *tertiary sector*.)

sex discrimination means preferring men to women applicants for a job or for promotion. Although it is illegal under the Sex Discrimination Act of 1975, it is still clear that it is happening, particularly in some sectors. Part of the problem is that proving it is difficult. Employers who discriminate are missing the opportunity to appoint the best person for the job and may have higher costs of production as a result. There is ample evidence that on average, full-time women employees are paid less than their male equivalents. The difference is not explained by differences in qualifications.

sexual harassment is distress caused by unwelcome verbal or physical advances of a sexual nature. Although the term usually refers to men harassing women, it may be vice versa. Sexual harassment can be a reason to claim *constructive dismissal* from an industrial tribunal.

shamrock organisation: a term invented by *Handy* to describe the modern business with three types of workforce:
- a permanent, highly valued and skilled core, assured of lifetime employment
- the contractual fringe (suppliers of services that can be contracted out, such as cleaning)
- a flexible labour force, hired and fired to cope with seasonal and cyclical changes in demand.

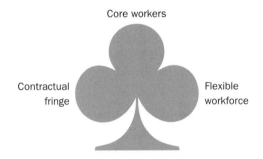

Core workers

Contractual fringe

Flexible workforce

Handy suggests that such an organisation will be slimmed down, with core staff taking on highly responsible tasks including the coordination of the fringe and flexible workforce. The shamrock organisation can be contrasted with the traditional paternalistic but *bureaucratic* corporation. (See *paternalistic leadership style*.)

share: a certificate entitling the holder to *dividends* and *shareholders' rights* in proportion to the number of shares owned.

share capital: the value of the sum invested into a company by ordinary and preference shareholders. As these investors cannot get their money back from the firm, the managers know that they can rely on these funds permanently into the future. Investors can, of course, sell their holdings to other investors through the *Stock Exchange*.

shareholder value: the euphemism used by company chairmen to save having to use terms such as 'profit' and 'capital gain'. The value shareholders get from owning shares is the total annual dividends they receive plus any capital gains they make, e.g. if the Tesco share price rises from 280p to 420p. Both are a function of the company's actual and potential profits, so company chairmen set their sights on 'maximising shareholder value' because they worry that customers and employees may object to the goal of 'maximising profits'.

shareholders' funds are that part of a firm's long-term finance owed by the company to its shareholders. It comprises the **share capital** invested by the shareholders plus the accumulated profits made by the firm over its years of trading (the **reserves**).

FORMULA: share capital + reserves = shareholders' funds

shareholders' rights are the legal entitlements of owners of ordinary shares. These include:

- the right to attend the **annual general meeting (AGM)**
- the right to vote on new directors
- the right to take part in a **vote of (no) confidence** in the **chairman (or chairperson)**
- the right to receive an **annual report and accounts** into the financial state of the business.

In practice, small shareholders have rights, but usually very little power. On occasions, however, they can exert considerable influence, as when Alan Sugar, founder of Amstrad, wished to end his company's Stock Exchange **listing** and return the company to the status of a **private limited company**. Sugar offered to buy Amstrad shares at a price which his shareholders considered derisory; they gathered together and turned the offer down.

share options: a financial incentive that offers managers the right to buy shares in the company they work for at a future date, at a price set today. For example, a director might be given an option to buy 250 000 shares at a price of 50p at any time between three and five years hence. If the share price rises to 90p, they can take up the option and sell the shares on the **stock market**. By buying at 50p and selling at 90p, a profit of 40p × 250 000 = £100 000 will have been made. Supporters of this kind of scheme believe that share options will provide key employees with the incentive to perform at their best. Critics suggest that it might lead to **short-termism** (when the options are due), and can lead to excessive financial rewards in the boardroom, when the workforce may deserve just as much credit as the directors.

share premium is that part of the **share capital** received in excess of the face value of the shares issued. For example:

- a firm is started up with 1000 £1 shares
- later, after a successful spell, it decides to issue a further 1000 £1 shares at the prevailing market price of £1.50 per share
- therefore it has a share premium of 50p × 1000 = £500
- plus share capital of £1 × 2000 = £2000
- giving a total share capital of £2500

share register: the list of all the shareholders in a company together with the size of their holding. Firms regularly check their share registers to see if a particular person or company is building up a large enough share stake to launch a **takeover bid**.

shift in aggregate demand: an increase in the amount of aggregate demand at all price levels. This is likely to happen because consumption, investment, exports or government expenditure, or some combination of these, has changed. If there is an increase in aggregate demand, it will be possible for output to increase so long as the appropriate resources are available (AD_2) (see diagram overleaf). If the economy is approaching **full-capacity output** (AD_3), pressure on resources will cause inflation to accelerate as **supply constraints** develop.

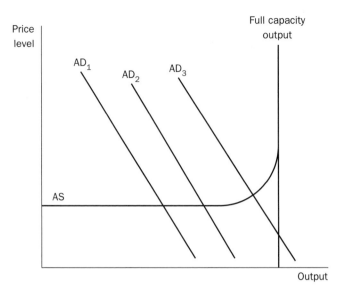

Shift in aggregate demand

shift in aggregate supply: a change in the potential of the economy to supply goods and services. Usually this will increase over time as technology and *investment* create new productive capacity. (See also *economic growth*.)

shifts in demand curves occur when something has an impact on the market which causes people to demand more (or less) of the product at its old price (see diagram below). This commonly occurs when:

● there is a change in taste or fashion
● there is a change in the price of substitutes or complements
● people expect prices to rise (or fall) some time in the future
● there is a change in people's incomes.

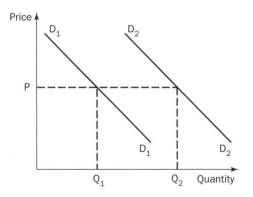

shifts in supply curves occur when something has an impact on the market which causes people to supply more (or less) of the product at its old price (see diagram opposite). This commonly occurs when:

- there is a change in the price of one of the inputs with which the good is made, e.g. when the price of a raw material rises, the supply curve shifts to the left (S_1 to S_2)
- there is a technological change, which enable producers to supply more at the same price, because costs have fallen (S_2 to S_1)
- taxes and subsidies are put on a good, e.g. the European Union subsidises farmers to make their beef competitive on world markets. Without the subsidy, the supply curve would shift to the left (S_2 to S_1).

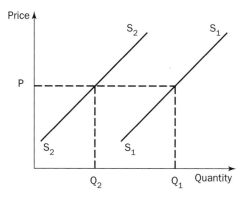

shift work is regular work that takes place during non-standard working hours. It may be a morning shift (e.g. 2a.m.–8a.m.) or a night shift (8p.m.–2a.m.). Shift work is essential in services such as the fire service and is often used in manufacturing, especially if there is an expensive, *flow production* process requiring high *capacity utilisation*. Some organisations recruit workers for a specific shift; others have a rotation of two weeks working days, two working evenings, etc. There may be shift payments that offer a higher rate of pay to compensate for the unsociable hours worked.

shocks are unexpected or unpredictable events which have a major impact on the economy. Examples include the reunification of Germany in 1989 and the oil price rises of 1974 and 1979. A change in commodity prices will be a major shock for a country which depends on export revenue from the sale of that commodity. The financial crisis of 2007/09 brought a widespread shock to the world economy. Shocks can initially affect demand or supply, or both. The financial crisis had a massive effect on aggregate demand. An oil price change affects supply in that it changes the cost of many inputs to the productive process. Natural catastrophes may affect supply. Once the impact of the shock is felt, both demand and supply will usually be affected.

shorting: selling a company's shares with the intention of buying them back once the price has fallen. 'Shorting a stock' can become self-fulfilling, with the share price forced down by the weight of selling. If the end result is a collapse in confidence in a bank or company, the sellers' profits may be at the cost of other people's jobs.

short run: a time period in which the level of output can change only to a certain extent in response to changing market conditions. For example, the short run may be the time in which inputs only of *variable factors of production* can be altered. The input of *fixed factors* cannot be changed. So more employees might be put to work with the same stock of equipment. In contrast, in the long run, inputs of all factors of production may be changed.

There can be investment and expansion, or a shut-down in production of items for which demand is diminishing. The definition of the short run may change according to the context in which it is being used.

short-termism is a phrase describing the state of mind of managers for whom rapid results are the top priority. Examples of short-termism include:

- expecting investments to pay for themselves quickly
- increasing prices up to their most profitable level (thereby attracting competition)
- cutting back on spending on research and development or training.

Such an approach can be contrasted with the Japanese pursuit of long-term goals such as total quality and technological superiority. It seems likely that the main causes of British short-termism are:

- the absence of a tradition of loyalty to one company, which may make executives too keen to make their mark quickly
- the greater number and influence of accountants in British boardrooms (compared with engineers in Germany and Japan)
- the threat of a *takeover* may encourage firms to keep short-term profit high in order to bolster up the share price: British firms are much more likely to have a majority shareholding available on the *stock market*, so this is a more important issue in Britain than in Germany or Japan.

simultaneous engineering means organising *product development* so that the different stages are carried out in conjunction with each other instead of in sequence. This reduces the time taken to get an idea to the marketplace, which cuts costs and provides a competitive advantage over slower rivals. Key elements include:

- project teams comprising specialists from the different business and engineering functions (such as *research and development (R&D)*, design, machine tools, materials handling, *market research*, cost accounting and so on)
- improved communications between functions
- simultaneous development of the product, the production and the marketing processes.

Simultaneous engineering is a crucial element in *lean production*.

single currency: the *euro* is the single currency of the 16 EU countries which have joined together in the *Economic and Monetary Union (EMU)*. In 2002, national currencies went out of use and the *European Central Bank* issued notes and coins. The costs and risks associated with foreign exchange transactions were eliminated within the member countries. The UK, Sweden and Denmark remain outside the euro area but only the UK has an opt-out agreement. The costs and benefits of the single currency are still hard to determine conclusively.

single European market: the agreement to create a unified market across the European Union. The overall objective was to make it genuinely possible for goods, people and capital to move around freely. Part of this entailed the removal of restrictions encountered when crossing member countries' borders. The overall effect of the measures was to make the EU much more like a single economy. They came into force at the start of 1993. Specific changes included the following:

- Foreign exchange controls were abolished, making financial integration much easier, so that capital could move around. This opened up the financial markets of all member countries to all the banks.

- Many regulations were harmonised, so that firms could produce to specifications common to all member countries. This meant that products could be standardised for the whole of the EU. It removed many **non-tariff barriers** to trade.
- Qualifications which are recognised in one member country are generally recognised throughout the EU.
- Common systems were established in the fields of transport and communication.
- Qualified majority voting was introduced in the **Council of Ministers** and the **European Parliament** was given added powers. This reflected the general view that closer economic integration would require more effective political systems.

In many respects, the single market is still incomplete because full harmonisation has not yet been achieved. However, movement towards the single market has been significant.

single status occurs when a firm has eliminated all the physical and contractual barriers between grades of staff. These forms of class discrimination might include: separate canteens, different working hours, different pay terms and conditions. Once a firm has removed such divisive features, it can hope to eliminate the feeling of '**them and us**' that pervades many organisations. Japanese firms go so far as to insist on the same overalls for all managers and workers, or even morning exercises. Both are to establish single status by demonstrating that all employees wear the same work clothes and participate in the same morning activity.

single union agreement means the recognition by a firm of only one workforce representative body for **collective bargaining** purposes. This removes the potential disruption caused by inter-union disputes and reduces the time spent on negotiations. Toshiba's agreement with the electricians' union (the EEPTU) in 1981 is believed to have been the first of its kind in Britain.

skill shortage: even when there is substantial unemployment, shortages may develop of people available for work and possessing the skills required. This is likely to happen if the economy has been growing and the employment of skilled people has been increasing. Employers may offer higher pay in order to attract the type of people they require.

Where skills are scarce, appropriately qualified people are in **inelastic supply**. An increase in pay may provide an incentive to acquire the skills but this will be a long-run process. This will help to reduce **occupational immobility**.

skills: any job-related competences possessed by an individual, who can use these to help produce a saleable product.

skills mismatch: a situation in which the people available for work have skills which are not those required by the employers who are seeking to hire people. This will be associated with **occupational immobility**. It occurs because people have been made redundant from **declining industries**. The skills required by growing industries are different. This is a feature of **structural change** and changing technologies.

skimming the market means pricing a new product at such a high level that it is only purchased by trend-setters, enthusiasts or the very rich. The firm may choose to hold this high price in the long term, or cut prices when competition arrives. Skimming the market is a viable option only for an innovative product. (See **market penetration (2)**.)

PROS: • a product's price affects consumer perceptions of its quality and desirability; pricing high can be an important element in establishing an up-market image

S

277

- skimming can be used as a form of **price discrimination**, ensuring that trend-setters pay the high price they are willing to pay, then lowering the price to attract the mass market later on

CONS:
- a high price may make it easy for a competitor to launch a successful, lower-priced imitation
- by failing to maximise sales at the start, the firm may not be able to hold on to a viable **market share** when competitors arrive

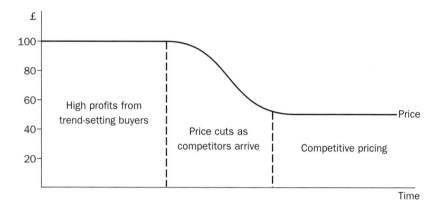

Skimming the market

sleeping partner: a contributor of finance to a business partnership who takes no active role within the firm, and therefore can arrange to hold **limited liability** status.

slogan: a catch-phrase used regularly by an advertiser to communicate a sales message in a highly memorable way.

slump is a period of low demand and investment, and high unemployment. It is a rather vague term used interchangeably with **depression** to mean a severe **recession** within the **economic cycle**. It is often seen in the context of 'booms and slumps' to indicate the way an economy tends to fluctuate between these two extremes. During a slump, **aggregate demand** is well below the level of **full-capacity output**. (See also **output gap**.)

Small Business Service: the agency set up in 1999 by the Labour government to promote and coordinate activities to develop entrepreneurial activity. **Business Link** has taken its place.

small claims court: a local court that will hear cases of dispute concerning sums of up to £5000. A typical problem might concern a householder claiming against an electrician over a £250 job that proved to be faulty. At the small claims court, individuals speak for themselves without the use of expensive legal advice.

small firm: a phrase that is taken to mean a firm with limited financial resources which has little or no power over its marketplace. The government uses the more precise definition of a firm with fewer than 50 employees. This, however, would allow firms with substantial earnings and high **market shares** to be termed small. As with every type of business, the attempt to define or generalise about them usually falls foul of their wide diversity. It is safer to consider the financial position and market strength of each firm individually than to overgeneralise.

small to medium-sized enterprises (SMEs) are all businesses with fewer than 250 employees, according to the **European Union (EU)**'s definition, which has also been adopted by the British government's Office for National Statistics. Small firms are those with fewer than 50 employees; medium-sized have between 50 and 250. In 2007, SMEs contributed over 50 per cent of all jobs in the private sector. This is shown in the table below:

Size of business (number of employees)	Total employed (000s)	% of workforce
Up to 49	10 803	47.5
50–249	2 653	11.7
250+	9 279	40.9
Total	22 735	100

Source: BERR Statistical Press Release, July 2008

SMEs: see *small to medium-sized enterprises (SMEs)*

Smith, Adam was the eighteenth-century author of much of the classical economic theory which still forms the basis of free-market economics. His best-known book *The Wealth of Nations* (Penguin, 1982) set out, in 1776, his faith in market mechanisms as a means of promoting efficiency and customer satisfaction. The book's key phrase referred to the *invisible hand* that ensures that customer *demand* can be matched by *supply* without needing a planning authority. The invisible hand is the *price mechanism*.

social audit: an independent quantification of the elements of a firm's activities that affect society, such as pollution, waste and workforce health and safety. A social audit can be used internally, by managers wanting to measure their degree of success at environmental improvement; or externally, by pressure groups or shareholders concerned about the firm's long-term health and reputation. The potential value of this technique can be seen in the example below. It shows how a social audit of two firms might lead to different conclusions about their real efficiency than a calculation of financial ratios might.

Worked example: bicycle manufacturing firms

	Firm A	Firm B
Financial ratios		
Trading profit margin	6.8%	8.8%
Return on capital	18.5%	19.8%
Social ratios		
Average lifetime of bike	5.5 yrs	3.0 yrs
% made from recycled material	60%	20%
Industrial accidents per 100 workers per year	1.5	8.0

social benefits are all of the benefits from consumption of a particular item, not just those received by the buyer. They therefore include the *external benefits* which may be obtained by third parties, i.e. people who neither bought nor sold the item. For example, the social benefits of a pretty front garden include the benefits obtained by the owner of it, together with the benefits for any passers-by who happen to enjoy looking at the garden.

FORMULA: internal benefits + external benefits = social benefits

(See also *marginal social benefits*.)

social capital: *infrastructure* which is provided by governments and is very necessary for economic growth, but cannot always be provided on a profitable basis by the private sector. It includes education, health care and some transport and communications facilities.

social cost measures the cost to the whole of society of a production process or business decision. This means that not only are the firm's *internal costs* accounted for, but also the costs imposed on society as a consequence of the action (such as pollution or unemployment). These latter costs are external to the company.

FORMULA: internal costs + external costs = social costs

(See also *marginal social costs*.)

social efficiency: the situation in the marketplace when output is at the level where *marginal social costs* and *marginal social benefits* are equal. At any other output, there will be external costs or benefits and an element of *market failure*. For example, any product that entails pollution or other kinds of environmental degradation will be overproduced if the social costs are greater than the social benefits. This could apply to electricity: the price is less than the full marginal social cost and so we all use more of it than we would if we had to cover the external as well as the *private costs* of generating it. This situation could be resolved by using only renewable sources of electricity.

social grade is the occupational category that shows the social class to which each household belongs. Interviewers ask respondents for the occupation of the head of the household and the answer is placed into one of the groupings listed below. This categorisation is used in *market research*, as evidence has shown that social class has a large effect on people's lifestyle and purchasing habits. The social grade bands are:

- GRADE A: top professional (e.g. lawyers) or directors of large companies
- GRADE B: senior managerial
- GRADE C1: clerical, e.g. secretary
- GRADE C2: skilled working class, e.g. welder
- GRADE D: semi- or unskilled working class
- GRADE E: state dependent, e.g. long-term unemployed.

socialism is a social and economic system which involves collective ownership of the means of production and a major role for the state in the provision of services which can improve people's welfare. In its extreme form of communism it dominated the *centrally planned economies* of Eastern Europe until 1989. In its social democratic form, socialism has been an important underlying principle for a number of left-of-centre political parties in Western Europe.

social responsibilities are the duties towards employees, customers, society and the environment that a firm may accept willingly, or may treat as a nuisance. The historical record of firms' acceptance of their responsibilities is patchy. Some religiously motivated firms such as Cadbury and Rowntree treated their workforce and customers with respect as far back as the nineteenth century. Yet at the same time, a brand of cigarettes called 'Heartsease' was promoted as an aid to recovery from illness. Such deceptions led to the passing of laws to protect consumers, workers and residents from socially irresponsible companies. Today, many firms believe it is in their best interests to behave correctly, since customer image and workforce contentment are important elements in business success. The key to a firm's attitude to its responsibilities is probably the timespan of its company objectives. A get-rich-quick building firm will have a very different approach to an established family business that thinks in terms of generations rather than months.

social security is the system by which governments provide for people in need – the **welfare state**. Unemployment benefits, pensions, income support and various other income supplements are payable to people in certain circumstances. Payments may be **means tested**, as with income support, or handed over as of right, as with pensions. Social security payments have increased enormously in all developed countries in recent years, partly because of ageing populations and partly because **unemployment** has been higher since 1980 than it was before.

social welfare concerns the well-being of the whole population and how it may be improved. Welfare economics explores the way in which resources should be allocated so as to maximise social welfare.

soft landing: if a prolonged period of economic growth has led to accelerating inflation, policy makers will aim for a soft landing, i.e. a downturn which leads to a slower, sustainable rate of economic growth but not a recession.

sole trader: an individual who may or may not employ other people, but who owns and operates the business. Sole traders generally have little capital for expansion, and are heavily reliant on their own personal commitment to make the business a success. Should the business be unsuccessful, there is no cushion from **limited liability**, as a sole trader is unincorporated; in other words, the firm's finances are inseparable from the proprietor's.

solvency is when a firm or individual's assets exceed its external debts. Therefore it has the financial stability that comes from positive asset backing. If external debts are greater than the asset values, a state of **insolvency** exists.

sources of finance indicate where an organisation might obtain the funds it needs, from internal or external sources. Before deciding between them, it is important to establish:
- The purpose – is short-term finance needed to help with the day-to-day running of the business, perhaps during a period of seasonally weak trading, or is long-term finance needed for the replacement of assets or to finance expansion?
- The size and type of the firm in question – clearly a **multinational** will not be using family and friends as a source, whereas a newly established firm may do so.

span of control: the number of subordinates answerable directly to a manager. It can be described as 'wide' if the manager has many direct subordinates or 'narrow' if there are few. Within an organisation, the span of control bears an inverse relationship to the number of layers in the management hierarchy. In other words, if the span is wide, fewer layers would be needed to manage a given workforce. This is illustrated overleaf, where a span of control of three results in five **layers of hierarchy**, while a span of nine requires only three layers (assuming a shop-floor workforce of 81).

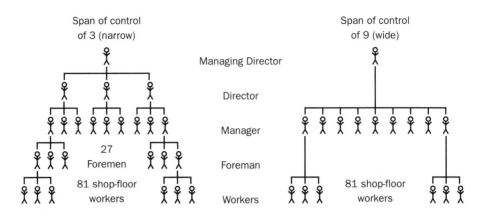

Advantages of a wide span of control include:
- the boss has less time for each subordinate, therefore must delegate effectively
- fewer layers of hierarchy are needed, therefore improving vertical communications
- allows subordinates 'the opportunity to use their ability', which is Professor **Herzberg**'s definition of *job enrichment*.

Advantages of a narrow span of control include:
- tighter management supervision may be necessary in a business where mistakes cannot be allowed (such as the production of components for passenger aircraft)
- less stress involved for each employee, as the scope of each job is limited
- more layers of hierarchy mean more frequent promotion opportunities, i.e. the career ladder has more rungs.

specialisation: the process by which individuals, firms and economies concentrate on producing those goods and services in which they have an advantage. Further specialisation is possible as production processes are broken up into a sequence of different tasks. This was described by *Adam Smith* in his account of the *division of labour* at the pin factory where each employee had a different job.

Specialisation has the potential to increase the output that can be obtained from a given quantity of resources. It is closely connected to the theory of *comparative advantage*. Scarce resources can produce more when specialising in the type of production to which they are best suited. For example, a farmer who specialises in arable crops such as wheat and sugar beet, because the land is most suitable for these, will probably make more money than when the farm also had dairy cattle. Aiming for self-sufficiency (as subsistence farmers must) is probably the least efficient and least profitable approach.

Taken to extremes, specialisation can involve some jobs becoming very repetitive and boring, for example, assembly processes in manufacturing. One management response to this has been *teamwork* and *multi-skilling* – which can provide employees with more variety and the firm with a more flexible *labour* force.

spectrum of competition: the range of market systems which can be anything between *perfect competition* and *monopoly*. At one extreme there is the situation of many competing producers with easy entry into the market; hairdressing would be one example. At the other extreme there is the single business which dominates the market and cannot be challenged because **new entrants** to the market have difficulty in getting started because of **barriers to entry**. Microsoft is currently the best-known example.

Perfect competition	Monopolistic competition	Oligopoly	Duopoly	Monopoly

speculation involves buying or selling something in the expectation of a price change and so making a profit. For example, foreign exchange dealers who expect the **exchange rate** to fall will sell quickly, then when the price has fallen they can buy back the currency at a much lower price than they sold at, so making a profit on the deal. Speculation may be suspected whenever a financial asset such as a share or a property is bought and then sold a short time later. (See also **shorting**.)

sponsorship is a form of promotion in which funds are provided for a sporting, cultural or social event in return for prominent display of the sponsor's company or brand name.

spot market: a term used to describe a commodity or foreign exchange market where the deals are made and completed there and then and delivery is immediate. In contrast, in the **forward market** deals are made in which the price is agreed now, but the delivery of the goods concerned takes place perhaps three months later.

spreadsheet is a set of numerical data inputted and displayed on a computer which is connected in such a way, via a number of formulae, that changing one figure will automatically update all the others. In business, spreadsheets are often used to predict events, because it is simple to ask **what if... ? questions** and immediately see a result. For instance, if it was suggested that sales might rise by 10 per cent next year, the company could see at a glance what the implications for sales revenue, costs and profits would be.

stabilisation policy aims to keep the economy growing in a sustainable way and prevent a cycle of **boom** and **recession**. It uses **fiscal policies** and **monetary policies** to influence the level of aggregate demand and prevent both overheating and rising unemployment. Stabilisation policies are not always successful because the time lags in the economy and weaknesses of some of the data can make it very difficult to predict how much policy change is required. Stabilisation policies can be used for electoral reasons in ways which are ultimately destabilising, but this has been made much less likely since the Bank of England became responsible for monetary policy in 1997.

stagflation is the economic phenomenon of stagnation and **inflation** happening simultaneously. This had been thought to be impossible, since the effect of stagnation would be to depress wages and hence prices. In practice, it was found during the mid-1970s that levels of inflation could rise to the point where people expected it to continue, and acted accordingly. Thus, although unemployment was rising, **trade unions** still negotiated for high pay rises because of the expected levels of prices next year.

stagging is the purchase of shares in a company **flotation** with the sole purpose of selling them quickly on the **Stock Exchange** for a profit. New issues are very often offered at an attractive price in order to ensure that all the shares are sold, thus offering stags a chance to make a quick profit. This was the case with many **privatisation** flotations.

stagnation: a situation in which the economy is growing very slowly or not at all.

stakeholder: an individual or group with a direct interest in an organisation's performance. The main stakeholders are: employees, shareholders, customers, suppliers, financiers and the local community. Stakeholders may not hold any formal authority over the organisation, but theorists such as *Handy* believe that a firm's best long-term interests are served by paying close attention to the needs of each of these groups.

standardisation is the production or use of products or components that are so identical as to allow them to be fully interchangeable. The achievement of standardised parts is a necessary condition for efficient *mass production* to take place. Without it, skilled workers would have to spend time filing down parts to fit them into the right slots. Standardisation is also a key element in *economies of scale*, as modern firms use the same components in different products to enable longer production runs to take place and to save on design costs.

standard of living is a rather imprecise term which refers to the ability of people to buy the goods and services they desire. It could be measured as people's real incomes, i.e. wage levels in relation to price levels. Increasingly it also takes into account non-quantifiable factors such as levels of crime, the time and ease of travelling to work and so on. This is sometimes referred to as the 'quality of life'. The UN's *Human Development Index (HDI)* provides an alternative approach.

statistics: in a business context, this means the statistical data that firms gather and may try to present in a light that favours themselves. When seeing numerate 'facts' presented, Benjamin Disraeli's famous statement should be borne in mind, that 'there are lies, damned lies and statistics'.

status: how highly a person is rated by other members of a group or workforce. This might derive from the individual's own abilities and achievements or from institutional factors such as job title or remuneration. *Maslow* regarded status as an important social need, while *Herzberg* considered it a *hygiene factor*, i.e. a potential source of dissatisfaction.

statutory requirements are those that are laid down by law and which every firm has to conform to. Laws are said to be 'in the statutes' or 'on the statute books'.

stealth taxes are taxes that the Chancellor of the Exchequer hopes people will not notice in the same way as they would notice a change in the standard rate of income tax. Examples include airport tax, insurance tax and the loss of tax breaks on pension contributions.

STEP: see *PEST analysis*

sterling is the name given to the UK's internationally traded currency, the pound sterling, to distinguish it from other countries which also use the word 'pound' for their currencies.

sterling exchange rate index: a measure of change in the foreign *exchange rate* which takes a weighted average of a basket of currencies. These are weighted according to their importance in the pattern of trade. It provides the simplest way of measuring competitiveness.

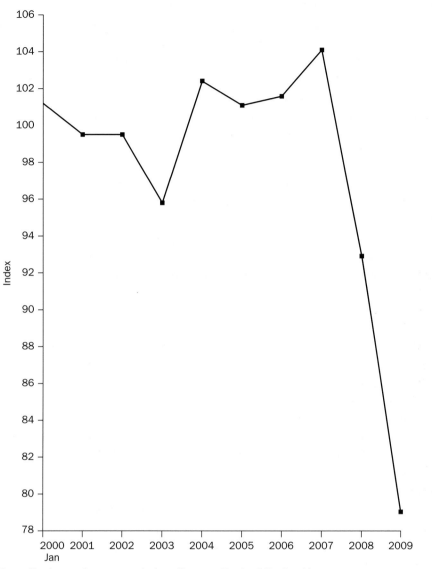

Sterling effective exchange rate index. (Source: Bank of England.)

Stern Review: a report written in 2005 by the then head of the Government Economic Service for the Treasury, on climate change. He concluded that the economic risks associated with climate change are potentially very serious, but that if 5 per cent of world GDP were to be devoted to tackling it, it would be possible to reduce greenhouse gas emissions by 80 per cent from their present level. He concluded that costs of managing climate change were significant but manageable, if a quick start could be made. The report was very influential. It is not clear how any action that might have been taken will be affected by the aftermath of the 2007/09 financial crisis.

stick to the knitting: a curious phrase that urges firms to concentrate on what they know best, rather than take the risks involved in diversifying into numerous other sectors.

stock: materials and goods required in order to produce for, and supply to, the customer. There are three main categories of stock: *raw materials* or components, **work in progress (WIP)** and finished goods. When aggregated for the whole economy, the level of stocks is important because it may reflect changes in the level of **aggregate demand** relative to output. Also, changes in stocks may impact upon the level of output. If demand has been falling, stocks will rise and destocking may become necessary. This means that the level of output will for a while fall below the level of demand and this may reduce the demand for *labour*, leading to rising unemployment.

stock appreciation: an increase in the value of a company's stocks, generally due to *inflation*. As company profits are boosted by increases in stock values, stock appreciation gives a rather artificial boost to profits (causing higher tax and perhaps dividend payments). The standard accounting procedure for preventing this distortion of real profitability is the adoption of last in, first out (LIFO) stock identification.

stockbroker: a person who trades in, and can give advice on the buying and selling of, shares.

stock control covers the procedures needed to ensure that stock is ordered, delivered and handled with efficiency, so that customer demand can be met cost effectively. This is achieved through careful stock rotation and may also involve a stock reordering system based upon predetermined minimum and maximum stock levels. (See **reorder level**.)

Stock Exchange is a market for securities (the collective name for stocks and shares). The London Stock Exchange is one of the biggest in the world after Tokyo and New York, with an annual turnover of over one million million pounds. Its main functions are to enable firms or governments to raise capital and to provide a market in second-hand shares and government stocks.

PROS: • offers firms a reliable source of investment funds, especially equity capital
   • by offering a second-hand market in shares it encourages people to channel their savings into industry
   • the Stock Exchange insists on stringent rules for admittance by firms and these, along with other legal requirements, offer a degree of protection to savers.

CONS: • the share price does not necessarily reflect the true value of a company. It may be the result of rumours, or the overall state of the market
   • being quoted on the Exchange removes some control from the management and may encourage **short-termism**, as directors focus upon **dividends** and the share price
   • recent scandals suggest that the degree of investor protection is in fact quite small, and call into question the ability of the Exchange to regulate itself.

stockholding costs are the **overheads** resulting from the stock levels held by a firm. These include:
• warehouse rental and insurance costs
• energy costs (refrigeration, for example)
• staffing costs, including security guards
• interest charges on the money tied up in the stock.

By moving to a **just in time (JIT)** system of minimal stock levels, all these costs could be cut dramatically.

stock market: see *Stock Exchange*

stock options: see *share options*

stockpiling: building up stock levels, perhaps in preparation for a seasonal sales peak or before the advertising launch of a new product.

stocks and shares is a general term for investments that are traded on the *stock market*. In this case, stocks means fixed interest securities such as *debentures* (*loan capital*), while shares give a part-ownership of a company (*equity capital*).

stocktaking: a periodical physical count of the items held in stock, usually carried out on the *balance sheet* date at the end of the financial year. This is to ensure accurate stock records and thereby determine the levels of *wastage* and pilfering that are occurring.

strategic alliance: see *joint venture*

strategic decision: a decision that will have considerable long-term effects on an organisation and therefore requires discussion and approval at a senior managerial level. An example might be whether to sell off a poorly performing division, or to invest sufficient extra capital to restore its competitiveness.

strategic objectives are wide-ranging, long-term goals of significance to the operations of a whole organisation. For example, a firm that has 70 per cent of its sales in Britain might set itself the strategic objective to reduce its dependence upon the home market to below 40 per cent within five years.

This might force a rethink about the location of its factories, the type of products it sells, the background or nationality of the staff it employs and so on. Among the most common strategic objectives are:
- to diversify
- to focus (un-diversify or *stick to the knitting*)
- to achieve a dominant market position
- to develop a technological advantage over rivals.

strategy: a medium- to long-term plan for how to achieve an *objective*. The plan itself would include not only what is to be done, but also the financial, production and personnel resources required.

stratified sample: a research sampling method that draws respondents from a specified subgroup of the population. An example would be a lager producer deciding to research solely among 18–30-year-old men, since they represent the heart of that marketplace. Within the chosen group, individuals might be chosen on a random basis, hence the term 'stratified random sample'. (See also *random sample* and *quota sample*.)

strike: a situation in which workers stop work in order to exert some power in an *industrial dispute*. Most often, this will be over pay but it can be about redundancies or unfair dismissal. Strikes may be official, i.e. sanctioned by the trade union, or unofficial. They are much more likely to occur in larger firms than in smaller ones. In recent years strikes have been fewer in number, partly because of the fear of unemployment and partly because the law now requires a secret ballot of union members as to whether they want to strike.

strike pay is a payment by a *trade union* to members who are on an official strike. This is usually of a sum that is far below the striker's regular wage.

S

structural change means a fundamental change in the way a business, a market or a whole economy operates.

- Economic change such as a switch from traditional, heavy industry to the 'sunrise' industries such as electronics can lead to **structural unemployment**.
- Structural change within a market might be caused by **privatisation**, two large companies merging or by the **liquidation** of a once-powerful firm.
- For an individual business, structural change might take the form of a shift to decentralisation or the decision to handle products on a global basis rather than country by country.

structural unemployment occurs when people are made redundant from **declining industries** but lack the appropriate skills to enter a growing industry or are located a long way from the jobs available. Many declining industries such as coal, textiles and iron and steel are localised, so that the large excess supply of **labour** in a place with limited opportunities becomes a real problem.

Occupational immobilities and *geographical immobilities* make it difficult for people to find alternative jobs. Supply-side policies such as training and retraining may be needed to deal with these. *Regional policy* and regeneration measures can be helpful too. There has been a long-term and substantial increase in structural unemployment in many developed countries which governments have had little success in reducing. Unskilled people are particularly vulnerable and despite recent improvements, the problem remains grave in many parts of the EU.

subcontracting: finding a supplier to manufacture part or all of your product. The main circumstances in which subcontracting is used are:

- when a firm is already operating at maximum capacity and therefore cannot meet further demand in any other way
- when there are elements of a product that the firm is ill-equipped to manufacture efficiently
- to cope with seasonal peaks in demand.

subcultures are formed of people who have interests or values in common, or who share a common background. They need have no formal structure or communication, although the internet has in many cases provided subcultures with on-line communities. They can be based around distinctions created by age, ethnic background, hobbies, life-style or just personal tastes and preferences. Religious groups form subcultures but they can just as easily consist of jazz enthusiasts or real ale drinkers. Some subcultures cut across international borders. They are of interest to businesses because they often form identifiable *niche markets*.

subjective decision: a decision that has been made either without, or in spite of, the evidence of researched data. Such decisions might be made by a lazy or prejudiced manager, or might be the result of an inspired **hunch**. A good example of the latter was the Sony chairman's support for the 'Walkman', despite research evidence that consumers saw no need for it.

subjective factors are those for which personal judgement is necessary since they cannot be quantified effectively. They may be very important in business decisions such as capital investment, though there is a tendency to treat figures as facts and therefore downgrade non-quantifiable issues. Subjective factors include: effect upon morale, expectations of competitors' actions, and the effect on, and importance of, the *corporate image*.

sub-prime mortgages: bank loans made to US borrowers with low incomes and/or with a poor credit history. The loans were secured against the value of the property, but falls in property prices from 2006 onwards led to a slump in the value of the mortgages. The original decisions to lend to low-income households were based on short-term bonuses and illusory profits.

subsidiarity is the idea that decisions which affect certain people should be made as locally as possible. The word has been much used within the context of the *European Union (EU)*. UK governments have used it as an argument to prevent what they see as the over-centralisation of power in the hands of the EU, and in particular the *European Commission*. Local authorities in England and Wales have also used it as an argument against the same UK governments for removing their traditional roles within local communities of looking after such things as health and education.

subsidiary: a business that is owned by another business (the *holding company*). The subsidiary is likely to be trading under its own name, but as the holding company owns more than 51 per cent of its shares, it is the latter that will have effective control. The subsidiary's financial figures will form part of the parent company's consolidated accounts.

subsidy is paid by governments to lower the costs of production, either for social reasons, or for strategic military reasons, or to raise incomes (e.g. hill sheep farmers), or to keep down the prices of essential goods.

substitute: a brand or product that fulfils the same function as another and can therefore be used in its place. For example, Persil is a substitute for Ariel and vice versa. Products that have several direct substitutes are likely to be highly *price elastic*, as consumers will switch to whichever of the competitors is the cheapest.

suggestion schemes are formal procedures for collecting ideas from the shop floor. The suggestions might relate to new products, improved working methods or cost-cutting measures. Often, such schemes offer financial or promotional bonuses to suggestions that are adopted by the company. Many firms have suggestion boxes for workers to place their ideas, but not many are successful. They lack the personal involvement and group spirit of *quality circles* or *kaizen* (improvement) groups.

sunk costs: costs which have already been paid for and which no longer figure in the decision-taking process. For example, once the product is brought to the market, research and development costs are sunk costs. The likelihood of sunk costs in some industries (e.g. mining) may mean that economies of scale are present.

sunrise industry: one positioned in a rapidly growing market, usually based on new technology and *innovation*.

sunset industry: one believed to be in terminal decline, with obsolete technology and an obsolete product.

supernormal profit: profit which is in excess of the amount needed to keep the resources in the industry, i.e. the full *opportunity cost* of all the resources used. When demand is rising, it will often be possible for the firm to make supernormal profit because it can raise the price and still sell the goods. This situation will continue until more firms have moved into the industry, thus competing and driving prices back down to the level where **normal profit** only is made. If there are **barriers to entry**, then the firm may make supernormal profit in the long as well as the short run, because the level of competition is reduced. In fact, any kind of market power will allow supernormal profits to be made; for example, brand names, such as Levi's, create loyalty which reduces the power of competition to force down profits. (See also **perfect competition** and **monopoly**.)

supplier relationships are important to firms which buy in many of their inputs from other businesses. In the context of a good relationship, it will be easier to negotiate quality improvements or **just-in-time** stock control procedures.

supply is one element in the market system: the market forces contributed by supply and demand together determine prices and quantities via the **price mechanism**. Firms will supply goods and services in a range of quantities, depending on the price they can get for them. At any given price level, quantity supplied will be affected by input costs in general, by technological change and by government policies which affect taxes and subsidies. Supply can be affected by producer cartels, e.g. **OPEC**. (See also **supply curve**.)

supply chain: the sequence of processes by which a final product is created. For many products, the supply chain takes in many different suppliers, often located in different countries. Many sophisticated manufactured products are built up in developed countries using intermediate products assembled in **developing economies** where wages are lower.\

supply constraints: shortages that occur because resources are not available. The most important supply constraint arises from **skill shortages**, indicating a need to train more people in scarce skills. Supply constraints can lead to wage rates and prices increasing and are significant when rising a**ggregate demand** leads to accelerating **inflation**.

supply curve: the curve showing the quantities producers wish to supply at a range of different prices. It is normally shown sloping upwards to the right. This is because a higher price gives a business more of an incentive to produce and indicates possible higher profits (as at p_2 and q_2 on the diagram.

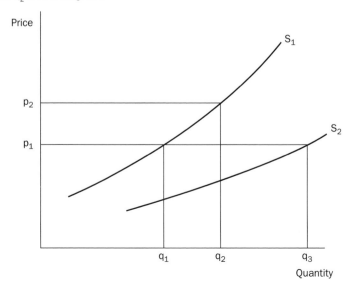

The supply curve will shift if there is a change in costs and it may then change its shape as well. For example, new technologies will tend to make the supply curve shift down and to the right, reflecting the fact that costs have fallen and possibly also **economies of scale** have been reaped. Then it may be possible to produce the larger quantity (q_3 in the diagram) at the original price.

Shifts in the supply curve may also be caused by changes in indirect taxation, or subsidies.

supply elasticity: the responsiveness of quantity supplied to a change in price. The formula is:

$$\text{FORMULA:} \quad \text{elasticity of supply} = \frac{\text{pecentage change in quantity supplied}}{\text{pecentage change in price}}$$

Inelastic supply will be less than one, while elastic supply will be greater than one. Supply may be perfectly inelastic (i.e. equal to zero) in the market period simply because there has not been time to mobilise the resources needed to increase supply or to disband them if the price is falling (see diagram).

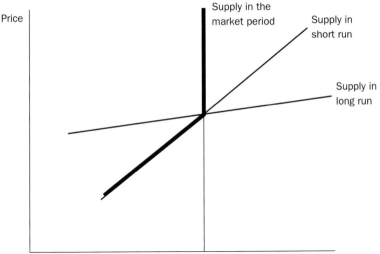

In the short run, supply can be increased by the addition of variable factors of production to the production process. In the long run, fixed factors of production can also be increased. So supply becomes more and more elastic the longer the time period. Housing is usually in inelastic supply: it takes time to build more; equally, if demand is falling the existing stock of housing will continue to stand for some time. This means that changes in demand may produce sharp fluctuations in price. Another example of inelastic supply occurs when scarce skills are in demand; it will take time to train more people and in the meantime the supply of the skills will be very inelastic.

If very scarce resources are needed to produce the item, then costs may rise as output increases, thus making supply rather inelastic. As depletable resources of mineral products are exploited, the price will rise and this means that supply is inelastic. In contrast, the supply of most manufactured products in the long run is highly elastic.

Firms will respond to a change in prices in different ways over time. In the market period they cannot change the quantity supplied but in the short run they can use more or less of the variable factors of production to increase or decrease output. The long-run response will take advantage of all possible ways to adapt to new conditions.

supply-side policies are based on the idea that economic growth can best be encouraged by helping markets to work more efficiently. They actually work to increase supply from a given quantity of real resources. There are many possible supply-side measures:

- Policies which make the *labour* market more flexible: these involve restriction of trade union activities, which has led in the past to overmanning and demarcation problems. Supply-side enthusiasts also argue for some reduction in *employment protection*.
- Training and retraining: these address directly the *supply constraints* which usually exist to some degree, increasing the supply of skilled labour able to respond to job vacancies.
- Competition policy: by encouraging competition, it is possible to force firms to organise their production systems more efficiently, increasing the output from a given input.
- Reducing disincentives to work: some people have suggested reducing unemployment benefit as a way to reduce the impact of the *poverty trap*. The *Working Families Tax Credit* tries to ensure that people with families are always better off working than not.
- Financial incentives to promote spending on research and development and encourage investment.
- Privatisation can help to increase general efficiency in the industries concerned.

Many supply-side measures have in fact secured widespread support from all political parties. Support is not confined to the original Conservative monetarist enthusiasts of the 1980s. Measures such as improving training and retraining, helping people to find jobs, and spending money on research and development can all help to increase *productivity* and employment, as well as fostering growth.

surplus: any excess of revenue over costs earned by a *non-profit-making organisation*.

survey: another term for quantitative market research; in other words, research among a large enough sample of consumers to provide valid data.

sustainable growth is a term used in two different contexts:

- Growth which can be kept up at a steady rate over the long term is said to be sustainable. In contrast, unsustainable growth requires resources which will become increasingly scarce as growth proceeds. In particular, shortages of scarce skills will develop and when they do, wage rates will be bid up, costs will rise and *inflation* will accelerate. This will lead the government to damp down the growth process and the result may be a swing into *recession* which will last until such time as people's inflationary expectations have been reduced by the threat of unemployment. Growth is sustainable if it can continue without leading to inflation.
- In the context of the environment, sustainable growth means growth which does not rely on exploiting resources which cannot be replaced. For example, the use of *depletable resources* such as oil can probably not be sustained indefinitely unless the rate of use can be slowed dramatically. The exploitation of hardwood forests cannot be sustained indefinitely unless the rate of use slows and more attention is given to replanting.

sweatshop: a workplace where exploitation is common, with low wages in return for high effort levels. Such a situation is most likely to occur if local unemployment is high and unionisation is low.

SWOT analysis is the assessment of a product, division or organisation in terms of its strengths, weaknesses, opportunities and threats. Its simple, four-box format makes it easy to use as a visual aid in a management meeting or conference.

SWOT analysis of British firms in the single European market

Strengths	Weaknesses
● expertise at financial services	● short-termist approach partly due to takeover threat
● low-cost production due to deregulated labour markets	● poor education and training within workforce
● influence of Japanese firms on British management	● high wage rates compared with newer EU members
Opportunities	**Threats**
● to gain market share or develop new markets within the European Union	● that foreign firms may prove more competitive, thereby taking a rising share of UK markets
● to build Europe-wide brands (such as Kit Kat) thereby enjoying large economies of scale	● that future European laws may restrict business decisions by British firms

The strengths and weaknesses reflect the actual position of the product or company, while opportunities and threats represent future potential.

synergy occurs when the whole is greater than the sum of the parts, i.e. when $2 + 2 = 5$. This is often anticipated in *takeover bids*, when directors assert that the purchase of a rival will provide such *economies of scale* as to make the combined firm a world-beater. Research evidence suggest that synergy is achieved far less often than it is forecast. There can be investment and expansion, or a shut-down in production of items for which demand is diminishing. The definition of the short run may change according to the context in which it is being used.

S

tacit collusion means that an understanding has developed between two or more competing firms, but without any kind of personal contact or formal agreement. It is characteristic of an *oligopoly*. The sellers will simply not take action in any way which might increase the level of competition between them. Because there is no actual agreement, this is hard to prevent, even though it may have considerable impact on the buyer.

It is possible for a long period of tacit collusion to follow a *price war* which the participants have found very damaging. They may just set their prices at similar levels and avoid further price competition.

tactical decisions are those based on short-term considerations such as meeting this year's budgets or plans. For instance, if a product's sales are 4 per cent below the annual forecast with one month until the year end, the sales manager might decide to run a *sales promotion* or cut the price. Usually, tactical decisions are made by middle management, though a decision to start the winter sale before Christmas would be a senior managerial decision for a clothes or jewellery retail chain.

tactics are the measures adopted to deal with a short-term opportunity or threat. Although managers would want to adopt tactics that fit in with the organisation's long-term strategy, there may be occasions when this is not possible.

takeover: obtaining full management control of another firm as a result of purchasing over 50 per cent of its *share capital*. This process is also known as acquisition. Usually, the bidder (*predator*) is sufficiently bigger than the target company to make the acquisition relatively easy to finance. However, it is possible for a small firm to raise the finance to buy a larger firm; this is known as a *reverse takeover*.

takeover bid: the attempt by a *predator* company to buy a controlling interest in another firm. This is done by offering the target firm's shareholders a significantly higher price for their shares than the prevailing market price. The offer can be made in any of the following ways:
- a cash bid, e.g. 150p per share
- a paper bid or share swap, e.g. three Firm A shares for every two of Firm B's
- a combination of cash and paper, e.g. 50p cash plus two Firm A shares for every two of Firm B's.

tall hierarchy: an organisation with many *layers of hierarchy* and a narrow *span of control* (see diagram opposite).

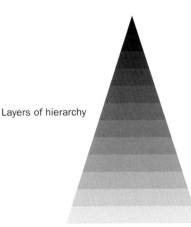

Layers of hierarchy

Chairman
Directors
Divisional directors
Senior managers
Regional managers
Area managers
Store managers
Assistant managers
Junior managers
Supervisors
Skilled workers
Shop-floor workers

tangibles: a term used to distinguish physical *fixed assets* such as land and machinery from *intangible assets* such as patents and *goodwill*.

target market: the precise profile of the customers a firm wishes to sell to. For a new cider, the target market may be working women aged 18–30; for an ice lolly it might be children aged 8–12. A firm will decide on its target market after conducting extensive *market research* including, perhaps, a *market segmentation* analysis. The choice of the target market will then affect every section of the *marketing mix*, including:
- distribution outlets: supermarkets or newsagents?
- pricing
- style of advertising and choice of advertising media
- product characteristics such as sweetness or colour.

tariff: a tax imposed on an imported good. This is likely to reduce demand, and makes any domestic competitor more attractive to consumers. The importer may seek to redress the imbalance by cutting *profit margins*, or by becoming more efficient, or in extreme cases by setting up a production plant inside the country itself. Import tariffs are banned between members of the *European Union (EU)*. Tariffs can be levied in one of two ways:
- an *ad valorem* tax, i.e. a percentage added to the price of the imported good
- a 'specific duty', such as £1 per item, regardless of whether the good is valued at £10 or £100.

The impact of tariffs depends on the elasticity of demand for the product. If demand is elastic, this implies that there are competing substitutes available from domestic producers and the tariff will cut imports considerably, as in diagram (a) overleaf. It may be impossible for the importer even to pass on the full amount of the tariff to the consumer. An example of this might be a tariff on steel products.

If, on the other hand, demand is inelastic, as in diagram (b) overleaf, the price increase brought about by the tariff will be quite high but the fall in quantity demanded will be less than proportional because people carry on buying the import as they see few or no satisfactory substitutes. This might happen with a tariff on sound systems.

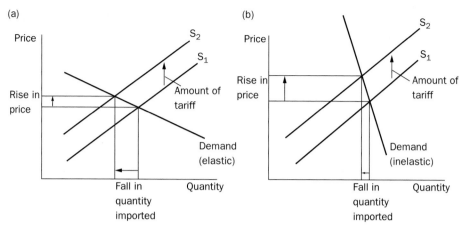

The impact of tariffs with (a) elastic and (b) inelastic demand

task culture involves a flexible approach to getting the job done, regardless of what roles individuals might have within the organisation. It contrasts with a ***role culture***, in which individual activities are defined by their position in the organisation. With a task culture, individuals will pick up responsibilities in the most appropriate way for the work in hand.

tastes can be an important element in the level of demand for a product; changes in tastes will bring about a ***shift in the demand curve***.

tax allowance: a specific amount which may be deducted from income before tax is calculated.

tax avoidance is the use of legal measures to minimise personal or corporate tax bills. Typical business examples include the use of tax havens and of ***transfer pricing***.

tax base includes all the sources of tax revenue. For example, profits are taxed to provide *corporation tax*, individuals are taxed to provide income tax and products are taxed to provide *VAT* revenues. Widening the tax base means devising ways of raising revenue which rely on different sources.

tax burden refers to the total amount of tax. When taken as a proportion of GDP, it is possible to compare the tax burden in different countries.

Current tax revenue as % of GDP, 2007

Australia	30.6
Belgium	44.4
France	43.6
Germany	36.2
Italy	43.3
Netherlands	38.0
Sweden	48.2
UK	36.6
US	28.3

Source: OECD

tax evasion means paying less tax than is legally due. For example, a person might not declare all of their income and thus pay less income tax than they should. Or they may claim allowances to which they are not legally entitled.

tax relief: a reduction in tax which is designed to create an *incentive*. For example, deducting investment expenditure from total profit can reduce tax payable on profits and encourage firms to invest.

tax revenue is the money which is paid to the government in tax. The total is important because it influences both the amount which the government may spend and the amount which has to be borrowed (*public sector net borrowing*).

The expected revenue from taxation is determined by the policies laid out in the *Budget*, usually in March. For 2009–10, income tax, VAT, National Insurance and corporation tax revenues were all forecast to fall because of the recession. (The figures are shown on the pie chart. The figure for borrowing shows the extra amount needed to cover total expenditure.)

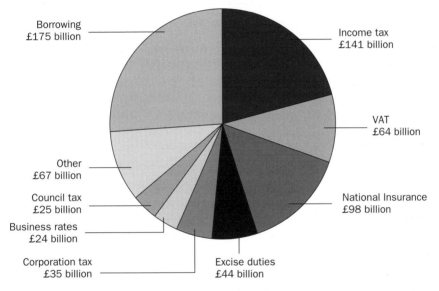

Expected tax revenue, 2009–10, £ billion. (Source: UK Treasury.)

tax thresholds are determined by the size of the personal tax allowance, which is the amount of income people are allowed to earn before tax becomes payable. An increase in the personal allowance means that the tax threshold rises. There is another threshold at the point at which the person becomes liable for tax at the 40 per cent rate.

Taylor, F W (1856–1915): an American engineer who invented work study and founded the scientific approach to management. He emphasised the duty of management to organise the working methods of shop-floor labour so as to maximise efficiency. Then, by setting financial incentives that would provide high rewards for hard work, both the worker and the business should benefit. Taylor used work study to analyse business efficiency, and advocated high *division of labour*, specialised tools, piece rate payments and tighter management control as the main methods for *productivity* improvement. Taylor's most important work with companies was between 1895 and 1905, though his widest contribution to management was through his 1911 book *Principles of Scientific Management*.

Taylor's methods had considerable impact in America and then in Britain, notably through **mass production** at the Ford Motor Company. His impact on shop-floor labour was equally substantial but far less happy. The alienation caused by **deskilling** and loss of power led to the drive for unionisation that characterised the industrial scene between 1925 and 1975. A biography of Taylor captured the essence of the man in its title *The One Best Way* (Robert Kanigel, Little, Brown & Co, 1997).

teamworking occurs when production is organised into large units of work, instead of by a high division of labour. The team of people working on the large task (such as making complete shoes, instead of just making the soles) will need to be:
- multi-skilled and therefore well-trained
- motivated to co-operate effectively.

technical economies: see *internal economies of scale*

technical efficiency: see *productive efficiency*

technological change refers to the process by which both products and the processes of production are developed and improved, as a result of increased scientific knowledge and the application of that knowledge to production.
- A technical breakthrough may make a new product development possible. Mobile phones are a relatively recent new product. This is **product innovation**.
- Equally, technical change leads to new and cheaper methods of producing and this leads to costs falling and sometimes also falls in relative prices. Telephone calls have become cheaper because of improved equipment. This is process innovation.

Technical change provides a substantial impetus to the process of **economic growth** because it makes it possible to increase **productivity**, e.g. to reduce the quantity of real resources needed to produce a particular item. The gains from technical change are most obvious in manufacturing, but there have also been major increases in productivity in the **primary sector** and in the service sector, for example as a result of using computer systems.

technological unemployment occurs where people have been made redundant as the business invested in labour-saving capital equipment. However, they will only remain unemployed if they are also affected by **occupational** or **geographical immobility**.

teleworking means working at home, though linked to the office by instant communications such as telephone, fax and e-mail and the internet. This can benefit the employer by reducing the **overhead** costs per worker, and provides a route back into work for employees who have been looking after dependent relatives.

tender refers to the closed bidding for a contract such as the construction of a building, where firms are asked to submit their price for a job and the lowest is accepted.

terms of trade: the price of **exports** relative to the price of **imports**. It is measured by the terms of trade index.

FORMULA: terms of trade index $= \dfrac{\text{index of export prices}}{\text{index of import prices}} \times 100$

The terms of trade improve if it becomes possible to buy more imports with the proceeds of a given quantity of exports, i.e. if import prices fall or if export prices rise. For example, if the price of copper rises, Zambian copper producers will receive a higher price for their exports and will be able to buy more imports. Similarly, if the price of copper stays the same but the price of imports rises, Zambia's terms of trade deteriorate.

There will be a change in the terms of trade if there is a change in the exchange rate. A *depreciation* leads to lower export prices and higher import prices. This implies a deterioration in the terms of trade. This leads to confusion, because the terminology suggests that deteriorating terms of trade are a bad thing. In fact, a depreciation may have the beneficial effect of making producers more competitive and lead in time to an improved trade balance.

tertiary sector is that part of an economy concerned with service businesses. It is the largest sector in terms of employment in the UK, accounting for around three-quarters of the workforce.

test market: the launch of a new or improved product within a tightly defined area, in order to measure actual sales potential. Launching a product nationally is so expensive in production costs, advertising expenditure and *opportunity cost* that many firms will not take the risk of assuming that successful *market research* findings will mean successful sales. They first want to test a promising idea out in an area that may be as small as a town or as large as the Midlands.

PROS: • provides more accurate sales forecasts, therefore the right-sized factory can be set up
• enables lessons to be learnt before the national launch

CONS: • gives competitors a chance to evaluate your product and decide how to respond
• management and *salesforce* focus on a small area, which may cause higher sales than are realistic nationally

them and us is a traditional statement of the divide between managers and workers. Managers see the workers as 'them'; workers see the managers as 'them'. This situation is perpetuated by the recruitment of graduate trainees who do not start at the factory floor, and perhaps by the very existence of *trade unions*. Many feel it originates in a class-obsessed society or in the school divide between grammar and comprehensive and state versus private education. Whatever its origins, most commentators would agree that its elimination is an important management task.

Theory X is *McGregor*'s term for the common management attitude that most workers have an inherent tendency to dislike work. In his own words:

'Behind every managerial decision or action are assumptions about human nature and human behaviours. A few of these are remarkably pervasive:
1 The average human being has an inherent dislike of work and will avoid it if he can.
2 Because of this human characteristic, most people must be coerced to get them to put forth adequate effort toward the achievement of organisational objectives.
3 The average human being prefers to be directed, wishes to avoid responsibility, has relatively little ambition, wants security above all.' (D McGregor, *The Human Side of Enterprise*, 1960)

(See also *Theory Y*.)

Theory Y is a managerial approach based on the belief that human beings can be stimulated by and energetic towards work, providing it has the potential to engage their interest. A common mistake is to believe that *McGregor*'s theory is about different worker types. It is not. His concern was to examine managerial attitudes and their effects. The main assumptions identified by McGregor as Theory Y were:

- 'The expenditure of physical and mental effort in work is as natural as play or rest…
- The average human being learns, under proper conditions, not only to accept but to seek responsibility…
- The capacity to exercise a relatively high degree of imagination, ingenuity, and creativity in the solution of organisational problems is widely, not narrowly, distributed in the population.' (D McGregor, *The Human Side of Enterprise*, 1960)

It has often been remarked that McGregor's Theory Y anticipated by more than ten years almost all of the management approach known as the *Japanese way*. (See also *Theory X*.)

third parties: individuals or groups which are not the main parties in a transaction, but are affected by it. For example, if a paint factory is polluting the atmosphere and people living nearby are affected by the pollution, those people are third parties in the transaction which takes place between the producer and the consumer of the paint.

tight (fiscal) policy is a government economic strategy which raises taxes and/or reduces public expenditure. Its purpose is to restrict demand, usually to keep *inflation* in check. It is usually combined with a tight *monetary policy*.

time-based management: focusing on time as a key business resource. In the 1970s price was the key competitive tool. In the 1980s it was quality. Now, speed of delivery, speed of response and speed of development are all-important. Speed adds value, as you can see in the price list of every photo-processing outlet.

time lag: a delay in the reaction of one *variable* to a change in another variable. For example, during the *economic cycle*, *unemployment* may start to fall only 12–18 months after output starts to rise at the end of a recession. An increase in *interest rates* will also have a delayed effect, spread over a period of perhaps a year, during which borrowers adjust their plans in response to the change.

time-series analysis is the processing of data into sequences of figures over time. Such data can consist of four main elements:

1 the longer-term trend, perhaps growth or decline
2 seasonal or cyclical factors, i.e. ups and downs that occur in a regular pattern
3 erratics: unpredictable fluctuations in the figures, caused by known elements (such as the weather) or by unknown ones (e.g. variations in the trendiness of a particular product)
4 responses: results of specific measures you have taken to affect the series (e.g. advertising spending causing a temporary sales increase).

To analyse this data effectively, it is necessary to process it by:

- smoothing out the erratics (by the use of *moving averages*)
- smoothing out the seasonal variations (by *seasonal adjustment*)
- identifying and measuring the responses.

This would make it possible to identify the underlying trend and then extrapolate it forwards in order to forecast the future position.

top-down management is a leadership style based on decisions and orders being issued from the top, without *consultation* or *delegation*; i.e. it is autocratic.

total contribution is the gross profit made on a sale, in other words before allowing for the fixed overhead costs:

> *FORMULA:*   total contribution = contribution per unit × quantity sold.

total cost: all the costs of producing a particular number of units, found by adding *fixed costs* to the total *variable costs*.

total quality management (TQM): the attempt to establish a culture of quality affecting the attitudes and actions of every employee. This is usually attempted by trying to get every work group (or department) to think of those they work for as customers, even if they are fellow employees. An example would be for the maintenance engineer to treat a shop-floor worker with a defective machine as a valued customer, rather than as a nuisance. Other main features of TQM include:

- the use of *quality circles*
- emphasis upon service and *after-sales service* quality as well as quality manufacture
- the idea that high quality (and low cost) stem from getting things right first time.

American firms with a long experience of TQM have reported that change occurs far more slowly than managers expect, leading to a phase of disenchantment with the process.

tradable permits: these allow certain businesses the right to pollute the atmosphere or water up to a certain point, but no more. The EU (and governments elsewhere) can cap the total amount of pollution allowed, gradually reducing the total. The permits are divided amongst the firms participating in the scheme.

The emissions trading system allows firms that can reduce their polluting activities below the level of the permit to sell it to another business, enabling it to pollute more. Allowing the permits to be sold to the highest bidder ensures that they go to the users that benefit most from the polluting activity. This means that 'the polluter pays'.

This scheme uses the price mechanism to turn an *external cost* into an internal one. Firms have an incentive to pollute less. However, the success of the scheme depends heavily on the number of carbon permits issued. The EU issued so many that their price fell up to 2007, i.e. for the first two years of the scheme. This ensured acceptance by the participating companies but greatly reduced the incentive to reduce pollution. However, if the allowable level of pollution is reduced over time, the system could become effective. Costs to firms will rise as firms adopt cleaner technologies, prices will rise, quantity of the products demanded will fall and pollution will diminish.

trade advertising: messages to retail, wholesale or industrial customers that are placed in trade media such as *The Grocer* magazine. Usually, consumer firms place advertisements in trade media in the week or two prior to the start of consumer advertising. This is to achieve retail distribution before consumers come in to search for the product.

trade association: an organisation set up to represent the interests of all the firms within an industry, notably for *lobbying* government and sharing information.

trade barriers: see *import controls*

trade creation occurs when a new *trading bloc* has been set up and businesses begin to take advantage of the opportunities arising from *free trade* between member countries.

Because there are fewer *trade barriers*, new markets open up and businesses will try to extend into them. There will be increased *specialisation* and more *trade*.

trade credit: providing business customers with time to arrange for the payment of goods they have already received. This period is one of interest-free credit, which helps the customer's *cash flow* at the cost of the supplier's. Although the typical credit period offered to customers is 30 days, the average time the customers take to pay is nearer 75 days.

trade cycle: see *economic cycle*

trade deficit occurs when visible *imports* are greater than visible *exports*.

trade diversion: when a new *trading bloc* is created, trade diversion takes place because some member countries will shift to buying more from other member countries rather than from non-member countries. For example, when the UK joined the European Union, it began to buy more butter from France and less from New Zealand. The absence of *trade barriers* between member countries and the *common external tariff* give people an incentive to switch. NAFTA, the *North American Free Trade Agreement (NAFTA)*, is demonstrating trade diversion at the present time, as people in the USA, Canada and Mexico will tend to buy more from each other and less from outside the area.

trade gap: a deficit on the *balance of trade*.

trade liberalisation: the process of limiting and reducing *trade barriers* and drawing closer towards a situation of free trade. The impetus for this has come from the *GATT/WTO* and it has been carried out through the various *trade agreements*. It has resulted in reduced tariffs on a wide range of goods and services and restrictions on the use of quotas and other non-tariff barriers. It has been a substantial element in the process of *globalisation*.

trade mark: a *logo* or symbol displayed on a company's products and advertising to distinguish the firm's brands from those of the competition. For exclusive use, a trade mark must be registered at the *Patent Office*.

trade not aid: the view that people in less developed countries would benefit more from help in starting and running businesses than from charity 'hand-outs' such as emergency food aid.

trade-offs: in making decisions people often have to consider that having more of one thing may mean having less of another.

- An important trade-off in *macroeconomic policy* is between inflation and unemployment. It is often the case that lower unemployment can be achieved but at the price of accelerating inflation. Other ways to reduce unemployment need to be found, e.g. *supply-side policies*.
- Another trade-off involves *equity* and *efficiency*. Increased wage *differentials* lead to improved incentives but less equity in the *distribution of income*.

In making a decision which involves a trade-off, there will be an *opportunity cost*. This is obvious when considering trade-offs as they affect consumers.

Trades Union Congress (TUC): the organisation that represents British *trade unions* at a national or international level. The TUC was formed in 1868 and has had periods of considerable influence on government decision-making, notably the 1970s. Its functions are to:

- be the voice of the union movement as a whole
- prevent or solve inter-union disputes
- promote international labour solidarity, especially within Europe.

trade surplus occurs when the value of visible *exports* is greater than the value of visible *imports*.

trade union: an organisation representing the interests and goals of working people. Membership involves the payment of subscriptions.

Advantages of trade unions to union members:
- collective bargaining on their behalf
- access to free legal advice and support.

Advantages of trade unions to businesses:
- communication link between management and workforce
- avoids the time-consuming need for individual bargaining.

trade war: a protectionist battle between governments in which *tariff* barriers against a country's imports lead to retaliation. If a trade war becomes serious enough it can cause a widespread downturn in world trade.

trading bloc: a group of countries that share *free trade* agreements between each other, but with *tariff* walls that discourage imports from countries outside the group. The *European Union (EU)* is a good example.

training is the provision of work-related education, in the form of either on-the-job training or off-the-job training.

training credit: an attempt at creating a market in training for young people, by giving school leavers a voucher worth £1500 which they can use to 'buy' the training they want from a local employer or college. This was hoped to provide more choice for the young person and therefore encourage the providers of training to improve the quality of their service. Critics suggested that £1500 was insufficient to provide a serious training programme.

transfer payment is where government income from one part of society is paid to another part. The best known are pensions and social security payments such as unemployment benefit.

transfer pricing is employed where no external market exists which would set a price. It is often used by large companies for internal purposes to control costs or, in the case of *multinationals*, to reduce taxation. This is achieved by one cost centre in a low-tax country charging another in a high-tax country a high transfer price. The first one will make a large profit on which little tax is paid, whilst the other will make low or no profits and so will also have a low tax liability.

transitional economies are those which have previously had *command economies* and are now allowing *market forces* to operate at least in parts of the economy. Russia, Poland and many other East European countries could be said to have more or less completed the transition process. China still has many state-owned enterprises.

transnational corporation: another name for a *multinational*.

transparency occurs when a deal or decision is made in an open manner, so that all those affected understand the reasons. Lack of transparency can mean that something illegal has happened and may mean that there has been some kind of *corruption*.

transportation links: the infrastructure that enables businesses to move exports and imports at a competitive cost. Both shipping and air freight services have become cheaper and more conveniently organised in recent years, e.g. by containerisation. This has encouraged *globalisation*.

Treasury: the UK government department responsible for executing the government's taxation and spending policies. It comes under the direct responsibility of the ***Chancellor of the Exchequer***, although the Prime Minister, as First Lord of the Treasury, has ultimate control. Because it has the power to withhold or spend money, it is the most influential of all departments. The Treasury operates a complex ***macroeconomic*** forecasting model which is designed to help decision-making, especially when devising the ***Budget***. Unfortunately the Treasury model has proved poor at spotting turning points in the business cycle.

trend: the underlying pattern of growth or decline within a series of data. This pattern can be projected forward as a prediction of the future in the process known as ***extrapolation*** of the trend.

trend rate of growth: see *long-run trend rate of growth*

trialling: see *market testing*

TUC: see *Trades Union Congress (TUC)*

turnover is an abbreviation for sales turnover, which means the same as ***sales revenue***.

two-factor theory: the view that the factors related to ***job satisfaction*** can be divided into two: those that only have the potential to provide positive job satisfaction and those that can only cause dissatisfaction. Professor ***Herzberg*** came to this conclusion in the late 1950s, after conducting research among accountants and engineers in America. The findings of his research are presented below. Many have criticised his research method, but many managers have attempted to put his theory into practice and have enjoyed considerable success.

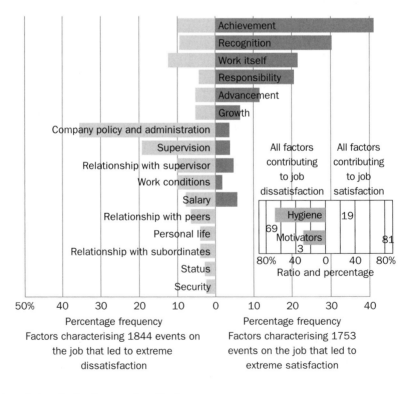

Herzberg's two-factor theory of motivation

uncertainty is the situation that underlies every business decision. This is because decision-making concerns changes that will have an effect in the future, and the future can never be predicted with certainty. An important issue that stems from this is that uncertainty increases over time. In other words, a forecast of next year's sales or costs has a lower chance of accuracy than an estimate of the figures for next week. Therefore decisions that rely upon circumstances in the distant future are subject to very great uncertainty. Examples of this include commercial failures such as supersonic aircraft and nuclear power.

underconsumption applies to *merit goods*, for which demand will be lower than is socially most efficient, if people are left to provide them for themselves. It is in the best interests of society for people to be educated and have access to health care, because in this way the population as a whole will be kept healthy and productive. However, both education and health care are expensive and people on low incomes will not be able to pay for them in the optimum quantities. They will therefore be underconsumed unless provided by the government. This is an example of *market failure*.

underemployment occurs where people nominally have jobs, but jobs that do not keep them fully occupied. This often results in very low wages, and is particularly prevalent in the agricultural sectors of less developed countries.

under-utilised capacity occurs when an organisation is producing below its maximum possible level. For instance, if a hotel has an average occupancy rate of 75 per cent, its level of under-used capacity is 25 per cent. This figure is important because it is only by making full use of capacity that *fixed costs* (and therefore total costs) per unit can be minimised.

undervalued exchange rate: an *exchange rate* which is below its long-term equilibrium value. This means that exports are very competitive and therefore high and imports appear relatively expensive and will be fairly low. The outcome is a current account surplus on the *balance of payments*. An undervalued exchange rate can be very helpful in encouraging the development of industries which export. China has been accused of keeping its exchange rate down and this could account for some of its success as an exporter.

underwriting is the acceptance of a business risk in return for a fee. Lloyd's of London has a worldwide reputation for its willingness to underwrite any type of insurance wanted by a client. For a *stock market* new issue, a *merchant bank* will underwrite it by guaranteeing to buy any shares which are not sold in the company *flotation*.

unearned income: income derived from interest, dividends and rents, i.e. from assets which are owned, rather than from employment.

unemployment exists when someone seeking work is unable to find any. Unemployment leads to loss of income and output.

The main types of unemployment are:

- structural, i.e. when the economy changes in a fundamental way, people are made unemployed. The coal and shipbuilding industries of the UK are examples
- cyclical, i.e. when demand is low at the bottom of the trade cycle
- seasonal, e.g. people in the building trade are often laid off during the winter when the weather is too bad to work
- frictional, which is when people are temporarily unemployed between jobs.

Cyclical unemployment can be reduced using *expansionary policies*. *Structural unemployment* can be addressed using *supply-side policies*. *Frictional unemployment* is reduced by improving information flows.

Unemployment can be measured in different ways, giving different results. The claimant count is the number of people who register as unemployed, which excludes some people who are available for work but do not qualify for unemployment benefit. The figures based on the *Labour Force Survey*, or the ILO definition of unemployment, will include these. The claimant count hovered around 5 per cent throughout the period 2000–07, and then rose sharply as recession set in.

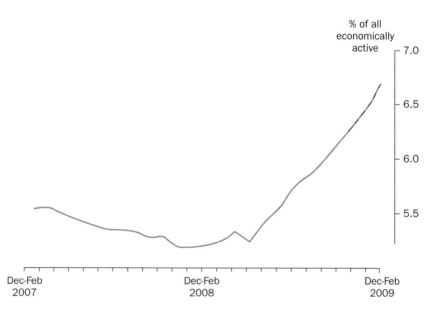

Unemployment rate, % of all economically active, claimant count, seasonally adjusted. (Source: ONS.)

In recent years attention has been focused on whether employment protection laws reduce the rate at which new jobs are created, especially for unskilled jobs. Policies have emphasised the need for *labour* markets to be flexible. Employers hesitate to take on more labour when it is hard to make people redundant later – they want hiring and firing to be easy. In the USA, unemployment has generally been lower than in most of the EU, where unemployment in a number of countries has been above 10 per cent for long periods.

In the UK and the Netherlands, unemployment has been higher than in the USA but lower than in the rest of the EU. Commentators have linked this to the more flexible labour markets of these three countries.

unemployment benefit is the social security payment made to people who have become unemployed. It has recently been renamed the jobseeker's allowance and is now paid for a maximum of six months. The intention is to create an enhanced incentive to find work.

unfair competition occurs when one or more firms use methods that are deliberately harmful to the interests of other producers and consumers. Good examples include *collusion* between firms, such as *cartels*, or a large firm using *predatory pricing* to drive a smaller firm out of business.

Uniform Business Rate is a tax paid by businesses to cover the use of local goods and services. It was introduced in 1990 and was the successor to the local rating system. It is set nationally but reflects local property values.

unincorporated means a firm that operates as a *sole trader* or partnership which has not applied to the *Registrar of Companies* for incorporation as a *joint-stock company*. Those running an unincorporated business have *unlimited liability* for the firm's debts.

union: see *trade union*

union recognition is the acceptance by an employer that bargaining on wages and conditions will be negotiated with the employees' *trade union* representatives. Employers must recognise a trade union if a majority of staff vote for union representation (as long as at least 40 per cent of workers cast their vote in favour). Firms with fewer than 20 staff are exempt.

unique selling point (USP): the feature of a product that can be focused on in order to differentiate it from all competition. The USP should be based on a real product characteristic, such as the advertising slogan used by Mars for one of its chocolate bars: 'Topic – a hazelnut in every bite'. Stronger still are USPs based on a patented technical advantage. Many firms, however, attempt to create USPs that are based purely on advertising imagery. This can be effective (better to be the sexiest chocolate bar than the hazelnuttiest) but usually at the cost of extensive TV advertising support. (See *differentiated product*.)

unit cost is the average cost of making one item, found by dividing total cost by the number of units produced. This sounds straightforward, but unit (or average) costs are among the trickiest concepts in business. This is because it seems as if you can use unit costs to work out the total cost of producing any specified number of units. In fact, however, unit costs comprise two elements: *variable costs* (which are a true cost per unit) and *fixed costs per unit* (which are only correct at one level of output). Therefore, before 'using' unit costs, it is necessary to strip out the fixed element.

C

Worked example: unit costs

At 400 units of demand, unit costs are £2, half of which are fixed. What are total costs if demand doubles?

Fixed costs stay at £1 × 400 = £400

Variable costs are £1 × 800 = £800

Therefore total costs at 800 units = **£1200** (*not* 800 × £2 = £1600)

unit elasticity means that *price elasticity* of demand is exactly equal to –1. The percentage change in quantity demanded is exactly the same as the percentage change in price. Price changes will make no difference to the amount of money spent on the product, because an increase in price will be offset by a decrease in quantity demanded. Someone who has a set amount of beer money to spend each week will have unit elasticity of demand.

unit trust: a fund that spreads small savers' investments over a wide *portfolio* of different *stocks and shares*. This is a popular and relatively inexpensive way of investing on the *Stock Exchange*. Unfortunately the slump in share prices between 2000 and 2002/03, and more recently in 2008/09, showed that even unit trust investment is not safe from losses.

unlimited liability means that because a business is trading without having become incorporated, its owners are liable for all the debts it may incur. If these debts are greater than the personal assets of the proprietors, they may be forced into *bankruptcy*. The main types of unlimited liability business are *sole traders* and *partnerships*.

unofficial strike: a refusal to work that has been agreed locally by *trade union* members, but has not been approved by the national union. As a result, strikers will not receive any *strike pay* and will have their legal case weakened should the firm dismiss them. Unofficial strikes are sometimes called *wildcat strikes* or walk-outs. Both terms give the correct impression of a dispute that has arisen so suddenly that workers act before getting official union approval.

unsecured loan: borrowing that is not backed by any form of security or *collateral*. This would be hard to obtain and would carry relatively high interest charges.

unsustainable growth: economic growth which is faster than the long-run trend rate of growth, which reflects the actual increase in the productive capacity of the economy. A period of unsustainable growth is likely to be followed by a period of slower than average growth. In 2007, the UK economy grew by 3 per cent. This was almost certainly not sustainable, regardless of what might have happened if the banking system had not collapsed. Inflation was rising towards 5 per cent and the Bank of England raised interest rates. This would have resulted in lower growth in 2008, even if the world economy had behaved normally.

An alternative definition of unsustainable growth would emphasise the environmental considerations. It would be growth at a rate involving the use of depletable resources which cannot be continued in the long run because these will become progressively scarcer and therefore more expensive. Sustainable growth involves the management of resources so that they are replaced as they are used. For example, trees are replanted and reliance on fossil fuels is progressively reduced.

up-market: a word used commonly in marketing to denote a product that is aimed at wealthier consumers. Its opposite is a *down-market* product.

upper turning point is the highest point in the *economic cycle*. It is usually reached where there are shortages of skilled labour and capital goods, and when expectations that the boom will continue begin to fade. The loss of confidence and rising costs reduce levels of investment and, through the *multiplier*, result in a downturn. (See diagram opposite.)

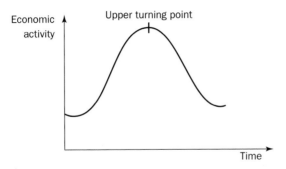

The upper turning point of the economic cycle

upstream activities are those that focus on earlier stages in the *production chain*. Therefore upstream integration is another term for backward *vertical integration*.

upturn is that point in the *economic cycle*, after a recession, where business confidence returns, investment restarts, unemployment falls and incomes begin to rise.

URL: uniform resource locator (URL) is the term for the address of a website. This usually begins: http://.

USP: see *unique selling point (USP)*

utilities are industries which provide the most basic services such as water and power. Before *privatisation* it was generally accepted that utilities were nationalised, not only because of their importance to the overall economy, but also because they operated on such a large scale they were *natural monopolies*. Now they are mostly regulated within the private sector.

Do you need revision help and advice ?

Go to pages 324–35 for a range of revision appendices that include plenty of exam advice and tips.

C

vacancies: job opportunities which are registered with job centres. This is not the number of job vacancies in existence, because many are not registered but are advertised independently in a wide range of publications and agencies. However, the changes in vacancies over time are a very useful indicator of the slackness or tightness of the *labour* market generally.

validity: measuring or judging the reliability of data such as the findings of *market research*. To assess the validity of research findings, the following should be considered:
- whether the questionnaire was biased
- whether the sampling method was appropriate
- whether the sample size was large enough to provide statistically valid data
- whether the interviewing was carried out consistently and without bias (overenthusiastic, for example)
- whether the research results can be related directly to customer actions (people may say they will try a product, but in practice they do not bother to do so).

value added is the difference between the cost of inputs and the price customers are prepared to pay for the finished product. It is value added that creates the surplus to pay wages, *overheads* and *dividends*. A product with high value added is likely to have been produced and/or designed with great skill, though it may also be the result of creating a very desirable brand image. Value added reflects the value of the services of land, labour, capital and entrepreneurship which have been used in the production process.

FORMULA: selling price – bought-in goods and services = value added

$$£4 \quad - \quad £0.80 \quad = £3.20$$

The diagram opposite shows how the £3.20 value added is distributed. It also indicates that value added can be expressed as a percentage:

% value added $\dfrac{\text{value added}}{\text{materials}} \times 100$

$= \dfrac{£4 - 80\text{p}}{80\text{p}} \times 100$

$= 400\%$

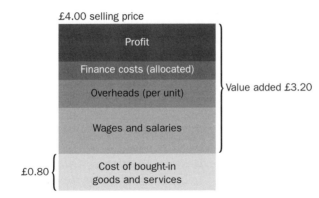

£4.00 selling price

Value added £3.20

£0.80

value added tax (VAT) is a percentage tax added on to the price of a good or service. It was introduced in 1973 to replace purchase tax and to harmonise with the rest of the *European Union (EU)*. Since each stage of production adds value (the difference between the cost of its inputs and the revenue gained from its output), the tax is added at each stage, and can be claimed back, until it reaches the final consumer, who cannot reclaim it. The tax is a *regressive tax* in that it takes a higher proportion of a poor person's income than it does of someone who is rich. In recent years, the UK government has broadened the VAT net, for example by taxing heating fuels.

value analysis: the study of each aspect of a product to see if it adds sufficient value to justify its cost. Companies conduct value analysis to find out whether new and existing products are designed in a way that satisfies the consumer in terms of what the product looks like, what it costs and how well it performs its job. Achieving this goal requires a combination of *market research*, cost information and engineering skills.

Generally, the term 'value analysis' is used to mean the identification of costs that could be cut, either by using cheaper materials or by redesigning a product to use fewer components. It is this negative approach that has led to value analysis being blamed for reductions in quality and workmanship; for example, cars being made with thinner body steel or window frames becoming much less ornate than in the past.

value judgement: an opinion based on beliefs rather than facts. Although the term could be used to describe *entrepreneurs* who make decisions in an unscientific manner, it is more commonly used as a criticism of student essays. Students often make the error of stating value judgements as if they are facts (for example, 'All firms profit-maximise').

values: ethical principles that guide one's actions, enabling one to identify decisions or actions that are morally unacceptable. (See *ethics*.)

variable: a variable is a factor that can cause changes to occur in a firm's plans or outcomes. Some variables are within the firm's influence, such as pricing levels, employee *motivation* and *advertising* effectiveness. An efficient firm will measure and evaluate these variables in order to decide what policies to adopt towards them. Others are wholly outside the firm's control, such as the weather, competitors' actions and consumer confidence. These variables should be measured and anticipated so as to aid the firm's planning process. In the macroeconomy, changes in variables may be predicted by economic models.

variable cost: one that varies in direct proportion to changes in output, such as *raw materials*, components, some labour and energy used in production. In other words, these are costs that should double if output doubles. Although *break-even charts* require the assumption that some costs vary in direct proportion to changes in *output*, in practice it is unlikely that any costs will be totally variable. For instance, raw materials are likely to cost less per unit when buying in bulk. Therefore the materials cost might not quite double when output doubles.

variable factors of production are those factors which can be varied in quantity in the short run. Raw material or component inputs are an example: the amount used will depend on the level of output and can be varied as necessary. *Labour* may be a variable factor, if the number of people employed or the hours worked can be varied according to the amount of work to be done. This might be the case if overtime was worked in order to increase output. Alternatively, labour may be a fixed factor, if the employees concerned will have to be kept on even if output falls.

VAT: see *value added tax (VAT)*

venture capital is risk capital, usually in the form of a package of loan and *share capital*, to provide a significant investment in a small or medium-sized business. The need for it arises when a rapidly growing firm requires more capital, but the firm is not yet ready for the *stock market*. In these circumstances, *merchant banks* might provide the funds themselves, or arrange for others to do so. A typical venture capital investment might provide £500000: half in loans and half in shares.

VER: see *voluntary export restraint (VER)*

vertical communication is the passage of information up and down the management hierarchy. It may be upward, as in a shop-floor complaint to managers about safety conditions, or downward, as in a manager-run team-briefing session. Successful vertical communication can overcome *them and us* barriers and can enhance the speed and quality of *consultation*. To achieve this, however, requires a clear sense of common purpose and a flat enough hierarchy to minimise the layers through which the communication must pass.

vertical integration occurs when two firms join together that operate in the same industry, but at different stages in the production/supply chain. The integration might come about through *merger* or *takeover*.

Backward (or upstream) vertical integration means buying out a supplier, e.g. a chocolate manufacturer buying a sugar producer. Forward (or downstream) vertical integration (*forward integration*) means buying out a customer, e.g. the chocolate firm buying up a chain of newsagents.

vested interest: a participant in a decision, action or statement who has a direct interest in the outcome and therefore may prove biased. For example, estate agents have a vested interest in suggesting that the housing market is strong enough for prices to rise.

visible balance: another name for the trade balance, i.e. visible exports minus visible imports.

visible trade is the export and import of goods only, services are not included. The difference between visible exports and visible imports is the *balance of trade*. (See also *balance of payments*.)

voluntary code of practice: a formal statement by a committee or organisation of the methods of working recommended as good practice for the firms and individuals within an industry. Such codes are often devised by the **employers' association**, which provides a symbol that participants in the scheme can display to potential customers. The code is voluntary if it has no statutory or legal backing. This is usually what employers say they want, though financial scandals within the City of London have led many within the financial sector to call for statutory and therefore legally enforceable codes of behaviour.

voluntary export restraint (VER): a quota placed on imports from a particular country, with the agreement of that country's government. (See **quotas** for explanation of the likely impact.) They have mainly been applied to developed countries' imports of manufactures from Asian countries. Their objective is to protect the domestic industry of the importing country. The exporting country may be persuaded to accept them if the alternative is a more damaging trade barrier. They are outside the rules of the **World Trade Organization (WTO)**.

voluntary liquidation: a decision by the company directors or shareholders to ask **receivers** to liquidate the business in the best interests of the shareholders. **Liquidation** meaning turning **assets** into **cash**. This process of winding up a company's affairs may be due to a financial crisis or simply because a firm's directors wish to retire and have no successors.

voluntary organisation: a *non-profit-making organisation* such as a charity or a youth group. The special difficulties of managing such organisations have been analysed by **Handy**. Key amongst them is the need for a management style that makes staff feel valued, since there is no financial reason for volunteer staff to work effectively.

vote of (no) confidence: this is the way in which shareholders who believe that their company has been mismanaged can demand that the current chairman resigns. A vote can be called at the **annual general meeting (AGM)** between the directors and the shareholders. Although this procedure is an important aspect of the theoretical **accountability** of company managements to their shareholders, in practice it is extremely rare for a vote of no confidence to succeed.

A vote of no confidence may also be carried out when a government policy has been so seriously called into question that the Speaker of the House of Commons accepts an Opposition call for a no-confidence debate. Should the government lose such a debate, it is accepted parliamentary practice that it resigns from office and a general election is held.

wage bargaining may occur collectively (between a trade union and an employers' association) or individually between employer and employee). The outcome depends heavily on the market power of individuals and the organisations concerned. Many people have no choice but simply to accept the going rate of pay, when neither they nor any trade union they might join has any bargaining power. Only a shortage of their particular skill, or of *labour* generally, will then raise their real earnings.

wage determination: assuming markets are competitive, pay will be determined by the interaction of supply and demand in the *labour* market. The important factors affecting demand are:

- the demand for the final product
- the price of capital equipment which could be substituted for labour
- the **productivity** of labour.

Factors affecting supply are:

- wage rates on offer in other occupations
- the non-monetary attractions of the work
- the amount of training required.

Some very unpleasant work is well paid because few people would accept it otherwise.

wage–price spiral: a phrase describing a situation in which wages chase prices, in turn causing prices to rise further, and so on. When *inflation* rises to such a level that workers see their *real incomes* falling, they respond by demanding wage increases to compensate. This is also known as *cost-push inflation*. Whether wages follow prices at the start of the cycle, or prices follow wages, is subject to a great deal of political debate.

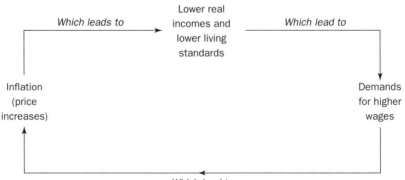

wage rate: the price of *labour*. When wage rates change, the change may be real or it may be just a change in money wages which maintains their existing purchasing power.

Wall Street Crash: the collapse in American share prices that began in 1929 and continued until 1932. It was the result of the American *stock market* rising so far during the 1920s that share prices no longer reflected reality. Investors took risks in highly speculative shares, such as land deals in the Florida Everglades and in Europe. Once rumours of the risks of these shares became common knowledge, the bubble burst and share prices plummeted, helping to bring about the *Great Depression*, which continued until the Second World War. The same pattern of share price boom and bust has happened several times since 1929, notably in the period 2002–2009.

Wal-mart: the world's biggest retailer and purchaser, in 1999, of Asda Food Stores in Britain. In the USA, Wal-mart sells largely on the basis of discount prices from enormous stores. British and continental European retailers are worried that Wal-mart may do exactly the same in the UK and Europe. That would be bad for profit margins but great for the consumer.

wastage is the rate of loss of resources within a production or service process, either necessarily (such as the weight loss when filleting a fish) or unnecessarily (such as sloppy work). Staff effort should be devoted to minimising the wastage that is within their control or influence.

In manufacturing, the main problems are:
- materials wastage
- reworking (due to poor quality first time)
- defective production (with products sold off as 'seconds').

In retailing, the main problems are:
- customer or staff theft and pilfering
- products passing their sell-by date (due to over-ordering or poor stock rotation)
- poor handling, leading to products becoming damaged.

waste disposal: the means used to dispose of all kinds of waste products. *Social responsibility* requires an *ethical code* to be in place, so that the business can avoid creating *negative externalities* for society.

waste management: ensuring that waste materials and emissions are kept within legal limits, at the lowest possible cost to the business. This process might be helped by environmental auditing, especially if the audit results are published each year.

wealth: the stock of *assets* held by an individual or organisation. These assets can be used to yield a stream of *income* in the future. They may consist of financial assets, such as bank balances or shares, or real assets, such as property.

wealth distribution: the way in which total *wealth* in the economy is shared out among the population as a whole. In most countries wealth is unevenly distributed, and becoming more so. In the UK, roughly 23 per cent of total wealth is owned by 1 per cent of the population, 52 per cent belongs to the wealthiest 10 per cent, and 94 per cent of all wealth belongs to 50 per cent of the population.

website: a location on the *World Wide Web* providing access to information. The *Financial Times* website will provide latest financial news, whereas the National Gallery's site may provide opening times and details of the latest exhibitions. Firms are interested in websites because of their potential to sell goods direct to the customer. Cutting out the middleman's 30–100 per cent profit mark-up could reduce prices to the customer and thereby boost market share.

weighted average: an average which takes into account the relative importance of its components. Weights can be regularly revised to ensure that they reflect current spending patterns (for price indices), output patterns or trade patterns – depending on the index concerned.

weighted index: the calculation of a data series with a base figure equalling 100 within which the principles of *weighted averages* are applied. Among the most widely used weighted indices in business and economics are the *retail prices index (RPI)* and the *Financial Times Stock Exchange 100 Index* (FTSE 100, popularly known as the *Footsie (FTSE 100)*).

The *retail prices index (RPI)* is a weighted average that gives larger weights to the prices of products on which a significant amount of income is spent. The *sterling exchange rate index* uses the same approach to give a weighted average of all exchange rates.

welfare: a term usually used to refer to people's well-being. It is hard to measure. *National income statistics* are an imperfect guide. Sometimes, other measures are used, which might include life expectancy, child mortality or the ownership of certain *consumer durables*.

welfare gain: the benefit to society of increasing consumption to the point where *marginal social benefits* are equal to *marginal social costs*. For example, when the government spends money on improving public transport, vehicle owners benefit from reduced congestion.

If the government does not subsidise public transport, the amount provided will be the amount that reflects the marginal private benefits, i.e. the fares paid by users. At the equilibrium point, this will be equal to the marginal private cost, determined by market forces. However, improving public transport will reduce congestion and pollution, with benefits for many groups of people. Welfare is optimised at the point where marginal social benefit is equal to marginal social cost. There is a clear welfare gain from the extra benefits obtained, over and above the extra costs, shown by the shaded triangle in the diagram.

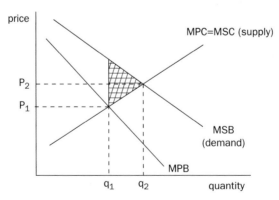

The triangle of welfare gain

welfare state: the system of social security benefits and health care which was set up in the UK after 1945. It was designed to help all those in need, but is constantly threatened by efforts to cut costs and avoid raising taxes. The capacity to provide is affected by the ageing population, which increases demands on the welfare state.

what if... ? questions are hypothetical considerations of:
- what might happen in the future
- what might result if things are done differently today.

What if... ? questions are the essential preliminary stage to **contingency planning**, i.e. to the process of preparing responses to possible opportunities or threats. These questions are made far easier to think through if a firm's sales, production, distribution and financial data is kept on a single computer model. This is the attraction of resource planning systems such as **manufacturing resource planning (MRP II)**.

whistle blower: an individual whose sense of moral outrage leads him or her to expose wrongdoing within an organisation, either to the authorities or to the press. The Public Interest Disclosure Act 1998 offered protection to whistle blowers from their employers. This protection only applies if the employee has tried to correct the concern internally before going public.

wholesale price index: a measure of changes in wholesale prices. It is useful because it may give an advance warning of impending changes in retail price levels.

wholesaling: the process of buying large quantities of product from suppliers and selling on in smaller volumes to retailers or business users. This is known as 'breaking bulk'. This role as the middleman is often looked down on because the wholesaler's profit margin appears to make goods more expensive for the consumer. As shown by the diagram below, however, without a wholesaler the number of journeys required for each manufacturer to service each retailer would become prohibitively expensive. Furthermore, there would be serious effects on traffic and the environment from the extra journeys necessary.

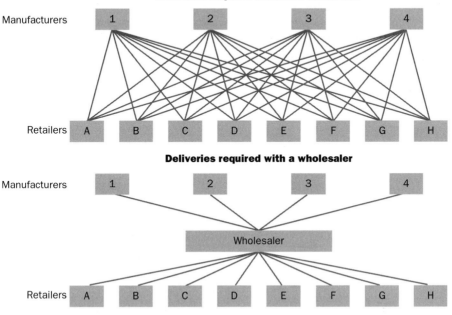

The role of a wholesaler

wildcat strike: spontaneous unofficial industrial action brought on by the sudden emergence of a major grievance such as the sacking of a respected shop steward.

windfall gain: a one-off gain that can aid this year's profit or cash position, but cannot be expected to recur in future.

winding up is the process of completing the *liquidation* of a business in order for it to cease trading in an orderly manner.

window-dressing: presenting the company accounts in such a manner as to flatter the financial position of the firm. This is a form of *creative accounting* in which there is a fine dividing line between flattery and fraud. In the overwhelming number of cases, window-dressing is no more misleading than tidying up before visitors arrive. Among the different ways of window-dressing accounts are:

- Masking a deteriorating *liquidity* position. This is in order to present a *balance sheet* that looks financially sound. This might be done via a sale-and-leaseback deal, bringing in an instant injection of cash.
- Massaging the profit figure. Although firms' revenue totals and cost totals sound like facts, there is scope for changing the figures. At the end of a poor year's trading, managers may be asked to bring forward as many invoices and deliveries as possible, to, in effect, push two months' revenue into the last month before the year-end.

withdrawals: see *leakages*

word of mouth: the spread of information or publicity through individuals' decisions to talk about a product or event. This is an especially important form of free *advertising* for fashion-based and/or children's products. Favourable word of mouth will spread if a product has been particularly well designed and made.

worker participation is the active involvement of the workforce in the ideas, decisions and actions of an organisation. It can be encouraged by structures such as *quality circles*, *kaizen* groups and *works councils*. Such structures are only successful, however, if senior management give full support to the suggestions that come up from the factory floor.

workforce planning means identifying a company's future staff needs, then devising a plan to achieve them. It is a three-stage process:

- Staff audit: finding out the skills and plans of current staff, e.g. how many speak French and how many would like to live in France.
- Staff targets: setting out the firm's staffing needs in one or two years' time, in order that the business can meet its objectives, e.g. Pizza Express wants to expand to France and needs 30 staff to move there.
- Staff plan: setting out the recruitment, training and re-training needs to move the business from the staff it has now to the staff it needs in the future.

working capital is the day-to-day finance available for running a business.

FORMULA: current assets – current liabilities = working capital

Working capital is used to pay for raw materials and running costs, and also funds the credit offered to customers (*debtors*) when making a sale. If a firm has too little working capital available, it may struggle to finance increased production without straining its *liquidity* position. Yet if a firm has too much capital tied up in the short term, it may not be able to afford the new machinery that could boost efficiency.

working conditions: the physical surroundings and atmosphere of a workplace, e.g. state of decoration and amount of pollution. Professor *Herzberg* regards them as *hygiene factors* since, whereas poor working conditions may be demotivating, good conditions become accepted as the norm and therefore give no positive satisfaction.

Working Families Tax Credit: a benefit paid to people with families whose pay is low. It helps to ensure that people on low pay do have some *incentive* to work.

working population: all those who are working or actively seeking work. The UK's working population is currently increasing, from 28.5 million in 1997 to 29.5 million in 2002 and 30.8 million in 2007. Some of this increase comes from immigration; some also from improved incentives to work through the *Working Families Tax Credit*.

Working Time Directive: the EU legal requirement that employees should work a maximum of 48 hours per week averaged over any 17-week period. Strangely, there is an opt-out from this rule. Any worker can volunteer to waive the right to this working time ceiling. The directive formed part of the social chapter of the *Maastricht* treaty.

work in progress (WIP): semi-completed components within the production process, either stockpiled or on the production line itself. This is one of the three types of stock; the others are raw materials and finished goods. Although in many factory contexts WIP is a minor element of stock, in others such as shipbuilding and construction, the long production time makes work in progress a heavy user of the firm's *working capital*.

works council: a regular forum for discussion between management and workforce representatives. Excluded from the agenda would be bargaining over wages, terms and productivity levels, as these matters would be left to *trade union* negotiations. The role of the works council is to look ahead at the company's plans and to draw ideas for improvements from the factory floor. A weakness of works councils has always been that because they include representatives from the whole firm, they lack the focus of a localised *quality circle* or improvement group. Germany has used works councils the most constructively.

The EU's European Works Council Directive revived works councils in the 1990s, as it forced large firms that operate in more than one European country to have regular works council meetings. Compulsion can never be successful, however, while managers see such meetings as disruptive rather than a positive opportunity to consult and learn from the shop floor. Nevertheless, some firms, such as Unilever, have taken impressive initiatives.

World Bank: see *International Bank for Reconstruction and Development (IBRD)*

world-class manufacturing is a term coined by R Schonberger to denote the characteristics of the world's top-performing companies. *Benchmarking* is the technique used most commonly to identify how well a firm's performance stands up against the world's best-performing manufacturers.

World Trade Center: the twin skyscrapers in Manhattan's financial district that provided office space for over 50 000 New York financial traders and bankers. The terrorist destruction of the 'twin towers' on 11 September 2001 caused a huge shock to American consumer confidence and destabilised politics and the world economy during the aftermath.

World Trade Organization (WTO): the grouping of over a hundred countries into an international free trade club. The member countries commit themselves to work towards the elimination of barriers to imports and thereby encourage free and fair trade. The WTO is a successor to the *General Agreement on Tariffs and Trade (GATT)*. Whereas GATT covered only trade in goods, the WTO also includes services and the protection of intellectual property (such as patents and copyright). China's acceptance as a member in 2002 represented the WTO's biggest-ever increase in economic importance worldwide.

Although the WTO has been highly successful in reducing tariff barriers on trade in manufactures, there are still major restraints on trade in agricultural products which are being reduced only very slowly, if at all. The **Doha Round** of trade negotiations began in 2001 and finally stalled in 2008. Agriculture and services figured large this time. It seems unlikely that governments will reactivate the talks while there is a worldwide recession. In the long run, there is still much scope for increasing standards of living through **trade liberalisation**.

The WTO has done much to promote trade. This has improved standards of living for huge numbers of people, including many who were very poor. However free trade does involve structural changes which can be painful in the short run; some people may lose out. This is a criticism of free trade rather than the WTO. However, there are other more direct criticisms of the WTO:

- Sometimes it appears to be defending the interests of the multinationals.
- Small, poor countries have little influence within the WTO.
- High levels of agricultural protection are still permitted in developed countries and these are detrimental to the interests of potential exporters in developing countries.
- In promoting economic growth, the WTO is probably increasing the use of resources in unsustainable ways.
- The WTO has worked to enforce intellectual property rights, which can be costly for developing countries, e.g. in terms of access to pharmaceutical products.

World Wide Web: a menu-based system of software that provides links to other information sources throughout the internet. It is where most of the information on the internet is posted for other users.

write off: the decision to cut the **book value** of an asset down to zero (or to a nominal sum such as £1). This would be done if it became clear that a physical asset had become worthless or a **debtor**'s item had become unrecoverable.

WTO: see **World Trade Organaization (WTO)**

x-inefficiency: the tendency for costs to rise because the organisation has few or no competitors. This is likely to occur if the producer has a degree of monopoly power, whether in the public or the private sector, which allows management to become careless about keeping costs to a minimum.

yield: another term for *dividend yield*.

zero defects: the goal of achieving perfect product quality, time after time. Many believe that this could only be feasible at an excessively high design and production cost.

zero hours contract: an employment contract stating that the employee's regular working week amounts to zero hours. This provides the employer with total flexibility, allowing the employer to tell staff at the start of each week the hours they are required to work. Such a contract might be given to a hotel receptionist, who might then have to work from 6.00 am to 2.00 pm Monday to Thursday and from 5.00 pm to 3.00 am on Friday and Saturday.

zero rated: products for which *VAT* declarations must be made, though the rate of tax is 0 per cent.

Edexcel revision lists

On the pages that follow, we have listed revision terms for the AS and A-level examinations for the Edexcel specification, which is the main awarding body in this subject. This is to help you use this handbook as effectively as possible. In addition, to help focus your revision, you can use the A–Z Online website to access these revision lists.

Log on to **www.philipallan.co.uk/a-zonline** and create an account using the unique code provided on the inside front cover of this book. Once you have logged on, you can print out the lists of terms together with their definitions for the particular exam you are taking.

AS Unit 1: Developing new business ideas

Entrepreneurs and identified opportunities (Section 1.3.1–1.3.2)

Autocratic leadership style

Characteristics of entrepreneurs

Demand

Democratic leadership

Entrepreneur

Equilibrium

Ethics

Leadership style

Management

Market orientation

Market price

Non-profit motives

Paternalistic leadership style

Profit

Profit maximisation

Profit motive

Supply

Theory X

Theory Y

Evaluating a business opportunity (Section 1.3.3)

Adding value

Bias

Competition

Competitive advantage

Customer behaviour

Differentiated product

Market

Mapping

Market niche

Market positioning

Market research

Market segmentation

Market share

Market size

Market structure

Opportunity cost

Primary data

Primary research

Product trial

Qualitative research

Quantitative research

Questionnaire

Repeat purchase

Sample

Sample size

Stakeholder

Test market

Unique selling point (USP)

Economic considerations (Section 1.3.4)

Consumer durables

Credit crunch

Deflation

Direct taxes

Economic cycle

Exchange rate

Export

Government expenditure

Import

Indirect taxation

Inflation

Interest rates

Real incomes

Recession

Unemployment

Planning and financing start-up (Sections 1.3.5–1.3.7)

Break-even chart

Business plan

Cash flow forecast

Contribution

Debenture

External financing

Fixed costs

Gross profit

Internal financing

Leasing

Limited liability

Margin of safety

Marketing plan

Operating profit

Overdraft

Private limited company

Profit

Profit and loss account

Profit margin

Public limited company (PLC)

Retained profit

Services

Sole trader

Trade credit

Unlimited liability

Variable cost

Venture capital

AS Unit 2b: Business Economics

How businesses respond to their markets (Section 2.3.1b)

Allocation of resources

Choice

Competitive advantage

Complementary goods

Consumer sovereignty

Demand

Dynamic markets

Equilibrium price

Incentives

Income elasticity

Marketing ethics

Marketing mix

Market share

Mixed economy

Opportunity cost

Price elasticity

Profit-signalling mechanism

Scarcity

Substitutes

Supply

How market structure affects businesses (Section 2.3.3b)

Allocative efficiency

Barriers to entry and exit

Branding

Collusion

Competition

Consumer sovereignty

Contestable markets

Differentiated product

Easy entry

E-commerce

Imperfect competition

Limit pricing

Long tail

Monopoly

Monopolistic competition

Monopsony

Normal profit

Oligopoly

Perfect competition

Predatory pricing

Price leaders

Price takers

Productive efficiency

Promotion

Spectrum of competition

What makes firms effective (Section 2.3.3b)

Capacity utilisation

Capital intensive

Cell production

Centralisation

Culture

Chain of command

Culture

Decentralisation

Delayering

Delegating

Efficiency

Empowerment

Hierarchical structure

Human capital

Human relations

Investment

Just in time (JIT)

Kaizen

Kanban

Labour intensive

Lean production

Matrix management

Multi-skilled

Net investment

New product development

Outsourcing

Productivity

Scientific approach

Span of control

Total quality management (TQM)

Businesses big and small (Section 2.3.4b)

Accountability

Average costs

Cost differential

Diseconomies of scale

Economies of scale

External economies

Global oligopoly

Inorganic growth

Internal economies

Market power

Market share

Micromarketing

Minimum efficient scale (MES)

Office of Fair Trading (OFT)

Organic growth

Profitability

Satisficing

Strategic alliances

Suppliers

Under-utilised capacity

Uncertainty and the macroeconomy (Sections 2.3.5b and 2.3.6b)

Aggregate demand

Aggregate supply

Bank Rate

Bankruptcy

Consumption

Contingency planning

Creative destruction

Depreciation

Euro zone

Exchange rates

Exchange rate movements

Exports

Forecasting

Government expenditure

Government intervention

Human capital

Immobilities

Income redistribution

International trade

Investment

Knowledge economy

Leading indicators

Monetary Policy Committee

Real income

Research and development (R&D)

Retail Price Index (RPI)

Risk

Shocks

Skill shortages

Social cost

Structural change

Supply constraints

Technological change

Uncertainty

Unemployment

A2 Unit 3: International business

International markets, including China and India (Sections 3.3.1 and 3.3.2)

Barriers to entry

Developing economies

Economic growth

European Union (EU)

Exports

Foreign direct investment (FDI)

Free market

Free trade

Infant industries

Infrastructure

Innovation

International competitiveness

Liberalisation

Outsourcing

Product life cycle

Protectionism

Single European market

Trade barriers

Trading bloc

World Trade Organization (WTO)

Trading internationally (Sections 3.3.3 and 3.3.4)

Balance of trade

Commodity prices

Comparative advantage

Cultural differences

Distribution channels

Economic growth

Emissions

Ethics

Exchange rate movements

Free trade

Global brands

Gross domestic product (GDP)

Human Development Index (HDI)

Infrastructure

International competitiveness	Quotas
Joint venture	Social responsibilities
Labour force	Specialisation
Natural resources	Stakeholder
Non-tariff barriers	Tariff
Opportunity cost	Technology
Pricing strategy	Working conditions
Promotional message	World Trade Organization (WTO)

Globalisation and multinationals (Sections 3.3.5 and 3.3.6)

Competition policy	Minimum wage
Developing economy	Multinational
Economies of scale	Pressure group
Exploitation	Real incomes
Globalisation	Subcultures
Global localisation	Sustainability
Global marketing	Sweatshop
Host country	Takeover
Level playing field	Target market
Living standards	Tax avoidance
Market niche	Transfer pricing
Market segmentation	Unsustainable growth
Merger	

A2 Unit 4b The Wider Economic Environment and Business

Do markets always work? (Section 4.3.1b)

Asymmetric information	Free rider problem
Cost–benefit analysis	Imperfect information
Climate change	Marginal social benefit
Demerit goods	Marginal social cost
Emissions trading schemes	Market failure
Equality	Merit goods
Equity	Misallocation of resources
External benefits	Negative externality
External costs	Non-excludability
Externalities	Non-rivalry
Free market system	Overconsumption

Overproduction

Polluter pays principle

Positive externality

Private benefits

Private costs

Public goods

Regulation

Social benefits

Social costs

Tradable permits

Trade-offs

Underproduction

Should markets be regulated? (Section 4.3.2b)

Anti-competitive activities

Cartel

Collusion

Competition Commission

Competition policy

Consumer protection

Contestable markets

Cost leadership

Discriminatory pricing

Dominant price leader

Economies of scale

Entry

EU Commission

Exit

Government failure

Interdependence

Limit pricing

Market power

Market-sharing agreements

Mergers and acquisitions (M and A)

Nationalised industries

Natural monopolies

Non-price competition

Office of Fair Trading (OFT)

Predatory pricing

Price fixing

Price wars

Process innovation

Product innovation

Public interest

Regulators

Regulatory capture

Restrictive practices

Smith, Adam

Tacit collusion

Can the government control the economy? (Section 4.3.3b)

Circular flow of national income

Consumer Prices Index (CPI)

Contractionary policies

Corporation tax

Cost inflation

Counter-inflation policies

Credit Crunch

Current account deficit

Demand inflation

Depreciation

Downward multiplier

Employment protection

European Union (EU)

Floating exchange rate

Forecasting

Full capacity-output

Geographical immobility

Government economic objectives

Injections

Keynes, J M

Leakages

Long-run trend rate of growth

Minimum wage

Multiplier

Occupational immobility

Policy conflicts

Public deficit

Quantitative easing

Saving

Shocks

Stabilisation policies

Supply constraints

Supply-side policies

Tax revenue

Time lags

Should government intervene in society? (Section 4.3.4b)

Absolute poverty

Disincentives to work

Distribution of income

Economic growth

Economic welfare

Property rights

Gini coefficient

Government failure

Imperfect information

Incentives

Income elasticity

Income tax

Inequality

Inferior goods

Kyoto Protocol

Lorenz curve

Marginal private benefit

Marginal social benefit

Marginal social cost

Overconsumption

Poverty

Poverty trap

Pressure groups

Progressive taxes

Redistribution of income

Regressive taxes

Relative poverty

Road pricing

Working Families Tax Credit

Examiners' terms

The following entries should help explain what examiners mean by the words they use in exam questions. It is important to remember, though, that the words are only half the story. The other key factor is the *mark allocation*. This not only gives an indication of the length of answer required, but also the depth. The higher the mark allocation, the more likely it is that the examiner is looking for the skills of analysis and, especially, evaluation – and the more likely that the exam question will be marked on the basis of levels of response.

Analyse: to break a topic down into its component parts. This should help to identify the causes and effects of the issue and to explain the process whereby the causes bring about the effects. This encourages more depth of study. It implies a writing style that uses continuous prose in fully developed paragraphs. Bear in mind the word 'why?' when analysing.

Assess: weigh up and thereby *evaluate* two or more options or arguments.

Assumptions: (see *state your assumptions*)

Comment: draw conclusions from the evidence, possibly in the form of a stated opinion. For example, in the first part of a question you might be required to analyse a company's financial position using ratios; part b) might ask you to comment on your findings. You might reach a conclusion about the firm's profitability and liquidity, then state your opinion about the firm's overall financial health. Also, it is often helpful to comment upon any further information needed.

Consider: another term inviting you to weigh up options or arguments in the form of continuous paragraphs of writing.

Critically analyse means to look in depth at an issue (analyse) from the perspective of a critic. In other words the examiner is encouraging you not to take the issue at face value; instead you should be questioning the assumptions or evidence involved. However, it is important to remember that film 'critics' may write a favourable review. You, too, should look at the strengths as well as the weaknesses involved.

Debate: put both sides of the case as forcefully as you can, then criticise each side from the perspective of the other. Take, for example, the essay title 'Debate the issue of whether cigarette advertising should be banned completely'. You should put forward the views both for and against, then tackle the arguments of those in favour from the point of view of opponents (and vice versa). You may decide, in the end, to 'vote' or abstain, as in a real debate.

Decide which: make a choice between the options, supported by your reasoning.

Define: explain the meaning of the term as precisely as you can; giving an example can help, but is not a substitute for explanation.

Discuss: put forward both sides of a case before coming to a conclusion. Discussion would require continuous writing and would be likely to be marked on a *levels-of-response* basis, with a high proportion of marks awarded for *evaluation*.

Discuss critically: a little different from 'discuss', though the examiner appears to be hinting that there may be a reason to be sceptical of the theory or question under discussion. Therefore you should look carefully for weaknesses in the logic.

Distinguish between: (as in 'distinguish between revenue and profit'). Here, you should explain each of the two terms and then look for the point of difference between them: 'the difference is that costs have been deducted from revenue to find profit'.

Draw a graph: it may sound absurd, but many Examiners' Reports state that students drew bar charts or even pie charts when asked to draw a graph. By 'graph' the examiner means line graph.

Evaluate: this vital term means to weigh up evidence in order to reach a judgement. In the context of an essay, you will have to present that evidence (pros and cons, perhaps) before reaching a conclusion. As the term invites your judgement, do be willing to state your opinion within the conclusion, e.g. 'In my view…'. It can be helpful to keep in mind the phrase 'to what extent…?'

Examine means to look in detail at the argument, evidence or theory presented. It requires continuous writing and should be rounded off with a conclusion.

Explain: expand upon in order to show your understanding of the term or theory being tested. The depth of explanation required will be indicated by the *mark allocation*. Giving a well-chosen example will often gain a mark.

Give: this means list, as in 'Give three current assets'. All you would need to provide in answer is 'stock, debtors, cash'. There is no requirement to explain the points you make. Point-form answers are acceptable.

How might: this phrase suggests a need to explain a process, as in 'How might a firm choose between two investment options?' You must explain the process with care, then consider the *mark allocation* before deciding whether a conclusion is required. If 5 marks are available, no conclusion would be necessary; with 25 marks, however, you would be wise to *evaluate* your answer.

Identify: to name one or more examples of the topic being examined. Usually this would require no more than a list, with one mark awarded per point made.

Justify your answer: present an argument in favour of the views you are expressing; for example: 'Should the Post Office be privatised? Justify your answer.' Although the question appears to be expecting a yes or no at the outset, it is better to wait until the end to state your opinion because you will have given the matter enough thought to be able to justify your decision.

Levels of response: a way of marking answers based upon different academic skills rather than the quantity of knowledge shown. This is the way in which most high-mark questions are examined. If ten marks are available for 'Explain the impact of higher interest rates upon firms', a levels-of-response marking scheme would put a ceiling on the number of marks available for listing points (see diagram). Therefore you are better off writing a full explanation of two or three points.

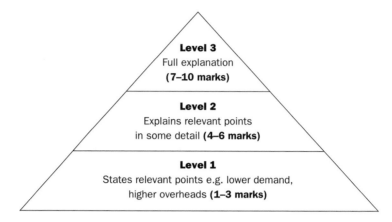

Level 3
Full explanation
(7–10 marks)

Level 2
Explains relevant points
in some detail **(4–6 marks)**

Level 1
States relevant points e.g. lower demand,
higher overheads **(1–3 marks)**

List: briefly state, not necessarily in a full sentence (same as *give*).

Mark allocation: the number of marks on offer for each part of a question.

Name: same as *list* or *give*.

Outline: provide a description of an event, theory or method. The length and the level of detail will be governed by the *mark allocation*.

Report format: see *Write a report*

Show your workings: this phrase is used often with numerical questions, but should never be ignored. In the pressure of the exam room, almost every candidate will slip up somewhere in a complex calculation. If there are 10 marks on offer for the answer '£24,800', the candidate who gives the answer '£248,000' with no workings will get 0, while a candidate with the same answer will get 9 marks if the workings show where the single slip was made. The secret with numerical questions is not to get 10 out of 10 one time and 0 the next. It is to get 8 or 9 marks every time.

Sketch a diagram: this suggests a quick drawing on the ordinary exam writing paper, paying little attention to precision in the lines being drawn. However, to convey any meaning, the sketch will need properly labelled axes and/or lines and a clear title. With sketches, the labelling may carry more marks than the diagram itself.

State: means the same as *give*.

State and explain: this should be tackled exactly in this way, i.e. give a reason (in perhaps 4–8 words) then explain it (in perhaps 4–8 lines).

State your assumptions: in a numerical question, tell the examiner the decisions you have made when there has been some uncertainty about the correct figures. To gain a mark, your assumption must be based on uncertainty and must be logical. For example, in a recent exam, many students calculating profit assumed that corporation tax would stay unchanged at £40,000 from one year to the next. As corporation tax is charged as a percentage of pre-tax profit, this was not acceptable. Do not confuse an assumption with a conclusion.

Suggest means to put forward an idea. If few marks are allocated, this might require no more than a list of points. The word is used more commonly, though, in the context of higher-mark case study or essay questions. In this case it would require a full explanation and justification for the suggestions made.

SWOT analysis: an investigation into an organisation's current strengths and weaknesses and potential opportunities and threats. It is usually presented in report format.

To what extent: this commonly used examining phrase requires you to reach a judgement about the degree to which a statement, theory or evidence is true. It is likely that the levels-of-response marking scheme will reward evaluation especially heavily. So focus on relatively few themes, deal with each in depth and then make a judgement about 'to what extent...'.

What do you understand by? (or **What is meant by?**): explain the meaning of the term or phrase given. An example may be helpful, but is not a substitute for explanation.

Why might: this phrase invites you to suggest possible explanations for why a firm or individual may have chosen a course of action. The use of the word 'might' gives you scope to stray outside the confines of, perhaps, a case study text. Any answer will be accepted as long as it is not too far-fetched; but remember that examiners want to reward your business understanding, so try to draw from relevant theories.

Write a memo: present your answer to a question in the form of a business memo (memorandum). This requires headings (To, From, Title, Date) and is likely to be a relatively brief statement of (or request for) factual information. The contents can be written in continuous prose or in point form.

Write a report: present your answer to a question in the form of a business report. A report is a document that is likely to provide a great deal of information (written and numerical) and is therefore broken down into sections, each of which is split into sub-sections. The users of the report expect to be able to refer to any part of it at any time and in any order. Therefore it has a contents page and frequent cross-referencing. A busy manager, for example, may just want to see what budget is being requested. When looking that up, a cross-reference to the financial returns expected would be helpful. The managing director may want to do no more than read a summary of the report's findings and recommendations, so most reports start with an 'executive summary'.

In the context of an exam, where only 30 or 45 minutes may be available, little of the above is possible. So the report need only have title headings (To, From, Title, Date) and a structure of numbered sections with numbered sub-sections. If time permits, it is valuable to start with a section on the background to the report and to end with recommendations/points for action.

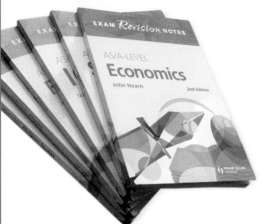